RECONCILIATION AND HOPE

LEON LAMB MORRIS

RECONCILIATION AND HOPE

*New Testament Essays on
Atonement and Eschatology*

presented to

L. L. Morris on his 60th Birthday

edited by

Robert Banks

*Research Fellow, History of Ideas,
Institute of Advanced Studies
Canberra, Australia*

1974

WILLIAM B. EERDMANS PUBLISHING COMPANY
Grand Rapids, Michigan

Copyright © 1974, The Paternoster Press Ltd
First American edition, July 1974, published by arrangement with
The Paternoster Press, Exeter, England

Library of Congress Cataloging in Publication Data

Main entry under title:

Reconciliation and hope.

CONTENTS: Hubbard, D. A. Leon Lamb Morris: an
appreciation.—Williams, D. Select bibliography of
L. L. Morris (p. 15-   )—Reconciliation: Gerhards-
son, B. Sacrificial service and atonement in the Gospel
of Matthew. [etc.]
 1. Bible. N. T.—Addresses, essays, lectures.
2. Morris, Leon. 3. Morris, Leon—Bibliography.
I. Banks, Robert J., ed. II. Morris, Leon.
BS2395.R4   234   74-5370
ISBN 0-8028-3349-3

Printed in Great Britain

CONTENTS

PART II – HOPE

EDITOR'S FOREWORD

THIS IS THE FIRST OCCASION ON WHICH AN AUSTRALIAN NEW TESTAMENT scholar has been honoured with a volume of this nature. His few predecessors who have also won for themselves international reputations have generally come to this country from other parts of the world or at a fairly early date become expatriates from it. Not so Dr. Morris who, apart from brief spells in the U.K. and U.S.A., has spent the whole of his life within its borders. In the midst of strenuous teaching and administrative responsibilities he has continued to write prolifically and seriously on various New Testament themes, particularly those upon which the essays in this volume are focused. His recognition is, I think, a sign of that theological "coming-of-age" which is taking place in Australia at present.

It was encouraging to find that a representative number of scholars from many different countries were only too willing to lend their support to this venture. The two publishers also readily consented to the appropriateness of such a Festschrift and have been of great help throughout its formation. As one for whom Dr. Morris's dedication to the task of Christian scholarship has been an incentive to persevere in the same direction, I would like to add my personal congratulations to those of the contributing essayists and publishers as well as many other scholars and laymen around the world.

ROBERT BANKS

LEON LAMB MORRIS: AN APPRECIATION

DAVID ALLAN HUBBARD

"LEON MORRIS HAS CONVINCED ME," THE DISTINGUISHED SCOTTISH professor acknowledged. "Every man must have a mercy-seat, a place of propitiation." That statement, awarding to Morris the laurels in his debate with C. H. Dodd as to whether *hilasterion* means propitiation or expiation, introduced me to Leon Morris's name nearly twenty years ago. It was not until several years after (1960, I think) that I met Dr. Morris for the first time in Santa Barbara, California. With fear and trembling, I awaited the arrival of the esteemed scholar, whose reputation had by then been enhanced by his *Apostolic Preaching of The Cross* and his commentaries on the Thessalonian letters. To my delight I discovered that my fears of awesome stuffiness were unfounded.

Here was a man humble in his discipleship, unimpressed by his own learning, cordial in his friendship. His relaxed attitude toward his accomplishments particularly impressed me. Immigration requirements insisted that he present the diploma of his Ph.D. degree (which he had earned at Cambridge in 1952) before he would be granted a visa to enter the United States as a visiting professor. Somewhat sheepishly Morris confessed to me that he had searched high and low before he found it. An academic document that some would have guarded like the crown jewels he had casually mislaid. Years of intimate, though intermittent, contact with Leon Morris have only deepened my admiration and affection for him. In fact, writing this tribute I find to be a hard assignment. Were I to say what I feel, the result would be sentiments too deep for public exhibition. Yet to say much less than I feel might seem to gloss over the depths of our friendship.

It takes a while to know the many sides of Leon Morris. His missionary background, for instance. His interest in the atonement and the theology of the cross do not derive alone from his concern that the evangelical tradition make a responsible contribution in the Anglican communion or in academic circles. It also stems from his personal commitment to the preaching of the cross as the power of God to salvation. This is a message which he has proclaimed through the years in the parish and in his missionary ministry in the Australian Outback where he served for five years (1940–45) as priest-in-charge of the Minnipa Mission, Diocese of Willochra, South Australia. There he held services in more than twenty centres which were like scattered dots on 40,000 square miles of bleak terrain.

Paved roads were almost non-existent. Leon and Mildred Morris (they were married in January 1941) usually followed other car tracks through the bush or made their own. Often Mildred drove while Leon read the books required by the London B.D., a bouncy, dusty way to gain an education. His concern for the isolated villages, homes, and stations normally beyond the reach of Christian preaching later led him to act as Victorian Secretary of the Bush Church Aid Society in 1952–53.

Before he became a missionary, he was a science student and teacher. His training at the University of Sydney (B.Sc., 1934) and at Sydney Teachers College prepared him for his first career - teaching school. It was during his first year at university that God called him to trust in Christ as Lord and Saviour. His study of sciences stood him in good stead when, after three years of teaching, the call of God came again. This time it redirected his career to ordination in the Anglican Church.

His scientific ability to weigh options and make sober choices he carried over to his theological training. He was granted the Th.L. by the Australian College of Theology in 1937. Not only was he awarded first class honours, but he won the Hey-Sharp Prize as the top Th.L. candidate in Australia. From the University of London he received the B.D. degree with first class honours in 1943 and the M.Th. in 1946. In 1951 he had the honour of becoming the first Australian scholar to be elected to membership in the international Society for New Testament Studies.

This record seems all the more remarkable when viewed in the light of his demanding administrative and pastoral responsibilities. During the past twenty-five years or so he has served as Vice-Principal of Ridley College, Melbourne (1954–59), as Warden of Tyndale House, Cambridge (1961–63), and Principal of Ridley College since 1964. In his quiet, unflappable way, he has carried out his duties with grace and efficiency. Hundreds of students in Great Britain, the United States, as well as Australia have been nurtured by his personal interest in them. Discussions over coffee have blended scholarly acumen, pastoral experience, innate commonsense, keen concern for persons. Individual counselling sessions have helped scores of students to find a way through their problems. At heart, administration is the service of people – not the shuffling of paper. At such service Principal Morris excels.

The "cure of souls" has been at the centre of his ministry through the years. His educational and administrative tasks have been enriched by his wide and varied experiences in the parish. Following his ordination as deacon (1938) and priest (1939) he served as curate of St. John's, Campsie, in the Diocese of Sydney (1938–40), of Holy Trinity, Coburg, in the Diocese of Melbourne (1948–49, 1953–55), of St. John's, Bentleigh (1957–58), and of St. George's, Bentleigh, in the Diocese of Melbourne (1958–59).

His credentials as a churchman continue to be impressive. Since 1964 he has served as Canon of St. Paul's Cathedral, Melbourne and was among the nominees for the Archbishopric of Sydney in 1966. He is at present Secretary of the Commission on Doctrine of the Church of England in Australia. As both a loyal Anglican and a sane ecumenist, he has laboured in many causes that cross denominational lines, including the chairmanship of Billy Graham's 1968 Melbourne crusade and the presidency of the Inter-Varsity Fellowship of Australia. During various sojourns in America he has served as a Visiting Professor at theological seminaries or divinity schools like Columbia (Decatur, Georgia), Fuller, Gordon-Conwell, Trinity, and Westminster. During one brief period in 1966 he also lent a hand to the editorial staff of *Christianity Today* in Washington, D.C. His presence was felt in interdenominational discussions on Biblical authority held at Wenham, Massachusetts in 1966 and on world evangelism at the Berlin Congress the same year.

The scholars whose essays in this volume pay tribute to Leon Morris are spokesmen for a vast host of academics, pastors, Bible translators and laymen to whom Morris's name has become a household word. Integrity of scholarship and clarity of expression combine in his writings with a reverence for the teachings of Scripture. This combination makes a marked impact on his readers whether through his more technical or his more popular writings.

The remarkable bibliography shows the range and variety of Dr. Morris's work. His weightier commentaries on Thessalonians and John have taken their place alongside the standard expositions of those books. His more popular commentaries on I Corinthians, Thessalonians, Revelation, and Ruth have been exemplary in their field, models of deep learning clearly and simply expressed. His critical works like *The Apostolic Preaching of The Cross* and *Studies in the Fourth Gospel* show his sense of strategy. It is the person and work of Jesus Christ on which his studies have centred. This focus has made Morris's work evangelical to the core. The Saviour and the good news he has brought are his chief interests. While appreciating all aspects of the academic task, he has personally chosen to test some of the main currents of Biblical scholarship, rather than to paddle in the backwaters. Not only my Scottish professor but a legion of Bible students have been convinced of the truth and power of the Gospel by Morris's scholarship.

Leon Morris's students and friends know sides of his life that his readers can only guess at: his puckish sense of humour, his deep personal piety, his quiet openness to his friends, his keen interest in sports, his thorough enjoyment of all of life. I have never met anyone from overseas who learned so quickly and followed so avidly American sports. Football, baseball and basketball have become as much a part of his interest as tennis, soccer and cricket. He knows not only the names of the star players but the intricacies of the rules. Some of my finest memories are recollections of hours passed at athletic events discussing theology and sports with Dr. Morris.

No tribute to Leon Morris would be complete without a mention of Mildred, his wife. From those days early in their marriage, when she drove the bumpy trails of the Outback while he studied, to the present, as she brings her warmth and grace to the faculty and students at Ridley, her gentle inspiration, her strong devotion, her unflagging courage, her readiness for new ventures have provided a fitting context for his ministries. In a sense these essays must be for her as well as for him.

A Select Bibliography of the Writings of L. L. Morris

Compiled by David Williams

1947

"The Atonement in Christian Thought," *Evangelical Action* (Melbourne), 61 (October 1947), p. 5.
"The Church and the Outback," *Coticula* (Ridley College, Melbourne), (1947), pp. 23–24.

1948

The Atonement: The Eclipse of Liberalism (Morris writes on the Atonement, and in conjunction with S. B. Babbage and J. A. Thompson on the Eclipse of Liberalism). Sydney: Theological Students' Fellowship of Australia, 1948, pp. 31.
"The Atonement," *Evangelical Action* 62 (November 1948), pp. 2–3.

1950

"A Ransom for Many," *Inter-Varsity* (Australia) 13 (1950), pp. 4–6.

1951

"The Use of ἱλάσκεσθαι etc. in Biblical Greek," *ExpT* 62 (May 1951), pp. 227–233.

1952

"The Biblical Use of the Term 'Blood'," *JTS* (NS) 3 (October 1952), pp. 216–227.
"The Idea of Redemption in the Old Testament," *The Reformed Theological Review* 11 (October 1952), pp. 94–102.
"Must We Believe in the Wrath of God?," *World Christian Digest* 39 (July 1952), pp. 13–16.
"The Wrath of God," *ExpT* 63 (February 1952), pp. 142–145.

1953

"The Epistles of John" (with R. J. Drummond in the 1st. and 2nd. eds), in *The New Bible Commentary*, ed. F. Davidson. London: The Inter-Varsity Fellowship, 1953; Grand Rapids, 1953. Repr. 1954. 2nd. ed. 1954. 3rd. ed. 1970.
"Here I Stand," *Evangelical Action* 67 (December 1953), p. 1.
"Theology and History," *Coticula* (1953), pp. 4–5.

1954

The Wages of Sin. (Tyndale New Testament Lecture, 1954.) London: The Tyndale Press, 1954. Pp. 30. Spanish ed. 1967.
"Church Union: Cloudland – or the Will of God?," *Coticula* (1954), pp. 14–15.
"Modern Trends in Biblical Criticism," *The Reaper* 32 (November 1954), pp. 344–348.
"The Passover in Biblical Literature," *Australian Biblical Review* 4 (1954/55), pp. 59–76.

1955

The Apostolic Preaching of the Cross. London: The Tyndale Press, 1955. Pp. 296.
"The Biblical Use of the Term 'Blood'," *JTS* (NS) 6 (April 1955), pp. 77–82.
"The Day of Atonement and the Work of Christ," *The Reformed Theological Review* 14 (February 1955), pp. 9–19.
"The Deity of Christ," *Evangelical Action* 69 (December 1955), p. 3.
"O Come, Let us Worship," *The Australian Churchman* 27 (1 September 1955), pp. 2–3.
"On Tying Labels," *Coticula* (1955/56), p. 12.
"The Relevance of the Bible," *The Living Church* 28 (July–September 1955), pp. 37–38.
"The Risen Lord To Worship," *Inter-Varsity* (New Zealand) 18 (December 1955), pp. 5–7.

1956

The Epistles of Paul to the Thessalonians: An Introduction and Commentary. (Tyndale New Testament Commentaries.) London: The Tyndale Press, 1956. Pp. 152. Grand Rapids: William B. Eerdmans Publishing Company, 1957. Pp. 152. Vietnamese ed. 1969.
A series of articles on basic christian doctrines appeared throughout the various issues of *Evangelical Action*, 70 (1956).

1957

Salvation. Sydney: Evangelical Tracts and Publications, 1957. Pp. 15. London: The Inter-Varsity Fellowship, 1958. Pp. 30 (under the title, *Good Enough?*).
The Story of the Cross. London and Edinburgh: Marshall, Morgan & Scott, 1957. Pp. 128.
"The Death of Jesus," *The Living Church* 36 (July–September 1957), pp. 29–30.
"Lo! He Comes," *The Australian Churchman* 29 (15 June 1957), pp. 10–12.

1958

The First Epistle of Paul to the Corinthians: An Introduction and Commentary. (Tyndale New Testament Commentaries.) London: The Tyndale Press, 1958. Pp. 249. Repr. 1960, 1963, 1964, 1966, 1969. Grand Rapids: William B. Eerdmans Publishing Company, 1958. Pp. 249.
The Lord from Heaven. London: The Inter-Varsity Fellowship, 1958. Pp. 112. Repr. 1960, 1964, 1966. Grand Rapids: William B. Eerdmans Publishing Company, 1958. Pp. 112. Japanese ed. 1964; Swahili ed. 1968.
The Truth of the Bible. (Inter-Varsity Papers No. 6.) Sydney: The Inter-Varsity Fellowship (Australian), 1958. Pp. 12.
"Asham," *EQ* 30 (October–December 1958), pp. 196–210.
"The Blood, Life or Death?," *Christianity Today* 2 (17 March 1958), pp. 6–7.
"Even Harder the Taxpaying," *Eternity* 9 (March 1958), p. 19.

1959

The First and Second Epistles to the Thessalonians. (The New International Commentary on the New Testament.) Grand Rapids: William B. Eerdmans Publishing Company, 1959. Pp. 274.
"Christ Victorious," in *Christian Education Kit* 3. Melbourne: General Board of Religious Education, 1959.

"Judgment and Custom," *Australian Biblical Review* 7 (December 1959), pp. 72–74.
"The Miracle at Cana," *Theolog News* (Theological Students' Fellowship of Australia) 3 (July 1959), pp. 2–3.

1960

The Biblical Doctrine of Judgment. (Tyndale Biblical Theology Lecture, 1960.) London: The Tyndale Press, 1960. Pp. 72.
The Dead Sea Scrolls and St. John's Gospel. (Dr. G. Campbell Morgan Memorial Lecture, 1960.) London: Westminster Chapel, 1960. Pp. 24.
Spirit of the Living God. London: The Inter-Varsity Fellowship, 1960. Pp. 102.
The Story of the Christ Child. London and Edinburgh: Marshall, Morgan & Scott, 1960. Pp. 128. Grand Rapids: William B. Eerdmans Publishing Company, 1960. Pp. 128.
"A Ransom for Many," *Eternity* 11 (May 1960), pp. 19, 23–24.
"The Biblical Doctrine of Judgment," in *Christian Reformed Ministers Institute Lectures 1960.* Grand Rapids: Christian Reformed Ministers Institute, 1960. Pp. 1–22.
"Bishop," "Blood," "Church Government," "Clergy," "Condemn," "Condemnation," "Deacon," "Episcopacy, Episcopal," "Eternal Punishment," "Mediation, Mediator," "Minister, Ministry," "Orders, Holy," "Orders, Minor," "Propitiation," "Punishment," "Sacrifice," "Sect," "Sprinkle, Sprinkling," in *Dictionary of Theology*, ed. E. F. Harrison. Grand Rapids: Baker Book House, 1960.
"Colossians," in *The Biblical Expositor* 3, ed. C. F. H. Henry. Philadelphia: A. J. Holman Company, 1960.
"Penal View of the Atonement," *His* 21 (December 1960), pp. 15, 16, 33.
"Where Shall Wisdom Be Found?," *The Evangelical Christian* (September 1960), pp. 22–24.

1961

"A Fresh Look at Jesus' Birth," *Decision* 2 (December 1961), p. 3.
"The Authority of the Bible Today," *The Churchman* 75 (July–September 1961), pp. 147–156.

1962

Christian Worship. London: Church Pastoral-Aid Society, 1962. Pp. 15.
"Abomination," "Antichrist," "Atonement," "Blood," "Death," "Devil," "Elect Lady," "Evil Spirits," "Expiation," "Faith," "Flesh," "Forgiveness," "Gift," "Heaven," "Jacob" (NT references), "Jeshua," "Judging," "Nephtoah," "Ordination," "Propitiation," "Reconciliation," "Redeemer, Redemption," "Restoration," "Resurrection," "Revelation, Book of," "Satan," in *The New Bible Dictionary*, ed. J. D. Douglas *et al.* London: The Inter-Varsity Fellowship, 1962. Grand Rapids: William B. Eerdmans Publishing Company, 1962.
"The Atonement," in *Basic Christian Doctrines*, ed. C. F. H. Henry. New York: Holt, Rinehart and Winston, 1962. Pp. 152–157.
"Christian Worship," *The Churchman* 76 (June 1962), pp. 74–82.
"God's Way is Grace," *Christianity Today* 6 (16 March 1962), pp. 14–16.
"History and Theology in the Fourth Gospel," *Faith and Thought* 92 (Summer 1962), pp. 117–129.
"The New Testament Doctrine of Ministry," *The Life of Faith* 86 (27 September 1962), pp. 803–804.

"Some Principles of Christian Worship," *World Christian Digest* 164 (December 1962), pp. 30–36.

"The Vocabulary of Atonement I: Redemption," *Themelios* 1 (October 1962), pp. 24–30.

1963

"The Atonement and Substitution," *TSF Bulletin* 37 (Autumn 1963), pp. 10–12.

"Blessed is the Man," *The Life of Faith* 88 (12 September 1963), pp. 913–914, 934.

"Christian Assurance," *The Christian* 4878 (13 September 1963), pp. 7, 21.

"The Church of God: Visible and Invisible," *Inter-Varsity* (Spring Term 1963), pp. 25–28.

"The Church of God: Church and Authority," *Inter-Varsity* (Summer Term 1963), pp. 27–29.

"The Church of God: The Church's Unity," *Inter-Varsity* (Autumn Term 1963), pp. 11–14.

"The Problem of Authority," *Bible League Quarterly* 252 (January–March 1963), pp. 65–70.

"The Vocabulary of the Atonement II: Reconciliation," *Themelios* 2 (October 1963), pp. 24–30.

"Why Be Afraid?," *The Christian* 4848 (15 February 1963), p. 7.

1964

The Abolition of Religion. London: The Inter-Varsity Fellowship, 1964. Pp. 111. Italian ed. 1970.

Ministers of God. London: The Inter-Varsity Fellowship, 1964. Pp. 128.

The New Testament and the Jewish Lectionaries. London: The Tyndale Press, 1964. Pp. 78.

Some Highlights in Current Theological Thought About the Bible. (Research Scientists' Christian Fellowship Papers No. 1.) Sydney: The Inter-Varsity Fellowship (Australia), 1964. Pp. 27.

"Apostle," in *The Encyclopedia of Christianity*, ed. E. H. Palmer. Marshallton: The National Foundation for Christian Education, 1964.

"The Church of God: The Church's Sacraments," *Inter-Varsity* (Spring Term 1964), pp. 6–9.

"Noel avec des yeux neufs," *Decision* (French ed.) 7 (November 1964), p. 10.

"The Reformers and the Unity of the Church," in *Stand Where the Reformers Stood*, ed. L. R. Shilton. Adelaide: Holy Trinity Church, 1964. Pp. 57–74.

"Synoptic Themes Illuminated by the Fourth Gospel," in *Studia Evangelica II*, ed. F. L. Cross. Berlin: Akademie – Verlag, 1964. Pp. 73–84.

"The Vocabulary of the Atonement III: Propitiation," *Themelios* 2 (April 1964), pp. 24–29.

"The Vocabulary of the Atonement IV: the Blood," *Themelios* 3 (October 1964), pp. 23–28.

1965

The Cross in the New Testament. Grand Rapids: William B. Eerdmans Publishing Company, 1965. Pp. 454. London: The Paternoster Press, 1966. Pp. 454.

"The Birth of Jesus," *The Christian* 4997 (24 December 1965), pp. 8–10.

"The Church of God: Systems of Church Government," *Inter-Varsity* (Spring Term 1965), pp. 32–34.

"The Church of God: The Church's Ministry," *Inter-Varsity* (Summer Term 1965), pp. 9–11.

"The Vocabulary of the Atonement V: Justification," *Themelios* 3 (April 1965), pp. 19–24.

1966

Glory in the Cross. London: Hodder and Stoughton, 1966, Pp. 94.

Jesus Lives. With Archbishop Frank Woods. Melbourne: General Board of Religious Education, 1966. Pp. 60.

The Problem of History and the Gospel. (Inter-Varsity Papers (NS) No. 2.) Sydney: The Inter-Varsity Fellowship (Australia), 1966. Pp. 19.

"History and the Fourth Gospel," *TSF Bulletin* 46 (Autumn 1966), pp. 16–21.

1967

"Biblical Authority and the Concept of Inerrancy," *The Churchman* 81 (Spring 1967), pp. 22–38.

"The Problem of History and the Gospel," *Interchange* 1 (April 1967), pp. 50–64.

1968

Judges and Ruth: An Introduction and Commentary. (Tyndale Old Testament Commentaries.) With A. E. Cundall. (Morris writes on Ruth.) London: The Tyndale Press, 1968. Pp. 217–318.

"Bishop," "Black Rubric," "Blass, Friedrich W.," "Blood," "Boanerges," "Book of Common Prayer," "Bread (Symbolic Usage)," "Canon of the New Testament," "Catholic," "Census," "Chester Beatty Papyri," "Church, Nature and Government of (Episcopalian View)," in *The Encyclopedia of Christianity* 2, ed. G. G. Cohen. Marshallton: The National Foundation for Christian Education, 1964.

"History and Interpretation in John," *The Reformed Theological Review* 27 (September–December 1968), pp. 89–97.

1969

The Revelation of St John: An Introduction and Commentary. (Tyndale New Testament Commentaries.) London: The Tyndale Press, 1969. Pp. 263. Grand Rapids: William B. Eerdmans Publishing Company, 1969. Pp. 263.

Studies in the Fourth Gospel. Grand Rapids: William B. Eerdmans Publishing Company, 1969. Pp. 374. Exeter: The Paternoster Press, 1969. Pp. 374.

1 and 2 Timothy, Titus, Philemon, Hebrews, James. London: The Scripture Union, 1969. Pp. 91.

"On Being the People of God", *Christianity Today* 14 (19 December 1969), p. 40.

"Reconciliation," *Christianity Today* 13 (17 January 1969), pp. 3–4.

1970

This is the Testimony. (Donald Baker Memorial Lecture, 1970.) Melbourne: Ridley College, 1970. Pp. 23.

"Are We Too Tolerant?," *Christianity Today* 14 (5 June 1970), p. 48.

"Christianity and Nationalism," *Christianity Today* 14 (21 August 1970), pp. 50–51.

"Objections to Evangelism," *Christianity Today* 14 (13 March 1970), pp. 58–59.

"The Optimist," *Christianity Today* 15 (4 December 1970), pp. 45–46.

"The Theme of Romans," in *Apostolic History and the Gospel*, eds. W. W. Gasque and R. P. Martin. Exeter: The Paternoster Press, 1970. Pp. 249–263.

"Two Hundred Years of Australia," *Christianity Today* 14 (3 July 1970), pp. 10–12.

1971
The Gospel According to John. (The New International Commentary on the New Testament.) Grand Rapids: William B. Eerdmans Publishing Company, 1971. Pp. 936.
"Assessment of the National Evangelical Anglican Congress," in *New Obedience,* ed. L. R. Shilton. Sydney: ANZEA Publishers, 1971. Pp. 86–93.
"The Authentic Gospel," in *Christ Calls us to a New Obedience.* Sydney: National Evangelical Anglican Congress, 1971. Pp. 41–47.
"Conservative Evangelical?" *Christianity Today* 16 (19 November 1971), pp. 50–51.
"Luke the Theologian," *Christianity Today* 15 (27 August 1971), p. 39.
"One Culture," *Christianity Today* 15 (21 May 1971), pp. 55–56.
"The Protestants and the Pope," *Christianity Today* 15 (26 February 1971), pp. 53–54.
"Studies in the Fourth Gospel," in *Explorations.* Melbourne: Ridley College, 1971. Pp. 19–34.

1972
Apocalyptic. Grand Rapids: William B. Eerdmans Publishing Company, 1972. Pp. 87.
"The Authentic Gospel," *Decision* 13 (November 1972), p. 7.
"God's Dice or God's Purpose?," *Christianity Today* 16 (11 August 1972), p. 42.
"Muting the Bible," *Christianity Today* 16 (12 May 1972), pp. 49–50.
"On the Third Day," *Christianity Today* 16 (18 February 1972), pp. 68–70.
"What is a Gospel?," *Christianity Today* 17 (10 November 1972), pp. 69–70.

1973
"Atonement," "Expiation," "Reconciliation," in *Baker's Dictionary of Christian Ethics,* ed. C. F. H. Henry. Grand Rapids: Baker Book House, 1973.
"Biblical Theology," *Christianity Today* 17 (19 January 1973), pp. 53–54.
"El Evangelio Auténtico," *Decision* (Spanish ed.) 5 (October 1973), p. 7
"Luke and Early Catholicism," *The Westminster Theological Journal* 35 (Winter 1973), pp. 121–136.
"The Serving Church," *Christianity Today* 17 (27 April 1973), pp. 49–50.
"World Out of Joint," *Christianity Today* 17 (20 July 1973), p. 50.

NOTE: A fuller bibliography of the Writings of L. L. Morris, including references to contributions in church newspapers and magazines, is housed in the Library of Ridley College, Parkville, Melbourne, VIC. 3052, Australia.

ABBREVIATIONS

ABR – *Australian Biblical Review.*

Apocrypha – *The Apocrypha of the Old Testament,* ed. R. H. Charles (1913).

Arndt – Arndt-Gingrich-Bauer, *A Greek-English Lexicon of the New Testament* (1957).

ATR – *Anglican Theological Review.*

AV – Authorized Version.

BDB – Brown, Driver and Briggs, *Hebrew and English Lexicon of the Old Testament* (1906).

BJRL – *Bulletin of the John Rylands Library.*

Blass-Debrunner – *A Greek Grammar of the New Testament,* E.T. (1961).

BNTC – *Black's New Testament Commentaries* (= Harper's).

CBQ – *Catholic Biblical Quarterly.*

CN – *Coniectanea Neotestamentica* (1947).

Gesenius-Kautzsch – W. Gesenius, rev. E. Kautzsch[28], *Hebräische Grammatik* (1909).

DSS – Dead Sea Scrolls.

EQ – *The Evangelical Quarterly.*

EvTh – *Evangelische Theologie.*

ExpT – *The Expository Times.*

HDAC – Hastings' *Dictionary of the Apostolic Church* (1926).

HJ – *Hibbert Journal.*

HTR – *Harvard Theological Review.*

Interp – *Interpretation.*

JBL – *Journal of Biblical Literature.*

JE – *Jewish Encyclopaedia,* ed. I. Singer, 12 vols. (1901–   ).

JJS – *Journal of Jewish Studies.*

JTC – *Journal for Theology and Church.*

JTS – *Journal of Theological Studies.*

Köhler-Baumgartner – *Lexicon in Veteris Testamenti Libros* (1953).

KNT – Meyer, *Kommentar über das Neue Testament.*

LXX – The Septuagint.

MGWJ – *Monatschrift für die Geschichte und Wissenschaft des Judentums.*

MH – Moulton-Howard, *Grammar of New Testament Greek* (1908, 1929).

Moule – *An Idiom Book of New Testament Greek* (1959[2]).

NEB – New English Bible.

NovTest – *Novum Testamentum.*

NTS – *New Testament Studies.*

PG – Migne, *Patrologia Graeca.*

Pseudepigrapha – *The Pseudepigrapha of the New Testament*, ed. R. H. Charles (1913).
PTR – *Princeton Theological Review*.
RGG – *Die Religion in Geschichte und Gegenwart* (1961³).
RHPR – *Revue d'Histoire et de Philosophie religieuses*.
RTR – *Reformed Theological Review*.
RSV – Revised Standard Version.
RV – Revised Version.
SJT – *Scottish Journal of Theology*.
Strack-Billerbeck – Strack and Billerbeck, *Kommentar zum NT aus Talmud und Midrasch* (1922–28).
TDNT – *Theological Dictionary of the New Testament* (E.T. of TWNT).
ThLZ – *Theologische Literaturzeitung*.
ThQ – *Theologische Quartalschrift*.
ThZ – *Theologische Zeitschrift*.
TNTC – *Tyndale New Testament Commentaries*.
TU – *Texte und Untersuchungen zur Geschichte der altchristlichen Literatur* (3 series), ed. Harnack *et al.* (1883–   ).
TWNT – *Theologisches Worterbuch zum Neuen Testament*, ed. G. Kittel, G. Friedrich (1933–   ).
WTJ – *Westminster Theological Journal*.
ZNTW – *Zeitschrift fur die neutestamentliche Wissenschaft*.
ZThK – *Zeitschrift für Theologie und Kirche*.
(Editions indicated by superior figures, e.g. RGG³)

PART ONE:

RECONCILIATION

CHAPTER I

SACRIFICIAL SERVICE AND ATONEMENT IN THE GOSPEL OF MATTHEW

Birger Gerhardsson

EVEN CLEARER THAN PAUL'S PRESENTATION IS THAT PORTRAYAL IN THE Epistle to the Hebrews of how Jesus Christ in lonely majesty once and for all (ἐφάπαξ) won an everlasting atonement. With this clear picture of a complete, exclusive and unique act of atonement at a decreed point of time in history, much in the New Testament can be understood. But not all: some passages still present us with difficulties. For example, the Matthean presentation of Jesus' ministry cannot be interpreted solely in the light of this picture of the atonement.

Certainly Matthew stresses, in quite explicit terms, that Jesus' ministry was for the purpose of taking away sin and creating righteousness. We will briefly call to mind three important passages:

(1) In 1:21 Matthew interprets the name of Jesus so as to characterize his ministry. The aetiological phrase "for he shall save his people from their sins (σώσει τὸν λαὸν αὐτοῦ ἀπὸ τῶν ἁμαρτιῶν αὐτῶν)" is only found in his Gospel. This is not a set formula which, so to speak, simply flowed from the writer's pen. According to Matthew, Jesus delivers people from many kinds of evil. His redeeming act could have been described in other ways if the writer had so wanted (cf. e.g. 11:4 f.). When he states that Jesus will save his people *from their sins*, he indicates just how much weight he ascribes to the atonement Jesus effects.

(2) In the pericope about the Last Supper Jesus says concerning the cup: "Drink of it, all of you; for this is my blood of the covenant which is poured out for many for the forgiveness of sins" (26:27 f.). The explanatory phrase "poured out for many" is taken over by Matthew from the tradition. But the additional words of interpretation "for the forgiveness of sins" (εἰς ἄφεσιν ἁμαρτιῶν) are his own. In this way also Matthew underlines the atoning significance of Jesus' activity.

(3) The logion, "the Son of man came not to be served, but to serve, and to give his life as a ransom for many (δοῦναι τὴν ψυχὴν αὐτοῦ λύτρον ἀντὶ πολλῶν)" (20:28), is one that Matthew has taken from Mark (10:45). However, as we shall see in a moment, it is an important passage for Matthew as well, though his interpretation differs somewhat from that in the earlier Gospel.

If we look more closely at the significance these three statements have within the framework of Matthew's Gospel, we will notice the following: (1) The interpretation of Jesus' name says nothing about the way in which Jesus saves his people from their sins. There is no suggestion that this is to happen exclusively through his sacrificial death. (2) The words interpreting the significance of the cup are not part of a general doctrinal statement about the death of Christ, but deal rather with the practical benefit participants in the church's Holy Communion can derive from it. (3) The saying about the service and sacrifice of the Son of man does not appear in the context of a discussion on atonement. What is said is not intended to present Jesus as the one, and only, exclusive Saviour. Jesus is here portrayed as the highest ideal for all who want to be great in the Kingdom of Heaven: they must serve those who are of least account in the eyes of men. This Son of man whom they are to emulate (note the Matthean ὥσπερ) saw his mission as that of giving his life as a ransom for many. The final words show how far his service extended. We shall come back to this later.

As a matter of fact, Matthew tends throughout his Gospel to present Jesus more as a typical than an exclusive figure, and to play down the historical "once and for all" in favour of heavenly ideals which have a timeless, or more correctly, a general and permanent validity. We shall see below how this tendency manifests itself in Matthew's presentation of the atonement theme. We shall also see that this way of interpreting the ministry of Christ is easy to understand if it is placed in its specific historical context. Matthew was educated by Jewish scribes and uses their way of speaking about "offering spiritual sacrifices" (λογικὴ λατρεία, πνευματικαὶ θυσίαι).

I

A well-known rabbinic tradition (ARN 4), which is said to date from the period just after 70 A.D., portrays the reactions of two pious rabbis to the ruined temple. Rabbi Joshua weeps: "Woe unto us, that the place where the sins of Israel were atoned for, is laid waste." But Rabban Johanan ben Zakkai comforts him: "We have another atonement as effective as this, and what is this? The deeds of mercy (gemilut ḥasadim), as it is said: 'For I desire mercy (ḥesed) and not sacrifice (zebaḥ)' (Hos. 6:6)."

This vivid picture reminds us of a series of facts which can be verified from other sources: that the desecration and destruction by the Romans of Israel's only legitimate place of sacrifice was a terrible shock to pious Jews. Nevertheless the religious life of the people still continued: its vital nerve was not struck. Much earlier, the teachers in Israel had realized that the decisive factor in Israel's worship of God ('abodah, λατρεία) does not lie in external sacrificial acts conducted in the temple, but in *obedience* to Him who has given the laws concerning the sacrificial services and other holy duties. That is why Israel's *abodah/latreia* could continue after the fall of the temple. However, the old idea that God was to be served by *sacrifices* ran very deep, as may be seen in their tendency to begin classifying all acts of obedience as sacrifices. It is these *spiritual* sacrifices which now bring about expiation for the sins of God's people. Those who pioneered this deepening and ethicizing of Israel's religion were not priests, but prophets, sages and scribes. It was only natural that the rabbis took over the leadership in Israel after the fall of the temple.

In Matthew's Gospel, we find, as is generally known, many direct and indirect traces of the revolutionary events that occurred around the year 70 A.D. Even Christian Jews were shaken at the thought of "the abomination of desolation, standing in the holy place", and their hearts also bled at the thought of what had happened on Mount Zion. However, expressions of their emotional loyalty to the holy city do not stand out so clearly as does their bitterness against those who had brought down God's judgement upon Jerusalem. In some respects, they viewed the matter from the outside. When Matthew's Gospel was written, Christian Jews had been thrust out from Israel's religious community and they too dissociated themselves from it. As they looked back on the destruction of Jerusalem they interpreted it as a logical catastrophe about which Jesus had prophesied and warned. It was the leaders of Israel and the people misled by them who had brought it upon themselves by rejecting Jesus and then hardening themselves against the apostles' message of his resurrection. The bitterness reflected in this attitude stems partly from the fact that it is *basically* not a reaction from outsiders but an essentially Jewish self-criticism of a genuinely prophetic kind.

Much has already been written on this subject and it does not need to be repeated in this connection.[1] I shall here try to answer the positive question as to how, in Matthew's Gospel, the sins of (the true) Israel are expiated. This issue could be approached by asking the complementary question: How, according to Matthew, does (apostate) Israel fill up the measure of its sins? Matthew is in the habit of working with sharp contrasts, and he does so in this case as well. I shall, however, limit myself to the positive side of the matter. Even so, other restrictions have to be made. Thus, only certain aspects of this complex problem will be taken up, and only a few key texts dealt with. An exhaustive treatment of the atonement theme in Matthew would require a whole monograph.[2]

[1] See particularly H. J. Schoeps, *Die Tempelzerstörung des Jahres 70 in der jüdischen Religionsgeschichte*, CN VI (1942), pp. 1–45; O. H. Steck, *Israel und das gewaltsame Geschick der Propheten* (Neukirchen-Vluyn, 1967); D. R. A. Hare, *The Theme of Jewish Persecution of Christians in the Gospel According to St. Matthew* (Cambridge, 1967).

[2] For some of the problems involved see, besides the works mentioned above, W. Trilling, *Das wahre Israel* (München, ³1964), G. Strecker, *Der Weg der Gerechtigkeit* (Göttingen, ²1966),

II

The Matthean Jesus does not disapprove of the temple and its outward sacrificial service, but he puts them in their place. This is most clearly expressed in the pericope about plucking ears of corn on the Sabbath day (12:1–8), where we come across the explicit statement: "Something greater than the temple is here". This rejoinder is part of that section of the pericope which is peculiar to Matthew (vv. 5–7). The argument is a conclusion of the *qal-waḥomer* type: the priests in their temple service can work on the Sabbath without incurring guilt. The sacrificial service (*abodah/latreia*) weighs more heavily in God's eyes than Sabbath-keeping, and the weightier matter sets aside the lesser. This traditional argument is now enlarged by Jesus' declaration: "Something greater than the temple is here!" It seems to me indubitable that the comparison here is between two kinds of worship: the *latreia* which the priests perform in the temple, and the *latreia* in which Jesus and his disciples are engaged. These two kinds of service are more closely defined in the Hosea quotation which follows: "I desire mercy (ἔλεος) and not sacrifice (θυσία)". That which is being contrasted here is, on the one hand, the outward sacrificial service, and, on the other, the perfect spiritual sacrifice that Jesus and his disciples are offering and which is characterized by "mercy".[1]

How deeply this conception of sacrifice is involved in the Matthean view of Israel's duty towards God, we find in a passage such as the pericope about prayer, fasting, and almsgiving in 6:1–6, 16–21. The Matthean Jesus is here giving instruction about the right way of "doing one's righteousness (δικαιοσύνη)". His three examples are examples of worship which is carried out with the heart (prayer), with the soul (fasting) and with one's property (almsgiving). A single idea is brought out here: these acts are to be carried out in such a way that from an earthly point of view they are "losses" i.e., they are to be pure *gifts* which do not bring in returns from men. It means simply this, that they are to be pure, whole, and unlimited *sacrifices* to God.[2] That every true sacrifice to God would receive its "reward" from the heavenly Father, was self-evident to Israel.[3]

[1] Cf. A. Cole, *The New Temple* (London, 1950), pp. 8–22, and Hummel, *op. cit.*, pp. 40–44, 90–103.

[2] To Matthew a sacrifice is basically a *gift* (δῶρον): 5:23 f.; 8:4; 15:5; 23:18 f. Cf. Hummel, *op. cit.*, pp. 94 f.

[3] See further my article "Geistiger Opferdienst nach Matth. 6, 1–6. 16–21", in *Neues Testament und Geschichte*, Festschrift O. Cullmann, ed. B. Reicke & H. Baltensweiler (Zürich & Tübingen, 1972, pp. 69–77).

R. Hummel, *Die Auseinandersetzung zwischen Kirche und Judentum im Matthäusevangelium* (München, ²1966), esp. pp. 76–108, and S. van Tilborg, *The Jewish Leaders in Matthew* (Leiden, 1972). For other aspects of the theme of spiritual service, cf. also J. R. Brown, *Temple and Sacrifice in Rabbinic Judaism* (Evanston, 1963), B. E. Gärtner, *The Temple and the Community in Qumran and the New Testament* (Cambridge, 1965), and R. J. McKelvey, *The New Temple* (Oxford, 1969).

When duties towards God are interpreted as spiritual sacrifices, it naturally follows that serving God tends to merge with serving one's fellowmen. Where are these sacrifices to be made – the giving, the "losses" – if not among men? *Latreia* tends to coincide with *diakonia* (cf. such passages as 7:12 and 19:16–22). They may, however, not completely coincide; one's duty to serve God does not cease when man is alone with God. The Matthean presentation is not inconsistent on these points.

III

In other studies I have tried to clarify the ethical dimension of Matthew's Christology. The model of thought can be stated in a short formula: Jesus is "the Son of God" who takes it upon himself to be the perfect "servant of God" in all things. The inmost secret of his attitude is love ('*ahabah*, ἀγάπη). Here we will only briefly deal with Jesus' "service". This is a serving of God (λατρεία) which becomes an ideal serving of man (διακονία). The opposite of this is "to seek one's own".

That Jesus, because of his origin, is the "Son of God" in a different sense than other "sons of God", is underlined in the story of the annunciation to Joseph (1:18–25), and his divine election is confirmed in the narrative describing his baptism (3:13–17). Then comes the temptation narrative (4:1–11). Here Jesus is tested in his capacity as "Son of God". The devil tries to provoke him into committing three acts: (1) To give in to the evil inclination in his heart and use his exousia to procure miraculous means of sustenance for his own benefit, (2) to force God to allow his angels to serve the "Son" and save his life from death, (3) to secure at the ordinary worldly price – service of Satan – power and riches in this world, indeed all the kingdoms of this world and their glory. But the answers Jesus gives show that he wholeheartedly places himself in subjection to what God has commanded in his law: (1) "Man shall not live by bread alone, but by every word that proceeds from the mouth of God", (2) "You shall not tempt the Lord your God", (3) "You shall worship the Lord your God and him only shall you serve (λατρεύειν)". The principle behind these answers is not hard to find. Jesus, "the Son of God", does not intend to "seek his own", but to "seek the things of God" (the Rule of God and his righteousness), to hear and do the will of his heavenly Father. This is the import of the Son's way of "serving" his Father. Notice how the term *latreuein* comes as a concluding climax in Jesus' last answer to the tempter's questions.

If, in the temptation narrative, we find Jesus' way of serving God (λατρεύειν) so interpreted, elsewhere we find demonstrations of his service of man (διακονεῖν). This theme is present in a concise but concentrated way in one logion we have already touched on, namely that the Son of man "came not to be served (διακονηθῆναι) but to serve (διακονῆσαι) and give his life as a ransom for many" (20:28).[1] The verb *diakonein* here occurs both in the active and in the passive, and we therefore gain a clear picture of its meaning: "attend to", "serve". Here it does not primarily refer to service of God but to service of men. The life programme of the Son of man is not "to seek his own" but "to seek the good of others". He uses his incomparable resources for serving his fellowmen (mainly by teaching and healing). We see here how obedience to God's word – worship in this transferred sense (*latreia*) – in practice becomes the service of men (*diakonia*). We see further that, from this perspective, Jesus' sacrifice of his life is presented as an act of obedience towards God, done on behalf of mankind. That which is to take place on Golgotha is not the offering of a sacrificial lamb to achieve a settlement between God and his people. Jesus himself will, in conscious obedience, give (δοῦναι) his life as a ransom for many.

Just how Jesus consciously "gives" his life in obedience to his heavenly Father's will, I have tried to analyse in other connections. The most significant passages are the three great predictions of the passion and resurrection (16:21; 17:22 f.; 20:17–19), the Gethsemane pericope (26:36–46) and the crucifixion narrative (27:32–50). The details which Matthew includes in his depiction of Golgotha are not arbitrarily collected historical reminiscences, nor are they chosen solely for the purpose of showing how the Scriptures are now being fulfilled. Matthew wants to show that that which is enacted on Golgotha is a "sacrifice". He wants to show, partly in explicit terms, partly by hints, that Jesus now presents himself as a perfect sacrifice, and that this sacrifice is complete and blameless even unto death. The "Son of God" takes it upon himself to subordinate his will to that his heavenly Father (*latreuein*), in order, by so doing, to benefit mankind (*diakonein*). Probably Matthew means that Jesus' unlimited obedience to God makes his sacrifice perfect, and that his divine identity gives the sacrifice universal application.

After the resurrection, Jesus proclaims the exousia "in heaven and on earth" which he has been given by his heavenly Father (28:18–20). This refers to his exaltation to the position of *Kyrios* at the right hand of Power (cf. 26:64), a throne on which no-one has sat before.[2] However, it is important to remember that Jesus has already previously had an incomparable exousia, namely on earth. As Matthew points out, when the "Son of God" enters into his public ministry (4:17), he has an exousia

---

[1] For a discussion of the background to this logion see J. Roloff, "Anfänge der soteriologischen Deutung des Todes Jesu" (Mk. X.45 und Lk. XXII.27), *NTS* 19 (1972/73), pp. 38–64, and H. Patsch, *Abendmahl und historischer Jesus* (Stuttgart, 1972), pp. 170–180.

[2] See A. Vögtle, *Das Evangelium und die Evangelien* (Düsseldorf, 1971), pp. 253–272, and cf. O. Michel, "Der Abschluss des Matthäusevangeliums", *EvTh* 10 (1950/51), pp. 16–26, G. Bornkamm a.o., *Ueberlieferung und Auslegung im Matthäus-Evangelium* (Neukirchen-Vluyn, ⁴1965), pp. 289–310, Trilling, *op. cit.*, pp. 21–51.

which enables him to teach, heal and cast out demons in a way which has no parallels in the history of Israel (note 12:42 and 9:33). When he is working in Israel he is not, according to Matthew, in a state of humiliation. He is the "Son of God" with exousia (cf. 11:25–30). But he *takes it upon himself* to hear and do God's word and to *humble himself* in order to serve. He already has the divine exousia to forgive sins (ἀφιέναι ἁμαρτίας), and by so doing, to heal (9:1–8). It is tempting to imagine that Jesus has this exousia in anticipation of the atoning sacrifice he is going to make. But this is probably not what Matthew means. When, in 8:16 f., he quotes Isa. 53 as a prophecy of this Jesus who *heals and casts out demons*, it is probably not intended in any anticipatory sense. Already by virtue of his origin and the spiritual service of sacrifice he carries out – love and deeds of mercy[1] – Jesus has the authority to forgive sins.

It is only in the final phase of Jesus' ministry that his irresistible exousia is taken from him. He is given over by God to extreme humiliation, suffering, and a violent death. And he accepts God's requirements and obeys. This is the sacrificial phase par excellence in Jesus' work. But, as has already been pointed out, Matthew undoubtedly believes that the spiritual sacrifice Jesus had made in the past already had an expiatory effect.

Matthew does not mean that Jesus' work is concluded at his exaltation. The exaltation he receives as a "reward" for his service gives him the exousia to continue the work he did on earth. The apostles go out to teach the peoples "whatsoever I have commanded you" and the risen Lord promises his presence in this service (28:18–20). The old conviction of the divine presence in Israel (particularly in the temple) is here transformed into belief in Christ's presence in the true Israel.

IV

For Matthew, Jesus' deed is not a sacrifice from which mankind is only to reap the fruits. Jesus invites Israel to participate in the deep spiritual temple service he himself carries out. Jesus' followers are to constitute a place of expiation, a sanctuary of atonement in Israel (and in its wider application, for all peoples),[2] and Jesus is not alone in carrying out the sacrifice which is to be made. All who have ears to hear must listen to

[1] To Matthew Jesus' mighty works are (advanced) *deeds of mercy*. Note σπλαγχνίζεσθαι in 9:36; 14:14; 15:32; 20:34, and cf. ἐλεεῖν in 9:27; 15:22; 17:15; 20:30 f.
[2] In this connection I also wish to call to mind how strongly the theme of reconciliation and mutual forgiveness is stressed in Matthew's Gospel. See J. S. Kennard, "The Reconciliation Tendency in Matthew", *ATR* 28 (1946), pp. 159–163, Trilling, *op. cit.*, pp. 121, 196–198, K. Stendahl, "Prayer and Forgiveness", *Svensk Exegetisk Årsbok* 22/23 (1957/58), pp. 75–86, W. G. Thompson, *Matthew's Advice to a Divided Community* (Rome, 1970), and G. Forkman, *The Limits of the Religious Community* (Lund, 1972), pp. 116–132.

God's word as it is now sounded in Israel and "do the will of my Father who is in heaven" (7:21–27). The decisive requirement of love to God (obedience) is so indissolubly fused with the requirement of love for one's neighbour (22:35–40) that the final inspection can turn out to be a question of how one has behaved towards one's fellowmen in need: in the final judgement "deeds of mercy" are asked after (25:31–46). *Diakonia* is counted as *latreia*.

According to Matthew, Jesus enjoins all children of the Rule of Heaven to be and behave as he does. In the Sermon on the Mount he sums up the requirements for citizens of the Kingdom of Heaven in the command to be perfect (τέλειοι, 5:48). The term undoubtedly retains its cultic associations. The word is an old characterization of the whole, spotless and blameless sacrifice (*tamim, tam, shalem*). And this requirement of "perfection" is made a general one for all who want to enter the Kingdom of Heaven.

Nowhere does Matthew state or assume that Jesus' sacrifice makes other offerings superfluous. The reflections in Matthew about Christ's death "as a ransom for many" are never given such an exclusive character that Christ's death has to be set against, and distinguished from, the violent deaths of other innocent and righteous people. On the contrary, the Matthean Jesus stresses forcefully that every true follower must be prepared to make even the utmost sacrifice, i.e. to give his life for Jesus' (the Rule of Heaven's) sake. The spiritual service of sacrifice must continue, even in its most extreme form. This is most clearly seen in the predictions about the suffering, death and resurrection of the Son of man. Throughout the synoptic tradition, predictions of the Son of man's rejection and violent death are connected with instructions to his followers to humble themselves and serve. The bearing of the cross in imitation of Christ is part of the lot the disciples have to take upon themselves. In Matthew, however, this theme has been outlined with exceptional clarity, particularly in the pericope concerning the first prediction of suffering (16:21–28; cf. also 10:16–39).

We have already been reminded that Matthew does not let Jesus distinguish the suffering of the actual atonement itself from that service of sacrifice into which the disciples must enter. He does not baulk at the thought that the great mystery of the atonement has a communal aspect. This is in itself nothing strange, if one takes into account Matthew's background. Sacrifice was of old a collective concern. It was an ancient conviction in Israel that sacrifice expiated sin, and that as a rule, this expiation held for a whole community. The sacrifice was not meant to just benefit the one who brought it, but also the family, relatives, tribe, people, town or land to which one belonged and which one wanted to represent. We are hardly true to historical circumstances if we understand spiritual sacrifices as being a purely individual matter.

I myself do not reckon that even the speech about a heavenly "reward" for such simple spiritual sacrifices as prayer, fasting and alms (6:1–6, 16–21) should be taken purely individualistically. When it comes to the advanced spiritual sacrifices, the sacrifice of life, the death of the martyrs, the communal aspect is undeniable. From early times the conviction was that the "death of the saints" was precious in the eyes of God and bore much fruit for others. This thought seems to lie behind certain elements in the Jesus-tradition, and not only in the logion about the grain of wheat in the Gospel of John. Also the parables about the mustard seed and the leaven (Matt. 13:31–33), and the metaphor about the salt which "dies" in the sacrificial meat in order to make the meat into a sacrifice pleasing to God (5:13), seem to deal with the secret behind the death of the saints for the sake of the Rule of Heaven.[1] In spite of his eagerness to demonstrate that Jesus' death was in all points perfect, Matthew shows no inclination to clearly distinguish Jesus' sacrificial death from the martyrdom of his followers.

V

We have seen that Matthew, by interpreting Jesus' ministry as a spiritual service of sacrifice, takes away the demarcation between Jesus and his followers, "the true Israel", the church, and between Jesus' work in the past and the church's work in the present. Jesus is primarily depicted as the perfect prototype for all "children of God" who want to be "servants of God". To balance the picture, however, we must remind ourselves that Jesus is in no less decisive a fashion portrayed as supremely exalted above the church, and that, according to Matthew, his activity constitutes the foundation upon which the church stands or falls. It is certainly true that the church has an extraordinary exousia. It can "bind and loose" (16:19; 18:18), it can forgive sins (9:8), it can heal the sick and cast out demons (10:1–8; cf. 7:21–23) etc. But it is quite typical that the church has received its exousia through Jesus, and that its mighty deeds are done "in the name of Jesus". When the church comes together for divine service it is "in the name of Jesus" and with Jesus as invisibly present (18:20; 28:20), and when one at the Holy Communion receives the forgiveness of sin, it is in remembrance of Christ's death (26:28). The Matthean baptismal formula – "in the name of the Father and of the Son and of the Holy Spirit" – is also worth considering from our point of view. Jesus' position as the church's incomparable *Kyrios* appears in countless ways in the Gospel of Matthew. What then, according to Matthew, constitutes the decisive differences between Jesus and his followers?

[1] See my article, "The Seven Parables in Matthew XIII", *NTS* 19 (1972/73), pp. 21–23.

There is one difference that Matthew is anxious to indicate: in all Jesus' followers is found a frailty and mortality – in the transferred meaning of the word – which was not found in Jesus. They are therefore required to repent, which Jesus never was (cf. 3:11, 14). They daily have to pray a prayer which Jesus did not need to pray: Forgive us our trespasses (6:9a, 12). They have to fall back on the perfect sacrificial service Jesus made whereas he never had to rely on anyone else's merits.

This theme is an authentic and common feature of the synoptic passion tradition, but it is Matthew who brings it out with particular clarity in his depiction of Jesus' ministry. Jesus enjoins it upon his followers to confess him before men (10:32 f.) and, when required to do so, to give up their lives for his (the Rule of Heaven's) sake (16:24–26; 10:38 f.). The twelve also promise to fulfil this requirement of faithfulness unto death. With Peter at their head, they protest that they would rather die than desert him (26:30–35). But when the test comes they all fail him and let him down (26:36–56), and Peter denies Jesus as coarsely as is at all possible (26:69–75). Thus even the church's leading men have forfeited their lives with Jesus and the heavenly Father (cf. 10:32 f., 39; 16:25). When Jesus gives up his spirit on the cross, the disciples are therefore in such a position that they need absolute forgiveness for themselves. This they also receive. That the risen Lord does not reject them after what has happened, but reveals himself to them and gives them his renewed confidence (26:32; 28:10, 16–20) signifies, *de facto*, fundamental forgiveness. It is striking that Matthew does not feel it necessary to comment explicitly on this. For him it was somehow self-evident that the repentant church can fall back on Jesus' mercy.

Throughout the whole passion narrative Jesus has a dark shadow behind him: the frail and failing church. One can ask oneself why the early Christian teachers so unsparingly told of how Jesus' foremost men – pillars in the church – failed in the moment of trial. Sometimes when the rabbis contemplated the great falls in the history of Israel, both that of the nation (worship of the golden calf) and that of individual great men (David's adultery), they drew the conclusion that this happened and was recorded in order to show coming generations that the road of repentance and atonement was open for the people of God, even for the vilest sinner.[1] Perhaps there was a similar consideration behind the early Christian teachers' presentation of the apostles' denial and failure. Matthew has no illusions about the church's infallibility. The church has an extraordinary exousia, but this has its source in Jesus, and it stands or falls on Jesus' position and presence (28:18–20). This is presented in symbolic form in the pericope relating Peter's attempt to walk on the water. Though he

[1] Ab. Zar. 4a, 5b. Cf. S. Schechter, *Aspects of Rabbinic Theology* (Schocken, New York, 1961), pp. 317 f.

can control the dangerous waves, he needs Jesus' command and Jesus' help (14:22–33).[1]

If we were to ask for the ultimate reason for this difference between the sinless Jesus and his imperfect followers, Matthew would presumably refer to what is said about Jesus' unique divine origin (1:18–25). Presumably this inherited conviction of Jesus' heavenly origin fills this function. We recognize this thought from Paul: The children of Adam are from the earth, men of dust; Christ is from heaven (1 Cor. 15:47). It was a deeply engrained idea in Israel that man's weakness and mortality was due to his earthly origin: "dust thou art and to dust thou shalt return" (Gen. 3:19). Over against this, Matthew – as does the tradition before him – sets the conviction that the "Messiah, the Son of the living God" was of heavenly origin. This mystery was able to explain why Jesus could carry out his service unto death without the least stain, and thus effect an atonement in which the church – all who want to be "the true Israel" – can trust.

[1] Cf. Bornkamm, *op. cit.*, pp. 48–53.

CHAPTER II

ESCHATOLOGICAL FAITH IN THE GOSPEL OF JOHN

JOHN PAINTER

I INTRODUCTION

NOWHERE IN THE NEW TESTAMENT IS THE RELATION BETWEEN HISTORY and interpretation, or history and faith, such an *obvious* problem as it is in the Gospel of John. John stands apart from the Synoptic Gospels with regard to chronology, content and style. None of the Gospels records bare history, but, in John, theological *reflexion* has progressed beyond the limits that we find in the Synoptics so that sources can no longer be detected with any certainty. The Gospel is a stylistic unity. Narrative and discourse passages are written in the same style and bear the impress of one mind. The language and style of the discourses differ greatly from the teaching of Jesus in the Synoptics. Certain words and phrases, frequently used in the Synoptics, rarely occur in John. "The kingdom of God", so important in the Synoptics, is to be found only in Jn. 3:3, 5. But there is a close theological relation because the seed of all the important Johannine themes can be found in the Synoptics, for example, Jesus as the new temple, the new birth, eternal life, the mission of Jesus, the glorification of Jesus and the faith of discipleship.

John develops the theme of believing, emphasizing the experience of salvation and the nature of the person of Christ. In doing this he becomes, with Paul, one of the leading theologians of the New Testament. Paul wrote of the permanent significance of the person and work of Christ, showing little *evidence* of interest in the historical Jesus. By writing a Gospel John shows that the Jesus of history and the Christ of faith are one, and gives a detailed treatment of the eschatological nature of faith in relation to the historical revelation in Jesus.

II THE VOCABULARY OF FAITH

John asserts that faith is the proper response to the revelation in Jesus. His understanding of the revelation has determined his understanding of faith. Statistical comparisons show the importance of believing in the Gospel.[1]

πιστεύειν is used in every chapter except 15, 18 and 21. In chapter 15 μένειν is used to express the abiding of faith in the allegory of the Vine. πιστεύειν is used only once in the passion narrative (19:35), because this is the record of the rejection of Jesus. But it is used six times in chapter 20, plus ἄπιστος and πιστός in 20:27, drawing attention to the centrality of the resurrection for faith.

There is a concentration on believing in chapters 1–12 where Jesus confronts the world with the challenge to believe. In chapters 13–17 the confrontation is past and the nature of authentic faith is developed by the use of other words, such as μένειν, τηρεῖν, γινώσκειν and εἰδέναι. While εἰδέναι is used more frequently than γινώσκειν in narrative passages, both words seem to cover the same semantic area except that εἰδέναι is never used in the formula of mutual knowledge, nor of the Father's knowledge.[2] John's more frequent use of εἰδέναι than γινώσκειν stands with the use of Paul, the Synoptics and the New Testament in general. The use of these two verbs as equivalents points away from Gnosticism to the use in the LXX.

John uses neither πίστις nor γνῶσις. The absence of γνῶσις is not surprising. It is used only twice in the Synoptics[3] and 29 times in the New Testament, of which 23 occur in the Pauline Corpus. γινώσκειν is used 221 times in the New Testament. The preference for the verb can hardly be regarded as an anti-Gnostic device. The books which reflect contact or conflict with Gnosticism are the ones in which γνῶσις is to be found, especially 1 and 2 Corinthians. If John was anti-Gnostic at this point we

---

[1] The following table gives a list of some of the words important in John, comparing the number of uses with other books in the New Testament. The different usage in discourse and narrative passages should also be noted as indicating the difference between the ideal and the actual. (For this see p. 41, n. 1.)

	John 1–12	John 13–17	John 18–21	John Total	Pauline Corpus	Synoptic Gospels	First John	N.T. Total
πιστεύειν	76	15	7	98	54	30	9	239
πίστις	0	0	0	0	142	24	1	244
γινώσκειν	33	21	2	56	49	61	25	221
γνῶσις	0	0	0	0	23	2	0	29
εἰδέναι	54	15	16	85	102	72	15	230
ἀγαπᾶν	7	25	5	37	33	26	27	142
ἀγάπη	1	6	0	7	76	2	18	118
φιλεῖν	4	3	6	13	2	8	0	25
μαρτυρία	12	0	2	14	2	4	6	37
μαρτυρεῖν	26	3	4	33	8	2	6	76

[2] But as the formula is used only in 10:14–15, and the Father is the subject of the verb "to know" on only one occasion (10:15), this is hardly significant. That γινώσκειν is always used where the future realization of knowledge is in view is only of grammatical importance (7:17; 8:28, 32; 10:38; 13:7, 35; 14:20, 31; 17:3, 23).

[3] Luke 1:77; 11:52.

would have expected γνῶσις to have been used, but with an anti-Gnostic meaning.

The absence of πίστις is more difficult to explain in the light of its frequent use in Paul and the New Testament as a whole. The fact that πίστις is used only twice in the Corpus Hermeticum has been noted as evidence that Gnostic association had not prejudiced its use.[1] Had there been Gnostic associations that John was countering we would have expected him to have used the word in a redefined sense.

There is a clear preference for πίστις in the Pauline Corpus and there is a concentration of use in contexts dealing with the conflict between faith and works as the way of salvation.[2] It is also used 16 times in a similar conflict in James. John was not concerned with this conflict.[3] In the Pastoral epistles πίστις is used 33 times, often to express the content of faith. While John does not disregard the content of faith, other elements are also prominent. He chose πιστεύειν because it suited his understanding of the proper response to the revelation, which is the primary theme of the Gospel and hence the concentration on πιστεύειν.

III THE πιστεύειν FORMULAE[4]

1. The verb followed by the dative of the person or object believed is used eighteen times, and expresses the most important aspects of belief on the basis of witness.[5] John wrote to emphasize the possibility of belief on the basis of witness (20:31).[6] There is a multiple witness which has a single point of focus, Jesus. Jesus' self-testimony and the witness of the Father to Jesus in his works stand apart from the rest (5:31–39; 8:13–18). The witness of the works may provide a transition (10:38; 14:11), but ultimately the scandal of Jesus' self-testimony cannot be avoided.[7] All but

[1] W. F. Howard, *Christianity According to St. John* (London, 1943), p. 155.

[2] In Romans 39 times, 26 in chapters 1–5; in Galatians 22 times, 14 in chapter 3.

[3] 6:28 f. does not deal with this subject.

[4] In 2:24 Jesus is the subject, but the verb is used in a sense different from the rest of the Gospel. Neither Jesus nor the Father is said to believe, nor does John use the verb in the Old Testament sense of the faithfulness of God. In 9:18 the verb is followed by ... περὶ ... ὅτι. The Jews refused to believe that the man in question had been blind. By discarding the miracle one possible way of coming to believe in Jesus was rejected. The construction used in 9:18 is not a straightforward πιστεύειν ὅτι construction, which is used in John to express the content of Christian faith.

[5] These include Jesus: 4:21; 5:38, 46; 6:30; 8:31, 45, 46; 10:37, 38; 14:11; Jesus' words: 2:22; 4:50; 5:47; Jesus' works: 10:38 (14:11); Him who sent Jesus: 5:24; the Scripture: 2:22; 5:46, 47; 12:38.

[6] There is a tenfold witness to Jesus in the Gospel. 1. The Baptist: 1:7, 8, 15, 32, 34; 3:26; 5:33; 2. The woman of Samaria: 4:38; 3. Jesus: 5:31; 8:18; 18:37; 4. Jesus' works: 5:36; 10:25; 5. The Father: 5:37; 8:18; 6. The Scriptures: 5:39 f; 7. The crowd: 12:17; 8. The Paraclete: 15:26; 9. The apostles: 15:27; 10. The beloved disciple: 19:35; 21:24. Only those instances where the terminology of witness has been used are listed.

[7] In 4:21 and 14:11 Jesus' appeal to believe him is followed by a clause indicating that to believe Jesus' self-testimony is to believe certain things about him, i.e., his place in salvation history (4:21), and his relation to the Father (14:11).

one use of this construction fall in chapters 1–12 where there is also a concentration of the use of the vocabulary of witness. After the resurrection the testimony of the eyewitnesses takes on a new significance. Because of this John uses the individual cases in chapters 1–12 as illustrations of the effectiveness of witness and in chapters 13–17 the basis of all future belief on the apostolic testimony is outlined (15:26–27; 17:20 f.).

2. There are two instances of the verb followed by ἐν (3:15; 20:31). In 3:15 the construction is in synonymous parallelism with the verb followed by εἰς in 3:16. The order of the words indicates that the meaning is "to believe in". There was a tendency in the New Testament period for εἰς and ἐν to overlap in meaning as in 3:15 f.[1] 20:31 is less clear because of the word order. But as believing in Jesus' name is elsewhere spoken of (1:12; 2:23; 3:18, using εἰς), and there is no reference to having life in Jesus' name, it should be taken as "believing in . . .". This is borne out by the parallelism between believing followed by ὅτι . . . and believing followed by ἐν. . . . Further, 1 Jn. 5:13, which is modelled on John 20:31, refers to those who believe in (εἰς) the name of the Son of God.

3. There are 36 instances where the verb is followed by εἰς[2] out of 47 uses in the New Testament. Of these 3 occur in 1 John, 3 in Acts and no other book has more than 1 use of this construction, which is peculiar to the New Testament.[3] This construction indicates belief in Jesus, except in 12:44 and 14:1 which refer to believing in the Father who sent Jesus. It is usually used with a personal object, but 6:29–30; 8:30–31; and 1 Jn. 5:10 are probable exceptions and Jn. 5:24, where the verb, followed by the dative case, has a personal object, and has much the same meaning as the verb followed by εἰς, for example in 14:1. Thus while there is a personal element in this faith other constructions can also express this.[4]

4. The verb is used absolutely 28 times,[5] but the contexts supply the objects of all but 16.[6] While 1:50 is a formal example of the absolute use, the context shows that only superficial faith in Jesus in current Messianic terms is involved. Such faith is challenged to reassess Jesus (1:51). The absolute use, like the verb followed by εἰς (2:23 f.) or by the dative case (8:31), can be used to express superficial faith. But the truly absolute use,

---

[1] See Moule, *Idiom*, pp. 69, 75, 80 f. This construction was used in the LXX and there is one clear instance of its use in Mk. 1:15.

[2] 1:12; 2:11, 23; 3:16, 18[(2)], 36; 4:39; 6:29, 35, 40; 7:5, 31, 38, 39, 48; 8:30; 9:35, 36; 10:42; 11:25, 26, 45, 48; 12:11, 36, 37, 42, 44[(2)], 46; 14:1[(2)], 12; 16:9; 17:20.

[3] Ecclus. 38:31 is not a parallel.

[4] Contrary to C. H. Dodd, *Interpretation of the Fourth Gospel* (Cambridge, 1953), p. 183 and L. L. Morris, *The Gospel According to St. John* (Grand Rapids, 1971), p. 336. Morris is also wrong in suggesting that this construction indicates a sense of mystical abiding.

[5] 1:7, 50; 3:12[(2)], 18; 4:41, 42, 48, 53; 5:44; 6:36, 47, 64[(2)]; 9:38; 10:25, 26; 11:15, 40; 12:39; 14:11, 29; 16:31; 19:35; 20:8, 25, 29[(2)].

[6] 1:7; 4:48, 53; 5:44; 6:36, 47, 64[(2)]; 11:15, 40; 14:29; 19:35; and probably also 20:8, 25, 29[(2)], referring to belief in the risen Lord which is at the heart of the meaning of "believe" used absolutely.

both uses with ἐν and many uses with εἰς or followed by the dative case, indicate authentic faith. These uses tend to fall in the discourses.

5. There are twelve instances where the verb, followed by a ὅτι clause, indicates the significance of Jesus.[1] The use of this construction often occurs with verbs of knowing, with εἰδέναι (16:30) and with γινώσκειν (6:69; 10:38; 17:8, 21; cf. 17:23). This construction is used to express the *perception* of authentic faith. The Gospel paradoxically shows that confessions of faith made in these terms by individuals (6:69; 11:27; 16:30), were not authentic at the time of making (6:70 f.; 13:36 f.; 11:39; 16:31 f.).

6. Twenty five uses of πιστεύειν fall in narrative passages, where rejection and partial faith in Jesus are stated.[2] Expressions of faith are brought into question by their contexts. All of the constructions are used to express both partial and authentic faith and the verb followed by εἰς is used more frequently than any other construction to describe partial faith.

7. Four instances describe activities which have the purpose of provoking belief (1:7; 17:21; 19:35; 20:31). Authentic faith was not a reality during Jesus' ministry, but the Gospel was written for a new situation when such faith had become possible.[3] Descriptions of those who came to partial faith during Jesus' ministry have become examples of the possibility of coming to authentic faith. Thus there is no difference in terminology in the narrative descriptions of partial faith and the descriptions of authentic faith that Jesus uses in his discourses.

IV SYMBOLIC PARALLELS OF BELIEVING

The idea of believing is also indicated by a number of symbolic parallels. The symbols do not have exactly the same meaning as πιστεύειν but focus on an aspect of what is a complex response to the revelation in Jesus. Most of the references occur in discourse passages and deal with an aspect of authentic faith, but in a few instances they occur in narrative passages and there are indications of the limitations involved. In other instances the narrative context indicates that the aspect in view is restricted to those who knew Jesus during the days of his ministry. The distinction between those who believed having seen Jesus and those who believed without having seen is also indicated using πιστεύειν (17:20; 20:29).

[1] That Jesus is the Christ the Son of God: 6:69; 11:27; 20:31; that "I am": 8:24; 13:19; that the Father sent Jesus: 11:42; 17:8, 21; that the Father is in Jesus and Jesus in the Father: 10:38; 14:10; that Jesus has come from God: 16:27, 30.

[2] Both 2:24 and 9:18 fall in narrative passages, as do two uses of the verb followed by the dative case, eleven uses followed by εἰς, seven absolute uses, and three uses followed by ὅτι.

[3] Debate about the tense of the verb to believe in 20:31 is not relevant because John was concerned that faith should be authentic, perceive the true nature of Jesus and thus lead on to real decision and obedience.

From the symbols certain aspects of what it means to believe may be outlined. Believing involves: 1. Perception, recognition, understanding; 2. Decision; 3. Dependence and obedience.[1] Some of the terms overlap from one group to another so that "to hear" and "to worship" can involve all three categories and "to follow" can involve obedience as well as decision.

In the category of perception, seeing and remembering are restricted to the situation of Jesus' ministry. Only those who had actually seen him with their eyes could see him in this way i.e., remember with new understanding what their eyes had seen.[2]

V   Dramatis Personae

The object of the verbs of believing is Jesus except where belief in God is expressed and then it is God as the one who has sent Jesus, as revealed in Jesus. Thus one is called to believe (in) Jesus, his words, his works, and certain facts about him concerning his relation to the Father. But these are not ultimate distinctions. For this reason John has designated Jesus as the Logos. Because his words are self-testimony, to believe him is to believe in him. He is the content of his own message.

[1] *1. Believing as perception, recognition, understanding.*
This aspect is emphasized when the verb is used with ὅτι and with verbs of knowing, as well as with the following symbolic descriptions.

	Narrative	Discourse
To see[1]	1:14	1:39, 46, 51; 6:40, 62; 11:40; 12:40; 14:7, 17.
To hear	4:42; 10:20	5:24, 25, 45; 8:43, 47[2]; 10:3, 8, 16, 27.
To remember	2:17, 22; 12:16	14:26.
2. Believing as decision.		
To come	1:39, 46	3:20, 21; 6:35, 37, 45, 65; 7:37; 14:6.
To receive or reject		1:5, 11, 12; 3:11, 32, 33; 5:43; 12:48[2]; 13:20; 14:17; 17:8.
To love or hate	(21:15, 16, 17)	3:19, 20; 8:42; 12:25, 43; 14:15, 21, 23, 24, 28; 16:27.
To confess or deny	9:22; 12:42; 18:25, 26	13:38.
To follow	(1:37, 38, 40) 6:2	1:43; 8:12; 10:4, 5, 27; 12:26.
3. Believing as dependence and obedience.		
To drink		4:13, 14 (6:35); 7:37.
To eat		(6:35); 6:51, 52.
To be a disciple	9:27	8:31; 13:35; 15:8.
To learn or be taught		6:45.
To keep		8:51(52); 14:15, 21, 23, 24, 28.
To abide		6:56; 8:31 (12:46); 15:4, 5, 6, 9, 10.
To serve		12:26.
To worship	9:38	4:23,24.

(*Note 1.* Bultmann is right in saying that the various verbs of seeing are used without any difference of meaning being intended (see *Das Evangelium des Johannes* (Göttingen, 1962), p. 45 n. 1). The difference of use is grammatical in that the different forms are used to supply different tenses.)

[2] Contrary to the views of most commentators. Both Bultmann and Dodd take this

Neither Jesus nor the Father is the subject of the verb to believe. Every other major and most other minor characters deny or affirm faith in the course of the Gospel. The disciples, as individuals (1:50; 6:69; 20:8, 29) or as a group (2:11, 22; 16:27, 30; 17:18), are described as the believers more frequently than any one else. But there are indications that, in the context of Jesus' ministry, they did not really believe (2:22), and Jesus even questioned whether they believed at all (16:31).

After the disciples "the many" are most frequently described as believers. This belief is normally in response to signs (2:23; 7:31; 8:30; 10:42; 11:45; 12:11) and is brought into question (2:23 ff.). In 8:30 "the many" are identified with the Jews of 8:31, who, more frequently than any others, are those of whom it is said that they do not believe (5:38, 47; 8:45–46; 9:18; 10:25, 26; 12:37).

VI   THE JOHANNINE SITUATION

John brings out the stark contrast between believing in and rejecting Jesus, making decision a prominent element in what he understands as believing. Judaism forms the background to the Gospel, Judaism fragmented by sects, the sect of the Way being the one which most threatened its life and faith. Pressure was brought to bear on all heretics and especially upon Jewish Christians. About A.D. 85 *birkath ha-minim* was published, providing a basis for excommunicating heretics from the Synagogue, with a clause designed to exclude Jewish Christians. In the New Testament, only in John is the technical word for excommunication, ἀποσυνάγωγος, used (9:22 (34); 12:42; 16:2). Excommunication lasted as long as the error of confessing faith in Jesus persisted. This sanction was designed to discourage converts to Christianity. According to 12:42, it achieved its aim reasonably well. The problem of the ostracism of Jewish Christians is apparent from the time of Paul but the basis for excommunication did not become fixed until later.

The threat of excommunication encouraged those who believed in Jesus to remain within the fold of Judaism as secret believers. Nicodemus is treated as a typical example (3:1 ff.; 7:50 ff.; 19:38 ff.). He is the typical *man* who believed on the basis of *signs* (2:23–25; 3:1–2).[1] He is the typical *ruler* who would not openly confess his faith for fear of excommunication (12:42). Even "the twelve" become secret believers because of fear of the

---

[1] Note the use of "man" and "signs" in both passages.

sight to be the vision of faith, open to all believers, though they differ on points of detail. But Dodd refuses to interpret Jn. 19:35 in this way saying that the evangelist was not the sort of person who could affirm the veracity of his evidence while offering only a suggestive symbol (cf. his *Historical Tradition in the Fourth Gospel* (Cambridge, 1963), p. 135). This comment is equally applicable to 1:14 (and 1 Jn. 1:1 ff.). Further, the Gospel clearly distinguishes seeing and believing (20:29).

Jews (20:19). The threat was also used to make timid believers recant. In John 9 the man who had been blind overcame intimidation and was ultimately excommunicated, becoming an example of the true believer in the Jewish situation.

The Gospel demonstrates that the revelation in Jesus justifies the cost of facing persecution. The revelation is the fulfilment and abolition of Judaism. The Prologue asserts that the revelation in the incarnate Word supersedes the Law of Moses. The Old Testament, like the Baptist, is rightly understood only in terms of its witness to Jesus.[1] The Jews' religion was surpassed by the new way (2:1–11).[2] The old Temple was made obsolete by the risen Christ as the new Temple for the meeting of God and man (2:13–22). The identification of Judaism with the citizens of the Kingdom of God is denied. Those who believe in Jesus enter the Kingdom (3:1–15). The true worshippers are those who receive the Spirit through believing in Jesus (4:23–24).

Believing is a response to the eschatological event. The coming of the Word made flesh in history brought about the judgement of the world, portrayed in terms of light coming into the darkness (3:19–21). The light was not conquered by the darkness, it overcame the darkness (1:5; 16:33). The judgement of the light causes division.[3] Those who believe, who come to the light, are divided off from those who reject Jesus.

VII The Judgement and Unbelief

Unbelief is the rejection of Jesus and his place in salvation history. Jesus came offering life and freedom. The Jews claimed that they had life and that they had never been in bondage (5:39 f.; 8:33). Because they *misunderstood* what Jesus offered they could not see the new possibility his coming had brought about. He came with knowledge of the unseen God. But the Jews claimed that they knew God and rejected the possibility of knowing him in Jesus. Their knowledge was based on the Scriptures (5:39, 45), which they used in proof-text fashion to avoid facing the claim of Jesus' works and words. They ruled out the possibility that Jesus had a place in salvation history on various grounds. There is a need to distinguish the intellectual arguments used to justify the rejection of Jesus from the moral and spiritual causes of unbelief.

The intellectual arguments form two groups. Firstly, there was the tendency to reject the reality of Jesus' miracles (7:4; 9:18). When the

---

[1] 1:7, 8, 15, 32, 34; 3:26; 5:33, 39, 46 f.; 8:56, 58; 12:41.

[2] The contrast is between poor and good wine. The best was kept until last. Compare Mk. 2:22.

[3] John uses σχίσμα in 7:43; 9:16; 10:19 to indicate the divisive effect of Jesus' words and works. But this theme is more pervasive than the word. See 3:19–21, 36; 7:31, 40–44, 45–52; 8:30 ff.; 9:16, 39–41; 10:19–20, 31–42; 11:45; 12:37–43.

miracles could not be denied their significance was misconstrued. Secondly there are arguments from Scripture which were used to deny Jesus any place in salvation history. 1. His origin (family) was known but the origin of the Messiah was to be unknown (7:27; 6:42). 2. His place of origin was wrong, Galilee not Bethlehem as foretold (7:41 f., 52). 3. His origin was not known whereas it was known that Moses came from God (9:29).[1] (There are inconsistencies in these arguments because they are rationalizations for the rejection which occurred for other reasons. The real problem was that Jesus did not fit into the religious pattern of life which they claimed had come from God.) 4. He broke the Sabbath law (5:10 ff.; 9:13 ff.). But the Old Testament gave precedents for the performance of certain works on the Sabbath (7:21 ff.). Jesus also argued that he only did what God was doing. God's creative works continued on the Sabbath (5:17 f.), a point acknowledged in the Rabbinic literature and Philo. In this way Jesus challenged the Jews to see God's ultimate revelation and act in him. His claim was rejected because it went beyond the bounds of the Old Testament and it was assumed that if a man claimed to be God he was a blasphemer. In the face of the scandal caused by his self-testimony Jesus appealed to the witness of the Father in his works (5:36; 10:31–39). If his words could not be accepted his works should show that he had some place in salvation history (9:16). Those who rejected both Jesus' words and works did so because their standard of judgement was perverted.

Our attention is turned to *the moral cause* of unbelief, which can be described as false or perverted love. Love is directed to the wrong object, indicating that man chooses wrongly. The element of choice is prominent when love and hate are used together or when it is indicated that love is directed wrongly. Both characteristics appear in 3:19–21. The first false love is love of the darkness. The darkness is the world apart from God, which rejects God's approach in the revelation of the light. The light is rejected because men prefer the world apart from God. They prefer their own evil actions to the change that accepting the judgement of the light would bring.[2] The second false love is love for the glory of man rather than the glory of God (5:41–44; 7:18; 8:50; 12:43); the choice of self-advancement and self-exaltation, of false greatness, greatness apart from God and opposed to God. The third false love is love for one's own life (12:25), love for self as opposed to love for God or anyone else. The fact that this love leads to death indicates that it is opposed to faith which leads to life.[3] These three loves involve the claim to already

[1] Johannine irony lies behind each of these arguments. The Jews did not know his father; he did come from Bethlehem; he had come from God.

[2] Love of the darkness may also be described as love of the world, 1 Jn. 2:15 f.

[3] Eternal life is the gift of God to those who believe (3:15 ff.). Life is no more to be equated with knowledge than it is with faith, contrary to Bultmann *op. cit.*, on 17:3. The meaning is that those who know God in Jesus receive eternal life as a consequence just as believers are given eternal life.

possess life, which made the Jews hostile to anyone who threatened their possession or called it into question. Jesus opposed and condemned this self-assurance because it prevented men from acknowledging his works and hearing his words: ". . . because you say 'We see', your guilt remains" (9:41). The Jews closed themselves against the revelation, willing self-preservation rather than knowledge of the origin of Jesus' doctrine. Those who seek to do God's will, who seek to honour God and honour from God, will know the origin of Jesus' doctrine (7:17).

The rejection of Jesus resulted from a moral failure. False standards produced false judgements. John suggests that the false moral standards have a *spiritual cause*. They have arisen because men are children of the devil (8:43 ff.); are not Jesus' sheep (10:26 f.); are not of the truth (18:37). It is not that some men are saved by nature, for all men, including "the twelve", were once in the darkness, in the world (15:19; 17:6, 9 f., 24). It is only through believing that one leaves the darkness and becomes a son of light (8:12; 12:35–36).

Are those who believe given to Jesus by the Father in such a way that they automatically believe (cf. 6:37–65 esp. 37, 44, 45, 65)? Are those who do not believe prevented from doing so by God (12:37–41)? On the contrary, 6:39 is balanced by 6:40 indicating that the Father gives Jesus those who believe in him, and 6:44 does not indicate *how* the Father *draws* men. 12:32 indicates that all men are *drawn* by the uplifted Son of Man.[1] The power of darkness prevents men from believing. Some men believed as a result of the coming of the light of the world, breaking the power of darkness.[2] Jesus gave the same reason for unbelief when he told the Jews who had refused his offer of freedom that they did so on the basis of the false standards which they had derived from listening to their father, the devil (8:38–44). They had false standards of truth, freedom, life, and God. Because of this they rejected the truth of the knowledge of God in Jesus and the freedom from sin, eternal life, which he came to bring. They rejected his words and his works. Had they given heed to his works their standards would have been changed. The transparently good nature of his works would have led to the conclusion that he had come from God (9:16). However, the majority of people failed to draw this conclusion.

The Jews did not believe because they failed to see the glory revealed in Jesus (12:40–41), primarily in his signs (12:37). 12:37 does not say that they *saw* the signs. Seeing signs is always related to believing. Though the Jewish authorities tended to be sceptical (9:18), they could acknowledge that Jesus performed signs i.e. miracles[3] (11:47), as did the crowd which

---

[1] The same verb is used in both verses and in Jer. 38(31):3 LXX where it is the love of God that *draws* men. The universal scope of the love of God is asserted in Jn. 3:16; 12:32.

[2] Compare Matt. 12:28 ff.

[3] Jesus never speaks of *signs*. He appeals to the witness of his *works* which indicate his authority because they are the works of the Father which he performs. In the situation of

failed to see the sign (6:26) and demanded one immediately after the feeding miracle (6:30). The repeated demand for a sign indicates the failure to see Jesus' miracles as signs of his authority (2:18; 4:48; 6:30). The Jews did not believe because they did not take Jesus' signs into account in their assessment of him (9:16). They denied his claims, the meaning of his miracles and the witness of those who believed in him. But those who believed insisted on taking the signs into account (9:16, 25, 30 ff.; 10:19–21). The failure to *see* the glory manifest in the signs, which witnessed to Jesus' authority, prevented faith.

In 12:37 ff. John has modified the text of Isa. 6:10 so that *the one who has blinded the Jews is distinguished from the one who would heal them*. The change from third person singular, for the agent of blinding, to the first person singular, for the agent of healing, is of the utmost importance as is the introduction of τυφλοῦν into this quotation. While a number of interpretations of 12:40 are possible,[1] only one fits the context, explains why the Jews did not see the glory of Jesus' signs and believe, and is consistent with the theology of the Gospel. "He", the prince of this world (12:31), has blinded the Jews so that Jesus may not heal them. This interpretation has the support of Origen[2] and a remarkable parallel in 2 Cor. 4:4:

> "... the god of this world has *blinded* the minds of the unbelieving, that the light of the gospel of the glory of Christ, who is the image of God, should not dawn upon them".

Paul was dealing with the problem of unbelief. The fault did not lie in the gospel or the preaching of it, but with Satan, who had made people insensitive so that they would not believe. Further, in 1 Jn. 2:11 the darkness is said to have *blinded* the eyes of those who walk in darkness. In Jn. 12:40; 2 Cor. 4:4; and 1 Jn. 2:11 we have the only three uses of τυφλοῦν in the New Testament. In none of these is it said that God is the agent of blinding and in 2 Cor. 4:4 and 1 Jn. 2:11 it is clear that he is not.[3]

[1] Other interpretations are ruled out for the following reasons: (1) "He" cannot refer to the prophet, whose words are quoted. (2) "He", God, has blinded the Jews so that the prophet may not heal them. But the prophet's failure does not explain the failure of the signs. (3) "He", God, has blinded the Jews so that Jesus may not heal them. Such opposition between the Father and Son is irreconcilable with Johannine thought (3:35; 5:19–20 *et al.*). (4) "They", the signs (the neuter plural would take a singular verb), have blinded the Jews so that Jesus may not heal them. One could compare the hardening effect of the parables according to Mark 4:12. But this interpretation fails to answer the question raised in the text in 12:38. "To whom...?" indicates that not all saw the signs performed by the arm of the Lord and 12:40 explains why they did not.

[2] Origen: Fragment XCII.

[3] The same point of view appears without the word in Lk. 8:12; Eph. 6:12; Col. 1:13; 1 Jn. 5:19.

Jesus' ministry signs are simply miracles as viewed by the crowds, as the formula "signs and wonders" of 4:48 indicates. But from the perspective of the resurrection and the coming of the Paraclete, signs operate as the works which bear witness to Jesus' leading men to authentic faith (20:31). Thus, while the signs produced misunderstanding during Jesus' ministry, they now provoke authentic faith. There is an ambivalence of meaning in the way signs are used in the Gospel because of this.

This dualistic interpretation is reinforced by the evidence of the Qumran Texts.[1] The general affinity of the Gospel with the Qumran Texts makes this parallel the more significant, especially as the affinity is nowhere more pronounced than with regard to the Johannine "dualism". In John, the prince of this world is the power of darkness (12:31; 14:30; 16:11). Having mentioned him (12:31), attention is drawn to the blinding effect of walking in the darkness (12:35 ff.).[2] Jesus, the light (8:12), was present for a short time. He exhorted his hearers to believe in the light that the darkness may not overwhelm them ($\kappa\alpha\tau\alpha\lambda\dot{\alpha}\beta\eta$). Jesus had not been overcome ($o\dot{v}\ \kappa\alpha\tau\dot{\epsilon}\lambda\alpha\beta\epsilon\nu$) by the darkness (1:5). He had conquered the world (16:33). Those who refused to believe had been overcome by the darkness. The only way to overcome the darkness was to believe in the light. The power of darkness still had its sway (12:39), but there were some exceptions (12:42).

John, like Paul and the Qumran Sect, acknowledged God's rule over the whole creation, but the power of darkness is not overlooked. The coming of the Word made flesh made belief possible (3:19–21). During the ministry of Jesus the signs had a limited effect, producing a limited faith (2:23 ff.), even among the leaders (12:42 f.). When Jesus was lifted up the power of evil was broken (12:31 f.) and faith on a universal scale became possible. The possibility is linked with Jesus' glorification (2:22; 12:16) and the coming of the Paraclete (14:26; 16:7). In the eschatological moment all men are called to believe (4:22 ff.; 5:25). Those who refuse definitively choose the darkness and are finally and irrevocably in the darkness (3:19 ff.; 9:39 ff.). Those who believe leave the world of darkness for the light.

VIII   REVELATION AND RESPONSE

John speaks of varying responses of faith, based on: 1. signs (2:23 f. et al.); 2. the witness of Jesus' works (10:37 f.; 14:10 f.); 3. Jesus' word (5:31; 8:18); 4. the apostolic witness (15:26 f.; 17:20 ff.).

1. Superficial faith

Faith expressed in the context of Jesus' ministry can only be understood as a partial faith. It expresses the attraction of people to Jesus as a miracle worker, teacher, prophet, or Messiah. The form of the statement in 2:23 reveals two characteristics of popular superficial faith.

---

[1] I QM XIII:1–XIV:9; 1 QS III:13–IV:26, especially 1 QS III:20, 24.
[2] Note 1 Jn. 2:11 and the relation of Jn. 12:27 to the Gethsemane prayer in which Luke (22:53) records Jesus' words, "but this is your hour and the power of darkness. . ."

i. πολλοὶ ἐπίστευσαν or variations using πολύς or πάντες are used.[1] The aorist tense is normally used,[2] drawing attention to the specific situation which attracted the crowds. Nothing is indicated about the quality or duration of faith by the tense of the verb. But the contexts show that this faith had yet to face the scandal of Jesus' claims about himself. In many cases it proved transitory. But there were those who went on to believe authentically.

ii. This faith arose out of seeing Jesus' signs.[3] While this was a real turning to Jesus, John indicates that it was inadequate (2:24), because these believers wanted to find the fulfilment of their own purpose in Jesus (6:15; 12:13 ff.).

Misunderstanding is also a mark of superficial faith. Those who are said to have believed are shown to have misunderstood Jesus' role and significance. This is an historical problem in that misunderstanding arose from the Jewish categories. Jesus was thought of as a prophet, miracle worker, or as the Messiah, understood as a political figure. Such faith had to meet the scandal of Jesus' self-testimony. The way John has used this understanding indicates the significance of a proper assessment of the person and work of Christ for authentic faith.

The misunderstanding motif has been recognized as a pedagogical technique used by John.[4] But it is not merely a literary device. It has the same function as the Messianic Secret in Mark, and expresses an appreciation of the historical situation of Jesus' ministry. The problem is not merely that the Jews did not know that Jesus was the Messiah, nor that they understood the Messianic role in terms of a conquering king rather than in terms of service and suffering. John emphasizes that Jesus is the one in whom God is present and active in his love for the world. Thus, the misunderstanding motif is historically based, dramatically developed and has a pedagogical purpose in the structure of the Gospel which was written to remove inadequate attitudes to Jesus which would not be able to stand the test of Jewish persecution. The Gospel was written to bring about authentic faith which perceives Jesus' unique place in salvation history as the incarnate Word (20:31). Misunderstanding is confronted by Jesus' self-testimony which scandalizes the crowds and produces murmurings.[5] The murmurings indicate the dissatisfaction of the believers with

---

[1] 2:23; 4:39, 41; (6:2) 7:31; 8:30; 10:42; 11:45, 48; 12:11, 42.

[2] In 6:2 and 12:11 the use of the imperfect tense anticipates rejection and in 11:48 the future tense is used in a prediction.

[3] 2:23 ff.; 3:2; 6:2, 14 ff.; 7:31; 9:16; 10:41–42; 11:45, 47 f.; 12:18–19, 37, 42.

[4] Bultmann *op. cit.*, p. 127, n. 1 etc. claims that this device was taken over from hellenistic revelation literature. He lists as examples of misunderstanding 2:20; 3:3 f.; 4:10 ff., 32 f.; 6:32 ff.; 7:34 ff.; 14:4 f., 7 ff., 22 ff.; 16:17 f. A number of other examples could be added, 1:49 ff.; 8:31 ff., 38 ff.; 11:11 ff., 23 ff.; 13:8 ff.; *et al.*

[5] γογγύζειν is used in 6:41, 43, 61; 7:38, half of the uses of this verb in the New Testament. It is used twice in 1 Cor. 10:10 to refer to the murmuring of the Israelites against Moses and Aaron, but ultimately against God, as in Ex. 16:2; Num. 14:2, 36; 17:6–15 LXX.

the one who has not measured up to their expectations. Jesus indicated that he did not intend to fulfil these expectations and brought about a direct confrontation of his way with theirs (6:26 ff.). This led to *division* (see earlier, p. 43, n. 3), the rejection of faith by some of those who had originally believed (6:64–66) and the affirmation of faith by "the twelve" through Peter (6:68 ff.; cf. Mk. 9:27 ff.).

2. *Authentic faith*

There are a number of statements which suggest the realization of authentic faith during Jesus' ministry (1:14, 49 f.; 2:11; 4:42, 53; 6:68–69; 9:35–38; 11:27; 16:29–30). But the fact that superficial faith cannot be distinguished from authentic faith by the formula used suggests that the contexts of these passages should be examined.

1:14 is part of the prologue and does not fit into the historical context of Jesus' ministry. It is a *reminiscence*, placed at the beginning of the Gospel to make the true nature of faith clear from the beginning.[1]

The confession of 1:49, which is shown to be inadequate by 1:51, was based on Jesus' miraculously acquired knowledge. The wording of the confession is capable of being understood at two levels: in terms of the Messiah of Jewish expectation or in terms of the unique, incarnate, Son of God of Johannine understanding.[2] Jesus responded that the faith of Nathanael would ultimately be based on the assessment of him as the exalted Son of Man, worshipped by men and angels (1:51).[3] The certainty, "you shall see . . .", should be compared with the hypothetical, "What if you see . . ." (6:62). The certainty of the one and the uncertainty of the other distinguishes the faith of Nathanael from the superficial faith of the multitudes. What distinguishes them at this stage is not so much greater perception, but the reality of Nathanael's decision to follow and his willingness to obey Jesus.

The confessions of 4:42, 53 and 9:35–38 are not modified by their contexts. Perhaps 4:42 looks forward to the fulfilment in the later Samaritan mission. In 4:53 the form of the statement should be compared with

---

[1] In 1:14 John asserts that the glory was *visible* to the eyewitnesses; that God was the *origin* of the glory; that the *nature* of the glory is the loving faithfulness of God seen in its fulfilment in Jesus.

[2] Understood in terms of Johannine irony the words "Rabbi, you are the Son of God. . ." express awareness of the incarnation, that the unique Son of God is to be known in a man, a mere Rabbi.

[3] "You will see the heavens opened", and the Son of Man will be revealed as the central figure with the angels converging on him. Compare Acts 7:56. The scene is set in heaven as in Rev. 4:1. The use of ἀνεῳγότα draws attention to the baptismal stories (Matt. 3:16 f.). But while the placing of 1:51 may suggest a relation with the baptism, the event spoken of is future, the lifting up of the Son of Man in his heavenly enthronement by the cross, receiving not only the worship of men (9:36–38), but also of angels (cf. Heb. 1:6 and Mk. 13:26; 14:62). His kingship does not await the future coming of the Son of Man but is revealed by his being lifted up to heaven by the cross.

Acts 11:14 and 16:14–15, 31, foreshadowing the Gentile mission. The man who had been blind becomes the example of the true believer in the Jewish situation who openly confessing his faith disregards the threat of excommunication.

The confession of Martha in 11:27 can also be understood at two levels. The words "who comes into the world" are Johannine and suggest the perception of authentic faith. But 11:39 indicates that this perception is lacking and that her understanding is as it was in 11:24, not having taken account of Jesus' self-testimony in 11:25 f.

Peter's confession in 6:68 f., and the disciples' confession in 16:29–30 are both couched in the terminology of authentic faith. But the prediction of the disciple's defection brings this into question (6:70–71; 13:2, 38; 16:31–32).

From the narrative confessions it is clear that authentic faith was not a reality during Jesus' ministry. These expressions foreshadow the development of the fullness of faith and are an assessment in retrospect which recognizes an integrity lacking in the superficial faith of the multitudes. Faulty perception led to the defection of the disciples, but the integrity of their faith led to reinstatement. The reason for stating faith in authentic terms in the context of Jesus' ministry is pedagogical. It is not an attempt to distort the historical perspective. There are many indications that this faith only came later and John develops, almost systematically, the reasons why it could only come later. The pedagogical purpose is based on the fact that the words and works of Jesus could not provoke authentic faith in the context of his ministry, but the reminiscence of them in the apostolic witness could. The difference between the situation of the ministry of Jesus and that of the apostolic witness is threefold and authentic faith presupposes:

1. The uplifting or glorification of the Son of Man (3:14 ff.; 12:23, 31 f.; 13:31, 32; (17:1)). The true glory of God in his love for the world was manifest in this event. Thus it was crucial for the coming of authentic faith. This event also brought about the effective judgement of the world by which Jesus overcame the blinding work of the power of darkness, making authentic faith possible.[1]

2. The coming of the Paraclete. This event is associated with the glorification of Jesus and the judgement of the world (7:37 ff.; 16:7 ff.).[2] The judgement began with the coming of Jesus, reached a critical stage at

---

[1] No account is taken at this point of the sacrificial interpretation of Jesus' death in such passages as 1:29; 6:51; 13; 17:19 etc. While the sacrificial element is clear in general terms there is no consensus of opinion on the precise meaning.

[2] 7:37 ff. deals with Jesus' offer of the Spirit. The appeal to Scripture is to be understood Christologically as is usual in John. This is confirmed by the clear statement concerning Jesus as the giver of the Spirit in 7:39. The same is true of 4:10 where the gift becomes the inexhaustible source of life in the believer (cf. 4:14). Jesus is the giver of the Spirit, the believer is the one who receives.

his glorification and continues to be made effective by the Paraclete whose coming Jesus' glorification made possible.[1]

3. The resurrection of Jesus. Thus great stress is laid on belief in the risen Lord (20:8, 18, 20, 25, 27–29). The resurrection is understood as an aspect of the glorification of Jesus. Through this event the disciples became aware of the true significance of Jesus and *remembered* crucial events in the life of Jesus so that they understood them in the perspective of salvation history, in relation to the Old Testament (2:22; 12:16). This *remembrance* is linked to the activity of the Paraclete (14:26).[2] While the events that were remembered were unchanged, the memory was modified by a new perspective, the resurrection of Jesus and the coming of the Paraclete (cf. Rom. 1:4).

Because the Gospel was written for this new situation the narratives frequently have two levels of meaning. One has its roots in the situation of Jesus' ministry and the other takes account of the new situation. The distinction between the eyewitness believers and those who believe on the basis of their testimony (cf. 15:26–27; 17:20 ff.; 20:29) is important because the Gospel is written eyewitness testimony. Thus there is a concentration on the terminology of witness and a complete absence of gospel and preaching terminology commonly found in the Synoptics, Acts and Paul. Because the Gospel is written testimony for this new situation there is no distinction in terms between the professions of faith and the descriptions of authentic faith in Jesus' discourses. The record of his words and works, which were largely ineffective during his ministry, is offered as that which can provoke authentic faith (20:30 f.).

IX   CONCLUSION

Believing is an eschatological phenomenon because it is a response to the eschatological event. It involves a *perception* that was possible only after the glorification of Jesus. It is a gift of the eschatological age, made possible by the coming of Jesus, but made actual by the coming of the Paraclete.

The *decision* involved in believing is set against the background of Jewish persecution. The necessity of this decision is only clear when it is recognized that the eschatological revelation surpassed all previous revelations. It is the decision to follow Jesus no matter what the cost. The reality of the decision is worked out in *obedience* to Jesus' word, in the willingness to confess him openly no matter what the cost, and in loving service

---

[1] While John emphasizes the eschatological fulfilment in Jesus' ministry (4:21, 23; 5:25) and glorification (12:23; 13:1, 31–32; 17:1), the complete fulfilment of the judgement on the last day remains in the future (5:28 f.; 6:39, 44, 54; 11:24).

[2] The accumulation of the terminology of remembrance is significant.

after the pattern of Jesus' own love (13:35). Both of these aspects of obedience are to be understood as the eschatological gifts of the Spirit to believers.

Faith is the eschatological gift to those who respond with integrity to the revelation in Jesus, whose coming potentially broke the grip of the power of darkness over men. To those who take advantage of the opportunity created by his coming, the Paraclete brings the gift of authentic faith.

All men are the creation of the Word. Response to the Word is a possibility given in creation. The problem concerns the origin of the rejection of the Word by men. John explains this in terms of the power of darkness, the prince of this world, who has perverted and blinded man. The coming of the incarnate Word in judgement broke the grip of the power of darkness so that men could leave the darkness for the light which had confronted them in Jesus.[1] Those who came to him were given the Paraclete, through whom authentic *perception, decision,* and *obedience* became actual in the world. This is a phenomenon of the eschatological age of salvation.

---

[1] It is important to distinguish the power of the revelation event and the witness to or proclamation of it from the activity of the Spirit in the lives of the believers, those who have accepted the revelation. John asserts the power of the revelation just as Paul asserts the power of the proclamation (1 Cor. 1:18; 2:4–5).

CHAPTER III

THE SPEECHES IN ACTS—
THIRTY YEARS AFTER

F. F. BRUCE

I

ON DECEMBER 19, 1942, I DELIVERED THE FIRST TYNDALE NEW Testament Lecture. It was later published in pamphlet form by the Tyndale Press, London, under the title *The Speeches in the Acts of the Apostles*.[1] The lecture was a by-product of a commentary on the Greek text of Acts, on which I was then engaged, and which was eventually published – again by the Tyndale Press – in 1951.

When that lecture was delivered I was a teacher of classical Greek, and treated Acts (together with Luke, of course) as a historical document in the tradition of Thucydides and Polybius. I have not renounced this understanding of the book, but have learned to make room for other perspectives to which in those days I was a stranger. When the lecture was published, it was greeted with general approval by my classical colleagues. They had little fault to find with my conclusion: "Taken all in all, each speech suits the speaker, the audience, and the circumstances of delivery; and this, along with ... other points we have considered, gives good ground, in my judgement, for believing these speeches to be, not inventions of the historian, but condensed accounts of speeches actually made, and therefore valuable and independent sources for the history and theology of the primitive Church."[2] My old teacher, Alexander Souter, professed himself to be in entire agreement with it – "but then", he added, "in my case you were preaching to the converted".[3] But these friends, being (like myself) classicists, did not perhaps appreciate the inadequacy of some of the arguments on which this conclusion was based. Another friend, a distinguished New Testament scholar and a student of Acts against its biblical background, found my convictions characterized by a "disarming ingenuousness".[4] Had he been a follower

---

[1] Later Tyndale New Testament Lectures dealing with aspects of this general subject are N. B. Stonehouse, *The Areopagus Address* (London, 1949), and H. N. Ridderbos, *The Speeches of Peter in the Acts of the Apostles* (London, 1961).

[2] *The Speeches in Acts*, p. 27.

[3] Private letter.

[4] J. Dupont, *Les Problèmes du Livre des Actes d'après les Travaux Récents* (Louvain, 1950), p. 47, reprinted in *Études sur les Actes des Apôtres* (Paris, 1967), p. 42.

of the Dibelius-Haenchen-Conzelmann line, I might have taken this criticism as a matter of course; as it is, I am disposed to treat it seriously and to concede that it has some substance.

If one valid perspective on Acts is to view it as a historical work in the tradition of Thucydides, the question immediately arises: Are the speeches Thucydidean? The answer, I think, must be Yes. But it is good to remind ourselves what "Thucydidean" speeches really are. Early in his *History of the Peloponnesian War*, Thucydides says:

> As to the speeches which were made either before or during the war, it was hard for me, and for others who reported them to me, to recollect the exact words. I have therefore put into the mouth of each speaker the sentiments proper to the occasion, expressed as I thought he would be likely to express them, while at the same time I endeavoured, as nearly as I could, to give the general purport of what was actually said.[1]

This last clause is the expression of Thucydides's historical conscience. Close attention has been paid to the probable meaning of his phrase "the general purport of what was actually said";[2] it seems clear, however, that while he disclaims anything in the nature of precise verbatim reproduction, he does claim to express the sense and intention of the speaker's words on each occasion. Thucydides chose his language with care. Naturally, since he reported the various speeches in his own language, a general similarity can be traced in the style of them all,[3] but this similarity of style does not extend to the sentiments expressed: Pericles expresses Periclean sentiments, while Cleon says the sort of things that Cleon would say.

The situation in Acts is analogous to that in Thucydides. Speeches freely composed as rhetorical exercises by lesser historians (like Josephus) and put into the mouths of *dramatis personae* with little regard for verisimilitude, are not Thucydidean speeches properly so called. The speeches in Acts are not mere rhetorical exercises, nor are they introduced simply as vehicles for the author's own reflections or interpretations. The critical attitude to the Jerusalem temple in Stephen's speech, for example, is not Luke's own attitude, which is much more positive. Again, we must bear Thucydides's last clause in mind when we read the following words of Hans Conzelmann on Acts 17:22-31:

> Inasmuch as Luke draws upon the form of secular historiography, we must interpret the Areopagus Speech first of all as a literary speech of Luke, not a real sermon by Paul. We take this procedure for granted in our interpretation of the speeches of Thucydides, for example. It is no less relevant for the

[1] Thucydides, *History* i. 22. 1 (B. Jowett's translation).
[2] Cf. M. Dibelius, *Aufsätze zur Apostelgeschichte* (Göttingen, 1951), pp. 122 f.; E.T., *Studies in the Acts of the Apostles* (London, 1956), pp. 140 ff.
[3] As was pointed out in the 1st century B.C. by Dionysius of Halicarnassus, *Epistula ad Pompeium* 3. 20.

interpretation of Acts 17. Luke makes Paul say what he considers appropriate to the situation.[1]

But, if the Thucydidean analogy be valid, we should also expect Luke to "give the general purport of what was actually said" and not to ascribe to the speaker sentiments or utterances out of keeping with his true beliefs and teachings.

II

As I re-read what I said thirty years ago, I note with interest the scholars to whom reference was made in the lecture. They include Israel Abrahams, B. W. Bacon, Friedrich Blass, F. C. Burkitt, F. H. Chase, F. J. Foakes-Jackson, Percy Gardner, J. Rendel Harris, Kirsopp Lake, Edward Meyer, J. H. Moulton, Eduard Norden, W. M. Ramsay, C. C. Torrey, Johannes de Zwaan and C. H. Dodd among the illustrious dead, and H. J. Cadbury who is still happily with us. All of them made distinguished contributions to the study of Acts, but most of them (to our impoverishment) receive but a bare mention when the problems of the book are discussed today. To the illustrious dead belongs also Martin Dibelius; the lecture contained a quotation from a work of his first published in 1926:

> These speeches, without doubt, are as they stand inventions of the author. For they are too short to have been actually given in this form; they are too similar to one another to have come from different persons; and in their content they occasionally reproduce a later standpoint (e.g. what Peter and James say about the Law in chap. xv).[2]

But, in the years that followed, Martin Dibelius made contributions to the study of the speeches in Acts of such quality as to exercise the profoundest influence on most subsequent work done on these speeches.

Already in 1939 he had communicated a paper on Paul's Areopagus address to the *Akademie der Wissenschaften* (*philologisch-historische Klasse*) at Heidelberg,[3] to which in the published text of my lecture I could give no more than a footnote reference.[4] Five years later he communicated to the same body a further paper on the speeches in Acts as a whole in the context of ancient historiography.[5] This latter paper, which was not published

[1] "The Address of Paul on the Areopagus", in *Studies in Luke-Acts*, ed. L. E. Keck and J. L. Martyn (Nashville/New York, 1966), p. 218.

[2] *A Fresh Approach to the New Testament and Early Christian Literature* (London, 1936), p. xv; E.T. of *Geschichte der urchristlichen Literatur* (Berlin und Leipzig, 1926).

[3] *Paulus auf dem Areopag* (Heidelberg, 1939), reprinted in *Aufsätze zur Apostelgeschichte*, pp. 29 ff.; E.T., *Studies in the Acts*, pp. 26 ff.

[4] *The Speeches in Acts*, p. 16, n. 3. (The outbreak of World War II in 1939 had impeded access to German literature.)

[5] *Die Reden der Apostelgeschichte und die antike Geschichtsschreibung* (Heidelberg, 1949), reprinted in *Aufsätze*, pp. 120 ff.; E.T. in *Studies*, pp. 138 ff.

until 1949 (the year after Dibelius's death), is one of the most important and influential studies of the subject ever to have appeared.

His thesis is that Luke has not only composed all the speeches in his own individual style but is responsible for their structure. In the first half of Acts, the speeches repeatedly begin with (i) an introduction relating the situation of the speech to its subject-matter; this is followed by (ii) an account of Jesus' ministry, death and resurrection. (In this last regard the personal testimony of the speakers is usually emphasized; oddly, however, Paul at Pisidian Antioch does not claim to be an eyewitness himself, but tells how the risen Christ "appeared to those who came up with him from Galilee to Jerusalem, who are now his witnesses to the people".[1]) After this account comes (iii) confirmatory evidence from the scriptures, the whole being concluded by (iv) an exhortation to repentance. This, Dibelius concludes, is how the gospel was preached when Luke was writing (c. A.D. 90, he thinks), and this is how Luke thought the gospel must always have been preached, by Peter or by Paul, to Jews or to Gentiles. But, of course, there were different categories of Gentiles: an approach which was appropriate to a God-fearer like Cornelius would have been inappropriate for people whose religious outlook was completely pagan, and so a different kind of structure is recognizable in the speeches at Lystra (Acts 14:15–17) and Athens (17:22–31). Again, quite different structures are discernible in the apologiae addressed by Stephen to the Sanhedrin (Acts 7:2–53) and by Paul to the elders of the Ephesian church (20:18–35), to the hostile mob in the temple court (22:3–21) and to the younger Agrippa (26:2–23).

The speeches, Dibelius notes, are introduced at crucial points in Luke's narrative, underlining and amplifying its dominant motifs, such as the Jews' refusal of the gospel and the Gentiles' acceptance of it. They are woven into the narrative by a repeated device in which one after another is brought to an end by some external factor such as an interruption or (as in the speech in the house of Cornelius) the descent of the Spirit. Thus to say as J. A. Bengel does at the end of Paul's Athenian speech, "He would have said more had they wished to hear more",[2] is to overlook the fact that the audience's breaking it off in Acts 17:32 is Luke's literary way of concluding a well-constructed and self-contained speech.

Dibelius does not go so far as to deny the historicity of the various speeches; he prefers to ignore it. On Paul's address to the elders from Ephesus he says: "Luke may have known of individual occasions when Paul spoke there. He may also have had information about the ξύμπασα γνώμη[3] (general purport) of the speaker or of the speech in individual instances; he may even have been an eye-witness . . ."[4] – but all these

---

[1] Acts 13:31.   [2] *Gnomon Novi Testamenti* (Tübingen, 1742), on Acts 17:31.
[3] Thucydides, *Hist.* i. 22. 1.
[4] *Aufsätze*, p. 141, n. 1; E.T., *Studies*, p. 164, n. 55.

possibilities are beside the point, since the author is not concerned with the historical relevance of the speeches but with their stylistic appropriateness. In dealing with another part of Acts Dibelius refers to "the older school of criticism, which thinks only of the event and not of the account."[1] With his emphasis on style criticism[2] Dibelius redressed the balance, but to such a degree that he lays himself open to the counter-charge of thinking only of the account and not of the event. The question of the historicity of the speeches is not beside the point in the study of a work which claims to be a historical narrative.

Dibelius does indeed allow that Luke incorporates into his speeches "older formulae of a kerygmatic or liturgical nature".[3] The type of presentation which they reproduce is an ancient one, as may be seen in the rather primitive christological titles which they contain.[4] The type, in fact, reappears in the summary of the preaching common to himself and the Jerusalem apostles which Paul quotes in I Cor. 15:3–5: "that Christ died for our sins in accordance with the scriptures, that he was buried, that he was raised on the third day in accordance with the scriptures, and that he appeared to Cephas, then to the twelve." On this ground, in fact, Dom Jacques Dupont associates Dibelius with C. H. Dodd,[5] but Professor Dodd makes a much more positive historical assessment of the speeches in Acts than Dibelius did. The author of Acts, he suggests, used his Thucydidean privilege "with considerable restraint". The Pauline speeches "in some cases at least . . . are not, indeed, anything like verbatim reports (for the style is too 'Lucan' and too un-Pauline for that), but are based upon a reminiscence of what the apostle actually said"; and "there is good reason to suppose that the speeches attributed to Peter . . . are based upon material which proceeded from the Aramaic-speaking church at Jerusalem, and was substantially earlier than the period at which the book was written."[6] With this estimate of the matter I find myself in substantial agreement, as I did in 1942.[7]

Dibelius's influence may be seen in much subsequent work produced on the speeches in Acts, especially by German-speaking scholars. The commentaries by E. Haenchen and H. Conzelmann provide illustrious examples of his influence. The situation is summed up by Eduard Schweizer:

[1] On the voyage and shipwreck narrative of Acts 27 (Aufsätze, p. 95; E.T., Studies, p. 107).
[2] His earliest contribution to the study of Acts was devoted to style criticism: "Stilkritisches zur Apostelgeschichte" in Eucharisterion für H. Gunkel, ii (Göttingen, 1923), pp. 27 ff., reprinted in Aufsätze, pp. 9 ff.; E.T., Studies. pp. 1 ff.
[3] Aufsätze, p. 10; E.T., Studies, p. 3.
[4] M. Dibelius, Die Formgeschichte des Evangeliums (Tübingen, ¹1919), pp. 7 ff. (³1959, pp. 15 ff.); E.T., From Tradition to Gospel (London, 1934), pp. 16 ff.
[5] J. Dupont, Études sur les Actes des Apôtres, pp. 135 ff.
[6] C. H. Dodd, The Apostolic Preaching and its Developments (London, ²1944), pp. 17 ff.; cf. his History and the Gospel (London, 1938), pp. 72 ff.
[7] Cf. I. H. Marshall, Luke: Historian and Theologian (Exeter, 1970), pp. 157 ff.

Ever since Martin Dibelius' essay about this subject, it has been more and more widely recognized that the speeches are basically *compositions by the author of Acts* who, to be sure, utilized different kinds of material for particular passages. This can be supported by *analysis of the speeches* which contain the missionary proclamation of the apostles to Jews and Gentiles.[1]

III

The treatment of this subject was carried farther in 1961 by Ulrich Wilckens in his monograph on the missionary speeches in the first half of Acts[2] – five delivered by Peter (2:14–36; 3:12–26; 4:8–12; 5:29–32; 10:34–43) and one by Paul (13:16–41). After a detailed analysis of all six, he concludes that they follow a common plan (as C. H. Dodd had pointed out a quarter of a century before), but that this plan is entirely Lukan and does not reflect an earlier kerygmatic tradition (as Dodd and Dibelius had held). The missionary speeches to pagans (delivered at Lystra in Acts 14:15–17 and at Athens in 17:22–31) are based on a schema which is attested in Paul's letters (cf. I Thess. 1:9 f.), but no such schema is attested for the missionary speeches to Jews and God-fearing Gentiles in the earlier part of the book.

The terms in which the gospel was presented to pagans may indeed be discerned in the letters of Paul and others, but these were addressed to Gentile churches. If we had letters addressed to converts from Judaism we should be able to judge more adequately if the missionary speeches in the earlier part of Acts are constructed on the pattern which was actually followed in the evangelization of Jews. As it is, the only New Testament letters which can with some show of reason be regarded as addressed to Jewish Christians are that of James and that to the Hebrews. The former does not indicate how its readers came to place their faith in "the Lord Jesus Christ, our glory" (Jas. 2:1); the latter was sent to people who had received the gospel from the lips of those who heard the Lord speak and experienced its confirmation by manifestations of the Spirit when they placed their faith in Jesus as Messiah and Son of God, but we have no detailed account of the form in which the saving message was presented to them. We are left, then, with the speeches in the early chapters of Acts as our sole means of information about the presentation of the gospel to Jews, and if Wilckens' analysis of these speeches were adequate, a verdict of *non liquet* would be the most that could be returned on the question of their relation to the primitive preaching to Jews.

But if the speeches to Jews in Acts are constructed on a constant pattern, it could be because this was the pattern on which the most primitive

---

[1] "Concerning the Speeches in Acts", in *Studies in Luke-Acts*, ed. Keck and Martyn, p. 208. Cf. G. Bornkamm, *Paul*, E.T. (London, 1971), p. xvii.

[2] U. Wilckens, *Die Missionsreden der Apostelgeschichte: Form- und traditionsgeschichtliche Untersuchungen* (Neukirchen, 1961).

preaching was regularly constructed. True, Luke recasts it to some extent in his own style, but there is much in the content that is not essentially Lukan. The regular appeal to Hebrew scripture in these speeches is not something otherwise characteristic of Luke's narrative. "He, at all events, does not turn aside to tell us that 'Then was fulfilled that which was spoken of by the prophet'. If Luke does not use the method of *Testimonies* on his own account, he is quite clear that it was the Apostolic method. It was either what they actually said or what they ought to have said".[1] It was, on the other hand, characteristic of the gospel presentation common to Paul and those who were apostles before him. If Paul proclaimed in Corinth – in the synagogue to start with, according to Acts 18:4 – that it was in accordance with the scriptures that Christ died and rose, we might *a fortiori* expect the same emphasis to characterize his preaching and that of his predecessors to Jews and God-fearers at an earlier date in Palestine and Asia Minor.

It may well be that in these earlier speeches, as Wilckens says, we miss the explicit ascription of saving significance to the *death* of Christ.[2] The reason for this could lie not in Luke's own theology but in the circumstances of the primitive community. That God had raised the crucified Jesus to life again was the great new fact which, in their eyes, dwarfed all others. The claims of Jesus, disallowed by his judges, had been confirmed by God: he was divinely vindicated as both Lord and Messiah, and as such he should be acknowledged by the whole house of Israel.[3]

Ernst Käsemann has contended vigorously that this emphasis bears the marks of primitive catholicism; the genuine *theologia crucis* has been displaced by a *theologia gloriae*.[4] But, essential to the authentic gospel as the *theologia crucis* is, can we say that historically it precedes the *theologia gloriae*? The *theologia gloriae* is implicit in the resurrection faith: God has exalted his Servant Jesus, who had been humiliated and put to death. Probably all evangelical Christians will sympathize with Professor Käsemann's insistence on the *theologia crucis*, whether or not they stand, as he does, in direct succession from Luther; but the vindication of the Crucified One is proclaimed at the threshold of the apostolic age. God forbid that we should glory save in the cross of our Lord Jesus Christ, but by virtue of that same cross *Christus patiens* is *Christus victor*. No cross, no crown. If the proclamation of *Christus victor* is a mark of primitive catholicism, then such catholicism is primitive indeed. The *theologia gloriae* ceases to be apostolic when it is maintained in a form which

---

[1] J. Rendel Harris, *Testimonies*, ii (Cambridge, 1920), p. 80. J. Dupont, in a review of Wilckens' monograph, points out that Acts 10:36–38 presupposes a unitive application of Isa. 52:7 and 61:1 (linked by the common verb εὐαγγελίζεσθαι) in a fuller form of this kerygma, of which Luke here preserves only an abridgement (*Études*, pp. 139 ff.).

[2] *Die Missionsreden*, pp. 184, 216.

[3] Acts 2:36.

[4] E.g. "Neutestamentliche Fragen von Heute", *ZThK* 54 (1957), pp. 20 ff.; E.T., *New Testament Questions of Today* (London, 1969), pp. 21 ff.

imagines that the church militant here in earth is already the church triumphant, as the Corinthian Christians mistakenly supposed (I Cor. 4:8). For believers on earth the fellowship in Christ's sufferings is now; participation in his glory lies in the future (Rom. 8:17). Luke knows this as well as Paul does: "through many tribulations we must enter the kingdom of God" (Acts 14:22).

IV

In two sections in the earlier part of Acts we have explicit evidence of a "Servant" Christology – in the sequel to the healing of the lame man in the temple court (3:11–4:31) and in Philip's encounter with the Ethiopian eunuch (8:26–40).

In the former of these two sections the "Servant" motif appears twice: in Peter's address to the crowd in Solomon's colonnade (3:12–26) and in the disciples' prayer after the release of Peter and John by the Sanhedrin (4:24–30). When Peter, at the beginning of his address, announces that "the God of Abraham, Isaac and Jacob, the God of our fathers, glorified his Servant Jesus" (3:13), we recognize an echo of the opening words of the fourth Isaianic Servant Song, "Behold, my Servant ... shall be exalted and highly glorified" (Isa. 52:13, LXX), with a gloss identifying the Servant with Jesus. The gloss is then expanded so as to show how the Servant's humiliation and exaltation were realized in history: "you denied the Holy and Righteous One, ... and killed the Author of life; but God raised him from the dead, and of this we are witnesses" (3:14 ff.).

The most substantial indebtedness to the Servant Songs is found in Philip's encounter with the Ethiopian God-fearer. This man was beguiling his homeward journey from Jerusalem by reading aloud part of the fourth Servant Song – in the Greek version, of course. When Philip approached his chariot, he heard the words of Isa. 53:7 ff. being read, and on being invited to join the reader in his chariot and explain their meaning to him, he made them the text from which "he told him the good news of Jesus" (Acts 8:30–35). The words quoted speak of the Servant's uncomplaining patience in face of humiliation, injustice and death: they do not explicitly mention his sin-bearing ministry. Yet it is difficult to think that either Luke or Philip would have ignored completely the context in which those words occur.[1] Wherein, we may ask, did the record of the Servant's suffering constitute "good news" for the Ethiopian if not in its atoning efficacy, in that he gave his life as an 'asham, a reparation-offering (Isa. 53:10)?[2] Luke indeed does not say this expressly, but it is a fair inference –

---

[1] Cf. E. Lohmeyer, "Vom urchristlichen Abendmahl", *Theol. Rundschau*, 9 (1937), p. 181.
[2] If Mark 10:45 ($\lambda\acute{v}\tau\rho o\nu$ $\grave{a}\nu\tau\grave{\iota}$ $\pi o\lambda\lambda\tilde{\omega}\nu$) echoes Isa. 53:10–12 (and even if it does not), it is significant that this note is absent from the parallel in Luke 22:24–27.

if we accept that it is a real historical incident that he is relating. We may agree with Professor Conzelmann that the way in which Luke uses Isa. 53 "does not prove ... the presence of any theory of atonement" in his thinking, but when he says that it "disproves" it, he outruns the evidence at one extreme as much as those who treat it as proof do at the other extreme.[1]

So far as Luke's Servant-terminology in general is concerned, C. F. D. Moule's conclusion is cogent: there is no clear evidence either that it was "exclusively primitive, or that Luke was inventing its application: it would appear, more likely, to belong by idiosyncratic use (perhaps Petrine) or by liturgical appropriateness on the lips on which it is, in fact, placed. The likelihood is that in Christian liturgical contexts, especially when under the influence of Jewish berakôth, 'thy Servant Jesus' was a common usage, perhaps for a considerable period".[2]

Twice in the early speeches Jesus is described by the title ἀρχηγός, which means something like "pioneer", the one who leads the way or blazes the trail for others.[3] G. W. H. Lampe has drawn attention to his identification in this rôle with the Servant; the Servant "suffers and ascends as the ἀρχηγός of his people. He goes on before as the guarantor of his followers' own entry".[4] The paradox of the Servant's passion is emphasized in Acts 3:15 in that it was the "Pioneer of Life" who was so unjustly put to death, while in 5:30 f. it is proclaimed that, after he was "hanged on a tree", God exalted him at his right hand as Pioneer and Saviour, to give repentance to Israel and forgiveness of sins".

Twice the crucifixion is referred to as "hanging on a tree" (ξύλον): in the apostles' defence before the Sanhedrin (5:30) and in Peter's preaching in the house of Cornelius (10:39). So also Paul at Pisidian Antioch says that after Jesus' death "they took him down from the tree" (13:29). The expression "hanging on a tree" is an echo of Deut. 21:22 f., where it is laid down that if the body of an executed criminal is hanged on a tree, "his body shall not remain all night upon the tree, ... for a hanged man is accursed by God". From Paul's application of these words to Jesus in Gal. 3:13[5] we may gather that the mode of Jesus' death was recognized as a stumbling-block in the way of accepting his Messiahship – a stumbling-block which Paul removes by the exegetical device of gezerah shawah. Behind Luke's use of the expression we may discern the recognition that

---

[1] H. Conzelmann, Die Mitte der Zeit (Tübingen, 1954), p. 202, n. 1; E.T., The Theology of St. Luke (London, 1960), p. 230, n. 1.

[2] "The Christology of Acts", in Studies in Luke-Acts, ed. Keck and Martyn, p. 170. Cf. the liturgical use of "thy Servant Jesus" in Didache 9:2 ff., 10:2 ff., and repeatedly in the Apostolic Tradition of Hippolytus.

[3] The other two occurrences of the noun in the NT are in Heb. 2:10; 12:2 (also in reference to Jesus).

[4] "The Lucan Portrait of Christ", NTS 2 (1955/56), p. 167.

[5] Cf. I Pet. 2:24. In all five NT passages where ξύλον is used in this sense NEB (1970) gives the rendering "gibbet".

the Deuteronomic passage was applicable to the death of Jesus. If (as is conceivable) the application was first made by those who found here an argument against his messianic identity, it was quickly accepted by Christians who must have found means of coming to terms with it – if not those which Paul found, then others which commended themselves as satisfactory. If, as the phrase "hanging on a tree" implies, Jesus submitted to the divine curse, an answer must have been given sooner rather than later to the insistent question: Why, or for whom, did he endure this curse?[1] It is difficult to avoid the conclusion that his endurance of the curse, as well as his subsequent exaltation in glory, provided the ground for the salvation and forgiveness of sins repeatedly announced in his name in those early speeches.[2]

V

At the end of the sermon in Pisidian Antioch not only is "forgiveness of sins" proclaimed through "this man" but "by him every one who believes is *justified* from all things from which you could not be *justified* by Moses' law" (Acts 13:38 f.). It may be that the reference to justification is added here because justification was known to be a key-term of Paul's, but that in the present context it means little more than being "freed", as the R.S.V. has it, and does not have the Pauline force.[3] It is misinterpreting Luke, however, to suppose that he is suggesting that Moses' law "justifies" from some things, but that faith in Christ avails to "justify" from those things – whatever they were – from which Moses' law provided no justification.[4] The only people whom Moses' law justified were those who kept it. The law-breaker was not justified by that law in any degree; he was condemned by it. But the justification which no sinner could find in Moses' law was available to every believer in Christ. Luke does not spell out the doctrine as Paul does, but if any doctrine of justification is implied in these words, it is the Pauline doctrine.

The style criticism to which Dibelius and Wilckens have subjected the speeches in Acts must be supplemented by studies of their form conducted along other lines. Mention should be made of J. W. Bowker's examination of some of them in the light of what can be discovered about early synagogue practice – his argument, for example, that the address of Pisidian Antioch (Acts 13:16–41) reveals, on analysis, indications of proem homily

---

[1] Cf. G. B. Caird, *The Apostolic Age* (London, 1955), p. 40: E. M. B. Green, *The Meaning of Salvation* (London, 1965), pp. 145 f.

[2] For the concept of salvation, comprising *inter alia* "forgiveness of sins and the gift of the Holy Spirit", as the central motif of Luke's theology, cf. I. H. Marshall, *Luke: Historian and Theologian*, p. 9 *et passim*.

[3] Cf. O. Bauernfeind, *Die Apostelgeschichte* (Leipzig, 1939), p. 177; H. Conzelmann, *Die Apostelgeschichte* (Tübingen, 1963), p. 77.

[4] Cf. B. W. Bacon, *The Story of St. Paul* (London, 1905), p. 103, n. 1.

form, based (it may be) on Deut. 4:25–46 as *seder* and II Sam. 7:6–16 as *haftarah*, with I Sam. 13:14 (apparently in Targum form) as the proem text, or that James's summing up at the Council of Jerusalem (Acts 15:14–21) is a genuine *yelammedenu* response and may even be understood as all that survives of a *yelammedenu* homily.[1]

Much, in fact, depends on the way in which one's mind has been conditioned to approach such a subject. I suspect that, despite years of intensive study of Paul's letters, my training as a classicist continues to influence me. For instance, when Professor Haenchen quotes my observation that Luke, being present when Paul addressed the Ephesian elders at Miletus, "may even have taken shorthand notes", the only comment which he can make on such a preposterous suggestion is a parenthetical exclamation mark. After all, Dibelius has "finally proved the speech to be Luke's work and evaluated it".[2] But, on reconsidering the matter, I remain of the same opinion as before, on the following grounds: (i) This is the only Pauline speech in Acts which can be paralleled (and that pervasively) from the Pauline letters, of which otherwise Luke betrays no knowledge; this suggests strongly that its content is Pauline, not Lukan. (ii) This speech is set in the context of a "we" section, and the most probable explanation of the "we" sections still seems to me to be that this is the author's way of indicating unobtrusively that he took part in the journeys which they record. (iii) Shorthand was not an unknown device in the first century A.D., and a man such as the author of Acts reveals himself to have been was just the kind of person to make use of it.

This speech contains the most explicit mention of the *redemptive* efficacy of the death of Christ to be found anywhere in the Lukan history. "Feed the church of God", says Paul to the elders of Ephesus, "which he won for himself by his own blood" – or rather "by the blood of his Beloved"[3] (verse 28). We may discern an echo of Psalm 74:2a, but the statement of the price of acquisition is added here. If the speech is composed by Luke, the reference to the blood of Christ is surprising. To say, with Professor Conzelmann, that it "probably adopts a turn of phrase current in the Church (perhaps to give a speech a Pauline stamp? – such tendencies are occasionally to be noted in Luke)",[4] is to admit that it is non-Lukan and ostensibly Pauline. True, Paul himself does not characteristically use the word "blood" in the sense of the "death" of Christ; where such language occurs in the Pauline corpus (as in Rom. 3:25; 5:9; Eph. 1:7) it has been thought to point in the majority of instances to

---

[1] J. W. Bowker, "Speeches in Acts: A Study in Proem and Yelammedenu Form", *NTS* 14 (1967/68), pp. 96 ff.; he refers to J. W. Doeve, *Jewish Hermeneutics in the Synoptic Gospel and Acts* (Assen, 1954), pp. 175 f., for a demonstration that the discourse of Acts 13:26 ff. was composed by someone who had "an excellent command of hermeneutics as practised in rabbinic Judaism".

[2] E. Haenchen, *The Acts of the Apostles*, E.T. (Oxford, 1971), p. 590.

[3] Taking τοῦ ἰδίου as dependent on, not qualifying, τοῦ αἵματος.

[4] *Die Mitte der Zeit*, p. 175; E.T., *The Theology of St. Luke*, p. 201.

the citation of a pre-Pauline formula, but the same might well be true of Acts 20:28. "This is Paul, not some other speaker; and he is not evangelizing but recalling an already evangelized community to its deepest insights. In other words, the situation, like the theology, is precisely that of a Pauline epistle, not of preliminary evangelism".[1]

VI

The treatment which the Areopagus speech receives from many scholars provides a good illustration of the tendency to be "more Pauline than Paul",[2] a tendency which, in this kind of situation especially, does less than justice to Paul's plain statement of his policy to make himself "all things to all men" (I Cor. 9:22).

Take the writer of Rom. 1:18–23, with his insistence that the Creator's "eternal power and divinity" can be recognized from his works, to a point where failure to recognize them is inexcusable. Bear in mind that his evangelization of the Gentiles thus far has been remarkably successful – a fact which (for all his modest disclaimer in I Cor. 2:1–5) implies considerable persuasiveness in speech and approach, including the ability to find an initial area of common ground with his hearers, apart from which any attempt at communication would be ineffective. Bring him to Athens and invite him to state his case against idolatry and for the true knowledge of God before an audience of Athenian citizens. What will he say? I find it difficult not to imagine him as saying something very much along the lines of the summary in Acts 17:22–31. Here he is talking to pagans, not writing to Christians; he will not cut off his hearers' ears as the first step towards gaining their attention. But he will say that idolatry is inexcusable, because the true knowledge of God was available to all men in his works of creation and providence; he may even point out that some of their own thinkers have perceived that men are the offspring of the supreme God who is the source and ground of their being. Even if the writer to the Romans is quoting a pre-Pauline form of words when he speaks in Rom. 3:25 of God's passing over former sins in his divine forbearance, he approves of the idea thus expressed; he may well therefore tell the Athenians that hitherto God has overlooked their culpable ignorance of his nature, but that the resurrection of Christ has introduced a new dispensation, in which God calls for their repentance in view of the coming judgement to be executed by the risen Christ. Here too we may discern a theme emphasized in the letter to the Romans, with its reference to "that day when, according to my gospel, God judges the secrets of men by Christ Jesus" (2:16).

[1] C. F. D. Moule in *Studies in Luke-Acts*, ed. Keck and Martyn, p. 171.
[2] Cf. H. Küng, "Der Frühkatholizismus im Neuen Testament als kontrovers-theologische Problem", in *Das Neue Testament als Kanon*, ed. E. Käsemann (Göttingen, 1970), p. 192.

Paul had ample precedent in the Hebrew scriptures for his exposure of the perverseness of idolatry and the folly of imagining that the most high God could be accommodated in a material building, as also for his insistence that God makes provision for all his creatures and allots the nations their living-space, while he himself is not dependent on anything that they can give to him. Naturally he will not refer his hearers to the testimony of the Hebrew scriptures, from which such liberal quotation is made in the Pauline letters and in the preaching to Jews and God-fearers in Acts; but if men whom his hearers do recognize as authorities have spoken to the same effect, he will quote their words – giving them a biblical sense as he does so. Many a Scots preacher has warned his congregation that "Pleasures are like poppies spread . . .", while he and they know quite well that Burns was no Christian moralist and that *Tam o' Shanter* was not seriously written to call sinners to repentance. It is underestimating Paul's versatility to suppose that he could not have presented the essence of Rom. 1:18–23 and 2:12–16 to pagans along such lines as those of Acts 17:22–31. True, Luke did not hear Paul address the Areopagus, but he knew how Paul was accustomed to adapt his *praeparatio evangelica* to an audience of this kind.[1]

VII

If in the Areopagitica the resurrection of Christ is the guarantee of coming judgement, elsewhere in Paul's speeches in Acts it is integral to the hope of resurrection.

At his interview with the leaders of the Jewish colony in Rome, recorded at the end of Acts, Paul tells them that "it is because of the hope of Israel that I am bound with this chain" (Acts 28:20). The "hope of Israel" is the hope of resurrection in general,[2] lately given concrete historical shape by the resurrection of Jesus, which declared him to be Lord and Messiah. So, before the younger Agrippa, Paul affirms (Acts 26:6–8):

> I stand here on trial for hope in the promise made by God to our fathers, to which our twelve tribes hope to attain, as they earnestly worship night and day. And for this hope I am accused by Jews, O king! Why is it thought incredible by any of you that God raises the dead?

When, in Rom. 1:3 f., Paul says that Jesus, son of David "according to the flesh", was "designated Son of God in power according to the Spirit of holiness by the resurrection of the dead", he puts the last word in the plural (ἐξ ἀναστάσεως νεκρῶν) because the resurrection of Christ

---

[1] See especially B. Gärtner, *The Areopagus Speech and Natural Revelation* (Uppsala, 1955). H. D. Betz, *Der Apostel Paulus und die sokratische Tradition* (Tübingen, 1972), p. 38, suggests that Luke depicts Paul in Athens as a latter-day Socrates.
[2] Cf. Acts 23:6.

in particular is part and parcel of the resurrection of the dead in general –
"Christ the firstfruits, then at his coming those who belong to Christ", as
he puts it in I Cor. 15:23. The same point as is made in Rom. 1:4 is made
in Acts 26:22 f., by means of the same Greek phrase, when Paul goes on to
assure Agrippa that his gospel consists of

> nothing but what the prophets and Moses said would come to pass: that the
> Christ must suffer, and that, by being the first to rise from the dead (ἐξ
> ἀναστάσεως νεκρῶν), he would proclaim light both to the people and to the
> Gentiles.

Christ, in short, is the hope of Israel, as he is the hope of all mankind,
by virtue of his rising from the dead. The salvation and eternal life which
his people have through faith in him are completely bound up with his
resurrection. "If Christ has not been raised, your faith is futile and you are
still in your sins. . . . If for this life only we have hoped in Christ, we are
of all men most to be pitied" (I Cor. 15:17, 19). Whatever other differences
may appear between these words of Paul and those quoted from Acts,
the founding of the wider resurrection hope on the particular resurrection
of Christ is common to both.

When, in Acts 24:15, Paul tells Felix that he shares the "hope in God"
cherished by many of his opponents, "that there will be a resurrection of
both the just and the unjust",[1] expression is given to an aspect of the
resurrection doctrine which is unparalleled in the Pauline letters. Paul may
well have believed, as many Pharisees did, that the unrighteous would be
raised from the dead in addition to the righteous, but in his letters –
perhaps because they were written to Christians – it is resurrection with
and in Christ that he expounds.

The earliest reference to the hope of Israel in the speeches of Acts
comes in Peter's address to the crowd in Solomon's colonnade after the
healing of the lame man. Here the exhortation to repentance is amplified
in a fashion unparalleled elsewhere in the book. "Repent, therefore", says
Peter, "and turn again, that your sins may be blotted out, that seasons of
refreshing may come from the presence of the Lord, and that he may send
the Messiah designated for you, Jesus, whom heaven must receive until
the times of the establishment of all that God spoke by the mouth of his
holy prophets from of old" (3:19–21). Then follows a quotation of the
prediction of the prophet like Moses in Deut. 18:15 ff. But the noun
rendered "establishment" (Gk. ἀποκατάστασις) is reminiscent of the verb
ἀποκαθίστημι used of the ministry of the returning Elijah in Mal. 4:6
("he will *restore* the father's heart to the son"), especially as interpreted,
e.g., in Mark 9:12, "Elijah indeed comes first and restores (ἀποκαθιστάνει)
all things". This contact with the Elijah expectation has led O. Bauernfeind to the view that the whole section beginning "whom heaven must

---

[1] For "the resurrection of the just" cf. Luke 14:14.

receive . . ." is drawn from a Jewish form of words (perhaps liturgical in character) originally referring to Elijah (who must remain in heaven, to which he was transported in a whirlwind, until the time comes for his eschatological ministry), now adapted to a Christian context by the substitution of "the Messiah designated for you, Jesus" for "Elijah" (perhaps amplified by a participial phrase as "Jesus" is in our present text).[1] J. A. T. Robinson, while recognizing that the Elijah expectation in some way underlies the passage, does not agree that Luke has adapted a Jewish form of words but discerns here "the most primitive Christology of all" in which Jesus in his earthly ministry as Servant (3:13) and Prophet (3:22 f.) is "the fore-runner of the Christ he is to be".[2] Thus far he is *Christus designatus*; only when he is sent back from heaven to earth will he be effectively the Christ. If it be asked how this interpretation can be squared with the expression in verse 18, "that his Christ should suffer" ($\pi\alpha\theta\epsilon\tilde{\iota}\nu$ $\tau\grave{o}\nu$ $\chi\rho\iota\sigma\tau\grave{o}\nu$ $\alpha\mathring{\upsilon}\tau o\tilde{\upsilon}$), the answer is that this is a well recognized Lukan form of words (cf. Luke 24:46).[3] In Acts 3:19–21, then, it is at his return from heaven that Jesus begins to exercise his messianic function; in 2:36, which expresses another christological perspective, it is his resurrection that proclaims him to be "Lord and Christ" (cf. Rom. 1:4), while for Luke he already suffers as the Messiah.

But this interpretation depends on our understanding of the participle $\pi\rho o\kappa\epsilon\chi\epsilon\iota\rho\iota\sigma\mu\acute{\epsilon}\nu o\varsigma$ in verse 20 and the noun $\mathring{\alpha}\pi o\kappa\alpha\tau\acute{\alpha}\sigma\tau\alpha\sigma\iota\varsigma$ in verse 21. As for the former word, Luke is the only New Testament author to use it, and its two other occurrences in his work refer to Paul's divine election to be a herald and witness of the risen Christ (Acts 22:14; 26:16). And here it is much more likely to denote Jesus' being foreordained to be his people's Messiah than to imply that, pending his parousia, he remains Messiah-designate.[4]

As for $\mathring{\alpha}\pi o\kappa\alpha\tau\acute{\alpha}\sigma\tau\alpha\sigma\iota\varsigma$, it must be understood in its whole setting. It cannot have the sense of "restoration" here, for "the restoration of all that God spoke by the mouth of his holy prophets from of old" is meaningless, whereas "the establishment of all that God spoke by the mouth of his holy prophets . . ." is not only intelligible but is in keeping with Lukan language elsewhere (cf. Luke 1:70, a specially close parallel; also 24:25–27, 44). But if "establishment" is the force of the word here, then the link with the Elijah expectation is superficial, not essential.

Luke is generally believed to reflect the outlook of the second Christian generation which had come to terms with the "postponement of the

---

[1] *Die Apostelgeschichte*, pp. 66 f.; cf. his "Tradition und Komposition in dem Apokatastasis-spruch Apostelgeschichte 3, 20 f." in *Abraham unser Vater*, ed. O. Betz, M. Hengel and P. Schmidt (Leiden, 1963), pp. 13 ff.

[2] "The Most Primitive Christology of All?" *JTS* n.s. 7 (1956), pp. 177 ff., reprinted in *Twelve New Testament Studies* (London, 1962), pp. 139 ff.

[3] Cf. also Acts 26:23, $\epsilon\mathring{\iota}$ $\pi\alpha\theta\eta\tau\grave{o}\varsigma$ $\mathring{o}$ $\chi\rho\iota\sigma\tau\acute{o}\varsigma$.

[4] Cf. C. F. D. Moule in *Studies in Luke-Acts*, ed. Keck and Martyn, p. 168.

parousia". For him the period of the church's existence has assumed independent significance as the sequel to the Christ-event at the mid-point of time.[1] It would be preferable to say that for Luke, as for Paul, the period which followed the Christ-event was the age of the Spirit, even if Paul's appreciation of the Spirit's anticipatory rôle is absent from Luke's thought. But one thing is certain: the eschatology of Acts 3:19–21 is neither Luke's nor Paul's. It implies that early repentance on the part of the people of Jerusalem would speed the parousia. In Luke's own perspective such an expectation finds no place, and if Paul does envisage a large-scale turning of Israel to the Lord, as the prelude to the parousia, it is as a sequel to the completion of the Gentile world-mission.[2] In Acts 3:19–21 we may not have "the most primitive Christology of all", but it might well be argued that we do indeed have the most primitive *eschatology* of all.

*   *   *   *   *

Leon Morris has made outstanding contributions to many areas of New Testament study. His main contribution to the study of Luke's writings is made in two chapters of *The Cross in the New Testament*. The second of these two chapters deals with the preaching of the cross in Acts, and naturally concentrates on the speeches. While he says truly of the earliest Christian preachers that "the wonder of the resurrection gripped their minds and their imaginations" and that "the new-found power of the indwelling Spirit of God transformed their innermost being", he also insists, with regard to their experience and their witness alike: "Nothing here makes sense apart from the cross whereon men's salvation was accomplished."[3] It is a pleasure to present these desultory reflections on Luke's record of the apostolic witness to one whom for many years I have admired as a scholar and valued as a friend.[4]

---

[1] This is the significance of the title of H. Conzelmann's *Die Mitte der Zeit*; it is obscured in the title of the English translation (*The Theology of St. Luke*).

[2] Rom. 11:11 ff.; cf. J. Munck, *Paulus und die Heilsgeschichte* (Aarhus, 1954), pp. 242 ff.; E.T., *Paul and the Salvation of Mankind* (London, 1959), pp. 247 ff.

[3] *The Cross in the New Testament* (Grand Rapids and Exeter, 1965), p. 108.

[4] This paper was completed and sent to the editor before I saw E. Kränkl, *Jesus der Knecht Gottes: Die heilsgeschichtliche Stellung Jesu in den Reden der Apostelgeschichte* (Regensburg, 1972).

One aspect of the speeches in Acts on which this paper has not touched is the possibility that in some of them, outstandingly Stephen's speech, Samaritan influence is to be discerned. This possibility has been ventilated in appendices by A. Spiro ("Stephen's Samaritan Background") and C. S. Mann (" 'Hellenists' and 'Hebrews' in Acts 6:1") in J. Munck, *The Acts of the Apostles* (Anchor Bible, 1967), pp. 285 ff., 301 ff., by M. H. Scharlemann, *Stephen: A Singular Saint* (Rome, 1968), and more recently by C. H. H. Scobie, "The Origins and Development of Samaritan Christianity", *NTS* 19 (1972/73), pp. 390 ff. The features to which these writers draw attention are perhaps features not of Samaritanism in particular but of a wider nonconformist tradition in Israel.

CHAPTER IV

"CHRIST CRUCIFIED"

E. Earle Ellis

OUTSIDE OF THE GOSPELS THE WORDS "CROSS" AND "CRUCIFY" APPEAR in the New Testament almost exclusively in the Pauline literature.[1] There, the latter term is found only in Corinthians and Galatians, the former additionally in Philippians, Colossians, and Ephesians. They are used primarily as theological concepts.[2] This is not to say that the historical event of the crucifixion has become less important, much less that the theological concept has displaced it. In accordance with Paul's thought generally the theological meaning arises out of and remains united with the historical occurrence, the "salvation history," to which it refers. Nevertheless, the meaning is more specifically determined by Paul's historical situation and by a somewhat unusual expression, χριστὸς ἐσταυρωμένος.

I

The phrase "Christ crucified" is found in two Pauline passages, I Cor. 1–4 and Gal. 3. In I Corinthians, the concern of this essay, it appears initially in I Cor. 1:18–31, a set piece of exposition:[3]

> For Jews seek signs and Greeks seek wisdom (σοφία)
> But we proclaim Christ crucified
> To Jews an offense (σκάνδαλον)
>   and to Gentiles foolishness (μωρία)
> But to those who are called – Jews and Greeks –
>   Christ, God's power and God's wisdom (σοφία)
>
> 1:22–24

The phrase occurs once more in the application of the exposition to Paul's Corinthian mission:

---

[1] Elsewhere, they occur only with a literal sense: Heb. 12:2 ("cross") and Acts 2:36; 4:10; Rev. 11:8 ("crucified").

[2] The theological meaning also occurs in the Gospels, e.g., Matt. 10:38; Lk. 9:23 ("daily").

[3] That is, theme and proem text (1:18 f.) + exposition + concluding text (1:31). Cf. W. Wuellner, "Haggadic Homily Genre in I Corinthians 1–3", *JBL* 89 (1970), pp. 199–204.

> . . . I did not come in excellence of word or of wisdom (σοφία)
> when I proclaimed to you the testimony of God
> For I decided to know nothing among you
> except Jesus Christ, that is (καί), him as the crucified one.[1]
> . . . And my word and proclamation
>   were not in persuasive words of wisdom
> but in a demonstration of spirit and power
> in order that your faith might not rest in the wisdom of men
> but in the power of God

2:1-5

The phrase "Christ crucified" is clarified in a number of ways by the
context. It appears to be an elaboration or explanation of the earlier
phrase, "the word of the cross" (1:18), that opens the section. Like that
expression it is equated with God's power. Specifically, it represents the
present mediation of God's power in two ways, in prophetic wisdom and
in miracle (δύναμις; 1:24), both of which have been manifested at
Corinth in Paul's inspired utterance and miraculous works (πνεύματος
καὶ δυνάμεως; 2:4).[2] It is the former, "God's wisdom", that is the
primary concern in I Cor. 1-4. As such, "Christ crucified" is set in
opposition to the "wisdom of the world" (1:20; cf. 3:18) or "of men"
(2:5) or "of word" (1:17; 2:4). It is not just a concept nor, as it is for
unbelievers, just a past reference to a crucified person. It refers primarily to
the exalted Lord who, in his exaltation, remains the crucified one. This
contextual understanding is confirmed grammatically by the use of the
perfect participle, ἐσταυρωμένος.[3]

In sum, "Christ crucified" is not only the message or "word" of Paul's
proclamation but also the one who speaks through and in that "word",
not only the historical content of the message but also the "wisdom" that
is active in it. That is, the term expresses the perspective from which the
risen Christ presently works and, thus, the perspective from which "God's
wisdom" is presently manifested.

II

I Cor. 1-4 begins with a thanksgiving for the Corinthians' rich charismatic endowment, especially in the pneumatic gifts of inspired speech
and discernment (1:5-7).[4] It then appeals to the Corinthians to put an end

---

[1] Cf. H. Conzelmann, *An die Korinther* (Göttingen, 1969), p. 69. On the explanatory καί
with οὗτος cf. Blass-Debrunner, p. 229 (§442, 9).

[2] For this interpretation of I Cor. 1:24; 2:4 cf. E. E. Ellis, "Christ and Spirit in I Corinthians",
Christ and Spirit, Essays for C. F. D. Moule, ed. S. S. Smalley and B. Lindars (Cambridge,
1973), pp. 262-70. Cf. Rom. 15:18 f.; II Cor. 12:12.

[3] Rightly, W. C. Robinson, Jr., "Word and Power," *Soli Deo Gloria, Essays for W. C.
Robinson*, ed. J. M. Richards (Richmond, 1968), p. 71.

[4] Cf. E. E. Ellis, " 'Spiritual' gifts in the Pauline Community", *NTS* 20 (1973/74), forthcoming.

to their dissensions and to "be united in the same mind and in the same judgment" (1:10). The relation of the two motifs is confirmed by the subsequent expository section (1:18–4:21) in which wisdom, one of the pneumatic gifts,[1] is a governing motif. The exposition presents a contrast between human wisdom and the wisdom that is "from God" (1:30; cf. 2:12) and leads to the conclusion that the Corinthians not go beyond "what stands written" (4:6), that is, in the Scriptures that Paul has expounded to them.[2] On the one hand the exposition is an attack on human wisdom, not merely on wisdom as a way of salvation[3] but on the inherent structure of "the wisdom of men" as such. As he shows in Romans (1:22) Paul regards human thought and human conduct to be not only bound together but also under sin and innately warped. For this reason Paul can infer that, since the Corinthians' claim to "wisdom" (cf. 3:18) is accompanied by "fleshly" ethical aberrations, their wisdom proceeds not from a wisdom "taught by the spirit" but only from words "taught by human wisdom" (2:13; 3:1 ff.).

The wisdom from God is "not fleshly ($\sigma\alpha\rho\kappa\iota\kappa\dot{\eta}$) wisdom but God's gift" (II Cor. 1:12). Furthermore, it has a cruciform manifestation, for it proceeds from the one who as the exalted Lord remains "Christ crucified." Thus it appears both as "power" and as "cross" in Paul and Apollos, the stewards of God's mysteries (2:7; 4:1). By their perceptive teaching they "build" God's temple (3:9 f., $\dot{\epsilon}\pi o\iota\kappa o\delta o\mu\epsilon\tilde{\iota}$) but also, like Christ, they manifest this wisdom of God in weakness and

> when reviled, we bless
> when persecuted, we endure
> when slandered, we try to conciliate.[4]

Such conduct is the ethical corollary, and indeed the proof, of the wisdom "that is from God".

---

[1] Cf. I Cor. 2:6–16; 12:8.

[2] Otherwise: M. D. Hooker, " 'Beyond the things which are written' . . . ", *NTS* 10 (1963/64), pp. 127–32.

[3] Otherwise: Robinson, *op. cit.*, pp. 74 f. The parallel with Galatians, which Robinson invokes, is attractive. (1) In both Corinthians (1:23) and Galatians (5:11) "Christ crucified", or the cross, is the indispensable *skandalon* of the Christian message. (2) In both it is associated with charismatic workings of the Spirit in the Church (I Cor. 1:26; 2:4; Gal. 3:5). (3) In both it is set over against the "fleshly" attempt to become mature Christians by human achievement, either by the wisdom of men (I Cor. 3:1 ff., 18 f.) or by the works of the law (Gal. 3:2 f.). (4) In both Paul condemns the attempt because it nullifies the "cross" of Christ (I Cor. 1:17; Gal. 2:21). And in both he does so by a biblical exposition that is similar to the midrashic patterns of Philonic and rabbinic exegesis. Cf. I Cor. 1:18–31; 2:6–16; Gal. 3:6–29; P. Borgen, *Bread from Heaven* (Leiden, 1965), pp. 47 ff.; see p. 74, n. 10. (5) In both Paul appears to identify or associate the "spirit" active in the two aberrations, *viz.* "the spirit of the world" and "the elemental spirits", with demonic powers (I Cor. 2:6, 12; Gal. 4:9). Nevertheless, even if there are important parallels, the problems addressed are different. In Galatians it is a question of the wrong use of something that is good (the law of God). In Corinthians it is the confusion of something that is good (the wisdom of God) with something that is at root perverse (the wisdom of men).

[4] I Cor. 4:12 f. Cf. I Pet. 2:23.

The basic problems in the Corinthian church manifest themselves in ethical attitudes: divisiveness (σχίσματα), strife, envy and, especially, conceit (φυσίωσις; cf. 1:10 f.; 3:3; 4:6, 18 f.; 5:2; 8:1; II Cor. 12:20). Such problems are specifically in the foreground in I Cor. 1–4. In responding to this deplorable situation, Paul is not content merely with exhortation.[1] He will not allow a separation of ethics and theology.[2] For he perceives theological ignorance and even misunderstanding to be an underlying cause of the unethical practices: faulty ethics reflect poor theological perception, even as bad theology corrupts good moral habits.[3] Therefore, Paul addresses the ethical problems with theological instruction.

III

What is the theological error in I Cor. 1–4 that Paul discerns beneath the faulty ethics of the Corinthians? Its general character, a wrong kind of "wisdom" (1:17; 2:4; 3:18), may be inferred from the theme of the section. But what, precisely, was its content? (1) According to some recent studies the Christians at Corinth espoused a "wisdom of men" that denied any soteriological significance to Christ's crucifixion; in the face of such teaching Paul set forth the message of the cross.[4] If the above analysis is correct, this view of the situation is mistaken in interpreting "the word of the cross" and "Christ crucified" primarily of the past fact of the crucifixion. Also, it is inconsistent with I Cor. 1:13 (cf. I Cor. 15:3) which presupposes that the Corinthians have, in fact, a positive view of the crucifixion. In the perceptive comment of W. C. Robinson, Jr., "Paul would hardly have sabotaged his whole argument by beginning it with the statement that (the Corinthians) would ridicule."[5]

(2) Is the Corinthians' error perhaps "a misunderstanding of the mode of possessing God's gifts"?[6] The opening thanksgiving (1:5) and the later section on the pneumatic gifts, I Cor. 12–14, lend some support to that interpretation. The gifts, including "the word of wisdom" (12:8), should be used above all for "edification" (οἰκοδομή, 14:26) so that there might be "no dissension (σχίσμα) in the body" (12:25). In the "hymn to love"

---

[1] Paul knows, of course, that in its concrete expression the Church is a *corpus mixtum*, containing both elect and reprobate, and that dissension and factionalism are in some measure inevitable "in order that those who are genuine among you might be recognized" (I Cor. 11:18 f.). Cf. II Cor. 13:5; Gal. 4:11.

[2] Cf. V. Furnish, *Theology and Ethics in Paul* (Nashville, 1968), pp. 224–27.

[3] Cf. I Cor. 15:33; Rom. 1:21 ff., 24 with I Cor. 3:20 (διαλογισμός). Paul does not use the Johannine idiom "to do the truth" (I Jn. 1:6), but the same implicit bond between thought and conduct is reflected in the phrase "obey the truth" (Rom. 2:8; Gal. 5:7).

[4] U. Wilckens, *Weisheit und Torheit* (Tübingen, 1959), pp. 20, 214.

[5] Robinson, *op. cit.*, p. 72.

[6] So, Robinson, *ibid.*, p. 75.

that is a "hymn to Christ"[1] the gifts, including "knowledge" (γνῶσις), are declared to be of no effect if they are not manifested in the context of a love that is not envious (ζηλόω) or conceited (φυσιόω).[2] In I Cor. 12–14 the wrong attitudes apparently are occasioned by a lack of understanding about spiritual gifts (12:1). They bear a striking similarity to the attitudes condemned in I Cor. 1–4, and it is probable that the underlying causes are not unrelated. However, Paul's different response to the symptoms in I Cor. 1–4 suggests that something more is involved than just a misunderstanding or misuse of the gifts.

(3) Somewhat similarly, it has been suggested that the Corinthians reflect "an over-realized eschatology". They suppose that the victory over sin and death has been consummated:[3]

> Already you have been filled
> Already you are rich
> Without us you have reigned.

This is the other side of the same coin that has been examined above: if the Corinthians have not discounted the crucifixion, they at least think that it is totally in the past. It remains for them only to share Christ's "reign". Indeed, according to this view they can in I Cor. 15 even deny a future resurrection because, like Hymenaeus, they think that "the resurrection is past already" (II Tim. 2:18).[4]

There are, however, certain problems with this understanding of the situation in I Cor. 1–4. First, the error in I Cor. 15 offers doubtful support for an eschatological interpretation of I Cor. 4:8. Even if it is a precursor of the teaching of Hymenaeus, it probably reflects more a Platonic anthropology than a "realized" eschatology: the immortal soul, released to eternal life at death, has no need of resurrection.[5] Secondly, in Paul's own teaching – and very likely in his teaching at Corinth – the Christian already has been (corporately) raised with Christ to resurrection life. Having come "alive to God in Christ Jesus", he is to "walk in newness of life".[6] As II Cor. 13:4 shows, because Paul himself "shares in Christ's

[1] I Cor. 13; cf. N. Johansson, "I Cor. xiii and I Cor. xiv", NTS 10 (1963/64), 386 f.
[2] I Cor. 13:1, 2, 4.
[3] E.g. F. F. Bruce, I and II Corinthians (London, 1971), pp. 49 f.; J. Munck, Paul and the Salvation of Mankind (Richmond, 1959), p. 165; E. Käsemann, Essays on New Testament Themes (London, 1964), p. 171.
[4] This view appears later in Gnostic theology. Cf. Tert., de res. 22 (perhaps alluding to I Cor. 4:8); Iren., Against Heresies 1, 23, 5 (re Menander).
[5] This also is part of later Gnostic thought. Cf. W. Schmithals, Gnosticism in Corinth (Nashville, 1971), pp. 157 f.; Justin, Dial. 80.
[6] Rom. 6:4, 11, 13; cf. Gal. 2:19 f.; II Cor. 6:9; 13:4. The expression "raised with Christ" (Col. 3:1; cf. 2:13; Eph. 2:6) is essentially no different, for this conception is presupposed in the phrase "to walk in newness of life" (cf. R. Tannehill, Dying and Rising with Christ (Berlin, 1967), p. 11). Cf. E. E. Ellis, Eschatology in Luke (Philadelphia, 1972), p. 15 n.; W. D. Davies, "The Moral Teaching of the Early Church", The Use of the Old Testament in the New, ed. J. M. Efird (Durham (N.C.), 1972), p. 318 n. Otherwise: E. Lohse, Colossians and Philemon (Philadelphia, 1971), p. 180.

resurrection life, he also shares in the power which is manifest in that life".[1] It is unlikely, then, that he would criticize the Corinthians merely for appropriating an eschatological perspective that he himself has taught and, indeed, has earlier applied to them: "in Christ you have been made rich" (I Cor. 1:5).

A mistaken eschatological perspective may indeed be involved in the false wisdom of the Corinthians. But the error is not in affirming the *reality* of a present participation in Christ's resurrection life and power, but rather in misconceiving the *way* in which that reality is presently to be manifested. In Paul's teaching Christ's followers have in the past been (corporately) "crucified with" him and "raised with" him.[2] And they are destined to actualize individually this corporate reality. But they will actualize the "resurrection with Christ" only at the parousia when, having been "found in him", they shall "attain to the resurrection from the dead" and shall "put on immortality".[3] In the present life they are called to actualize the "crucifixion with Christ". As imitators of Paul[4] they are to seek not their own benefit but that of others,[5] to endure suffering

> as sorrowful, yet always rejoicing
> as poor, yet making many rich
> as having nothing, yet possessing all things.[6]

In imitating Paul they are, in fact, imitating Christ,[7] completing "what is lacking in Christ's afflictions for the sake of his body, that is, the Church."[8]

This *imitatio Christi* is, moreover, the context in which Christ's resurrection power is presently manifested. For Christ's "power is made perfect in weakness."[9] The Corinthians have not followed this path. They have engaged in competitive wrangling.[10] Having "been made rich" in Christ's gifts of words and knowledge, they "boast" as though the gifts were

---

[1] Tannehill, *op. cit.*, p. 99.

[2] Gal. 2:19 f.; Rom. 6:4; Col. 3:1; cf. E. E. Ellis, *Paul and His Recent Interpreters* (Grand Rapids, 1961), pp. 37–40 (= *NTS* 6 (1959/60), 212–16).

[3] Phil. 3:9, 11; I Cor. 15:53; cf. II Cor. 5:3 f. There is, of course, a present *ethical* imperative "to walk in newness of life" that is related to the Christian's identification with Christ's resurrection.

[4] Cf. I Cor. 4:16; 11:1; Gal. 4:12 f.; I Thess. 1:6; II Thess. 3:9.

[5] I Cor. 10:33 f.; cf. 15:31; Rom. 12:1.

[6] II Cor. 6:10.

[7] I Cor. 11:1; I Thess. 1:6. On the primacy of the Christological motif in Paul's ethic cf. Davies, *op. cit.*, pp. 314–32.

[8] Col. 1:24; cf. I Cor. 3:9–17; Gal. 2:20 (συνεσταύρωμαι!).

[9] II Cor. 12:9 f.

[10] Perhaps along the lines of the Jewish practice of "discussions with associates [and] argument with disciples" (Pirke Aboth 6:6) about the meaning of Scripture. So, Wuellner, *op. cit.*, p. 203, who follows D. Daube and S. Liebermann in identifying λόγος σοφίας (I Cor. 2:4) with the *debar ḥokmah* in rabbinic discussions. Cf. Rom. 2:17–24; Acts 18:15; I Clem. 45:1.

their own attainment.[1] Having been endowed in order to "build" God's temple, they are instead destroying it by their boasting, envy, strife, and dissension. In consequence, their cherished wisdom, in a subtle transformation that even they have not discerned, has become mere cleverness, a manifestation of human words rather than of divine power.[2] And, apparently, they have failed to distinguish the resulting "wisdom of this age" from "the wisdom from above."[3] The apostle wishes to call them back from this disastrous course. To do so, he invokes among other things an image of Christ that he has used earlier in his letter to the Galatians. In a word he reminds them that the Christ who manifests God's wisdom and God's power is the one who in his exaltation remains "Christ crucified," the serving and the sacrificing one. And this exalted Christ manifests these divine gifts among his followers only under the sign of the cross.

[1] I Cor. 1:5; 4:7. Since this attitude would be equally wrong after the parousia, I Cor. 4:8 cannot refer merely to a mistaken eschatological perspective. It is primarily an ethical aberration that Paul addresses.

[2] I Cor. 3:18 ff.; 4:19 f.

[3] Cf. Jas. 3:13–15, 17, where the same kind of critique of "wisdom" is made.

CHAPTER V

THE EARLIEST CONFESSION OF
THE ATONEMENT IN PAUL*

HERMAN RIDDERBOS

WHEN I SPEAK OF THE EARLIEST CONFESSION OF THE ATONEMENT, I have in mind the earliest form preserved for us in which the *kerygma* of the atonement came to a certain fixed interpretation and functioned in that form as an authoritative tradition. The formula in I Cor. 15:3, in which Paul describes the redemptive significance of the death of Christ (i.e. "Christ died for our sins in accordance with the Scriptures") can be distinguished as such. The purpose of the following contribution, through which I am happy to associate with those who desire to honour the person and work of Leon Morris, is not only to study the content of this earliest confession as preserved by Paul but also to investigate how this traditional confession functions in the wider context of Paul's preaching.

That in these words, quoted from I Corinthians, we do indeed meet with an old, already existing, formula, and that they are not an original statement of Paul himself is evident in several ways from the text itself. Paul speaks here about the *tradition* which he has delivered to the church as the point of departure[1] for his preaching and which he himself had also received as such. He adds, and from this its fundamental significance is evident, that the church, if it is not to lose its firm foundation, must hold on to this tradition in the manner (literally: in the words[2]) in which he has preached it. Both the circumstantial paradosis-terminology,[3] and the emphasis on the necessity to keep this tradition untainted, point to an earlier, authoritative formulation. This is also clear from the words with which Paul quotes the tradition in the verses 3 ff.,[4] and which together form the λόγος of verse 2. It has been frequently pointed out that in this passage we come across a number of expressions which are not characteristic of Paul's phraseology[5]. Above all, however, the content of verse 3

---

* Translated by J. W. Deenick, Geelong, Victoria.

[1] ἐν πρώτοις, v. 3.

[2] τίνι λόγῳ, v. 2.

[3] παρελάβετε, παρέδωκα, παρέλαβον, but also ἑστήκατε and κατέχετε in vv. 1 and 2 belong to these (cf. Mk. 7:4; II Thess. 2:15).

[4] Expositors disagree on how far this traditional λόγος continues and where Paul himself begins to speak again.

[5] See for this, e.g. Jacob Kremer, *Das älteste Zeugnis von der Auferstehung Christi* (1967), p. 25.

is itself remarkable. In I Cor. 15 Paul addresses those who deny the resurrection of the dead. One would therefore expect that he would direct his argument exclusively to the resurrection. Instead he begins to speak of the *death* of Christ, of the significance of his death, of the evidence for it in the Scriptures, and further of Jesus' burial. All the more clearly this proves that Paul appeals to traditional formulas, traditions delivered at the beginning when he founded the church, and which he now brings to their remembrance.

The importance of this observation will become even clearer when we take further note of the content of this tradition. We limit ourselves to verse 3 i.e. to the part that refers to the death of Christ. Of great significance is the manner in which the redemptive character of Christ's death is expressed both in the words: *for our sins*, and in the addition: *in accordance with the Scriptures*, which is repeated in verse 4 when the resurrection is mentioned. In this way the tradition explicitly gains the character of an *interpretation*. One could argue that this applies to all of the tradition, as, for example, it comes to us in the synoptic gospels. Yet the words: "died for our sins in accordance with the Scriptures", contain something like a "systematic" or "confessional" summary which distinguishes itself in this regard from the historical kerygma as we find it in the synoptic gospels and as Paul, for example, quotes it in I Cor. 11:23 ff. It is for this reason that we believe we may characterize these words as the earliest *confessional* statement concerning the atonement.

The element of atonement is naturally included in the manner in which in these words the death of Christ is related to "our sins". The expression "for our sins" or "for the sake of our sins"[1] is more specific than the more general formula "for us" or "for our sake" which also frequently occurs in statements relating to the death of Christ (cf. Rom. 5:8; II Cor. 5:15; I Thess. 5:10; also Rom. 5:6; 14:15; I Cor. 1:13; II Cor. 5:14; I Peter 3:18). The expression "for our sins" relates the death of Christ to our existence burdened with sin and guilt, and expresses no less than that by his death our sins have been done away with, eradicated and atoned for.[2]

This is confirmed by the addition "in accordance with the Scriptures", which must be taken in close connection with the words "for our sins". Because, even though the Scriptures are mentioned in general and no special passage of Scripture is referred to (which could well indicate again the early period from which the statement originates), most scholars assume that the words "for our sins" have been derived from Isa. 53:5. Most probably these words were already applied to the death of Christ in the Aramaic-speaking church[3]. Against this background of Isa. 53:5 the

---

[1] ὑπὲρ τῶν ἁμαρτιῶν ἡμῶν.
[2] See, for example, H. Riesenfeld, *TWNT* VIII, p. 515 (E.T., p. 512).
[3] See J. Jeremias, *Die Abendsmahlsworte Jesu*[3] (1960), p. 95 His argument is directed against the objections of H. Conzelmann, who wants to explain the formula from the LXX and so from the Greek-speaking church ("Zur Analyse der Bekenntnisformel I Kor. 15:3-5", *Ev.*

words "for our sins" gain a very clear context and one may reckon it to be evident that the interpretation of Jesus' death as an atoning death already belonged to the very early kerygma which in this fixed form has been delivered to us.

It is all the more clear that the words used in I Cor. 15:3 must indeed be understood in this sense from what Paul says a little later about Christ having been raised. There he writes to the church: if Christ has not been raised your faith is futile and *you are still in your sins* (v. 17). Christ's resurrection is the indispensable complement of His death for our sins. Christ's death alone is for that reason insufficient. That is to say, His death is not merely the means of grace that is applied *to us*, viz., in the contrition and penance which His death works *in us* and so, through repentance, delivers us from a guilty conscience and the burden of our sins. No matter how much the death of Christ also imparts itself as a power to us and in us, his death has, in relation to our sins primarily an "objective" significance. It was an event that happened to, was executed upon, Christ before God's face and on our behalf. It was in His death that He atoned for our sins and in this He was recognized and accepted by God in His resurrection. For that reason we would "still be in our sins" had Christ not been raised. Christ's resurrection is the public recognition and acceptance by God of His (Christ's) sacrifice as the eradication and expiation of our sins.

The very same thought is expressed, even more explicitly, in another word central to Paul's kerygma: "who (Christ) was put to death for our trespasses and raised for our justification" (Rom. 4:25). These words have been related closely to Paul's statement in I Cor. 15:3, and quite properly so. Many consider these words also as an already existing formula used by Paul to conclude his argument in Romans 4. However this be, the words "for our trespasses"[1] in Rom. 4:25 are in any case merely a variant to "for our sins" in I Cor. 15:3, and thus an alternative rendering of Isa. 53:5, where also for that matter in the *parallelismus membrorum* two different expressions are used. The preposition: "because of" ($\delta\iota\acute{a}$ + acc.) in Rom. 4:25 and "for the sake of" ($\upsilon\pi\acute{e}\rho$ + gen.) in I Cor. 15:3 will have to be understood as two different renderings of the Hebrew *min* or the Aramaic *be*. It is further obvious that the more causal "because of" in Romans 4:25 does not merely mean that "we" (the human race) are the cause of His death, i.e., because "we", represented by the Jews, killed Him. No matter how much people have been responsible for Christ's death the logical subject of the words "put to death for our trespasses" is not Jesus' murderers but God himself. The expression "was put to death", or as the AV has it more accurately "was delivered", is thus an established passion formula (cf. Rom. 8:32; I Cor. 11:23; Gal. 2:20; Eph. 5:2) in which either

[1] $\delta\iota\grave{a}$ $\tau\grave{a}$ $\pi\alpha\rho\alpha\pi\tau\acute{\omega}\mu\alpha\tau\alpha$ $\acute{\eta}\mu\hat{\omega}\nu$.

Th. 25, 1965, pp. 1–11), maintained and expanded by E. Klappert, "Zur Frage des semitischen oder griechischen Urtextes von I Kor. XV. 3–5", *NTS* 13 (1966–1967), pp. 168–73.

God Himself (Rom. 8:32) or Christ (Gal. 2:20) is the acting person. Here, in view of the passive form being used and Jesus being the object of the delivering, only God Himself can be meant. In that case, our sins are *the reason why* He was delivered, i.e., our sins moved God to deliver Christ, namely to make Him atone for our sins; or, if one would take "because of" (διά) a little more final: in order to free us from our sins. But in both cases the real point is that Christ (suffering and dying) substituted for us so as to carry our sins and to atone for them, wholly in accordance with Isaiah 53.

Only in this way are the two parts of the statement in Romans 4:25 in agreement with each other. The second part, as we remember, speaks of Jesus having been raised by God for the sake of (διά) our *justification*. This last word has, as always with Paul, a forensic meaning. It speaks of our being *acquitted* by God. The resurrection of Christ is therefore here also (as in I Cor. 15:4) the divine reverse of Christ's deliverance by God into death. As He executed His judgement over sin in delivering Christ up to death so God executed our acquittal and justification in Christ's resurrection.

We are therefore free to say that Rom. 4:25, whether it is in this formulation originally Pauline or (as in I Cor. 15:3) an already fixed formula, makes completely transparent, in so far as that would still be needed, the meaning of the earliest Christian confession concerning the redemptive effect of Christ's death. It interprets this effect in accordance with Isaiah 53, it points to God as the acting person in the surrender and death of Christ, and it points to our sins as the cause and the motive for this action. So it characterizes Christ's death as a subjection to the divine judgement for our sake and in our place, and thus as the accomplishment of atonement for our sins.

★　　★　　★　　★　　★

How much this basic thought of the earliest Christian kerygma functions in *Paul's whole preaching and theology* can be made clear in various ways. But here again we have to distinguish between different formulations of the kerygma which in turn may flow together or appear side by side. Relevant here are the thought of *atoning sacrifice* derived from the O.T. cultus; the concept, so characteristic in Paul's gospel, of *forensic justification*; and the idea of *substitution* combined with these last two conceptions.

The concept of the *atoning sacrifice* occurs in a passage that is particularly important for Paul's whole doctrine of redemption i.e., Rom. 3:21 ff., where it says in verse 25 that God has put forward Christ as an expiation which receives its efficacy from "his blood". Even though the atoning sacrifice is mentioned explicitly only here in Paul's letters, we find the same thought in places where "the blood of Christ" is referred to i.e. apart from Rom. 3:25 also in Rom. 5:9; Eph. 2:13 and in Col. 1:20. It has quite rightly been pointed out that we have to understand this expression in *sacrificial* terms.[1] Crucifixion was not itself a particularly bloody execution. When therefore *the blood* of Christ is regularly referred to, it is not so much because of the manner of His death but because of its significance as a sacrifice, especially as an atoning sacrifice, in which the blood was shed to cover and eradicate sin. In that sense Paul speaks in I Cor. 5:7 of Jesus' death as a paschal sacrifice and as an offering for the eradication of sin; and, in the words of the Holy Supper, Paul speaks of the New Testament or covenant that is founded in the blood of Christ (I Cor. 11:25, cf. 27). We are therefore able to interpret the shorter formulations, to which we referred earlier, in the same light; such as *"for our sins"* (I Cor. 15:3; cf. also Gal. 1:4) or simply *"for us"* (Rom. 5:8; 14:15; II Cor. 5:14), *"for the ungodly"* (Rom. 5:6) and other such phrases in which the death and self-surrender of Christ for our sake are expressed (Rom. 8:32; Gal. 2:20 *et al.*).

As mentioned already, the idea of atoning sacrifice is in Paul closely related to the concept of forensic justification. So, for example, in Rom. 3:25 where it is said that God has put forward Christ as an expiation to show His righteousness (vv. 25, 26), God manifests Himself in the death of Christ as the righteous Judge, who in Christ's death judges and condemns sin (cf. also Rom. 8:3) and who at the same time justifies and acquits "him who has faith in Jesus". Therefore it can be said that we are justified "through his blood" (Rom. 5:9). In both concepts Christ appears as the substitute; e.g., when it is said that "one has died for all" in II Cor. 5:14, where the "for us" of the atoning sacrifice is very closely related to the substitution[2] by the "One" for the "all". We find the same thought elsewhere, when the justification of the ungodly is founded on their sins having been accounted to Christ and when He thus substitutes for them; e.g. (and again in close correspondence to the terminology of Isaiah 53), in II Cor. 5:21: "for our sake He made Him to be sin who knew no sin, so that in Him we might become the righteousness of God". In both parts of this statement Paul uses the *abstractum pro concreto*: God made the sinless One the carrier of sin so that we in Him would be righteousness before God. Substitution and justification are closely related so that it can be said that Christ has delivered us from the curse of the law by becoming a curse (i.e., one cursed by God) for us (Gal. 3:13).

[1] J. Jeremias, *Der Opfertod Jesu Christi* (1963), p. 16.
[2] H. Riesenfeld, *TWNT* VIII, p. 516 (E.T., p. 513): "τῷ ὑπὲρ αὐτῶν ἀποθανόντι καὶ ἐγερθέντι in v. 15 is based on a kerygmatic formulation like that in I Cor. 15:3, and the prep. thus has the primary sense of "on behalf or in favour of". But in the more forensic expression εἰς ὑπὲρ πάντων ἀπέθανεν in v. 14 the sense "in the place of" is predominant, as is shown by the development of the thought in the following clause: ἄρα οἱ πάντες ἀπέθανον."

From this whole complex of pronouncements, to which still others could be added, also from the so-called deutero-Pauline letters, it becomes very clear that Paul's kerygma entirely agrees with what has been delivered to us as the earliest Christian confession concerning the atoning power of Christ's death and presents with rich nuances a broad unfolding of it. The basic thought behind it is found in the cultic-juridical aspect, the deep significance of which consists in this that God Himself gives the atoning sacrifice that is needed to cover sin (Rom. 3:25) and that He in order to condemn sin where it demanded condemnation i.e., in our human existence, sent His own Son so as to condemn sin and to atone for it in Him (Rom. 8:3). The initiative of the atonement rests with God's grace. It is He who in Christ reconciles the world unto Himself. Yet sin must be atoned for, must be eradicated and condemned. That is the atoning power of Christ's death according to the earliest Christian confession, and according to Paul's kerygma and doctrine as well.

*   *   *   *   *

It has been frequently argued that, while Paul took over the tradition concerning the redemptive character of Christ's death which had already been established before his time, yet with him all of this gained different dimensions in depth and breadth. E. Käsemann, for example, writes[1] that Paul often expressed what he really had in mind with the help of traditional formulas. Also according to Käsemann I Cor. 15:3 ought to be referred to in this connection. There the words "for us" represent the central motif, containing both meanings i.e., "for our sake" and "in our place", and establishing our inability to work out our own salvation.[2] In this way a certain shift occurred with Paul, respecting the tradition, characterized by Käsemann as a "radicalization".[3] Particularly the sacrifice motif as interpretation of Christ's death is moved completely into the background. Paul certainly knew the concept of sacrifice and used it without objection (*bedenkenlos*), but other interpretations moved so much to the forefront that for that reason alone the sacrifice motif is given very little real significance.[4] The same applies to the early concept of the vicarious suffering of Christ, the carrying of the punishment for our sins. According to Käsemann, Paul's texts give no support to this idea. Paul knew the concept of substitution (*Stellvertretung*) but not in the sense that Christ offered the sacrifice in our stead, or carried the punishment for sin in our place. The effect of the cross on *people* so much determined Paul's thinking that its effect upon *God* does not come into the picture at all. The substitution consists in the deep *shame* of Christ's incarnation as the price of redemption, accomplished as it is without our help.[5] On the cross

---

[1] "Die Heilsbedeutung des Todes Jesu nach Paulus", in H. Conzelmann, E. Flesseman-van Leer, E. Haenchen, *Zur Bedeutung des Todes Jesu. Exegetische Beiträge* (1967), pp. 11–34.
[2] *Op. cit.*, p. 18.   [3] *Op. cit.*, p. 22.   [4] *Op. cit.*, p. 21.   [5] *Op. cit.*, p. 21.

it becomes manifest that the true God alone is the Creator who has to accomplish His purpose with the help of that which is nothing, as the One who raises from the dead; and also on the cross it becomes evident that man is sinner, who cannot save himself or conquer the distance between God and himself. Paul interpreted the received tradition of the cross of Jesus in the sense of his own doctrine of justification.[1] And this justification is to be understood as atonement because it makes an end to the enmity, and grants peace from God to those who otherwise would remain enemies but are now through the *pax Christi* led back to obedience.[2] Here too the current tradition is used in order to present the theology of Paul himself in clearer outline, and in this way the tradition itself is given a different emphasis. Did the tradition speak of forgiveness of earlier trespasses because of the atonement accomplished through Jesus' death (Rom. 3:25; II Cor. 5:19)? For Paul, salvation is not primarily the end of perdition and guilt, which once separated us from God, but (acc. to Rom. 5:9 ff.; Rom. 8:2) salvation is *liberty from the power of sin*, death and divine anger; it is more particularly the possibility of the new life. "Er hat die von ihm aufgegriffene Überlieferung also radicalisiert".[3]

★   ★   ★   ★   ★

In his *Theology of the New Testament*, Bultmann is of the opinion that Paul's interpretation of the redemptive character of Christ's death indeed follows the tradition dating from the earliest Christian church, but that for him the most typical concept is *not* contained in that tradition.[4] With regard to the first – the tradition – Bultmann also points to those statements in which Paul describes the death of Christ as the atoning sacrifice designated by God, and refers to Rom. 3:25 ff. and Rom 5:9 as well as to I Cor. 15:3. However, for Bultmann too, this tradition does not represent the most essential and typical elements in Paul's concept. We see rather that in other places Paul enhances the categories of cultic-juridical thinking (*gesprengt*). The death of Christ is then no longer merely a sacrifice that takes away the guilt of sin, i.e., eradicates the punishment evoked by sin, but also becomes a means by which one is liberated from the powers of this aeon, of the law, of sin and of death.[5]

Bultmann believes that Paul describes these concepts, so typical for him, in terms which he borrowed from the Hellenistic mystery religions (in which the initiated also participate in the death and resurrection of the deity) and which he then further interprets in the categories of the Gnostic myth. According to these Gnostic notions there would exist a kind of cosmic unity between the redeemer and the believers redeemed by him, a *soma*, so that what happens to the redeemer (or has happened to

[1] *Op. cit.*, p. 20.   [2] *Op. cit.*, p. 22.   [3] *Op. cit.*, p.22.
[4] *Theologie des Neuen Testaments* (1953), p. 291.
[5] *Op. cit.*, p. 292.

him) also happens to those who belong to his *soma*. By using Gnostic categories Paul would have been able to characterize the redemptive significance of Christ's death and resurrection not only as a sacrifice offered once and for all on our behalf or as a punishment suffered in our place, but also as a redemptive event that can be interpreted as *an event that indeed happens to man.*[1]

In the theology of both Bultmann and Käsemann, we find a tendency to establish a certain distance between the oldest Christian tradition concerning the death of Christ on the one hand and Paul on the other. Paul would link up with the tradition but it would not be typical for his own thinking. While the tradition emphasized what once "objectively" happened for us but without us, Paul was more interested in the liberating effect of the death of Christ as an event that in reality happens *to man*. While Käsemann, in the essay from which I quoted, tries to make this clear particularly with terms derived from the Pauline doctrine of justification (the death of Christ sets us free because it robs us of presumptuousness and places us under God's liberating regime), Bultmann refers to the categories of Gnosticism as the means preferred by Paul to express the existential liberation which the death of Christ means to the individual man.

★   ★   ★   ★   ★

In my opinion one will indeed have to distinguish, in Paul's doctrine of the atonement, between a twofold explication of the earlier tradition as we have it in I Cor. 15:3 – or, more precisely, one will have to recognize that Paul endeavours to unfold the full content and consequence of the "Christ died for our sins".

The epistle to the Romans in particular gives us a clear insight in the development of Paul's thinking. In studying this letter we have to remember all the time that here Paul unfolds his kerygma in constant confrontation with the redemption pattern of the Jewish synagogue. Therefore, when he expresses the redemptive nature of Christ's death above all in the juridical-cultic categories of expiation and justification (as in the central passage of Romans 3:25 ff.) it is not merely an adaptation to a tradition which would be hardly, if at all, characteristic for his own train of thought but it far rather expresses what is fundamental to his whole gospel, which is partly also determined by this confrontation with the equally juridical elements at the basis of the Jewish doctrine of redemption. That also explains why the doctrine of justification receives such disproportionately strong emphasis. This in itself is no "radicalization" of the tradition, nor is it a shift (concerning the effect of the atonement) from what once happened for our sake (the removal of the guilt

[1] *Op. cit.*, p. 295.

and punishment of sin) to that which now and constantly again happens to us (the liberation from sin as an actual power and the possibility of the new life in liberty). With Paul the doctrine of justification even in its most radicalised form remains rooted in what Christ once accomplished for us and without us (*pro nobis et extra nos*). With a full range of motifs and metaphors it points to this "objective" significance of Christ's death and resurrection as the only and unrepeatable act of atonement, as becomes unmistakably clear, for example, from the idea of reckoning and imputation elaborately worked out in Romans 4 and from the concluding statement in Romans 4:25; "who was put to death for our trespasses and raised for our justification."

★   ★   ★   ★   ★

To be sure the Apostle does not leave it at that: he also explains the redemptive significance of Christ's death as a liberation of the whole life of the believer. I do not think one ought to say that in this respect Paul transcends the earlier tradition, because there is no reason to believe that the tradition of the death of Christ would have to be understood *exclusively* in the juridical and cultic categories. Already the words of I Cor. 15:3, oriented as they are to Isaiah 53, have – we may say – a naturally wider implication than one limited to the juridical. However, this does not detract from the fact that we find in Paul – particularly in the letter to the Romans – a far clearer and far more extensive explanation of the all-embracing import of the atonement.

Here too we have to take into account that he wishes to maintain the gospel of the atonement and justification by faith over against the Jewish doctrine of redemption. Even this Jewish doctrine did not limit itself to the juridical aspect. In relation to this we observe, beginning with Romans 5, a clear progress and extension of thought. Here Paul does his best to clarify the fact that justification by faith as proclaimed by him is not just an isolated, abstract juridical judgement that would not effect any concrete change in our human life which is full of temptation and strife, such as could easily create among his opponents the impression of a mere assertion not in agreement with the reality of life. Over against this he contends that precisely this justification by faith controls all of life and also as "peace with God" gives foundation to the hope of participating in the total liberation of life, the glory of God. For that purpose he appeals precisely to the forensic character of Christ's death as a death for the ungodly. For if the death of Christ, while we were yet sinners, reconciled us with God, how much more shall we, now that we have been reconciled, be saved by His *life*? Therefore justification is not merely a divine acquittal, once executed in the death of Christ; it is also an invitation into a relationship with the saving power of the life of Christ (Rom. 5:10) or, as

Paul calls it in the remainder of chapter 5: "justification to life"[1], and "justification to eternal life"[2] through Jesus Christ our Lord (Rom. 5:18, 21).

So here we see an expansion of the concept of justification or, rather, a connexion between "justification" and "life", whereby on the one hand the concept of "justification" wholly retains its forensic meaning, whereas on the other hand, through its connexion with the concept of "life", it is further and more directly qualified as a *life giving* and *life related* justification.

Added to this we find in Rom. 5:12 the highly remarkable parallel between Adam and Christ. The fact that Paul introduces this here is obviously related to the argument in Romans 5:1–11 – that justification by faith is not an *abstractum*, not merely a divine acquittal, but that it also constitutes the foundation of hope for the future and grants participation in the life of Christ. This is clarified through the participation of "the many" in "the One", on the one hand Adam, on the other Christ whose type Adam was (5:14). Now while the participation of the many in Adam means participation in sin, so the participation of the many in Christ is participation in the abundant grace of God and in the grace of that one man Jesus Christ (Rom. 5:15). This also means participation in the triumphant *life* of Christ – "those who receive the abundance of grace and the free gift of righteousness reign in life through the one man Jesus Christ"[3] (v. 17) – which leads Paul twice to qualify justification as a justification that grants life (vv. 18 and 21).

As we see, this concept of justification also remains predominantly the foundation in the Adam-Christ parallel (cf. also v. 20). At the same time, this parallel serves to extend the idea of the atonement (vv. 10, 11) which is being worked out, particularly in chapter 6. It is precisely this anti-thetical parallel between Adam and Christ which enables Paul to involve the church in a more comprehensive manner in the death and resurrection of Christ. What is effected in the obedience or the disobedience of the One applies also to the many. They, Adam and Christ, represent the two turning points in human history. They include in their person all who belong to them. It is not merely a question of one or more isolated acts, which the One does to the advantage or disadvantage of the others, but it is the totality of life which they represent and in which the many are included with them.

This expansion of the concept is also demonstrated in the terminology. While the juridical-cultic notion of the substitution is generally expressed in the prepositions ὑπέρ and περί, whereby Christ is the subject ("Christ

---

[1] δικαίωσις ζωῆς (Rom. 5:18).
[2] δικαιοσύνη εἰς ζωὴν αἰώνιον (Rom. 5:21).
[3] ἐν ζωῇ βασιλεύσουσιν (cf. v. 21: ἡ χάρις βασιλεύσῃ διὰ δικαιοσύνης εἰς ζωὴν αἰώνιον).

has died for us"), now the participation of the church in Christ's death is also further expressed with the help of the preposition σύν, whereby the church is the subject ("crucified, died, raised with Christ" etc.). For the transition from the one concept to the other, scholars have often appealed to II Cor. 5:14: "one has died for all, therefore all have died." However, this transition can also be traced in the course of the argument in Romans 5 and 6. In Rom. 5:6 ff. Paul still uses the traditional formulation: "Christ died for us," in which the cultic-juridical significance of Christ's death comes to the fore: "we are justified by His blood". Yet, after having introduced the concept of the One and the many he speaks in chapter 6 of our having been crucified and our having died with Christ. And so we are no longer dealing merely with justification but specifically with the church having been redeemed from the *power* of sin. For the church is included in the death and resurrection of Christ and thus has died *to* sin[1] (Rom. 6:2) and now is dead *to* sin and lives for God (v. 11).[2] In that way he lays the foundation for his further exposition in chapters 6, 7 and 8, in which he interprets the redemptive nature of Christ's death and resurrection not merely in terms of justification and acquittal, but also in those of liberation from the power of sin, of renewal of life and of sanctification.

According to Bultmann, Paul borrowed this idea of the participation of the many in the death and resurrection of the One from the Hellenistic mystery religions and from the Gnostic concept, which envisaged a cosmic inclusion of believers in the *soma* of the Redeemer. From this it would then be evident that the typically Pauline elements in the doctrine of atonement ought be explained from the Gnostic-Hellenistic *Lebensgefühl* of subjection to the powers of sin and death, rather than from the tradition which interprets the redemption given in Christ's death in juridical and cultic categories.

Now the Gnostic background of the Pauline conception of the *soma* of Christ has, on closer examination, proven to be a very dubious *interpretamentum* for Paul's doctrine of redemption, as also the reference to the cultic-myths of the Hellenistic mystery religions and the so-called "myth of the redeemed redeemer".[3] Yet, however that may be, it seems to me that in this way – in the footsteps of the old liberal tradition[4] – an increasing distance is posited, improperly, between Paul's thinking and the early Christian tradition concerning the death of Christ. For although it is true that in chapters 6–8 the essential point of the argument has shifted, since from here on all emphasis is placed on the fact of liberation from the power

[1] ἀπεθάνομεν τῇ ἁμαρτίᾳ.
[2] νεκροὺς μὲν τῇ ἁμαρτίᾳ, ζῶντας δὲ τῷ θεῷ.
[3] See, for example, H. M. Schenke, *Der Gott "Mensch" in der Gnosis: Ein religionsgeschichtlicher Beitrag zur Diskussion über die paulinische Anschauung von der Kirche als "Leib Christi"* (1962); C. Colpe, *Die religionsgeschichtliche Schule: Darstellung und Kritik ihres Bildes vom gnostischen Erlösermythus* (1961).
[4] Cf. H. N. Ridderbos, *Paulus: Ontwerp van zijn Theologie*³ (1973), pp. 10 ff.

of sin in our human existence, yet this transition is to be understood again in the context of Paul's confrontation with Jewish thinking and not with the Hellenistic-Gnostic climate of thought, whatever that may be. What Paul introduces as an objection against his doctrine of justification and grace (Rom. 6:1: "are we to continue in sin that grace may abound?") is precisely the classic and fundamental *Jewish* objection against this doctrine (cf. Rom. 3:8).[1] And when in what follows in chapters 6, 7 and 8 he further emphasizes the fact that Christ has also liberated us from the power of sin, then this is done because in the Jewish synagogue's doctrine of redemption the battle against the power of sin in the life of the faithful did certainly receive as much attention as the question of how one is justified (on the ground of the works of the law) in God's future judgement. It is for that reason that in chapters 6–8 (especially in chapter 7) the law according to Jewish thinking is once again brought into the picture in the apostle's argument, but now from a point of view that differs from that in chapters 2–4. For according to Jewish thinking the law was given for a double purpose: on the one hand so as to derive from the works of the law the ground for acquittal and justification in God's judgement, but on the other hand, and no less so, to assist man in his battle against the power of sin and to give him, in the inner conflict between good and evil (the good and evil *yetzer*), the moral strength to obtain victory over the evil inclination (which Paul calls "the flesh").

Over against this Paul (in chapters 6–8) puts it in an argument, as sophisticated as it is basic, that also in this battle against *the powers* of sin the believer lives not under the law but under grace (cf. 6:14; 7:5). Here too he emphasizes first of all (cf. 6:1–12) the decision which has occurred in the death of Christ: for Christ in His death obtained for His own not only acquittal from sin but also broke once and for all the power of sin. Once[2] He died to (the power of) sin. That is to say, by dying He disposed of the power of sin (Rom. 6:10) because He who has died has paid the toll. He is free from sin (6:7).[3] One may say, therefore, that the believer's liberation from the power of sin is founded in the same way in the death and resurrection of Christ as is his liberation from the guilt and punishment of sin. Only the representation and the terminology are different. Whereas in the last instance One dies *in the place* of all, in the first instance there is mention of a dying of the many *together* with the One because they have been incorporated in Him through baptism[4] (Rom. 6:5; cf. I Cor. 12:12) and thus what once has happened to Christ is now applicable to them. In both cases, however, the same unique redemptive event is meant. One cannot distinguish between that which once ("objectively") happened

[1] See, for example, Strack-Billerbeck IV.i (1928), pp. 466 ff.
[2] Dative τῇ ἁμαρτίᾳ ἀπέθανεν, v. 10 (cf. v. 2).
[3] ὁ γὰρ ἀποθανὼν δεδικαίωται ἀπὸ τῆς ἁμαρτίας.
[4] σύμφυτοι γεγόναμεν.

for our sake and that which now ("subjectively") happens to us; not only our justification from guilt but also our liberation from the power of sin resides on Calvary. *There* Christ died for our sins, but *there also* our old nature has been crucified with Him. *There* He bought us free from the curse of the law (Gal. 3:13) but *there* also did we escape from the slavery of the law and *there* have we been brought under the new dominion of the Spirit (Rom. 7:6; Gal. 2:19 ff.). In both cases the unique and unrepeatable redemptive event of Christ's death remains central.

From the other point of view, one may also argue that the death of Christ can be interpreted in *both* respects as an event that is in reality executed *in the life of man*. In this context, the gospel of the death and resurrection of Christ is proclaimed in both respects not merely as an indicative but also as an imperative. Because Christ has been made to be sin for us (the justification), therefore comes to us the call: "be reconciled to God" (II Cor. 5:20, 21). And because we have died with Christ and so have died to the power of sin, therefore it is said to us: "let not sin reign in your mortal bodies" (Rom. 6:8, 12). In both instances the point in question is the effect which the atonement has in the believer's life, the liberation from the law; and in both instances life under the dominion of the Spirit is signified. For since the forgiving love of God has been poured out into our hearts through the Holy Spirit who has been given to us (Rom. 5:1–5, 21), justification is life also; peace with God; and boasting in suffering and hope. On the other hand, liberation from the power of sin consists in this, that we live no longer under the impotent regime of the law but through the power of the Spirit. This matter of the second confrontation with the law is raised by Paul in a most vivid way in Romans 7 and 8. First we are confronted with the moral impotence and conflict of the man sold under sin, who in his battle against what he does not want still seeks his power in the law; after that in chapter 8 we are shown the power of the Spirit who leads us out of the bondage of sin into the liberty of the children of God.

Thus there develops, in close connexion and parallel with each other, a double confrontation with the law as a means of redemption. This can be described on the one hand as the contrast between *the law and faith*, on the other hand as that between *the law and the Spirit*; on the one hand as being delivered from "the law of works" and brought under "the law of faith" (Rom. 3:27), on the other hand as a being freed from "the law of sin and death" and as a life under "the law of the Spirit of life" (Rom. 8:2).

*   *   *   *   *

Summarizing, we may conclude that the earliest confession concerning the atonement: "Christ died for our sins according to the Scriptures", constitutes the point of departure for Paul's doctrine of the atonement. He provides for this confession, that had been delivered to him, an exposition which possibly remains without peer in all of the New Testament. If we could include in our field of study the letters to the Ephesians and the Colossians, still wider and even cosmic dimensions would come into view. However, Paul remained faithful to the original Christian confession and his explication of it, no matter how grand and vast it becomes, does *not* mean its liquidation or the repeal of its original character. By understanding the death of Christ in the light of the Scriptures, the earliest Christian church did not start from its own experience, but from the significance of the person of Christ and from the history of the divine work of redemption. It is precisely this redemptive–historic character of the death of Christ that dominates and directs Paul's preaching as well as his explication of the atoning power of Christ's death and resurrection. In various ways, no doubt, he makes the transition from the history of redemption to our human existence, from the *historia salutis* to the *ordo salutis* and he translates the redemptive effect of Christ's death and resurrection in a rich variety of anthropological categories; but his christology determines his anthropology, and not the other way round. This does not merely apply to his doctrine of justification which derives its deepest tones from the fact that Christ once died for the ungodly as a manifestation of the divine judgement executed upon Him and of the divine acquittal granted in Him. Not improperly, therefore, one could speak, and has spoken, of the eschatological character of Paul's doctrine of justification. Yet also when he describes the effect of Christ's death in the liberation of man from the power of sin, Paul refers back to what once happened in Christ to those who have been incorporated in Him through baptism. In Romans 6, Paul starts as it were all over again from the beginning, i.e., he derives *every* effect of the atonement in the lives of people from what happened to and with Christ.

To preserve that order, to remain faithful to the earliest Christian confession, and to the explication which Paul gave of it in increasingly wider concentric circles, is the not so simple but, as I see it, highly necessary task – and one of the greatest relevance – of Christian theology in our time – a task to which he too to whom we dedicate this book has given his energies, and for the fulfilment of which we desire to recognize and to honour him.

CHAPTER VI

THE REVELATION OF CHRIST TO PAUL ON THE DAMASCUS ROAD AND PAUL'S DOCTRINE OF JUSTIFICATION AND RECONCILIATION A STUDY IN GALATIANS I*

Günther Bornkamm

I

THE INCLUSION OF THE ONLY AUTOBIOGRAPHICAL REPORT OF ITS KIND left us by Paul in a reflection on his doctrine of justification and reconciliation seems to break an elementary rule of hermeneutics.[1] This rule obliges the exegete and historian not to impose on any given text a theme which is alien to it, and to note carefully not only what it says but what it does not mention. What can we expect a passage from which the concepts of justification and reconciliation are entirely absent to contribute to our understanding of them? The passage has its own theme: attacked and challenged by the false teachers in Galatia, the apostle, in a broad, comprehensive review of his own life-story, defends the legitimacy of an office which was entrusted to him not by men but directly by God, and thus also the truth of his controversial gospel for the Gentiles.

It is from this that the passage derives its incomparable value, which secures it the historian's keen attention. For this compressed, authentic account of Paul's, which virtually has the accuracy of minutes of proceedings, provides us with detailed information about a long and otherwise largely obscure period not only in Paul's own career immediately after his conversion but, at the same time, in the history of earliest Christianity. From the recollection of his Jewish past (1:13 f.) and his turning to Christ on the Damascus road (1:15 f.) to the apostolic conference in Jerusalem (2:1–10) and farther on to the conflict with Peter in Antioch (2:11–21), this autobiographical report spans about two decades. That is in any event far longer than the later period of his mission in the

* Translated by the Rev. Dr. J. M. Owen, Principal of the Presbyterian Theological Hall, Perth, Western Australia.

[1] I gratefully avail myself of the opportunity provided by this *Festschrift*, celebrating our esteemed colleague's sixtieth birthday, of developing further some thoughts already put forward in my *Paulus* (E.T. *Paul*, 1971). In order not to broaden unnecessarily the compass of this paper (and being in any case cut off from libraries at the time of writing), I have cited relatively little special literature and have also refrained from mentioning many passages which will immediately come to the reader's mind.

Aegean lands. That later period lasted scarcely more than half a decade, and we can form a reasonably clear picture of it, especially from all his indisputably genuine letters, which were composed at that time, but also from individual reports in Acts, although their historical value does not match that of the letters.[1] Historically valuable, however, as the first two chapters of Galatians are, this does not entitle us to demand from them theological ideas which, in accordance with the plain structure of the letter, do not come under discussion until chapters 3–6.

Critical misgivings about the recourse to the story of Paul's life favoured by many expositors are all too well justified. This recourse has often proved to be a disastrous flight into psychologizing fantasy, which introduces its own modern impressions into the texts, where what we have to do is to think the apostle's theological thoughts after him. This modern excess of zeal for tracing Paul's inner development and spiritual history is seldom aware how much it sins against Paul's own statement: "We preach not ourselves, but Christ Jesus as Lord" (II Cor. 4:5) and, so to speak, disregards the proportions of his overall thought. No wonder, then, that in consequence of such treatment the Pauline theology is inevitably seen as a personally conditioned, accidental or necessary product of the course of his life, so that its claim to truth becomes a relative one.

These basic considerations draw attention to a "Scylla" of Pauline interpretation. But they contain an equally dangerous "Charybdis" into which exegesis will just as surely steer if it tears the apostle's life and his message – his career and his theology – apart. As a rule, his life-story then regularly becomes a mere succession of historical facts and dates, successes and sufferings, good fortune and ill fortune, while his theology, conversely, becomes a system of timeless insights of faith. Yet Paul, more than any other figure in primitive Christianity, is distinguished by the incomparable energy and consistency with which he has made the message of Christ committed to him into his own personal concern, right into the concrete decisions of each day and into the content of the thought of all his letters. It is in this sense that he speaks of himself as continually carrying around in his body the stigmata and death of Jesus (Gal. 6:17; II Cor. 4:10). What else does this mean than that his life is to be understood as theology transposed into concrete history and that his theology is viewed aright only when its constant relation to his life is kept in sight?

II

When we recall the current exegesis of Galatians 1, it appears (as far as I can see) not yet to have escaped the two danger zones of Scylla and Charybdis; it tends either to overload Paul's autobiographical statements

[1] Cf. *Paul*, pp. xiv ff.

with psychological reflexions or to underestimate the theological motifs which they contain and not to make them sufficiently visible.

In this connexion we can confine ourselves to a brief criticism of the false idea, still widely held, that Saul, the one-time Pharisee and persecutor of Christians, had even before his conversion secretly become aware that his zeal for the law was a great fiasco and that, due to the overwhelming influence of Jesus, he finally broke down under the pangs of conscience. This stereotyped picture has been transferred to the apostle from the life-story of Luther and from the realm of experience of the pietist fathers, but it does not really fit his case. Wherever Paul mentions his Jewish past, whether in passing or in greater detail, he speaks of it not as a contrite sinner but with pride – and that applies even to his persecution of the church of Christ. What he once regarded as wealth and gain, his faultless righteousness by the standards of the law, he has sacrificed; he now regards it as loss and refuse (Phil. 3:4 ff.). The same tone is maintained in Gal. 1:13 f. to provide a foil for Paul's statements about his conversion and call in 1:15 f. The well-known passage in Rom. 7:7–25, which is often mis-takenly understood as biographical, is no proof to the contrary. In it Paul uses the stylistic form of the "I" with universal sense to portray the misery of man "in the flesh", unredeemed, held prisoner under Sin, Law and Death, and he does so retrospectively, in the light of the Christ-event. Here the traditional picture of Paul has been radically corrected by more recent exegetical research.[1]

On the other hand, the opinion remains virtually unshaken that in Gal. 1:15 f. Paul, in repelling his opponents' attacks on his gospel and his apostleship, bases his faith and commission exclusively on the subjective experience of the vision of the risen Christ vouchsafed him on the Damas-cus road, and – this continuation belongs inseparably to what has gone before! – that from then on he maintained his own preaching of salva-tion on the basis of the "revelation" received through this vision, with a sovereign rejection of all humanly mediated tradition about Jesus. Since Paul names himself among the resurrection witnesses (I Cor. 15:8; 9:1) and, as no one will deny, has experienced the appearance of the Risen One on the Damascus road, a corresponding interpretation seems to be required for Gal. 1:15 f. also. The correctness of such an interpretation is virtually never doubted. To avoid its consequences, or at least to tone down the curious abruptness of Paul's thoughts, expositors have made every imaginable effort to make them psychologically comprehensible. At the very least they have tried to present the apostle's short, two weeks' visit to Cephas "after three years"[2] (Gal. 1:18 f.) as the sort of opportunity

---

[1] Cf. W. G. Kümmel, *Römer 7 und die Bekehrung des Paulus* (1929); R. Bultmann, *Existence and Faith* (E.T., 1960), pp. 152 ff.; G. Bornkamm, *Early Christian Experience* (1969), pp. 87 ff.

[2] Since the ancient counting of years, months or days included the first along with the rest of the series, a period of at least more than two years can be meant by μετὰ τρία ἔτη.

which Paul would have sought and grasped, by which after a strange delay to be sure, he rectified his omission and obtained from the first disciple whom Jesus called, the leader of the Jerusalem church, the basic information necessary for faith and proclamation. But these and similar efforts come to grief on his actual wording. They do not get rid of the puzzling fact that Paul, immediately after his conversion, did not get in touch with those at Jerusalem (as might have been expected) but, in all probability, began at once to carry out his apostolic commission in non-Jewish Arabia.[1] An interval of at least more than two years remains extremely odd, too, when one considers that Paul had not known the earthly Jesus (II Cor. 5:16) and that, in his situation, it could well be seen as the most natural and urgent thing for him to set off at once, in penitence and curiosity, to see the original apostles.[2] Similarly, no exegesis should overlook the contrast between the equally glib and ineffective filling in by some interpreters of that brief visit to Cephas and the reserve which characterizes Paul's account of it. Neither should sight be lost of the fact that the apostle in any case spent the next decade and a half conducting a mission in Syria and Cilicia off his own bat before finally setting off with Barnabas and Titus to the apostolic conference. Paul's description of events in Galatians 1, which he even confirmed with an oath (1:20), is, further, headed by his unambiguous and unmistakable protestation of his complete independence of the Jerusalem apostles (1:12). Galatians 2 dovetails neatly into this, for in this continuation of his story Paul says: At that conference even the original apostles confirmed the freedom and independence of my gospel to the Gentiles, and later I fought for it uncompromisingly in the conflict with Cephas at Antioch.

Is all this based on an obstinate appeal to his "Damascus-experience" – in other words, to his vision? One is astounded that the exegetes who hold this customary interpretation to be the only right one do not frankly spell out its consequences and implications in quite a different way. If this is right, if this is what the text demands, it means that here a singular and stubborn individualist, with an unyielding view of himself which is downright fanatical, has set out to do battle with the original apostles and the primitive church, has jeopardized the church's unity, has finally got his way after bitter struggles and now, years later, is attempting to fight the same battles over again in his controversy with the Galatian Judaizers.

Initially at least, this will have been the impression which Paul in fact gave his opponents and which, very probably, he had already given to those who took part in the Jerusalem conference. He did not really shun the odium of it. But the decisive question concerns the grounds on which

[1] "Arabia" surely means the territory east and south of Syria, belonging to the Nabataean kingdom. Paul, it is true, does not expressly say that he preached there, but this is most probably implied by the ἵνα clause. We do not know when he came back to Damascus.

[2] Acts, which passes over Paul's sojourn in Arabia, gives rise to the false impression that he left Damascus for Jerusalem as soon as possible (9:20 ff.).

he defended his gospel and his apostleship to the Gentiles. If it had merely
been for him a matter of the appearance of the Risen One which he had
experienced on the Damascus road, the question would arise how he
could, then as now, claim this as something peculiar to himself and so
treat his "Damascus experience" as absolute. Primitive Christianity was
and remained united in its assurance of the resurrection of Jesus Christ:
this includes the teachers of false doctrine with whom Paul had later to
contend in his congregations. Where, as in I Cor. 15:8 and 9:1, he appeals
to his being an eyewitness of the resurrection, he expressly includes himself in the great circle of all the others and especially the original apostles:
"Whether then it is I or they, so we preach and so you have come to
believe" (I Cor. 15:11). This consideration compels us to assume that
Paul could scarcely have defended his special apostleship to the Gentiles on
the bare ground of his being an eyewitness of the resurrection – a status
which he shares with the other apostles and on which the faith of all is
founded. Yet exegesis must not operate with mere postulates; it must
submit to verification by the text. The text appears to contradict our
assumption. But the appearance is deceptive. A closer examination[1] of
Paul's use of the words "revelation" and "reveal", especially in the Epistle
to the Galatians, shows us that here as elsewhere he does not use these
terms in a uniform sense and that their meaning in each case follows from
the words with which they are associated and from their immediate
context. Moreover, in none of the four passages in which the noun or
verb for revelation is used (1:12, 16; 2:2; 3:23) is the subjective element in
the vision or experience a constituent part of the concept itself.

The first of the passages mentioned (1:12) combines the noun of
action, ἀποκάλυψις, with the objective genitive Ἰησοῦ Χριστοῦ. That
we have to understand it in this sense is established beyond any doubt by
the way in which the same thing is expressed immediately afterwards
(1:16) with the verb: God resolved in accordance with his decree to reveal
his Son to me. The Christological title "his Son" here replaces the proper
name Ἰησοῦς Χριστός as an interpretative extension of it. It is not possible to determine whether the additional phrase ἐν ἐμοί is supposed to stress
the special mode of experience. The prepositional construction can also
replace the simple dative.[2] But it would not involve an essential alteration
to the meaning. In either event, the sentence describes a divine action of
which Paul is the recipient. However, that does not yet settle the question
whether, in 1:15, Paul is setting his subjective, visionary Damascus-road
experience in opposition to tradition and teaching mediated through
men. Is an answer to this question to be found in the further statements
about revelation in the epistle? Obviously not in the note in Gal. 2:2

[1] For what follows cf. the excellent monograph by D. Lührmann, Das Offenbarungsver-
ständnis bei Paulus und in paulinischen Gemeinden (1965), especially pp. 67 ff.
[2] Cf. Arndt, p. 260; Blass-Debrunner, section 220 (1), p. 118.

where he says that it was on the grounds of a revelation that he went up (to Jerusalem) with his companions for the apostolic conference. The phrase κατὰ ἀποκάλυψιν means here, in all probability, nothing other than divine instructions voiced by Spirit-filled charismatics in the gathered congregation at Antioch, in the same sense as Paul speaks elsewhere, in conformity with general Christian usage, of "revelation" as one charisma among others (I Cor. 12–14; cf. especially 14:6,26; Phil. 3:15) and as Acts 13:2 depicts the sending out of the representatives of the congregation.

The fourth passage in which "revelation" is once again mentioned (Gal. 3:23) is all the more important for our question. In expounding it, attention must be paid to the fact that the great theological section of the epistle, in which the statement stands, serves a purpose no different from that of the first two "autobiographical" chapters – viz. the defence of the law-free gospel for the Gentiles, which Paul's opponents in Galatia have pilloried as base opportunism and as a sordid concession to his Gentile hearers (1:10). In their opinion, Paul has suppressed the law and circumcision in order to get a better reception and has thus corrupted the message of salvation. It is against this charge that the apostle directs his apology – or rather his sharp counter-attack. It is in truth the Judaizing agitators who have distorted the gospel and become backsliders, and the Galatian congregations have let themselves be seduced by them (3:1). This is developed in the train of thought in Gal. 3–6, which is concerned with salvation-history and eschatology: God has made an end of the old aeon, in which all men were held captive under the law and the world powers (στοιχεῖα τοῦ κόσμου) and has led us, by the sending of his Son, to the promised freedom of the sons of God. It is in this context that the significant statement stands: "But before faith came, we were kept in custody under the law, all locked up together until faith should be *revealed*. So the law has become our taskmaster, in order that we should be justified by faith" (3:23 f.).

This is not the place to enter into a detailed exegesis of the whole passage. We confine ourselves to noting the following features and motifs which are of special importance for the understanding of Gal. 1:15 f.:

(*a*) The section Galatians 3–4, which prepares the way for the Epistle to the Romans, develops the apostle's doctrine of justification in broad, universal dimensions.

(*b*) The tools with which this is done have been borrowed from the conceptual world of apocalyptic tradition. This is obviously the source of the two-aeons model but equally, also, of the concept of "revelation". It means in Gal. 3:23, as it does already in Jewish apocalypticism, a freshly commencing, aeon-changing, eschatological act of God, in the sense of an objective event not brought about by men.[1] The word πίστις, too,

[1] In other places too Paul repeatedly speaks of revelation in this traditional apocalyptic

requires to be understood in this way in our passage – not as a human
attitude or a concern of the individual, but as the "principle of salvation"
(H. Schlier) opposed to the νόμος, made possible and set in force by God
and announced to the world as a whole. Paul therefore speaks just as
objectively of the "coming" of faith (i.e. of the message of faith) as he
does in 4:4–7 of the sending of the Son and of his Spirit. Indeed, he has
already been able in 3:2 to tackle the Galatians on the ground that the
word of the Crucified One has been proclaimed to them and that they
have received the Spirit, although he really has to describe them as
"bewitched".

(c) This is as much as to say that the apostle gives the apocalyptic idea a
radical new twist, by relating it no longer to a saving event which is yet
to come but to that which has already been realized.

(d) This saving event is established and inaugurated by the sending of
the Son of God to earth as a man, who has borne the curse of the law on
the cross and "redeemed" us by his death from servitude to the world
powers (3:1, 13; 4:4 f.).

Certainly none of these thoughts is expressed before Galatians 3–4, but
they have already given Paul's statements in Gal. 1:12–16 about his
conversion and call their peculiar character.

(1) The ideas of his doctrine of justification underlie these statements
too, and are illustrated in the person of the apostle. God, by the revelation
of Jesus Christ, has put an end to the former Pharisee's proud zeal for the
law, has brought him to surrender his own righteousness from the
works of the law, and at the same time has given his life and activity a
new beginning and a new goal. Gal. 1:12 ff. and Phil. 3:5 ff. are very
closely connected. But so are Galatians 1 and Galatians 3–4, yet with the
difference that the change of the aeons which is to be spoken of later is
dealt with here as the turning-point in the apostle's life.

(2) Paul, however, does not merely understand himself as a model and
paradigm of justification by faith alone; he knows himself also to be chosen
and called as the bearer of this gospel to the Gentiles. As is shown by the
tightly-packed statement in Gal. 1:15 f., with its echoes of the calling of
Old Testament prophets (Jer. 1:5; Isa. 49:1), its emphasis lies not, as in
Philippians 3, on his conversion, but on his call – in other words, on the
commission given him to proclaim among the Gentiles this gospel which
is summarized in his message of justification. This is what is really
peculiar to *his* apostleship.

How closely the salvation-event and the preaching of salvation belong
together for Paul has already been made clear in our discussion of Galatians
3–4. There, the sending of the Son in the fulness of time and the "coming"

---

sense – in connexion with the last judgement (Rom. 2:5; I Cor. 4:5; II Cor. 5:10), with the
glory which is to follow the sufferings of this present time (Rom. 8:18 f.) or with Christ's
parousia (I Cor. 1:7).

of the message of faith are spoken of in parallel sets of statements – the two are not distinguished as a "saving fact" and subsequent information about it, but together signify an aeon-changing, saving act originating from God and effected by him. Similarly, in II Cor. 5:17 ff., Paul brings together God's act of reconciliation in Christ and the "ministry of reconciliation", i.e. the preaching of it, and therefore he qualifies the word of Christ's ambassadors with the same "Now" of salvation-history (II Cor. 6:1 f.). The passion with which, in the autobiographical account in Galatians 1, Paul defends himself against the "personal" attacks of his opponents obviously requires to be understood against this background of ideas, for what is at stake is really not his personal integrity but the cause of the gospel committed to him. It is when it is seen in this connexion that the concept of "revelation" in Gal. 1:12, 16 also receives its full weight. Even though Paul here designates himself as its recipient, there exists not the slightest occasion for reducing it in this place to the sense of "vision", against Paul's dominant usage, and denying that its meaning, far from being restricted to the person of Paul, relates to the change of the aeons in Christ. It requires rather (as in the statement of 3:23 and its context) to be understood in the light of its content, i.e., with regard to the divine authorization of the apostle to proclaim the gospel which applies equally to the Gentiles – the gospel in which "the righteousness of God is revealed from faith to faith" (Rom. 1:17). There can be no talk, then, of Paul's claiming in Galatians 1 to be autonomous *vis-à-vis* the entire early church on the ground of his individual ecstatic experiences or of his being – in common with the original apostles and other witnesses of the resurrection (I Cor. 15:5 ff.) – a witness of the resurrection himself. But in Gal. 1:15 f. he must indeed insist on the commission given to *him*, because the content of the gospel demands it.

(3) This content is indicated in a single expression: "But when it pleased (God) to reveal *his Son* to me", and it is explicitly repeated in the attached final clause: ἵνα εὐαγγελίζωμαι αὐτὸν ἐν τοῖς ἔθνεσιν. The christological title "Son of God" is not encountered in the indisputably genuine Pauline epistles nearly so frequently as the two other titles ὁ Κύριος and Χριστός, the latter of which has largely, although by no means invariably, become a proper name.[1] Of the fourteen occurrences of ὁ υἱὸς (θεοῦ), no fewer than eleven are to be found in Romans and Galatians alone, which are very closely related in theme; and it is significant, at that, that they occur above all in the context of the Pauline doctrine of law and grace, works and faith (Gal. 1:15 f.; 2:20; 4:4, 6; Rom. 5:10; 8:3, 29, 32). In all these passages the use of the title is connected with the thought of Christ's pre-existence. But this latter term, borrowed from dogmatics, expresses only imperfectly what Paul has characteristically in mind. At no point does Paul's use of the title "Son of God" contain

[1] Cf. Lührmann, *op. cit.*, pp. 76 f.

any reflection on Christ's divine nature *per se* before all time, or imply the thought of his supernatural birth. (The same is true of the Gospel of John and the Epistle to the Hebrews.) On the contrary, it refers to the Incarnation; and, for Paul, that means at once that it refers to Jesus' death, through which he was to "redeem those under the law, so that they might receive sonship" (Gal. 4:4 f.).

In contrast to the Gospel tradition, Paul has actually little interest in Jesus' human existence, but all the more in his *incarnation* and *redeeming death* on the cross (Gal. 2:20; 3:1, 13; 6:14, 17). It is in the latter that God's act of love is concentrated: he "did not spare his Son, but gave him up for us all" (Rom. 8:32). If Gal. 1:15 f. is set in the context of these thoughts, as is required by the line of argument and terminology of the whole epistle, the important consequence emerges that here, too, the christo-logical title "Son of God" denotes not, as usually interpreted, the Risen and Exalted One, but the Son of God "sent" as *man*, who was made subject to the law and died on the cross to redeem all men. His resurrection has validated and manifested him as such, and has set his death for all in force. As such, correspondingly, he is to be proclaimed like a divine decree before all the world by the preaching of the Crucified One (Gal. 3:1).

III

If this interpretation is correct, it throws a significant light on the apostle's initially surprising behaviour, after his call, *vis-à-vis* the Jerusalem church and its leaders, and similarly on his attitude to the congregations of Hellenistic-Jewish and Gentile Christians in Syria. From the Epistle to the Galatians in particular, but also from certainly reliable accounts of which Luke has made use – admittedly strongly harmonizing use – as well as from other New Testament witnesses[1], it can safely be concluded that the Palestinian and Hellenistic-Syrian congregations represented very different types of early Christianity, even if it did not come to a final break between them, despite the persecution of Stephen's supporters and their mission in non-Jewish territory. At the risk of being perhaps a little too crudely schematic, one might assume that each of these types of Christianity was marked not only by the loss of a sense of Jesus' earthly story, but also by the loss of a sense of the historical and temporal charac-ter of one's own personal existence. The faith of those who remained in

[1] The differences between the Palestinian Jewish churches and the Hellenistic churches are presupposed also, for example, in the Gospel of Matthew. Cf. my studies, "Der Aufer-standene und der Irdische. Mt. 28, 16–20" in *Zeit und Geschichte: Dankesgabe für R. Bultmann* (1964), pp. 171–92, and "Die Binde- und Lösegewalt in der Kirche des Matthäus", in G. Bornkamm, *Geschichte und Glaube*, zweiter Teil (*Gesammelte Aufsätze* iv, 1971, pp. 37–50 = *Festschrift für Heinrich Schlier*, 1970, pp. 93–107).

Jerusalem obviously derived its vitality from the memory of Jesus' ministry and death, which was mediated and kept awake by his first disciples, and from the ardent expectation of the Risen and Redeemed One as the coming "Messiah" and "Son of Man". The faith of those separated from Jerusalem, on the other hand, was kept most intensively alive by their certainty that Jesus was already installed as Kyrios-Kosmokrator and as victor over the world powers – the One who manifested his presence and power through the experience of the Spirit and the spiritual gifts enjoyed by the charismatics in the congregation. Jesus' shameful death thus largely became a merely transitional stage – "through the cross to the crown", "through night to light!"[1] As regards the believers' self-understanding, it meant that the primitive Jerusalem church was experiencing something like a *vacuum*, which had to be obediently endured in loyal adherence to the temple worship and Jewish traditions, and at the same time in constant expectation of the parousia; while among the "Hellenists" faith was characterized by an *enthusiastic fulness*, by a pleromatic assurance which often enough burst its banks tempestuously.

Paul is not to be classified without further qualification under one or the other of these types of early Christian faith. From those in Jerusalem he could not expect to secure full agreement immediately on the subject of his law-free gospel for the Gentiles. That is why he kept well away from them for so many years. On the other hand he did not acknowledge one of the Hellenistic congregations as his new mother-church. His activity in Arabia (which was most probably of a missionary character) preceded his return to Damascus, and his independent mission in Syria and Cilicia (Gal. 1:21) preceded his journey to Antioch (Acts 11:26). His stay in this metropolis of Hellenistic Christianity was similarly of short duration and soon came to an end with his departure for his subsequent missionary journeys. Paul's "Damascus", we might say pointedly, lies between Jerusalem and Antioch not only in a geographical but also in a deeply symbolical sense.

So far as it is possible in the framework of this study, I should like to elucidate this at least by means of a few comparative observations and point to certain basic thoughts in Paul's Christology and soteriology which, in

---

[1] The statement that in the whole of the N.T. Jesus' crucifixion is understood as the vicarious death of the Sinless One for sinners and that it has to count as a "steady constant" of early Christianity (cf. J. Jeremias, *Der Opfertod Jesu Christi*, 1963, p. 11) is an inadmissible over-simplification. It should rather be observed that the thinking of the first disciples and of certain later groups in the early church was unable immediately, without more ado, to bring out saving significance from the cross of Christ itself. They were satisfied, for a start, to confess that Jesus' shameful death did not conflict with God's holy will but rather took place in accordance with it. In Luke's historical work, therefore, God's action in raising Jesus is simply set in sharp contrast to the action of men: "*You* delivered him up and had him nailed to the cross, but *God* raised him up and exalted him to be the Christ" (Acts 2:23 f., 36; 3:14 f.; 4:10; 5:30). Cf. W. Schrage, "Das Verständnis des Todes Jesu Christi im N.T." in *Das Kreuz Jesu Christi als Grund des Heils* (1967), pp. 60 ff.

contrast to other theological conceptions of the primitive church, characterize his understanding of the saving event and had their effect on his
world-wide mission.

(a) As we have said already, the christological title "Son of God"
acquires special significance in the Epistles to the Galatians and Romans.
It was not Paul who introduced it into early Christian thought. Apart
from numerous other New Testament writings, a number of passages in
Paul's own letters, which show no specific features of Pauline Christology,
make this plain. The short summary of the gospel in the introduction to
the Epistle to the Romans is specially instructive. As recent research has
shown,[1] arguments based on its language and content indicate that in
Rom. 1:3 f. Paul reproduced a kind of credo of the early Jewish-Christian
church. Taken by itself, the compressed formula says that the earthly
Jesus, legitimated as Messiah by his Davidic· descent, is since his resurrection – or *because of* his resurrection? – exalted to be the Son of God.
The idea of pre-existence is absent, as also is any mention, or soteriological interpretation, of his death, so that we have (in the admittedly
misleading language of the later history of dogma) a decidedly "adop-
tionist" Christology. In a similar way, I Thess. 1:10 speaks, in the characteristic idiom and expectation of primitive Christian missionary preaching
in general, of the Risen One as the Son of God who will save us from the
wrath to come. The piece of eschatological teaching in I Cor. 15:20–28
belongs here, too: Christ, raised from the dead as "the Son", must reign
until the end of the world; finally he will hand over his dominion to the
Father and, after victory over his enemies, subordinate himself to God.
None of these statements is specifically Pauline in language or ideas; they
simply reproduce the expectation of the End common to primitive
Christianity.

But the idea of pre-existence, with its focus on the incarnation and
saving death of Christ, is also broadly attested apart from Paul.[2] From this
we should not too hastily draw the conclusion that in early Christian
theology it was common property right from the start. Yet it is indis-
putable that, at a relatively early time and independently of Paul, it was
especially the saving significance of Christ's death that increasingly and
variously became the object of theological reflection and the subject-
matter of preaching. As examples from the Synoptic Gospels, we might
adduce above all Mark 10:45 and the passages about the Lord's Supper.
It is rightly assumed that the common expressions about the "blood" of
Christ and his atoning death "for us", which are not specifically Pauline,

---

[1] Cf. R. Bultmann, *Theology of the N.T.* (E.T. 1952), i, pp. 49 f.; E. Schweizer, *Lordship
and Discipleship* (E.T. 1960), p. 37; W. Kramer, *Christ, Lord, Son of God* (E.T. 1966), pp. 108 ff.;
G. Bornkamm, *Paul*, p. 248.

[2] It plays a familiar and important role in the Gospel of John (cf., among other passages,
1:34, where Lamb of God = Son of God; 3:16–18); in I John 4:9 and in the Epistle to the
Hebrews (2:6 ff.; 4:14 ff.; 5:8; 10:29).

had their origin in these primitive Christian themes.[1] What begins to be unmistakably Pauline is the apostle's interpretation of these ideas in the framework of his message of justification and reconciliation.

(b) This indicates the soteriological aspect from which Pauline Christology requires to be considered. In a general sense, of course, soteriology is part of every christological conception in primitive Christianity. But the understanding of the saving event as God's justifying and reconciling act is distinctively and genuinely Pauline. Here it must be noted that the apostle's thoughts turn in particular on the δικαιοσύνη θεοῦ χωρὶς νόμου (Rom. 3:21)[2] which is grounded and revealed in Christ, in much larger measure than on reconciliation. Reconciliation is not under discussion in Galatians or Philippians 3, nor yet in Romans until chapter 5 (verse 10) – and then as nearly synonymous with δικαιοῦσθαι. The doctrine of justification itself is not in every aspect a new creation of Paul's; in support of it he himself appeals expressly to the witness borne to it by the law and the prophets. That its central motifs solo deo and sola gratia could already find expression in Judaism, in more extreme statements, is shown by such a passage as IV Ezra 8:36: "For your righteousness and goodness, Lord, become manifest therein, that you take pity on those who have no store of good works." The Qumran texts have supplied plenty of further examples of this.[3] Yet statements of this kind must not be interpreted in a Pauline sense without further examination. For in Paul's letters it is only through the solo Christo and sola fide that these motifs gain their full meaning and significance. Once again, a passage within the context of the first great development of the doctrine of justification (Rom. 3:21–31) is specially instructive. As recent investigations have shown,[4] the apostle has here, in two parallel, compressed and overloaded sentences, taken up a piece of Jewish-Christian tradition and then offered his own commentary on it and developed it further. This is clearly recognizable in the similar beginnings to verse 25 (εἰς ἔνδειξιν τῆς δικαιοσύνης αὐτοῦ) and verse 26 (πρὸς τὴν ἔνδειξιν τῆς δικαιοσύνης αὐτοῦ). In the first, the righteousness of God means the covenant faithfulness shown by God in Christ's atoning sacrifice, through which, by the forgiveness of Israel's sins, he has renewed the covenant which Israel had broken. In the second, on the other hand, this limited sense of δικαιοσύνη θεοῦ is transcended as it is extended to all who accept salvation through faith in Jesus. Similarly new and highly significant is the way in which

[1] Cf. H. Conzelmann, An Outline of the Theology of the N.T. (E.T. 1969), pp. 69 ff.

[2] Cf. E. Käsemann, "Erwägungen zum Stichwort 'Versöhnungslehre in N.T.'" in Zeit und Geschichte: Dankesgabe an R. Bultmann (1964), pp. 47–59; D. Lührmann, "Rechtfertigung und Versöhnung", ZThK 67 (1970), pp. 437–52.

[3] A critical report of the extensive literature on the doctrine of justification in the Qumran texts and in Paul is to be found in H. Braun, Qumran und das N.T., ii (1966), pp. 166 ff.

[4] Cf. especially E. Käsemann, ZNW, 43 (1950–51), pp. 150–54 (= Exegetische Versuche und Besinnungen, i (1960), pp. 96–100); further discussion in D. Lührmann, op. cit. (see p. 101, n. 2) pp. 437 ff.

God is seen to be righteous in his justifying act. This act has *now* taken place; it does not only apply retrospectively, in God's not reckoning the sins committed by his people in the past, but has opened up a fundamentally new possibility of life – by faith alone, not by the works of the law (3:27 ff.). In this way, God has shown himself to be the God of all men, Jews and Gentiles, and has shown both groups on an equal footing the only way of salvation. As Paul says with special emphasis in Romans and Galatians (but also in other contexts and varying terminology in Philippians and the letters to Corinth), to deliver this message is the task which has been especially assigned to him; this has become the theological foundation of his entire missionary activity.

It should be noted in this connexion that the apostle (paradoxical as it may seem) has also allotted to the law an abiding and essential significance, broadening its scope to apply to the Gentiles as well. He therefore firmly opposes every kind of antinomianism. It is for the same reason that he closes the section Rom. 3:21 ff. with the words: "Are we then annulling the law? No, we are rather establishing it" (v. 31). But Paul no longer understands the function and effect of the law in the genuinely Jewish and traditionally Jewish-Christian sense. From now on, the significance of the law no longer lies in its showing the way to salvation and life, but rather in its pronouncing all men guilty before God – and that not only because they fell short of its demands, but because even for those with a zeal for the law it has become the basis of their self-assertion before God and the object of their "boasting". Through Christ and the revelation of his righteousness "without law", God has met this need of the unredeemed and has thus put an end to the law as a *way of salvation* (Rom. 10:4). All that the law is capable of – all that it is meant to do – is to bring about recognition of sin (Rom. 3:20). But precisely in this way it points beyond itself and bears witness to the righteousness of God.

In Paul's letters this doctrine of justification is developed in all directions and in the language appropriate to the hearers of the moment; the idea of reconciliation also is integrated with it and subordinated to it. As is evident from the rest of the New Testament,[1] the idea of reconciliation too was known to primitive Christianity before Paul and apart from him. That is demonstrated not least by the ἱλαστήριον-motif,[2] which is found in Paul only in Rom. 3:25. The idea of καταλλαγή, which stems from the Old Testament and Jewish tradition, does not really add anything new to his doctrine of justification, and in his thought it is not allowed to develop into an independent dogmatic topic. But it stresses in a special – one might say, objective – way the new "state" of peace (Rom. 5:1) into which those justified by God are brought, and thus, at the same

---

[1] Cf. (apart from Rom. 3:25) Heb. 2:17; I John 2:2; 4:10.

[2] Paul introduces the term ἱλαστήριον as a familiar concept, probably in the general sense of an atoning sacrifice or means of atonement.

time, it stresses the world-embracing effect of God's saving act in Christ (II Cor. 5:18 f.). As a result, two things can be said about the relation of justification and sanctification in Paul. On the one hand, the motif of καταλλαγή belongs to the tradition to which the apostle, in his doctrine of the δικαιοσύνη of God, gives a new interpretation, oriented towards faith. On the other hand, the idea of reconciliation, which Paul has freed from all Jewish particularism, interprets his doctrine of reconciliation and makes its world-embracing significance recognizable. This is done in Romans 9–11 in very concrete relation to the enigmatic fate of Israel, which had been chosen by God and yet, for the time of the Gentile mission, rejected on account of its enmity to the gospel. Even if God's chosen people has missed its destiny of living by grace alone, yet, according to Paul, it is not eternally lost. Its rejection for the time being has rather served to bring about the καταλλαγὴ τοῦ κόσμου (Rom. 11:15), in which those who now are still hardened will finally participate.[1]

★   ★   ★   ★   ★

Let us look back once more at the passage of scripture from which this study set out. It need scarcely be said that our intention was not to portray the apostle as the "Great Solitary One", but rather to put his autobiographical account in Galatians 1 into the context of his doctrine of justification and reconciliation. When one reads the passage in this light, it appears that Paul's reason for insisting so tenaciously on the independence of his apostleship was not that he held his own vision of Christ on the Damascus road to be more important than all other traditions, even if that meant the shattering of the church's unity. It was much more that the message of salvation, intended for all men, counted in his eyes as the true foundation of the one church made up of Jews and Gentiles. Charged with this gospel he accepted, from the time of his call onwards, the responsibility of endangering the existing unity of the church, and for this reason he remained suspect in the eyes of the Jerusalem congregation to the end of his days. In truth, however, he fought his whole life long, as no other ever did, for the unity of the church. His words in I Cor. 15:10 hold good for this agitated struggle too: "I have laboured harder than any of them; yet not I, but the grace of God which is with me."

[1] D. Lührmann shows in the article cited on p. 101, n. 2 (pp. 440 ff.) that, in the deutero-Pauline Epistle to the Ephesians, the doctrine of justification has already become traditional, while the idea of reconciliation as the establishment of cosmic peace serves to interpret it (so the situation is quite the reverse of what we find in Paul). The Pauline dialectic of law and gospel has therefore been given up in Colossians and Ephesians. Cf. G. Bornkamm, "Wandlungen im alt- und neutestamentlichen Gesetzesverständnis", in *Geschichte und Glaube*, zweiter Teil = *Gesammelte Aufsätze*, iv, 1971), pp. 73–119, pp. 114 ff.

CHAPTER VII

RECONCILIATION AND FORGIVENESS
IN THE LETTER TO THE COLOSSIANS

RALPH P. MARTIN

I

Introduction

THE CHRISTIAN COMMUNITY AT COLOSSAE WAS PERSONALLY UNKNOWN to Paul (2:1) at the time of his writing to it.[1] It is clear that he had learned of the success of Christian preaching only at second-hand (1:4, 9). Presumably this initial evangelism was undertaken by Epaphras who sends greetings (in a later part of the epistle) to the Colossian believers as "one of yourselves" (4:12) and he was evidently commissioned by Paul to be his spokesman and ambassador to the town of Colossae (1:7). It is Epaphras who has come from the congregation to visit Paul in his confinement and has brought news of the establishing of the church in that part of the Lycus valley (1:8).

Paul rejoices, in this letter, over the ready welcome which these people had given to the message of his colleague who had carried "the word of truth" (1:5). Part of their response was that they had "received Christ Jesus the Lord" (2:6) and had "come to fulness of life in him" (2:10). More specifically, they had understood the meaning of the grace of God (1:6, 7) as Epaphras' preaching announced to them the availability of God's offer to include them along with other Gentile peoples within the scope of his mercy (1:27). The consequence of this understanding of the "mystery" (1:26, 27) was that by their faith-response to the overture of God's truth in the gospel they had entered a new humanity in which all religious disadvantages and racial distinctions were done away (3:10, 11). They had entered into the heritage of God's ancient and covenant people as his elect ones (3:12; cf. 1:26; 2:13) and they had come to share in the inheritance of the family of God, a company embracing men and angels (1:12 and possibly 1:26).

They had been rescued from the dark domain of evil powers and brought over to the kingdom of Christ (1:13). Included in that transference these men and women had known the freedom of deliverance

---

[1] The following essay makes certain assumptions regarding the authorship and provenance of the epistle. Some justification for these assumptions, with a bibliography of the current debate, will be found in the present writer's *Colossians: The Church's Lord and the Christian's Liberty* (Exeter, 1972; Grand Rapids, 1973).

from evil and evil forces as their sins were forgiven (1:14; 3:13) and they were reconciled to God (1:22). God had graciously accepted them as pardoned sinners (2:13) and had himself removed every impediment to their restoration to his favour (2:14). In particular, the demonic powers of angels and spiritual beings which held their lives captive in a web of superstitious dread were compelled to relinquish their grip, since God in Christ who was their liberator had already broken the power of these malign spiritual forces on the cross of Christ where he won a resounding victory over them at a time when it seemed he was their helpless prey (2:14, 15).

In that death of Jesus Christ, these Colossian believers had died to "the elemental spirits of the universe" (2:20); and in his resurrection triumph over them they too had a share (3:1), with its promise of liberty from all the enslavement and inhibitions they had previously known as pagan Gentiles in a society where demons and taboos kept people in a twilight of fear and uncertainty. Formerly they had lived in their society as "men of the world" (2:20) doomed under God's righteous sentence (3:6, 7) and held prisoner to evil passions and practices which had their origin in a mind at enmity with God (1:21). Now, they had experienced not only a forgiveness which cut off the entail of the past and gave them a fresh start, but a moral transformation which is likened to the imparting of a new nature (3:9, 10). This is both God's gift and an expression of his character demonstrated in Christ (3:10, 11).

The dramatic "moment" when this life-changing transference from the realm of evil to God's kingdom in the company of Christ's people took place is located in an act of renunciation, described as "putting off the body of flesh in the circumcision of Christ" (2:11; cf. 3:9). In the next breath, Paul proceeds to talk about baptism with its symbolic actions of burial and being raised out of the water (2:12). Then, as though to show that these actions have their counterpart in religious experience, he applies these baptismal motifs to the acts of God who both passes sentence of death on transgressors and vivifies them in a spiritual renewal so that they are lifted out of the realm of death into new life (2:13). The offending sentence of condemnation is obliterated, and the baptized Christian is brought by this faith-response-in-baptism to a new relationship with God and a new standing before him. The newly baptized neophyte has come to fulness of life in Christ (2:10) and has been enrolled in the congregation of God's people as a member of the "saints" (1:2) and given a part in "one body," the church (3:15; cf. 1:18; 1:24), the new "Adam" (3:10).

From this cursory survey of the epistle to the Colossians the main lines of Paul's description of how new life came to the readers are fairly well drawn. We do not anticipate that there would be much quarrel among modern interpreters that Paul's writing adds up to this. It is different, however, when we ask about the situation at Colossae which occasioned the form and style as well as the specific content of the apostle's teaching. Our purpose is to examine two extended passages (1:12–23; 2:13–15) with a view to setting them against the background of their historical context (as far as we may determine it today) and in the light of the recent discussion of the redactional use Paul makes of traditional elements which putatively underlie the epistle.

II

1:12–23: Christian Experience and the Hymn to Christ

"He has delivered us from the dominion of darkness" (v. 13) is a translation which, while it accurately conveys the thought of the writer, fails to bring out the syntactical connexion with the foregoing part of Paul's statement. Paul's sentence is participial (ὅς), referring back to the Father who has enabled his people to escape from their former sad condition as Gentiles and to take their appointed place among the saints who dwell in light (v. 12). "Appointed place" is a phrase which combines in translation two separate items: μερίς is a share or a part, and κλῆρος a lot. These terms are often juxtaposed in the Old Testament, e.g. Deuteronomy 10:9, LXX: "Therefore Levi has no portion or inheritance with his brothers" (διὰ τοῦτο οὐκ ἔστιν τοῖς Λευίταις μερὶς καὶ κλῆρος ἐν τοῖς ἀδελφοῖς αὐτῶν). The terms have an original reference to the apportionment of the land of Canaan (Deut. 32:9; Jos. 19:9),[1] but the thought is really a single one and relates to the tribes' occupancy of their promised inheritance. A spiritualized meaning of "appointed lot" is already found in the Old Testament (e.g. Ps. 15:5, LXX: "The Lord is the portion of my inheritance": κύριος ἡ μερὶς τῆς κληρονομίας μου); and this process of spiritualizing paves the way for the extended usages of the metaphor in the Qumran literature (e.g. 1 QS xi. 7 f.)[2] and in Paul. The Qumran text is interesting because it throws some light on the Pauline allusion to "saints who dwell in light." The section from the Community Rule runs:

> God has given them to His chosen ones
> as an everlasting possession,
> and has caused them to inherit
> the lot of the Holy Ones.
> He has joined their assembly
> to the Sons of Heaven
> to be a Council of the Community (Vermes' translation)[3]

As E. Lohse points out, in this citation the phrases, "Holy Ones" and "the Sons of Heaven" are in parallelism; and this fact settles the issue of the

[1] Further examples of the way in which the two terms are combined are given by W. Foerster, *TDNT* III, pp. 759–61.
[2] For this material see E. Lohse, *Colossians and Philemon* (Philadelphia, 1971), pp. 35 f.
[3] G. Vermes, *The Dead Sea Scrolls in English* (Harmondsworth, 1962), p. 93.

meaning of the former term. The "holy ones" are the angels. If this is the correct background of the Pauline passage, the meaning of verse 12 will be: God the Father has authorized you as his "holy ones" (1:2) to share in a heavenly life in company with the angels who dwell in light. And this translation has bearing on the verse immediately following, because strictly this too continues the same thought. The same God who is praised for his election of his people and his appointment of believers to their eternal destiny also delivered them from their fate in bondage to satanic powers and placed them in the domain of his beloved Son (v. 13). The church's confidence in being already part of the heavenly realm is renewed in a later part of the letter (3:1–4), and the church's possession of a title to the world of angels (implied also in the contrast of 1:26 f.) prepares the ground for Paul's later and more explicit polemic against the false teaching at Colossae which venerated the angels as mediators (2:18).

Paul's emphasis on the present reality of the Christians' share in the heavenly world leads him to expound a doctrine of deliverance and reconciliation. At verse 13 the Old Testament-Qumranic background is again much in evidence. "Deliverance" ($\dot{\rho}\acute{v}\varepsilon\sigma\theta\alpha\iota$) is exactly the connotation of the language used of Israel's salvation from the hands of the Egyptians (Ex. 6:6; 14:30; Jud. 6:9, 13) as a prelude to their possession of the land as their inheritance. The Qumran hymns extol God as the deliverer of the faithful from their enemies (1 QH ii. 35; iii. 19). The enemy in verse 13 is "the power of darkness", which is a Hebraic expression to be understood as "the domain of evil powers"; it is parallel with the Qumran teaching on the "dominion of Belial" (1 QS i. 18, 23 f.; ii. 19; 1 QM xiv. 9; xvii 5 f.) which is described as the dominion of his wickedness which inflicts persecution on the children of righteousness (1 QS iii. 22 f.). This time of suffering for the saints is called the "dominion of falsehood" (1 QS iv. 19) where the Angel of Darkness is in command. But at length deliverance will come for "the sons of light", God's holy ones (1 QS i. 9; ii. 16; xi. 7 f.).

The contrast between darkness and light is intended, in Paul's writing (cf. Acts 26:18), to point to the issues of bondage to satanic or demonic powers and the freedom which Christians have known within the rule of Christ, God's Son. The two verbs which dramatically describe the release and the new allegiance and freedom are: $\dot{\rho}\acute{v}\varepsilon\sigma\theta\alpha\iota$ (to set free) and $\mu\varepsilon\theta\iota\sigma\tau\acute{a}\nu\alpha\iota$ (to transfer). Israel had been delivered from her Egyptian slavery and transplanted in the land of Canaan. There may be another historical allusion in Paul's mind as he writes to the churches of the Lycus valley (2:1; 4:16). Antiochus III in the early part of the second century BC had brought several thousand Jews from Mesopotamia and Babylon and settled them in Lydia and Phrygia (Josephus, *Ant.* xii. 149). But the metaphor of servitude and release, followed by a newly found liberty, is common enough. The Qumran community rejoiced in its deliverance from its enemies and its place in the company of the children of light.

There is one final part of the Christian's experience to which Paul calls attention. As a climax in verse 14 he announces, though again in a relative clause, that in Christ "we have redemption, the forgiveness of sins". Membership of the elect community which is nothing else than passing under the present lordship of Jesus Christ is made possible by the redeeming power of God. Once more there are anticipations of this thought in the Old Testament and Qumran traditions in spite of the lack of attestation of the noun ἀπολύτρωσις (redemption) in biblical Greek.[1] It is true that in the Colossians text the cost or the price of the redemption is not alluded to, but the connexion of thought with the foregoing probably requires us to supply the meaning of the payment of a ransom in order that the captives held by the power of evil might be set free (v. 13).[2]

Paul's use of the word redemption usually contains an eschatological dimension, but this is not present here. Rather, the promise is that re- demption is a present experience within the church's fellowship and under the regime of Christ. Its content is crisply defined as consisting in the forgiveness of sins. A reason may be sought for this change of emphasis; and it is this enquiry which will guide us to the heart of the issue in the exegesis of 1:13–23.

Recent study of the passage 1:15–20 has reached a fairly settled consen- sus, especially regarding the literary genre and form of the verses.[3] E. Käsemann speaks for most modern interpreters: "The hymnic character of Col. 1:15–20 has long been recognized and generally acknowledged."[4] Less agreement is forthcoming on the matters of the background and meaning of the hymn; and even more problematical is the issue of Paul's redaction of an independently existing hymn written as an aretalogy in praise of the cosmic Lord.[5] There are two concerns which have dominated

---

[1] Cf. L. L. Morris, *The Apostolic Preaching of the Cross* (London, 1955), p. 37; F. Büchsel, *TDNT IV*, p. 352, who refers to the sole LXX example of the word in Dan. 4:34 (καὶ ἐπὶ συντελείᾳ τῶν ἑπτὰ ἐτῶν ὁ χρόνος μου τῆς ἀπολυτρώσεως ἦλθε) and concludes that, since this text refers to Nebuchadnezzar's restoration from this madness, "this verse shows that there does not have to be a ransom". But Morris adds a corrective to this con- clusion (*op. cit.*, pp. 11, 25, 39) in the light of the context of Daniel's exhortation to the king to "redeem all his iniquities with almsgiving" (4:27).

[2] So J. B. Lightfoot, *Saint Paul's Epistles to the Colossians and Philemon* (London, 1897), *ad loc.* Cf. L. L. Morris, *op. cit.*, p. 43.

[3] I may refer to an article, "An Early Christian Hymn (Col. 1:15–20)", *EQ* 36, 4 (1964), pp. 195–205 for some discussion and bibliography. For a useful summary of the more recent debate, see J. G. Gibbs, *Creation and Redemption* (Leiden, 1971) pp. 94–114.

[4] E. Käsemann, "A Primitive Christian Baptismal Liturgy", *Essays on New Testament Themes* (London, 1964), p. 149.

[5] Or, in a more complex formulation, the issue is what is the paraenetic purpose of the post-Pauline author of the epistle in the use he makes of a gnostic hymn which later became transformed into a baptismal homology? This is the question which Käsemann poses regarding the genesis and application of the Christ-hymn. I have considered this theory briefly in *Colossians: The Church's Lord and the Christian's Liberty*, pp. 40 ff. and for further criticism based on Käsemann's acceptance of some concepts which are patently non-gnostic in the

current study, viz. an endeavour to set the text into a versified pattern which is as nearly symmetrical as possible, and an interest in isolating a pre-Pauline (i.e. precanonical) hymn which Paul has taken over and adapted to his use in the letter to the Colossians.[1] Significantly these two concerns bear upon each other and inter-penetrate. Because they are so intimately related, any solution to the problems of the passage which can offer help in both areas simultaneously is more likely to be correct than any proposal which deals with only one matter of the tandem partnership. Our purpose is to attack the problem on this double front. First, we shall see if it is possible to detect a pre-Pauline hymn of recognizably symmetrical form; and then, we try to suggest why the apostle may have been driven to break the symmetry by his additional material which formerly had to be removed from the present text in order to secure a neat scheme of versification.

The structure of the pre-Pauline traditional composition[2]

Strophe I

Verses 15, 16

ὅς ἐστιν εἰκὼν τοῦ θεοῦ	He is the image of the invisible God
τοῦ ἀοράτου,	the firstborn of all creation;
πρωτότοκος πάσης κτίσεως;	
ὅτι ἐν αὐτῷ ἐκτίσθη τὰ πάντα,	For in him all things were created
ἐν τοῖς οὐρανοῖς καὶ ἐπὶ τῆς γῆς.	in heaven and on earth.
τὰ πάντα δι᾽ αὐτοῦ	All things were created through
καὶ εἰς αὐτὸν ἔκτισται.	him and for him.

This stanza consists of three lines which hail the cosmic Christ as Lord of creation. He is the one who is uniquely related to God as his manifest

---

[1] For the latest discussion of the issues involved in the principle of pre-Pauline tradition and a Pauline redaction, see B. Vawter, "The Colossians Hymn and the Principle of Redaction", *CBQ* 33 (1971), pp. 62–81. His analysis of the formal structure of the hymn and its pre-Pauline theology is, however, obfuscated by his insistence (following Käsemann, *loc. cit.*, p. 153) that the writer of the epistle already found 1:13, 14 connected with the hymn and that therefore the redaction of the hymn had already taken place before the author of Colossians took it over. This assumption which destroys all semblance of symmetrical form in the *Urtext* makes it possible for Vawter to regard the redactional changes as "slight" and not substantive (*loc. cit.*, p. 76).

[2] This section is based on E. Schweizer's work: "Die Kirche als Leib Christi in den paulinischen Antilegomena", *ThLZ* 86 (1961), cols. 241–56 = *Neotestamentica* (Zürich/Stuttgart, 1963), pp. 293–316. Cf. his essay, "The Church as the Missionary Body of Christ," *Neotestamentica*, pp. 317–29; and most recently "Kolosser 1, 15–20", *Beiträge zur Theologie des Neuen Testaments. Neutestamentliche Aufsätze* (1955–1970), (Zürich, 1970), pp. 113–45. There is a handy summary of Schweizer's contributions in H. J. Gabathuler, *Jesus Christus. Haupt der Kirche-Haupt der Welt* (Zürich, 1965), pp. 110–18.

---

original form of the hymn, see E. Lohse, *Colossians*, pp. 45, 60, n. 205. In particular, E. Schweizer is quoted (*TDNT* VII, 1075, n. 474): "Reconciliation of the material world with heaven is the precise opp[osite] of the Gnostic hope."

presence (εἰκών); he holds the primacy over all the orders of creatio
He stands over against God's handiwork as the agent through whom
the forces of the universe came into being; indeed, he is creation's sove
eign Lord (πρωτότοκος). He also is the rightful "soul" or sphere
which the world exists and he is the one who guides its destiny. Creatio
is both "in him" and "for him", so that he becomes the key to explain
that is. The stanza declares that "it is all there with Christ in view".[1]

Strophe II

Verses 17, 18a

[καὶ] αὐτός ἐστιν πρὸ πάντων,   He is before all things,
καὶ τὰ πάντα ἐν αὐτῷ συνέστηκεν;   And in him all things hold togethe
[καὶ] αὐτός ἐστιν ἡ κεφαλὴ τοῦ
σώματος.   He is the head of the body.

The first line partly recapitulates the previous stanza with its emphasis o
his pre-existent activity. Then, the hymn's thought proceeds with th
assertion that the same cosmic Lord is the unifying principle which estab
lishes the units of the cosmos and holds the particles of matter togethe
This is the sense of the verb συνέστηκεν.[2] As the centre around which a
things revolve and which gives coherence to the whole creation, he is th
head or ruler of the cosmic body.

Strophe III

Verses 18b–20

ὅς ἐστιν ἀρχή,   He is the beginning,
πρωτότοκος ἐκ τῶν νεκρῶν,   the firstborn from the dead,
ὅτι ἐν αὐτῷ εὐδόκησεν   For in him all the fulness of God
πᾶν τὸ πλήρωμα κατοικῆσαι   was pleased to dwell;[3]
καὶ δι' αὐτοῦ ἀποκαταλλάξαι   And through him to reconcile to
τὰ πάντα εἰς αὐτόν.   himself all things.

The final section celebrates the triumph of the cosmic Lord who embodi
the divine "fulness" (πλήρωμα). God's plan is executed through him wh
as the risen one marks a new beginning of world history. He also effec
God's design to bring the universe into harmony with the divine purpos
(reconciliation).

[1] A. M. Hunter, *Interpreting Paul's Gospel* (London, 1954), p. 60.
[2] See the references to Plato, Philo and Sirach supplied by Lohse, *ad loc.* He concludes i
regard to Philo: "The divine Logos, indeed God himself, is the unifying bond which includ
all things and holds them together."
[3] The subject of the verb εὐδόκησεν is disputed. To the discussion of C. F. D. Moul
The Epistles to the Colossians and to Philemon (Cambridge, 1957), pp. 70 f. may now be adde
G. Münderlein, "Die Erwählung durch das Pleroma. Bermerkungen zu Kol. I. 9," *NTS*
(1962), pp. 264–76 and following him J. G. Gibbs, *Creation and Redemption*, pp. 99 f., 10
for whom the implicit subject is the Spirit. See the full survey in N. Kehl, *Der Christushymn*
im Kolosserbrief (Stuttgart, 1967), pp. 110–25. The translation given above follows E. Schwei
zer, *Neotestamentica*, p. 294, n. 3.

Paul's redaction

It will be clear that certain parts of the received text in our Bibles have been omitted from the above reconstruction of the verses. By these omissions it is possible to secure a hymn of noticeable symmetry, with each stanza consisting of three lines and with a discernible rhythmical pattern which is partly accounted for by the use of special rhetorical devices.[1] If this is soundly based, it should be possible to inspect the lines and phrases which were left out and to see whether Paul had a special reason for wishing to insert them into a putatively original hymn. In this view, Paul has supplemented the hymn which was in circulation prior to his writing to the Colossians. He has taken over this already existing *Vorlage* and edited it by the addition of extra lines.

These extra phrases are put in as Paul wished to stress points which this extant piece of Christian liturgy, conceivably used at baptism to celebrate Christ as cosmic Lord world ruler and giver of new life to the world, did not do.[2] Or else he wished to correct some misplaced emphases in the original version of the hymn.[3] This emendation was made, not by striking

---

[1] Correspondences in the lines of the strophes are most obviously seen by comparing strophes I and III:

Who is the image of the invisible God,	Who is the beginning,
the first born of all creation;	the first born from the dead;
For in him were created all things	For in him all the
in heaven and on earth.	fulness willed to dwell;
All things through him and to him	And through him to
were created.	reconcile all things to him.

These correspondences in the lines are not accidental, but are designed to bring out the main emphases in the two orders of creation and redemption. The use of the relative pronouns (ὅς), the repetition of πρωτότοκος (verses 15b and 18b) and ὅτι ἐν αὐτῷ (in verses 16a and 19) and the frequent mention of "all" (i.e. Norden's *Allmachtsformel: Agnostos Theos. Untersuchungen zur Formengeschichte religiöser Rede* (Berlin, 1913), pp. 240 f.) are all features which betray a carefully composed *Urtext*. See J. M. Robinson, "A Formal Analysis of Colossians 1:15–20," *JBL* 76 (1957), p. 286.

The most revealing example of a rhetorical form is the presence of chiasmus in verses 16c and 20:

a τὰ πάντα	*b* καὶ δι' αὐτοῦ
b δι' αὐτοῦ καὶ	*a* τὰ πάντα

For an attempt to carry through a systematic chiastic analysis, see E. Bammel, "Versuch zu Col. 1:15–20," *ZNTW* 52 (1961), pp. 88–95; and for a detailed comment on this attempt, see H. J. Gabathuler, *op. cit.*, pp. 118–21.

On a tripartite division of the text into three stanzas, with strophes I and III covering the aspects of creation and redemption, it is a problem to know how to treat strophe II (verses 17, 18a), as Gabathuler notes (*op. cit.*, p. 128). One proposal would be to take this *Mittelstrophe* as proclaiming Christ's work of preservation (based on the line τὰ πάντα ἐν αὐτῷ συνέστηκεν) with line 1 recapitulating the first strophe and line 3 looking forward to his reconciling work as head of the cosmic body. It is thus a *Scharnierstrophe* uniting what has gone before and what is to follow in the acclamation of the cosmic Christ.

[2] As in the case of the *carmen Christi* in Phil. 2:6–11 where most modern commentators trace the hand of Paul in the insertion of the phrase θανάτου δὲ σταυροῦ in verse 8.

[3] As in the case of the pre-Pauline Romans 3:24, 25 which *ex-hypothesi* represents a Jewish Christian formulation, modified by Paul's addition of verse 26 in order to bring it into line with this theological position. See E. Käsemann, "Zum Verständnis vom Römer 3:24–26",

out the offending parts but by juxtaposing some corrective lines or sentences, whose presence is known most obviously by the way in which
they break the poetic structure of the piece as a whole.

Of all the hypothetical additions supplied by Paul's hand our attention
is concentrated on two specimens.[1] At verse 18a he has added (in a way
whose grammatical form clearly betrays the fact that it is an after-thought)
the words: "the church" to the affirmation, "He is the head of the body."
This suggestion is no speculation, since we have in 1:24 an illustration of
the way Paul would normally write the phrase, "his body, that is, the
church" and it is quite different in 1:18. Obviously, at verse 18a, the words
τῆς ἐκκλησίας are an explanatory addendum.[2] But the addition has
drastically and dramatically altered the meaning of the entire sentence
and all that follows. In its pristine form, the line declared that Christ was
the head of the body of the universe. By this additional gloss Paul has
effected a transformation of meaning, and turned a cosmological statement
into an ecclesiological/eschatological one. This turns the course of the
subsequent stanza from being a continuation of Christ's authority in the
universe into a new channel; and it boldly appropriates the statements
about Christ the cosmocrat so that now, in Paul's revision, they do service
in the interests of Christ's authority in the church. A piece of cosmic
aretalogy in celebration of Christ the world ruler has been adapted by
Paul and transformed into a *carmen Christi* extolling him as redeemer of his
people and God's reconciling agent.

The second example makes the point even sharper. At verse 20 Christ's
achievement is described as one in which God was pleased to reconcile
(ἀποκαταλλάξαι) all things to himself. At the end of the stanza at a point
far removed from its antecedent (τὰ πάντα) comes an explanatory phrase,
"whether on earth or in heaven." This unusual placing of the gloss is
one more sign that it is Paul's thought. He has appended it in order to
amplify the scope of "the All" which is the object of God's redeeming
enterprise. Paul's annotation makes it plain that no part of the cosmos
stands outside the compass of the divine reconciling work.

[1] These two parts of the text which appear as Paul's addenda to the *Vorlage* are most
commonly accepted as such even by those scholars who are sceptical of the other Pauline
additions (suggested by J. M. Robinson and E. Schweizer, among others). See E. Käsemann,
"A Primitive Christian Baptismal Liturgy", pp. 151 f.; Lohse, *Colossians*, p. 45 and Vawter,
loc. cit., p. 75. The exception is that these scholars are anxious to retain the verb εἰρηνοποιήσας
in verse 20c as part of the *Urtext*, as well as to treat the phrase εἴτε τὰ ἐπὶ τῆς γῆς εἴτε
τὰ ἐν τοῖς οὐρανοῖς in the same way.

[2] To be sure, this submission ought not to be taken as axiomatic since it creates a problem
seen by Kehl, *op. cit.*, p. 41, viz. how can a universe which already is united to Christ as its
head (κεφαλή) stand in need of a "reconciliation"? The answer must lie in the sense to be
given to the verb ἀποκαταλλάξαι in the *Urhymnus*, which Paul has adapted to his own
purpose by the significant addition of εἰρηνοποιήσας. See later p. 113.

ZNTW 43–44 (1950–51), pp. 150–54. For discussions of this theory, see A. M. Hunter,
Paul and his Predecessors[2] (London, 1961), pp. 120–22, and J. Reumann, "The Gospel of the
Righteousness of God," *Interp* 20 (1966), pp. 432–52.

But the more significant addition is found in the interpretative clause rendered, "making peace by the blood of his cross" (v. 20c). The effect of this addendum is once again to transform radically the meaning of the reconciliation. In the original statement of the hymn the cosmic theology proclaimed a universal harmony because of the creator's work in Christ the Lord. That harmony which re-united the fractured and fragmented elements of the world was seen as the restitution of Christ as the head of a cosmic body, according to an attested understanding in hellenistic thought which announced that the body of the universe was ruled by Zeus or Logos.[1] The Christian version of this concept of a world-body under the control of a dominant head is seen in verse 18a. As Paul felt impelled to modify this emphasis and to re-cast the statement as an assertion of Christ's lordship in the church, so he could not leave the hellenistic idea untouched. He must ensure a fuller understanding of reconciliation as a soteriological reality by relating it closely to the death of Christ on the cross. Only in this way can he insist that redemption comes, not in knowing the cosmic secrets of the universe or by indulging in speculation, but by the forgiveness of sins (1:14). And that forgiveness, made possible by the costly death of Jesus as an historical event, is mediated to men and women who are consciously committed to the lordship of Jesus Christ not as a statement about his control of the cosmos but as a personal confession of their being in his kingdom and under his rule (1:13). This was the point and purpose of Paul's citation of the hymn at verse 15, introduced as it was by a description of the way in which his readers became members of Christ's body, the church. At the close of the hymn, Paul adds a final interpretative comment to make certain that its revised meaning will not be lost.

Reconciliation for him is not to be thought of as a cosmic miracle which merely changed the state of the universe outside of man. By the insertion of a reference (εἰρηνοποιήσας) which is unique in his writing and which is marked by a certain syntactical awkwardness in the verse, Paul has ensured that the moral transformation of the "reconciliation of all things" shall not be overlooked. Implicit in his addition of the line, "making peace by the blood of his cross" are the several ways in which Paul achieves this objective.

First, he has shown that reconciliation is primarily concerned with the restoration of relationships. Accepting the premise that the earlier hymn was an existing part of the tradition and that the pre-Pauline tradition really represents a type of thinking which was current coin at Colossae, as seems likely, it declares that Christ is the restorer of the universe to its true harmony. Paul, however, goes on to insist that

[1] See E. Schweizer, *TDNT* VII, p. 1037 for quotation from an Orphic fragment to this effect, and his discussion in *Lordship and Discipleship* (London, 1960), Appendix B. The "Body of Christ", pp. 119 ff.

speculative interest is not enough to match a moral problem. This is why he can move directly from the quotation of the hymn (which contains not a single personal reference) to an application of what the hymn (in its revised form) teaches. The link between 1:15–20 and 1:21–23 is close-knit, with the personal pronoun at verse 21, "And you" and the verb at verse 22, "he has now reconciled by his death" standing in an unusual and emphatic position. Quite evidently this is Paul's set purpose.[1] Having shown how the scope of Christ's work reaches every part of creation, he can apply this teaching to his readers. But this modification of the hymn has made it clear that the reconciliation really matters because it touches human lives and produces the effect of a changed human character. Hence the purpose of reconciliation is spelled out: "in order to present you holy and blameless and irreproachable before him" (v. 22b), a purpose which says nothing about mastering the hidden secrets of the universe or indulging in gnostic speculation about the *pleroma*. To be sure, Paul will later in this epistle offer a rationale of the way in which the evil powers were overcome and forced to surrender their claim on Christ and his people (2:14, 15). But at this point Paul's teaching remains within the orbit of the personal effect of reconciliation by which its moral power is known, in the restoration to the favour of God of men and women who formerly were estranged and hostile in mind and open transgressors (v. 21). And the sum of that experience is: the Lord has forgiven you (3:13; cf. 1:14) by his incarnation ("his body of flesh") and sacrificial death on the cross ("the blood of the cross" . . . "by his death").

The second way in which the meaning of the term reconciliation in verse 20 is more sharply defined by Paul's theology of the cross is more obviously polemical and designed to answer the needs of the Colossian church. Part of the "Colossian heresy" (as Lightfoot called it) was evidently a promise that salvation could be enjoyed "instantly" with an immediate offer of immortality and with very little said by way of the ethical demands of the new life. Against that distortion Paul is quick to insist that his (and the apostolic) understanding of the gospel is different on the important ground that it does not pass lightly over the moral

---

[1] Not the least obvious sign of Paul's deliberate intention is his use of the verb ἀποκαταλ-λάσσειν in 1:22 (the textual question does not materially affect the issue), which is picked up from the *Vorlage* of the hymn at 1:20. The evidence shows that this form of the verb is uniquely Christian (see Arndt) and that it occurs in the New Testament only in these two Colossians texts and Ephesians 2:16. The supposition of F. Büchsel (*TDNT* I, p. 258) that it is Paul's own coinage will need modification if the reference in verse 20 derives from a pre-Pauline source. Moreover, in our statement, there are several meanings to be attached to the verb, notably in Colossians where at verse 20 in the hymn the reconciliation describes the unifying of the cosmos under its true head (cf. J. Michl, "Die 'Versöhnung' (Kol. 1, 20)", *ThQ* 128 (1948), pp. 442–62), whereas in Paul's hands the verb takes on a soteriological meaning, which embraces *both* the "overcoming of the cosmic hostility through the lordship of Christ" (explained in 2:15) *and* the restoration of sinful men to God's favour and family (1:22). This is the sense given to 1:20 by Dibelius-Greeven, *An die Kolosser* (Tübingen, 1953), p. 19 quoted in the above line.

demands whether of God's nature or of man's response to his offer. A gnosticizing version of redemption and reconciliation apparently was content simply to assert that God works by non-moral fiat and automatic process. A christianized account of the divine activity (if we may see the evidence for such in the earlier draft of verse 20) stated simply that Christ fills the universe as its head and so leaves no room for competing agencies in the celestial hierarchy to make their bid for man's allegiance. In that sense the spiritual super-beings (later called "the elemental spirits of the universe," (2:8, 20)) are "reconciled" by having their power to oppose Christ and set up a rival claim nullified. By their enforced submission to the lordly Christ who alone expresses the divine fulness (1:19; 2:9) and who by divine appointment is the head of all these angelic hosts (2:10) they are brought to an acknowledgement of his authority and of their rightful place under him. This is described as God's design for the cosmos in which there should be no discord, since it is the divine good pleasure that all things shall be brought under the undisputed headship of Jesus Christ (Eph. 1:10 states this design in clear fashion). This is the meaning of cosmic reconciliation in the *Grundschrift*. But for Paul this statement of Christ's relation to the powers was not adequate. For him – and we shall inspect his thought more fully when we come to 2:13–15 – these cosmic forces are not simply neutral agencies which need to find their true place in the hierarchy over which Christ presides. Their bid for man's allegiance shows that they are rebel forces and it is needful that their hostility should be drawn out and neutralized.[1] So Paul expounds the need for their rebellion to be put down and for peace to be restored in a universe which is at odds with its creator. Moreover the creator-God in a moral world cannot deal with rebel spirits with a wave of the hand. In some way they have to be exposed, with their evil intentions brought out into the open and their claim to human obedience answered. Only then will there be true reconciliation as these usurping powers are called to a trial of strength and shown to be weak and impotent (see Gal. 4:8, 9) in the face of God's wisdom displayed in Christ's cross. That engagement, for Paul, took place at the cross where the issue of God versus the powers

---

[1] It is feasible that, since *evil* spirits are not mentioned in the text of Colossians, those whose theology is represented in the tradition of the hymn may have seen the cosmic powers in a neutral light and in a non-dualistic way. Then, it would be Paul who has given a moral character to the powers since, in the Colossian false teaching and practice, they were becoming a rival to Christ (2:8, 18) and so setting up a dualistic tension which Paul could not tolerate for the reason given in Romans 8:38 f.

The antagonistic motif behind Paul's use of the verb ἀποκαταλλάξαι and his imagery of 2:15 may well be accounted for on this assumption. Because of the situation at Colossae, "The Powers are no longer instruments, linkages between God's love, as revealed in Christ, and the visible world of creation. In fact, they have become gods (Galatians 4:8), behaving as though they were the ultimate ground of being, and demanding from men an appropriate worship. This is the demonic reversal which has taken place on the invisible side of creation. No longer do the Powers bind man and God together; they separate them" (H. Berkhof, *Christ and the Powers* (Scottsdale, Pa., 1962), p. 23).

was joined; and peace is now proclaimed throughout the whole universe because of what Christ did both in his submission to the evil spirits and in his triumph over them. But the emphasis which Paul makes at 1:20c is clear: reconciliation is not secured easily nor is it accomplished as a physical miracle which changes the state of the cosmos outside of man. It "does not work like, to use a Gnostic image, a magnet put up in heaven and drawing those who are brought into its magnetic field irresistibly after it. The effect of Christ's death is the effect of a deed of love bringing its fruit in a human life which is touched by it".[1]

III

2:13–15: New Life in Christ and the Hymn of the Saviour

These verses form a compact section in which Paul is applying the acts of God to his readers' situation. One dominant act was his appointment of his Son as "head of all rule and authority" (2:10), i.e., the elemental spirits of the universe. This headship of Christ confirms the original sense of 1:18a. Attempts have been made to see in this short paragraph (in particular in verses 14, 15) a snatch of hymnody which celebrates the redeeming and victorious power of God in Christ.[2] Clearly there is a break in thought at verse 13. From the initial statement of verse 10 that Christ is Lord of all the powers, the apostle's discussion moves on to consider various ways in which the readers came to an experience of "fulness of life" (verse 10). Three aspects of their experience are mentioned as figures under which the Christian initiation is described: circumcision, baptism, and new life in a resurrection. The section which follows verse 13b: "God has made you alive in union with him (Christ)" is evidently intended to be a paean of praise to the Redeemer who achieved the believers' new life. If there is the insertion of a hymnic fragment at this point, it is an open question whether the subject of the verbs is continued from verse 13b, i.e., God the Father, or whether the "hymn of the Redeemer" beginning at verse 13c or verse 14 more naturally extols Christ the Lord. We shall see grounds on the exegetical level for preferring the latter suggestion.

The lines of the fragment may be set down, noting the same poetic features as we observed in the case of 1:15–20. Moreover, at one place, it is possible to detect a Pauline insertion which interrupts the flow of

[1] E. Schweizer, *The Church as the Body of Christ* (Richmond, Va., 1964), p. 70.
[2] The most ambitious attempt at tracing a hymnic form in ch. 2 is that of G. Schille, *Frühchristliche Hymnen* (Berlin, 1965), pp. 31–37. He thinks that verses 9, 10b, 11b and 13b–15 were all part of a traditional hymn on which the author of Colossians has commented. But it is unnatural to bring verses 9 and 10 into a hymnic scheme, as critics of Schille have noted e.g. R. Deichgräber, *Gotteshymnus und Christushymnus in der frühen Christenheit* (Göttingen 1967), pp. 167 f. and E. Lohse, *Colossians*, p. 99, n. 43. Much more probable is the view that sees the hymnic material beginning at verse 13c; or, as we prefer, to ensure a three-line metrical symmetry, at verse 14.

the text. This comes at verse 14 where the phrase τοῖς δόγμασιν (RSV "with its legal demands") is an awkward pendant and occurs disconnectedly in the middle of the sentence.[1] In addition, the following phrase ὃ ἦν ὑπεναντίον ἡμῖν complicates the meaning and has been regarded as tautologous in view of the preceding καθ' ἡμῶν which is descriptive of τὸ χειρόγραφον. It is then a plausible suggestion that these two phrases are insertions by Paul himself, added to clarify the special sense in which he wishes τὸ χειρόγραφον to be understood. There is also the problem of knowing exactly the point at which the hypothetical hymn begins. We are inclined to treat the participial clause, "who forgave us all our trespasses"[2] in verse 12 as Paul's climactic and triumphant declaration at the close of his recital of the benefits conferred by the gospel message since he identifies himself ("us all") with his erstwhile Gentile readers ("you . . . were dead in the uncircumcision of your flesh").[3] This would also be in keeping with his consistent stress on forgiveness in the epistle (1:14; 3:13) and would give some justification for the quoted passage which follows directly. That hymnic period tells the story of the Saviour whose dramatic actions have dealt with the accusing powers. He emerged victorious after his engagement with them and as a direct consequence he is the mediator of pardon to his people.

The structure of the pre-Pauline traditional composition

Strophe I

Verse 14

ἐξαλείψας τὸ καθ' ἡμῶν χειρόγραφον,
καὶ αὐτὸ ἦρκεν ἐκ τοῦ μέσου,
προσηλώσας αὐτὸ τῷ σταυρῷ.

Who cancelled the bond of debt which stood against us,
And he removed it,
Nailing it to the cross.

These lines explore the rationale of Christ's forgiveness. He is the one who confers the blessing of pardon, as explicitly mentioned in 3:13, "As the Lord (Christ) forgave you . . ."[4] The problem posed by the "certificate of indebtedness" (τὸ χειρόγραφον) which was inimical to men's hopes of restoration to God is met by what Christ did. He wiped the record clear

[1] So Lohse, op. cit., ad 2:14.
[2] The verb "to forgive" (χαρίζεσθαι) is attested in Paul at 2 Cor. 2:7, 10; 12:13 in very personal passages, though the full expression "to forgive trespasses" is not found elsewhere in his undisputed writings.
[3] The explanation which R. A. Wilson gives " 'We' and 'You' in the Epistle to the Ephesians", Studia Evangelica II TU 87 (Berlin, 1964), pp. 676–80, "The paragraph passes from the second to the first person when Paul wishes to emphasize that what he is describing to his hearers has been the experience of all Christians" (p. 677), holds good for this section of Colossians.
[4] At 3:13 P.46 A B D G and the Latin Bible read "the Lord"; but this meaning is clarified as referring to Christ in a weighty body of textual evidence.

(ἐξαλείφειν)[1] of the list of men's transgressions and then he took that discharged document and affixed it to his cross.

Strophe II

Verse 15

ἀπεκδυσάμενος τὰς ἀρχὰς καὶ τὰς ἐξουσίας, ἐδειγμάτισεν ἐν παρρησίᾳ θριαμβεύσας αὐτοὺς ἐν αὐτῷ.	Who divested himself of the principalities and powers, He made a public display of them, Triumphing over them in it (the cross).

Even more dramatically the work of the Redeemer is described in vivid language. On the assumption that the translation given above is defensible,[2] the first line declares how the crucified Christ dealt effectively with the enemies which conspired to cause his death. These demonic agencies (as in 1 Cor. 2:6–8) tried to cling to him (or his flesh) but he stripped them from his person and discarded their pretended authority over him, as a person divests himself of clothing. In so doing he disgraced them by showing them up in their real character, as usurpers and rebels against God.

[1] The verb ἐξαλείφειν means to smear out, obliterate (Moule) as writing on wax or papyrus was rubbed out. But it is fanciful to see here an allusion to the washing of baptism, as H. G. Marsh (*The Origin and Significance of the New Testament Baptism* (Manchester, 1941), p. 134) does.

[2] The chief difficulty centres on the meaning to be given to the participle ἀπεκδυσάμενος. The RSV assumes that God is the subject of the sentence, going back to verse 13b, and its translation, "he disarmed the principalities and powers" gives to the middle verb an active and transitive sense to denote the personal interest of the one who acts. See Arndt, *s.v.* and A. Oepke, *TDNT* II, p. 319. But this translation is open to question on the score that the evil powers are more likely to be stripped of their rule and so exposed to ridicule rather than to be disarmed of their weapons (so Lohse). H. Schlier, *TDNT* II, p. 31, n. 2 follows Lohmeyer in treating the verb as a "divestment of dignity rather than despoiling of weapons". If the verb is given its true meaning of "to strip off" – and this is preferable in the light of Lohmeyer's insistence that the imagery is not drawn from the battlefield but from a royal court in which public officials are degraded by being stripped of their honour – it is still an open question whether the full force of the middle voice should be given. The choice is between taking the verb to mean, he stripped the evil powers of their dignity and authority (so Lohse), or by giving the full meaning to the deponent, he divested himself of the principalities and powers of evil. The latter is the sense taken by the Greek fathers and preferred by Lightfoot: "The powers of evil, which had clung like a Nessus robe about His humanity, were torn off and cast aside for ever." This interpretation makes ἀπεκδυσάμενος govern τὰς ἀρχάς κτλ and yields the translation found in the RV. There is a third view, adopted by the Latin fathers and in recent times by J. A. T. Robinson, *The Body* (London, 1952), p. 41, which would make Christ's action relate to a divesting of his flesh. Yet again it is possible to combine these early Greek and Latin interpretations in the manner taken by C. A. A. Scott, *Christianity According to St. Paul* (Cambridge, 1927), pp. 34 ff. This is the line we have followed in the text. It unites the view that Christ (who is the subject of the participle) stripped off from himself the evil forces which attacked him and that he stripped off his flesh, since it was his flesh (i.e., his frail humanity) which the evil powers assaulted. Flesh in this context means "the medium through which He had become involved in the human experience of the hostility of the evil Potentates and Powers, the spirit-forces which had usurped authority over men" (Scott, *op. cit.*, p. 35). As Moule, *Colossians*, p. 102 points out, the transition between these two views is one that Paul may well have made in spite of the absence of any precise term for "flesh". Paul's description of Christ's reconciliation in 1:22 ("in his body of flesh by his death"), however, makes clear his close association of Christ's death and the medium of his bodily "flesh". For the phrase "body of flesh" see p. 123, n. 1.

They presumed to attack him as weak and helpless (apparently regarding him as a mortal man, identified with the human race over which they claimed their rights). But he repelled that assault by turning them into captives and conquered rebels whose bluff had been called. He led them in a public procession, just as the victorious Roman general paraded his captives of war in chains through the streets of the city at the conclusion of a foreign campaign.[1] So these demonic powers are Christ's "prize of war," held up to public spectacle as he mounted the cross. From that cross he reigns and receives the homage of his foes, who are now "reconciled" and subjugated.

As was the case with the hymn in 1:15–20 there are areas of interpretation, where the hypothesis of tradition-and-redaction helps in elucidating the meaning of a passage. In 2:13–15 we are assuming with several modern interpreters that Paul has used a piece of traditional material, possibly set in hymnic form, and has inserted it as part of his continuing polemic against the Colossian false teachers. It is not difficult to imagine how impressive this citation would be if it represented a species of agreed teaching in the churches, to which Paul could appeal as part of the tradition which the Colossian Christians had received (2:6). He would then be able to use this fragment as an effective way of checking the gnosticizing proposal that the angelic powers were to be venerated as powerful intermediaries in the Colossians' quest for religious certainty.

Paul's redaction

The apostle, as on the occasion of his use of 1:15 ff., has taken over an already extant piece of liturgy and edited it for his own purpose. The presence of symmetrical forms is seen in the way in which two stanzas of three lines each can be detected, with correspondences of participial style and the main verbs carefully arranged. Moreover, it cannot be accidental that, as 1:15 and 1:18b begin their respective strophes in a similar way and 1:16 and 1:20 conclude their stanzas on the same note (with a recurrence of τὰ πάντα), so in this hymn of the Redeemer the last line of strophe I and the last line of strophe II match each other, with a participial clause and a reference to the cross. Also the first lines of both stanzas are participial, and the second line in each stanza contains the prominent main verb. We have now to enquire into the purpose of Paul's redactional activity. This is seen in his additions at verse 14 where the original hymn stated that Christ "cancelled the certificate of indebtedness which stood against us".

We have already seen the difficulty which the received text presents with its overloading of the sentence by the inclusion of "because of regulations" (τοῖς δόγμασιν) and its repetition of the otiose phrase "which was against us" (ὃ ἦν ὑπεναντίον ἡμῖν). By recourse to the theory of an *Urtext*

[1] G. Delling, *TDNT* III, p. 160.

which did not have these phrases we are able to see why Paul needed to add in these glosses. By the addition of τοῖς δόγμασιν he wished to stress how it was that the χειρόγραφον was the ground of the accusation levelled by the demonic powers. Also we propose that the second phrase marks the beginning of a new sentence which Paul includes to re-iterate how the work of Christ consisted in taking away "that which was inimical to us" (ὃ ἦν ὑπεναντίον ἡμῖν). These two matters require some comment: and we shall take them in reverse order.

On the second point, Lohmeyer's suggestion is deserving of attention.[1] He proposes to place a period after τοῖς δόγμασιν and to treat the phrase ὃ ἦν ὑπεναντίον ἡμῖν as the object of the verb ἦρκεν. The text now reads: "That which was hostile to us, even that (referring back to the *cheirographon*) he has removed". This re-punctuation certainly makes for a simpler and smoother flow of the sentence, and the unusual position of the phrase coming before the verb can be explained by the expedient that it is a Pauline addendum, added to make clear the evil character of the document which Christ has not only wiped clear but also removed (from the divine presence?).

The meaning of τὸ χειρόγραφον is well-attested in both the Jewish and Graeco-Roman world. It represents a statement of obligation written by a debtor with a promise to pay what is due. The qualifying τοῖς δόγμασιν apparently suggests the reason why this document contains a record of human failure before God, though perhaps unconsciously many inter-preters seem to be influenced by an identical phrase in Ephesians 2:15 where a reference to the standard of the divine law is clear. Under this influence, τὸ χειρόγραφον is taken to be a bond of debt which records its damaging indictment of mankind "because of regulations", i.e., by the strict requirements of God's law man is convicted of his failure to attain the standards set by that law and branded as a transgressor. In that way the law has become an instrument of judgement which the obedient Christ took responsibility for in our name and so "paid the debt" on behalf of sinners. He did this by his close identification with human need, even to the point of his vicarious death on the cross.

There is, however, a difficulty with this view, viz. that it is awkward to equate a certificate of indebtedness signed by men with a divine exhibi-tion of condemnation in the bond which was nailed to the cross. Some recent interpreters have, therefore, suggested that the χειρόγραφον refers not to a document of human guilt in respect of the Mosaic law but to an

---

[1] E. Lohmeyer, *Die Briefe an die Philipper, an die Kolosser und an Philemon* (Göttingen, 1953) *ad loc.* He renders the text:

> Was uns feind war,
> Ja, das hat er weggeräumt,
> das an das Kreuz genagelt;

But Lohmeyer's exegesis which makes the χειρόγραφον refer to a document on which is inscribed a man's pact with the devil is an eccentricity.

indictment presented at the heavenly court.[1] The original text referred simply to a *cheirographon* hostile to man; Paul's addition of the explanatory gloss, "consisting of ordinances. That which was against us" amplifies the nature of the charge which the angelic indictment brought against mankind.

The reason for believing that this is Paul's designation of the bond as the work of evil spirits is primarily to be sought in 2:20. There he makes it plain that the false ideas and prescriptions which formed the basis of the errorists' appeal and which entailed a worship of the angels (2:18) consisted in the regulations or ordinances imposed on the Colossians. To the simple believer, caught by this spell, the ascetic requirements of 2:23: "don't handle, don't taste; don't touch" may have seemed harmless enough and even laudable as inculcating a self-discipline. For Paul this line of reasoning is demonic and is to be utterly refused. His challenging rebuke τί . . . δογματίζεσθε; admits of no compromise. The reason for his stringent rejection is given in the preceding verses. This asceticism substitutes for a way of life κατὰ χριστόν a rival system of religion and ethics which is not only κατὰ τὴν παράδοσιν τῶν ἀνθρώπων (2:8) and κατὰ τὰ ἐντάλματα καὶ διδασκαλίας τῶν ἀνθρώπων (2:22), but κατὰ τὰ στοιχεῖα τοῦ κόσμου and so οὐ κατὰ χριστόν (2:8). For Paul this is deadly heresy, and the recourse to δόγματα is the surest sign that the evil spiritual forces are threatening to engulf the church and rob it of its freedom in the gospel. Paul must therefore proclaim that the indictment which the evil powers bring against the Colossians as they consent to submit to a way of life which is a deliberate return to astral tyranny has already been answered in the heavenly court by the Christians' advocate who has both wiped the account clear and removed it as a liability facing man.

The way that Christ did this is the theme of the second stanza of 2:15. But it is impossible to see the full relevance of Paul's use of the rare participle ἀπεκδυσάμενος in this verse in isolation from what he has said in 2:11 and what will follow as part of his paraenetic counsel in 3:9. The middle term is still *cheirographon*, which in this context takes on a special meaning as a virtual equivalent of Christ's human body which, in Pauline thought, is closely linked with his death on the cross (2 Cor. 5:21; Gal. 3:13; Rom. 8:3). This is the argument proposed by O. A. Blanchette[2] in order to link *cheirographon* with Christ's body bearing our sins. Additional support for this view comes from the *Gospel of Truth*[3]

[1] A. J. Bandstra, *The Law and the Elements of the World. An Exegetical Study in Aspects of Paul's Teaching* (Kampen, n.d. around 1964), pp. 158 ff. cites the evidence from L. Koep, *Das himmlische Buch in Antike und Christentum: Eine religionsgeschichtliche Untersuchung zur altchristlichen Bildersprache* (Bonn, 1952).

[2] O. A. Blanchette, "Does the *Cheirographon* of Col. 2,14 represent Christ Himself?" *CBQ* 23 (1961), pp. 306-12.

[3] The passage in the *Gospel of Truth* is 20:22-28. The translation in *Evangelium Veritatis*, ed. M. Malinine, H.-Ch. Puech, G. Quispel (Zürich, 1956) reads:

where the text speaks of Jesus taking or wearing a book as his own and as being nailed to the cross where he affixed the ordinance of the Father to that cross. The choice of sense: bearing or wearing the book is evidently settled by a subsequent text (20:34) which remarks: "Having divested himself of these perishable rags (his flesh), he clothed himself with incorruptibility, which it is impossible for anyone to take away from him."

The association of "wearing" and "divesting" recalls the previous verse 11 where the key phrase is "putting off the body of flesh in the circumcision of Christ". This is a disputed verse, but the likelihood is that we should understand ἐν τῇ περιτομῇ τοῦ χριστοῦ to mean the circumcision which Christ himself underwent when he stripped off from himself the clinging attack in his flesh of the spiritual powers which assaulted him. Verse 15 relates to the same event and shows how on the cross the engagement with the evil powers led to his victory over them. By taking χειρόγραφον as a personalized allusion to the charge-list of guilt which Christ assumed in his body we are now in a position to understand why these evil powers attacked him. They accused him as though he were a sinner – or, as the gnostic would put it, because he was fleshly and obviously out of harmony with the divine because he was suffering[1] – and indicted him. But he repelled this charge first by receiving the full force of their malevolence and "wearing" the charge as he took responsibility

[1] Paul's answer to this charge may be inferred from his use of the adverb σωματικῶς in 2:9 on which W. L. Knox, *St. Paul and the Church of the Gentiles* (Cambridge, 1939), p. 168, n. 3 comments: "It seems to be a summary reply to the argument that Jesus could not have been divine, for He had a real body and was really crucified, which is impossible for a divine being."

> This is why, Jesus appeared (and) took that
> Book (cf. 20: lines 3 ff.) He was nailed
> to a (cross of) wood (and) He attached the
> deed of disposition
> of the Father to the Cross
> Oh! great, sublime Teaching.

The points of similarity and distinction between this section of a gnostic document and Col. 2:14 were first pointed out by W. C. van Unnik "The 'Gospel of Truth' and the New Testament", *The Jung Codex*. Three studies by H.-Ch. Puech, G. Quispel and W. C. van Unnik, ed. F. L. Cross (London, 1955), pp. 108 ff. and have been noted by later writers. Cf. the discussion of Sasagu Arai, *Die Christologie des Evangelium Veritatis* (Leiden, 1964), pp. 100–105.

The key text comes in line 24 which most translators render: "He took that Book". However, the *Note critique* in *Evangelium Veritatis*, p. 53, draws attention to the suggested ambiguity of the underlying Greek ἀναλαμβάνειν which the Coptic translator read as "to take up" "to take upon oneself" (cf. W. W. Isenberg's renderings: "He took that book as his own" in *Gnosticism: An Anthology*, ed. R. M. Grant, London, 1961). The Greek may also mean "to clothe" – a translation already preferred by H. M. Schenke, *Die Herkunft des sogenannten Evangelium Veritatis* (Göttingen, 1959), p. 37: "Er bekleidete sich mit jenem Buche", and now argued for by Bandstra, *op. cit.*, p. 161, n. 173 and Cullen I. K. Story, *The Nature of Truth in "The Gospel of Truth" and in the Writings of Justin Martyr* (Leiden, 1970), p. 129.

for it and, then, by rejecting it as he discarded his "body of flesh",[1] now a dead thing and so fit to be abandoned on the cross (1:22; cf. Rom. 6:6, 7). However, this was not the end, since he was raised in a spiritual body and vindicated by God, thus reversing the sentence which these evil forces levelled at him. He stripped off their hold and overcame them. Even more, he turned the tables on them and led his erstwhile overlords in captive as *his* prize of war at the very place – ἐν αὐτῷ – (the cross) where they imagined that their victory was won.

This is a highly dramatic and picturesque account of the historical events of Good Friday, with which we may find it hard to relate. Paul's first readers must have understood it all, and we are encouraged to believe this by the way in which he proceeds to apply the teaching to their new life. All that Christ did both in submission to death and overcoming his foes has personal and experiential relevance in the light of 3:9, 10: "seeing that you have put off (ἀπεκδυσάμενοι) the old nature . . . and have put on the new nature." The Christians' "putting off" (ἀπέκδυσις) exactly matches Christ's "putting off",[2] and points back to 2:11. When the Lord consented to yield to the regime of the astral powers and then to triumph over them, Christians too were involved in that representative act and by their faith union with him (expressed in baptism) they were united with him in his death and victory. The result is clear: You died with Christ out from under the elemental spirits of the universe (2:20).[3] They are now an enemy which brings its accusations and indictment against you in vain, for they have done their worst to Christ and been foiled in the attempt to succeed in their clinging attack. He has neutralized their malevolence and holds them as his spoils of war.

Paul finally drives home the point: Therefore do not allow any false teacher encroaching on the life of your congregation to carry you away as a prize of war (2:8).[4] You are assured by Christ's victory that he has "reconciled" (i.e., drawn the hostility of) these malign spirits; and the sure token of that victory is proved by the new life which the Colossians already have as men and women risen with Christ and as part of the heavenly world (1:12–14; 3:1–4). Specifically their sins are forgiven and no accusing angel can bring charges against them. The cosmic reconciliation is certified by the knowledge and assurance of divine forgiveness.

---

[1] For the phrase "body of his flesh", see 1 QpHab ix. 2 and the other Jewish allusions suggesting a man's frail physical nature, cited by K. G. Kuhn, "New Light on Temptation, Sin, and Flesh in the New Testament", *The Scrolls and New Testament*, ed. K. Stendahl London, 1958), p. 107.

[2] Lightfoot comments (p. 189): "The ἀπέκδυσις accomplished in us when we are baptized nto His death is a counterpart to the ἀπέκδυσις which He accomplished by His death."

[3] J. A. T. Robinson's forceful attempt to render Paul's Greek at 2:20: *The Body*, p. 43.

[4] I suggest that there is a parallel intended by Paul's use of the rare verb συλαγωγεῖν (to carry off as a captive of war) in 2:8 and his use of the verb θριαμβεύειν (to lead in a triumphal procession someone as a captive) at 2:15.

To have (this) forgiveness of sins . . . means to be free from the powers and principalities, who on the cross of Christ were subjected to ridicule and shame (2:15). Whoever is baptized into Christ is placed under the dominion of the beloved Son of God, who as Lord holds in his hands the authority over the whole world as well as the salvation of those who belong to him – freed for the new life of obedience that confesses his rule.[1]

[1] Lohse, *op. cit.*, p. 131.

CHAPTER VIII

PAUL'S UNDERSTANDING OF THE DEATH OF JESUS

James D. G. Dunn

THERE IS LITTLE DOUBT IN MY MIND THAT DR MORRIS'S CHIEF contribution to New Testament theology has been his work on the doctrine of the atonement. His treatment of various aspects of the subject in several journals, including the *Expository Times*, *Journal of Theological Studies* and *New Testament Studies*, reached its climax in what for me is still his single most important work, *The Apostolic Preaching of the Cross* (1955) – followed since then by the more popular *The Cross in the New Testament* (1965).

In this birthday offering to Dr Morris, I wish simply to draw attention to an aspect of Paul's theology which is much more important as a key to Paul's thought than works on Pauline theology would suggest. I refer to Paul's understanding of Christ as representative man (I). When we correlate this with Paul's understanding of Jesus' death as a sacrifice we gain an insight into Paul's theology of sacrifice (II) which certainly strengthens Dr Morris's interpretation of Paul but which also calls for some qualifications (III).

I *Jesus as Representative Man*

The fact that Paul tells us next to nothing about the historical Jesus has always been at the heart of one of the most intractable problems in New Testament theology and Christian origins – the relation between the gospel of Jesus and the theology of Paul. The discontinuity between the two had been stressed by Liberal Protestantism and by the History of Religions school, particularly W. Heitmüller and W. Bousset.[1] And although R. Bultmann shared many of their conclusions he did attempt to demonstrate a significant element of continuity between Jesus and Paul.[2] More recently the probable influence of particular sayings of Jesus

[1] W. Heitmüller, "Zum Problem Paulus und Jesus", *ZNTW* 13 (1912), pp. 320–37; W. Bousset, *Kyrios Christos* (²1921, ET⁵ Nashville, 1970). See also W. Wrede, *Paul* (1905, ET London, 1907).

[2] R. Bultmann, "The significance of the Historical Jesus for the Theology of Paul" (1929), ET in *Faith and Understanding: Collected Essays* (London, 1969), pp. 220–46; "Jesus and Paul" (1936), ET in *Existence and Faith* (London, 1960), pp. 217–39.

on Paul has been highlighted,[1] and a link is still possible along the lines of *imitatio Christi* (I Cor. 11:1; Eph. 4:20; Col. 2:6; I Thess. 1:6).[2] Perhaps we should also mention that at the other end of the spectrum Paul's apparent lack of knowledge of the historical Jesus has been made the major plank in an attempt to revive the nevertheless thoroughly dead thesis that the Jesus of the Gospels was a mythical figure.[3]

What does not seem to have been adequately appreciated is that for Paul the Jesus of history is integral to his soteriology; it is of vital significance for Paul that Jesus actually lived and died in history. Paul calls men not to take up some timeless ideal, not merely to believe in a divine being contemporary with him, but to believe in the Jesus who lived and died and now lives again. The contemporary Christ is one and the same as the Jesus of history. If it is not the same Jesus, then his gospel falls in ruins. It is the Jesus of history now exalted who challenges self-sufficient and self-indulgent man; it is the presence here and now of the Jesus who lived and died which brings men to the crisis of decision. Paul's soteriology therefore hangs on the wholeness of his Christology;[4] separation of the Jesus of history from the Christ of faith does not characterize Paul's soteriology, it destroys it.

Why is this so? Because for Paul the earthly Jesus was not significant primarily for what he *said* or *did* during his life, but for what he *was*. And what he *did* by his death and resurrection gains its significance for salvation primarily from what he *was*. The key idea which runs through his Christology and binds it to his soteriology is that of solidarity or *representation*.[5] *Jesus became one with man in order to put an end to sinful man in order that a new man might come into being. He became what man is in order that by his death and resurrection man might become what he is.*

The most sustained expositions of Jesus' representative significance come in Rom. 5:12–21 and I Cor. 15:20 ff., 45–9. In both instances Jesus is compared and contrasted with Adam. The point of the comparison and contrast lies in the representative significance of the two men. Adam means "man", "mankind". Paul speaks about Adam as a way of speaking about

---

[1] For example, D. M. Stanley, "Pauline Allusions to the Sayings of Jesus", *CBQ* 23 (1961), pp. 26–39; H. Riesenfeld, "Parabolic Language in the Pauline Epistles", *The Gospel Tradition* (Oxford, 1970), pp. 187–204; D. L. Dungan, *The Sayings of Jesus in the Churches of Paul* (Oxford, 1971); C. K. Barrett, "I am not Ashamed of the Gospel", *New Testament Essays* (London, 1972), pp. 116–43.

[2] Though see H. D. Betz, *Nachfolge und Nachahmung Jesu Christi im Neuen Testament* (Tübingen, 1967), pp. 144, 168.

[3] G. A. Wells, *The Jesus of the Early Christians* (London, 1971), pp. 131–51.

[4] Cf. A. E. J. Rawlinson, *The New Testament Doctrine of the Christ* (London, 1926), chapter 5; W. D. Davies, *Paul and Rabbinic Judaism* (London, 1948), pp. 41 f., 49–57; M. Black, "The Pauline Doctrine of the Second Adam", *SJT* 7 (1954), pp. 170–79; D. E. H. Whiteley, "St. Paul's Thought on the Atonement", *JTS* n.s. 8 (1957), pp. 242–46; R. Scroggs, *The Last Adam* (Oxford, 1966), pp. 92–112.

[5] See also G. Delling, "Der Tod Jesu in der Verkündigung des Paulus", *Apophoreta: Festschrift für Ernst Haenchen* (Berlin, 1964), p. 86.

mankind. Adam represents what man might have been and what man now
is. Adam is man made for fellowship with God become slave of selfish-
ness and pride. Adam is sinful man. Jesus too is representative man. He
represents a new kind of man – man who not only dies but lives again.
The first Adam represents physical man (ψυχὴ ζῶσα, σῶμα ψυχικόν) –
man given over to death; the last Adam represents pneumatic man
(πνεῦμα ζωοποιοῦν, σῶμα πνευματικόν) – man alive from the dead.

Now it is clear from the I Corinthians passage that Jesus only takes up
his distinctively last Adam/man role as from the resurrection; only in and
through resurrection does he become life-giving Spirit.[1] How then can
we characterize his representative function in his life and death? The
answer seems to be that for Paul the earthly Jesus represents *fallen* man,
man who though he lives again is first subject to death. Adam represents
what man might have been and by his sin what man is. Jesus represents
what man now is and by his obedience what man might become. This is
most clearly expressed in three passages.

(a) Rom. 8:3 – "What the law could not do, because it was weakened
by the flesh, God has done – by sending his own Son in the precise likeness
of sinful flesh (ἐν ὁμοιώματι σαρκὸς ἁμαρτίας) . . .". ὁμοίωμα here as
elsewhere in Paul means a very close likeness – a mirror image, a twin likeness, an exact replica. In Rom. 1:23 its use with εἰκών must signify an in-
tensifying of the idea of likeness/image, otherwise the phrase ἐν ὁμοιώματι
εἰκόνος is tautologous; thus, "changed the glory of the incorruptible
God into what was *nothing more than* the image of corruptible man . . .".
In Rom. 5:14: "death reigned from Adam to Moses even over those who
did not sin *in precisely the same way* as Adam (ἐπὶ τῷ ὁμοιώματι τῆς
παραβάσεως Ἀδαμ)". In Rom. 6:5 the "likeness of Christ's death" does
not mean baptism nor the death of Christ itself but the convert's experience of death to sin and life to God beginning to work out in himself,
which Paul characterizes as a sharing in Christ's death and so as an
experience which is *precisely like* (and dependent upon) Christ's death to
sin (6:10).[2] So in Rom. 8:3 ἐν ὁμοιώματι σαρκὸς ἁμαρτίας must mean
'in the very form of sinful flesh".

But is Paul saying then that Jesus became guilty of sin? No! As is
generally recognized, σάρξ in Paul is not evil, otherwise he could not use
it in a neutral sense, or speak of it being cleansed (2 Cor. 7:1).[3] Flesh is not
evil, it is simply weak and corruptible. It signifies man in his weakness
and corruptibility, his belonging to the world. In particular it is that

---

[1] See J. D. G. Dunn, "I Corinthians 15:45 – Last Adam, Life-giving Spirit", *Christ and
Spirit in the New Testament: Studies in Honour of C. F. D. Moule* (ed. B. Lindars and S. S.
Smalley, Cambridge, 1973), pp. 127–41.

[2] J. D. G. Dunn, *Baptism in the Holy Spirit* (London, 1970), pp. 142 f.; On ὁμοίωμα
cf. J. Schneider, *TDNT*, V, pp. 192–97.

[3] H. W. Robinson, *The Christian Doctrine of Man* (Edinburgh, ³1926), pp. 114 f.; W. D.
Stacey, *The Pauline View of Man* (London, 1956), p. 162; E. Schweizer, σάρξ, *TDNT*, VII,
p. 135.

dimension of the human personality through which sin attacks, which sin
uses as its instrument (Rom. 7:5, 18, 25) – thus σὰρξ ἁμαρτίας. That is
to say, σὰρξ ἁμαρτίας does not signify *guilty* man, but man in his *fallen-*
ness – man subject to temptation, to human appetites and desires, to death.
The "sinful flesh" is nothing other than the "sinful body" (Rom. 6:6), the
"body doomed to death" (Rom. 7:24).

Thus in Rom. 8:3 Paul is saying simply that God sent his Son in the
very form of fallen man, that is, as representative of fallen men. ὁμοίωμα
in other words does not distinguish Jesus from sinful flesh or distance
him from fallen man, as is often suggested; rather it is Paul's way of
expressing Jesus' *complete identity* with the flesh of sin, with man in his
fallenness.[1] So far as Paul was concerned Jesus had to share fallen humanity, sinful flesh, otherwise he could not deal with sin in the flesh. It was only
because he shared man's sinful flesh that his death was "a sacrifice for sin"
(NEB) and so served as God's act of judgement on sin in the flesh (see
further below).

(*b*) Phil. 2:7 f. It is very likely that the Christ-hymn of Phil. 2:6–11 uses
an Adam Christology, probably influenced to some extent by the Primal
Man speculation current within Hellenism at that time.[2] The lines of the
hymn which are most relevant to us are:

> μορφὴν δούλου λαβών
> ἐν ὁμοιώματι ἀνθρώπων γενόμενος
> καὶ σχήματι εὑρεθεὶς ὡς ἄνθρωπος.

In the first of these three lines the choice of δοῦλος is the significant point.
It may be sufficiently explained as a means of heightening the contrast
with κύριος in v. 11. The suggestion that it refers to the servant of Isa. 53,
though attractive, is not convincing.[3] But it is probable that it was also
deliberately chosen as a description of Jesus' earthly state, and that Paul
would understand it in this way. In this case Paul in taking over the hymn
would intend to signify that Christ by his incarnation became a slave of the
elemental powers of the universe (cf. Gal. 4:1 ff.) – that is, he fully shared
the bondage and limitation of man's earthly state.[4]

This is surely confirmed by the second and third lines quoted above.
The second line gives us the only other occurrence of ὁμοίωμα in Paul:
he became the precise likeness of men; he became just what men are.
Indeed, he came ὡς ἄνθρωπος, that is, not just as one man among many,
but *as man*, as representative man[5] – man, who, be it noted, is immediately
described as subject, obedient to death.

[1] Cf. P. Althaus, *Der Brief an die Römer* (NTD 6, Göttingen, 1932, [10]1966), p. 85; C. K.
Barrett, *The Epistle to the Romans* (London, 1957), p. 156; O. Kuss, *Der Römerbrief* (Regensburg, 1957, 1959), p. 495; R. Jewett, *Paul's Anthropological Terms* (Leiden, 1971), pp. 150 ff.
[2] R. P. Martin, *Carmen Christi* (Cambridge, 1967), pp. 116–33, *et passim*. See also Jewett
op. cit., pp. 230–36.
[3] K. H. Rengstorf, δοῦλος, *TDNT*, II, p. 278.
[4] Cf. those cited by Martin, *op. cit.*, pp. 177–81.   [5] Cf. Martin, *op. cit.*, pp. 209 ff.

(c) I Cor. 15:27: Paul explicitly quotes Ps. 8:6 – "He has put all things
n subjection under his feet" – and refers it to the exalted Christ. Since
's. 8:4–6 was widely used in the early Church as a testimonium to Christ
Eph. 1:22; Phil. 3:21; Heb. 2:6–9; I Pet. 3:22) it is probable that Paul had
he whole passage in mind.[1] That is to say, it is probable that Paul under-
tood Ps. 8:4–6 with reference to Jesus in the same way as the writer
o "the Hebrews". Jesus was the man who fulfilled the destiny God had
riginally intended for man.[2] Man had been made "lower than the angels",
ut had not yet been crowned with glory and honour and granted
ordship over all things. But in contrast, Jesus *had* fulfilled that destiny.
He too was man "for a short while lower than the angels", but had now
een crowned with glory and honour "because he suffered death"
Heb. 2:9). That this train of thought is in Paul's mind in I Cor. 15:27 is
ikely in view of the explicit Adam Christology in the immediate context
f the quotation. In other words, Jesus enters his role as New Man only
fter living and suffering as Man. Adam had missed his destiny because of
in and his destiny had become death (I Cor. 15:21 f.). Only after living
ut that destiny (death) and through it creating a new destiny (resurrec-
ion) can the original destiny be fulfilled. Only by living out the destiny
f Adam can the destiny of the Last Adam become a reality.

Space prohibits an elaboration of this aspect of Paul's theology – that
*or Paul Jesus in his life and death is representative man, representative of fallen
man – by living out that fallenness to the death and overcoming it in resurrection
e becomes representative of new life, of new man.* It must suffice to refer
riefly to other passages where the same Christology is reflected. Rom.
:3 – as man he lives, like man, $\kappa\alpha\tau\grave{\alpha}\ \sigma\acute{\alpha}\rho\kappa\alpha$ – through flesh, and to some
xtent anyway, in terms of flesh.[3] Gal. 4:4 – as man of flesh, like men, he
nows subjection to the law. Rom. 6:9 f. – as man of flesh, like men, he is
ubject to death. In short, as representative man he shares the weakness and
orruptibility of man's flesh, as representative man he knows the power of
he powers, law and death, that enslave man. "Christ dies the death of the
lisobedient, of sinners" (Rom. 5:6, 8; 2 Cor. 5:21).[4]

We might mention also Paul's use of the title $X\rho\iota\sigma\tau\acute{o}\varsigma$. It is frequently
ssumed that Paul uses the title quite conventionally and adds nothing to
t.[5] This is not in fact true. And the way in which Paul does use it is of

[1] Cf. C. H. Dodd, *According to the Scriptures* (London, 1952), pp. 32 ff., 120 ff., 126; B.
indars, *New Testament Apologetic* (London, 1961), pp. 50 ff., 168.
[2] C. K. Barrett, *The First Epistle to the Corinthians* (London, 1968), pp. 359 ff.; F. F. Bruce,
& 2 Corinthians (London, 1971), pp. 147 f.
[3] J. D. G. Dunn, "Jesus – Flesh and Spirit: an Exposition of Romans 1:3–4", *JTS*, n.s. 24
1973), pp. 40–68.
[4] Delling, *op. cit.*, p. 88.
[5] See, for example, the treatments of R. Bultmann, *Theology of the New Testament* Vol. I
ET London, 1952); O. Cullmann. *The Christology of the New Testament* (1957, ET London,
959); R. H. Fuller, *The Foundations of New Testament Christology* (London, 1965). But see
lso F. Hahn, *The Titles of Jesus in Christology* (1963, ET London, 1969), p. 186; W. Kramer,
Christ, Lord, Son of God (1963, ET London, 1966), pp. 133–50.

especial interest for us. For, on the one hand, he nails it firmly to Jesus in his death: the Christ is the Crucified One (I Cor. 1:23; 2:2; Gal. 3:1). And on the other, it becomes the chief vehicle for Paul's expression of Christ's representative capacity, the solidarity of believers with the risen Christ: he is baptized in the Spirit *into* Christ (Rom. 6:3; I Cor. 12:13; 2 Cor. 1:21; Gal. 3:27); he has died *with* Christ, is crucified *with* Christ, his life is hid *with* Christ in God etc. (Rom. 6:3 f., 8; 8:17; Gal. 2:19 f.; Eph. 2:5; Phil. 1:23; Col. 2:20; 3:1, 3; I Thess. 5:10); his present life in all its aspects is lived *in* Christ (e.g., Rom. 6:11; 8:39; I Cor. 15:22; 2 Cor. 5:17, 19; Gal. 2:4; Phil. 2:1; Col. 1:28; I Thess. 2:14); he is a member of the *body* of Christ (Rom. 12:5; I Cor. 12:12, 27 etc.); Christ is the offspring of Abraham to whom the promise has been made, and all who identify themselves with Christ are counted as Abraham's children (Gal. 3:16, 26–9). The two distinctively Pauline emphases in Paul's use of Χριστός cannot be unrelated. *Christ is representative man precisely as the Crucified One.*[1]

2 Cor. 5:14 now becomes clearer as one of the most explicit expressions of Paul's understanding of Jesus as representative man – "one man died for all; therefore all mankind (οἱ πάντες) has died".[2] When we talk of Christ as representative man we mean that what is true of him in particular is true of men in general. When we say Adam is representative man in his fallenness, we mean that *all men* are fallen. So when Paul says Christ died as representative man he means that there is no other end possible for men – all mankind dies, as he died, as flesh, as the end of sinful flesh, as the destruction of sin. Had there been a way for fallen man to overcome his fallenness and subjection to the powers Christ would not have died – Christ as representative man would have shown men how to overcome sinful flesh. But Christ, Man, died because there is no other way for man – any man. His death is an acknowledgment that there is no way out for fallen men except through death – no answer to sinful flesh except its destruction in death. "Man could not be helped other than through his annihilation".[3] Only through death does the New Man emerge in risen life. In other words, if we may follow the train of thought a little further, Christ's identification with fallen men is up to and into death. But there it ends, for death is the end of fallen men, the destruction of man as flesh – Christ died, all died. Beyond death he no longer represents all men, fallen man. In his risen life he represents only those who identify themselves with him, with his death (in baptism), only those who acknowledge the Risen One as Lord (2 Cor. 5:15). Only those who identify themselves with him in his death are identified with him in his life from death. Hence it is a

---

[1] For further material in Paul where Adam Christology provides the basic structure of the thought see Black, *op. cit.*, pp. 174 ff.; Scroggs, *op. cit.*, pp. 95 ff.

[2] Cf. H. Windisch, *Der zweite Korintherbrief* (Göttingen, 1924), pp. 182 f.

[3] K. Barth, cited by G. C. Berkouwer, *The Triumph of Grace in the Theology of Karl Barth* (Grand Rapids, 1956), p. 135.

mistake to confine the "all" of 5:14 to believers. The "all" of 5:14–15 are not identical with "the living" of 5:15. Jesus' representative capacity before resurrection (sinful flesh – Rom. 8:3) is different from his representative capacity after resurrection (spiritual body – I Cor. 15:44–45). All die. But only those "in Christ" experience the new creation (2 Cor. 5:17). In short, as Last Adam Jesus represents only those who experience life-giving Spirit (I Cor. 15:45).

II *Jesus' Death as a Sacrifice*

We must now attempt to view Jesus' death through Paul's eyes from another angle and then bring the two viewpoints together to give us a fuller picture of Paul's thinking about the cross. I refer to Paul's understanding of Jesus' death in terms of cultic sacrifice. The idea of blood sacrifices and of divine-human relationships being somehow dependent on them is so repellent to post-Enlightenment man that many commentators have instinctively played down or ignored this side of Paul's theology. The most recent example is E. Käsemann who reacts against undue emphasis being given to the idea of sacrificial death by firmly denying that Paul ever definitely called Jesus' death a sacrifice, and who sums up, "The idea of the sacrificial death is, if anything, pushed into the background . . .".[1] An examination of Paul, however, makes it difficult to escape the conclusion that Käsemann's own (certainly valuable) demythologizing of Paul's theology of Jesus' death nevertheless falls into the trap of making Paul's language less foreign and less distasteful and so misses both the offence of Paul's thought and its point.

In Rom. 3:25 *ἱλαστήριον* cannot have any other than a sacrificial reference. Since the word is used so often in LXX for the lid of the ark, the "mercy-seat", the only real debate has been whether it should be understood as *place* or *means* of expiation/propitiation – the latter ("means") being clearly more appropriate.[2] And even if the verse is a quotation,[3] Paul gives it such a central place in a key passage of his exposition that it must be very expressive of his own thinking; indeed in such a case one quotes from an earlier text or source because it puts the point as well or better than one can oneself. The attempt has sometimes been made to see as the immediate background of Rom. 3:25 the martyr theology which

[1] E. Käsemann, *Perspectives on Paul* (1969, ET London, 1971), pp. 42–45; cf. V. Taylor, *The Atonement in New Testament Teaching* (London, ³1958), pp. 185–90. It is astonishing that G. Bornkamm, *Paul* (1969, ET London, 1971), hardly discusses what Paul means by the gospel of the cross as a whole, let alone the concept of Jesus' death as sacrifice.
[2] For the debate see L. L. Morris, "The Meaning of *ἱλαστήριον* in Romans 3:25", *NTS* 2 (1955–56), pp. 33–43; K. Kertelge, *"Rechtfertigung" bei Paulus* (Münster, 1967), pp. 56 f.
[3] R. Bultmann, *Theology*, p. 46; E. Käsemann, "Zum Verständnis von Rm. 3:24–26", *ZNTW* 43 (1950–51), pp. 150–54; Kertelge, *op. cit.*, pp. 51 ff. E. Lohse, *Märtyrer und Gottesknecht* (Göttingen, ²1963), p. 149 restricts the pre-Pauline tradition to v. 25.

finds its clearest expression in 4 Macc. 17:21 f., where ἱλαστήριον is used
to describe the atoning significance of the Maccabean martyrs' deaths.[1]
This is certainly possible; but two qualifications are necessary. First,
martyr theology is itself an application of sacrificial metaphor; the reason
why the death of martyrs can be thought to carry such weight of atonement is because their death can be seen as a kind of sacrifice. Indeed in
Diaspora Judaism martyr theology is sacrificial precisely because it served
as one of the substitutes for the sacrificial cult in faraway Jerusalem.[2]
Second, in Rom. 3:25 the ἱλαστήριον is presented by God himself. This
thought is not present in Jewish martyr theology but is quite common in
connection with the sacrificial cult in the Old Testament.[3] Thus, whether
or not Paul was consciously alluding to martyr theology here, it is most
likely that the primary reference of his metaphor was to Christ's death
as cult sacrifice.[4]

Rom. 8:3 – "God sent his Son in the precise likeness of sinful flesh and
for sin (περὶ ἁμαρτίας)". NEB translates the last phrase, "as a sacrifice for
sin". And this is wholly justified since περὶ ἁμαρτίας is regularly used in
LXX to translate the Hebrew ḥaṭṭā'th (sin offering – e.g. Lev. 5:6 f., 11;
16:3, 5, 9; Num. 6:16; 7:16; 2 Chron. 29:23 f.; Neh. 10:33; Ezek. 42:13;
43:19; in Isa. 53:10 it translates the Hebrew 'asham, "guilt-offering").[5]
It is likely that Paul draws the words from this background as a deliberate
allusion, since otherwise the phrase is unnecessarily vague.[6] Some commentators object that such a reference confuses Paul's thought at this
point,[7] although Paul never has been noted for his unmixed metaphors
(see e.g. Rom. 7:1–6; Gal. 4:1–6, 19). But is the charge just? When Paul
says, God sent his Son περὶ ἁμαρτίας "in order that the just requirement
of the law might be fulfilled in us . . .", does he not include the law of the
sin offering as part of "the just requirement of the law"?

I Cor. 5:7 – Paul explicitly states, "Christ, our paschal lamb, has been
sacrificed". It is frequently remarked that "the Paschal victim was not a

---

[1] See D. Hill, *Greek Words and Hebrew Meanings* (Cambridge, 1967), pp. 41–45, and those
cited by Lohse, *op. cit.*, p. 152, n. 4.

[2] Lohse, *op. cit.*, p. 71.

[3] Cf. Kertelge, *op. cit.*, pp. 57 f.

[4] Cf. Kuss, *op. cit.*, pp. 165 f. On the question of whether the Gen. 22 tradition about Abraham offering up Isaac (as sacrifice) has influenced Paul here and elsewhere (Rom. 8:32; Gal.
3:13 f.) see N. A. Dahl, "The Atonement – An Adequate Reward for the Akedah? (Rom.
8:32)", *Neotestamentica et Semitica: Studies in Honour of Matthew Black*, ed. E. E. Ellis and M.
Wilcox (Edinburgh, 1969), pp. 15–29.

[5] The more usual phrase is περὶ τῆς ἁμαρτίας.

[6] C. K. Barrett, *Romans*, p. 156, thinks Paul means nothing more precise than Gal. 1:4 –
Jesus Christ gave himself "for our sins" (ὑπὲρ τῶν ἁμαρτιῶν). But LXX in Ezekiel usually
uses ὑπέρ instead of περί in reference to the sin offering, and Paul may well regard περὶ
ἁμαρτίας and ὑπὲρ τῶν ἁμαρτιῶν as equivalent phrases. In the mind of a Jewish Christian
could "for our sins" have any other reference than to the cult? NEB has, quite rightly,
"Jesus Christ, who sacrified himself for our sins". See further below.

[7] E.g. A. Schlatter, *Gottes Gerechtigkeit* (Stuttgart, 1935), p. 257; O. Michel, *Der Brief an
die Römer* (Göttingen, ¹²1963), p. 190, n. 2; Lohse, *op. cit.*, p. 153, n. 6.

sin-offering or regarded as a means of expiating or removing sins".[1] However, the Passover is already associated with atonement in Ezek. 45:18–22, and this link is firmly forged in the words used by Jesus in the last Supper. He interpreted their Passover meal in terms of "blood poured out (ἐκχυννόμενον) for many". The language is unavoidably sacrificial and signifies atonement.[2] This tendency to run together different meta-phors and descriptions of Jesus' death so that old distinctions are blurred and lost is clearly evident elsewhere in the early Church (I Pet. 1:18 f.; Jn. 1:29), and Paul's language in I Cor. 5:7 and elsewhere hardly suggests that it was otherwise with him.

2 Cor. 5:21 – "God made him into sin, him who knew no sin". The antithesis "made into sin", "sinless", makes it difficult to doubt that Paul had in mind the cult's insistence on clean and unblemished animals for the sacrifices. A more specific allusion to the Day of Atonement's scapegoat is probable.[3] Perhaps there is also an allusion to the suffering servant of Isa. 53;[4] but this should not be seen as a way of lessening the sacrificial allusion since Isa. 53 itself is studded with sacrificial terminology and imagery and the role of the Servant cannot be fully understood apart from the sacri-ficial background of his death.[5]

Similarly the several passages in which Paul uses the phrase "in or through his blood" cannot be understood except as a reference to Christ's death as a sacrifice (Rom. 3:25; 5:9; Eph. 1:7; 2:13; Col. 1:20). Again attempts have been made to avoid the full offensiveness of the allusion.[6] But the emphasis on blood can hardly have come from the tradition of Jesus' death since it was not particularly bloody[7] and must be drawn from the under-standing of Jesus' death in terms of cult sacrifice.[8] Likewise Paul's talk of Jesus' death as "for sins" (Rom. 4:25; 8:3; I Cor. 15:3; Gal. 1:4) or "for us" etc. (Rom. 5:6–8; 8:32; 2 Cor. 5:14 f., 21; Gal. 2:20; 3:13; Eph. 5:2, 25; I Thess. 5:9 f.) probably reflects the same influence, even if, in the latter case, it is mediated through martyr theology.[9]

Granted then that Paul sees Jesus' death as a sacrifice, what light does this throw on Paul's understanding of Jesus' death? The obvious way to answer the question is to inquire into the Old Testament or Jewish theology of sacrifice. But here we run into a considerable problem. For,

---

[1] G. B. Gray, *Sacrifice in the Old Testament* (Oxford, 1925), p. 397.

[2] J. Jeremias, *The Eucharistic Words of Jesus* (³1960, ET London, 1966), pp. 222 ff.

[3] Windisch, *op. cit.*, p. 198.

[4] Cullmann, *op. cit.*, p. 76; J. Jeremias, *The Servant of God* (rev. ET London, 1965), p. 97, n. 441.

[5] Taylor, *op. cit.*, p. 190; M. Barth, *Was Christ's Death a Sacrifice?* (Edinburgh, 1961), pp. 9 f.

[6] See, for example, those referred to by Davies, *op. cit.*, pp. 232 ff.

[7] E. Schweizer, *Erniedrigung und Erhöhung bei Jesus und seinen Nachfolgern* (Zürich, ²1962), p. 74 (6e).

[8] So e.g., Taylor, *op. cit.*, pp. 63 f.; Davies, *op. cit.*, p. 236; Lohse, *op. cit.*, pp. 138 f.; Barth, *op. cit.*, p. 7; contra Delling, *op. cit.*, pp. 89 f.

[9] H. Riesenfeld, ὑπέρ, *TDNT*, VIII, pp. 509 ff.; cf. Delling, *op. cit.*, p. 87.

as is well known, there is no clear rationale in Judaism concerning sacrifice. No doubt the sacrifices were very meaningful to the pious and penitent worshipper in Israel.[1] But just what the essence of atonement was for the Jew remains an unsolved riddle. "It seems necessary to admit", sums up M. Barth, "that we do not know or understand what the Old Testament and 'Judaism' really believed and taught about the mystery of expiating sacrifice".[2]

On the other hand, in view of the passages cited above, particularly Rom. 3:25; 8:3 and 2 Cor. 5:21, it seems likely that Paul himself had a fairly well defined theory of sacrifice. Moreover, whereas rabbinic thought had begun to play down the importance of sacrifice and to recognize other means of expiation,[3] Paul seems to retain an important place for the category of sacrifice in describing the effect of Jesus' death.[4] This too suggests that, however obscure Jewish theology was, Paul himself could give a fairly clear exposition of atoning sacrifice. One possible way forward is to read back Paul's understanding of sacrifice by correlating the two conclusions we have already reached – Paul thinks of Jesus dying both as representative man and in terms of cultic sacrifice – and by examining the sacrificial ritual in their light. The exercise is necessarily speculative, but it may help to illuminate Paul's understanding of Jesus' death.

(a) First, we note that the *sin* offering, like Jesus' death in Rom. 8:3, was intended to deal with sin. In some sense or other, the ritual of killing the sacrifice removed the sin from the unclean offerer. Now it is true that the sin offering dealt only with inadvertent sins – according to Old Testament ritual there was no sacrifice possible for deliberate sins. But at the same time the fact that a death was necessary to compensate for even an inadvertent sin signifies the seriousness of even these sins in the cult. The others were too serious for any compensation to be made. In such cases the sinner's *own* life was forfeit – no other life could expiate his sin.[5]

(b) Second, as Jesus in his death represented man in his fallenness, so presumably Paul saw the sin-offering as in some way *representing* the sinner in his sin. This would probably be the significance for Paul of that part of the ritual where the offerer laid his hand on the beast's head. Thereby the sinner identified himself with the beast, or at least indicated that the beast in some sense represented him;[6] that is, represented him *as*

[1] H. H. Rowley, *Worship in Ancient Israel* (London, 1967), chapter 4.
[2] Barth, op. cit., p. 13. See also G. F. Moore, *Judaism* (Cambridge, 1927), Vol. I, p. 500; E. Sjöberg, *Gott und die Sünder* (Stuttgart, 1938), pp. 175, 256 ff.; Davies, op. cit., p. 235; Lohse, op. cit., p. 21; G. von Rad, *Old Testament Theology*, Vol. I (1957, ET Edinburgh, 1962), pp. 251–55; R. de Vaux, *Studies in Old Testament Sacrifice* (Cardiff, 1964), p. 91.
[3] Davies, op. cit., 253–59; Lohse, op. cit., pp. 21 ff.
[4] "In an age of spiritualization and moralization of cultic terms, Paul is conspicuous by his insistence upon the message that only sacrifice and blood make pure and righteous" (Barth, op. cit., p. 33).
[5] See most recently de Vaux, op. cit., pp. 94 f.
[6] G. Nagel, "Sacrifices", *Vocabulary of the Bible*, ed. J. J. von Allmen ([2]1956, ET London,

sinner, so that his sin was somehow identified with it, and its life became forfeit as result – just as Christ, taking the initiative from the other side, identified himself with men in their fallenness (Rom. 8:3), was made sin (2 Cor. 5:21).

It is by no means widely held that this was the generally understood meaning of the act. The laying of a hand on the head of the beast is usually given a far less significant role – simply indicating ownership, or signifying the readiness of the offerer to surrender that which belongs to him.[1] I am no expert in this field, but this conclusion does seem to me to be rather too sophisticated. For one thing, it hardly seems an adequate explanation of the importance attached to this action in the detailed instructions of Lev. 4. For another, if that was all the action meant we would have expected it to be repeated in all sacrifices, non-bloody ones as well; whereas, in fact, it only occurs in the case of sacrifices involving blood. Again, where the same action is used outside the sacrificial ritual, identification seems to be the chief rationale. Thus, Num. 27:18, 23; Deut. 34:9 – Moses lays hands on Joshua thereby imparting some of Moses' authority to him, that is, conveying some of himself in his role as leader to Joshua, so that Joshua becomes in a sense another Moses. Num. 8:10 – the people lay their hands on the Levites so that the Levites become their representatives before the Lord, in particular taking the place of their first-born. Finally, Lev. 24:14, where hands are laid on a blasphemer prior to his execution by stoning. The whole people perform the execution, but only those who witnessed the blasphemy lay their hands on his head. This suggests that they do so to identify themselves with the blasphemer insofar as by hearing the blasphemy they have been caught up in his sin.[2]

The only place where the significance of laying hands on an animal in cultic ritual is explained is Lev. 16:21, where the High Priest lays both his hands on the second goat in the Day of Atonement ceremony – thereby explicitly laying the sins of the people on the head of the goat.[3] Of course, it was the first goat which was sacrificed as a sin offering, whereas the second goat was not ritually killed, only driven out into the desert. But were the two layings on of hands seen as quite distinct and different in significance? Could it not be that the two goats were seen as part of the one ritual, representing more fully and pictorially what one goat could not? Perhaps part of the significance of the Day of Atonement ritual was that the physical removal of the sins of the people out of the camp by the second goat demonstrated what the sin offering normally did with

---

[1] See particularly W. Eichrodt, *Theology of the Old Testament*, Vol. I (⁶1958, ET London, 1961), pp. 165 f.; de Vaux, *op. cit.*, pp. 28, 63.

[2] Cf. D. Daube, *The New Testament and Rabbinic Judaism* (London, 1956), pp. 226 f.

[3] Cf. M. Noth, *Leviticus* (ET London, 1965), who speaks of "the transference to the animal of the guilt, conceived in some quite solid sense" (pp. 38 f.).

1958), p. 379; J. S. Whale, *Victor and Victim* (Cambridge, 1960), pp. 49 f.; Rowley, *op. cit.*, p. 133.

their sins anyway. Sin offering and scapegoat were two pictures of the one reality. Rom. 8:3 and 2 Cor. 5:21 certainly suggest that Paul had such a composite picture of Jesus' death as sacrifice.

Against this view, that the sin offering was thought to represent the offerer, it is sometimes argued that if the beast became laden with the offerer's sin it would be counted as unclean and so could not be used in sacrifice.[1] But does not this objection miss the point? The animal must be holy, wholly clean precisely so that priest and sinner may be certain that its death is *not its own*, that it does not die for any uncleanness of its own. Only a perfect beast can represent sinful man; only the death of a perfect animal can make atonement for imperfect man.

Alternatively the argument is put that the sin offering could not embody sin since the priests ate the meat left over from some of the sin offerings. Since they could not eat contaminated flesh, the sacrifice could not have been contaminated by sin.[2] But again this seems to miss a key point – viz. that the life of the animal was regarded as its blood (Lev. 17:10–12; Deut. 12:23). The priests did not of course eat the blood. On the contrary, the blood was wholly used up in the ritual: indeed, the blood played a more important role in the sin offering than in any other sacrifice;[3] and the sprinkling of the blood "was regarded as the essential and decisive act of the offering up";[4] Lev. 17:11 – "it is the blood, that is the life, that makes expiation". Thus, since the life *is* the blood, so the *life* of the sacrifice was wholly used up in the ritual. The equivalence between the life of the man and the life of the beast lay in the *blood* of the victim, not in the whole victim. And, since the blood was wholly used up, the use made of the carcase did not affect its role as sin offering; that role was completed in the blood ritual.

(*c*) Third, if we extend the line of reasoning in the light of Rom. 8:3 and 2 Cor. 5:14, 21, the conclusion follows that Paul saw the death of the sacrificial animal as the death of the sinner *qua* sinner, that is, the destruction of his sin. The manner in which the sin offering dealt with sin was by its death. The sacrificial animal, identified with the offerer in his sin, had to be destroyed in order to destroy the sin which it embodied. The sprinkling, smearing and pouring away of the sacrificial blood in the sight of God indicated that the life was wholly destroyed, and with it the sin of the sinner.

One can hardly fail to recognize what we may call the sacrificial chiasmus:

By the sacrifice the *sinner* was made *pure* and *lived free of that sin;*
By the sacrifice the *pure* animal *died.*

[1] Eichrodt, *op. cit.*, p. 165, n. 2; Nagel, *op. cit.*, p. 378.
[2] Eichrodt, *op. cit.*, p. 165, n. 2; de Vaux, *op. cit.*, p. 94.
[3] R. de Vaux, *Ancient Israel* (ET London, 1961), p. 419; *Sacrifice*, p. 92.
[4] A. Büchler, *Studies in Sin and Atonement* (New York, 1928), pp. 418 f.

nd we can hardly fail to fill out the rest of the second line by adding: y the sacrifice the *pure* animal was made *impure* and *died for that sin* – y its death destroying the sin. That this is wholly in accordance with aul's thought is made clear by 2 Cor. 5:21, the clearest expression of 1e sacrificial chiasmus:

"For our sake God made the *sinless one* into *sin* so that in him *we* might become the *righteousness* of God."

o too Rom. 8:3:

God "condemned *sin* in the flesh (of *Jesus*) in order that the *just requirement of the law* might be fulfilled in *us*."

o too Gal. 3:13, although here the metaphor is not directly sacrificial:

"*Christ* redeemed us from the *curse* of the law having become a *curse* for *us*".

In short, *to say that Jesus died as representative of fallen man and to say that esus died as sacrifice for the sins of men is for Paul to say the same thing.* His eath was the end of fallen man, the destruction of man as sinner. But only hose who, like the offerer of old, identify themselves with the sacrifice, 1ay know the other half of the chiasmus, the life of Christ beyond the eath of sin, the righteousness of God in Christ.

III   *Conclusions and Clarifications*

This recognition of the representative and sacrificial character of Jesus' leath in Paul's theology seems to me to confirm Dr Morris in his central ffirmations about the atonement over against those who would weaken ne or other element. "If it is true that their death is made his death, it is lso true that his death is made their death;" this is how he sums up his reatment of the death of Christ in Paul in his most recent work on the ubject.[1] On the other hand our exposition suggests that some qualifica-ion, or better, sharper definition, is necessary at two points on which Dr. Morris strongly insists. I refer to the words "propitiation" and "substitu-ion".

(*a*) *Propitiation.* Should we translate ἱλαστήριον in Rom. 3:25 as "pro-itiation" or "expiation"? Those familiar with Dr Morris's work will eed no introduction to the debate on this question and I certainly cannot nter into it here. Suffice it to say that the studies of Dr Morris, R. R. Nicole and D. Hill[2] make unavoidable at least some retreat from C. H.

[1] Morris, *Cross*, p. 224.
[2] L. Morris, "The Use of ἱλάσκεσθαι, etc. in Biblical Greek", *ExpT* 62 (1950–51), pp. 227–33; *Apostolic Preaching*, chapters 4–5; R. R. Nicole, "C. H. Dodd and the Doctrine of Propitiation", *WTJ* 17 (1955), pp. 117–57; Hill, *op. cit.*, pp. 23–36.

Dodd's rejection of all propitiatory significance for the ἰλάσκεσθαι word group in the LXX.[1] Dr. Morris's reminder that the context must be considered as well as the individual usage is particularly important.

Nevertheless, in view of the larger understanding of Jesus' death which we have gained above, and without neglecting the context, "expiation" does seem to be the better translation for Rom. 3:25. The fact is that for Paul God is the subject of the action; it is God who provided Jesus as a ἰλαστήριον. And if God is the subject, then the obvious object is sin or the sinner. To argue that God provided Jesus as a means of propitiating God is certainly possible, but less likely I think. For one thing, regularly in the Old Testament the immediate object of the action denoted by the Hebrew *kipper* is the removal of *sin* – either by purifying the person or object, or by wiping out the sin; the act of atonement "cancels", "purges away" sin. It is not God who is the object of this atonement, nor the wrath of God, but the sin which calls forth the wrath of God.[2] So for example, 2 Kings 5:18: Naaman prays, "May *Yahweh* expiate (ἰλάσεται) your *servant*"; Ps. 24:11: "For the honour of thy name, O Lord, expiate (ἰλάσῃ) my *wickedness*"; Ecclus. 5:5–6:

> "Do not be so confident of pardon (ἐξιλασμοῦ)
>   that you sin again and again.
> Do not say, 'His mercy is so great,
>   he will pardon my sins, however many' " (ἐξιλάσεται).

And for another, if we have indeed gained an insight into Paul's understanding of the rationale of sacrifice, then it follows that for Paul the way in which Christ's death cancels out man's sin is by destroying it – the death of the representative sacrifice is the destruction of the sin of those represented, because it is the destruction of man's sinful flesh, of man as sinner. NEB therefore correctly translates Rom. 3:25: "God designed him to be the means of expiating sin by his sacrificial death".

On the other hand, we must go on to recognize that a secondary and consequential result of the destruction of a man's sin in the sin offering is that he no longer experiences the wrath of God which his sin called forth. At this point we must give weight to Dr Morris's reminder that this section of Romans follows immediately upon the exposition of God's wrath "against all ungodliness and wickedness of men" (Rom. 1:18). Almost inevitably therefore, the action of God which makes righteousness possible for men does involve the thought that wrath need no longer apply to them. As C. K. Barrett notes: "It would be wrong to neglect the fact that expiation has, as it were, the effect of propitiation: the sin that

---

[1] C. H. Dodd, "Atonement", *The Bible and the Greeks* (London, 1935), pp. 82–95, reprinted from *JTS* 32 (1931).
[2] "The subject of the ἰλάσκεσθαι is not man, but Christ and in him God, and he who receives the ἰλασμός is not God but man" (Schlatter, *op. cit.*, p. 145). See also Dodd (as n. 1), and F. Büchsel, *TDNT*, III, pp. 314 ff., 320 ff.

might have excited God's wrath is expiated (at God's will) and therefore no longer does so".[1]

But we must be clear what we mean by this. As Rom. 1:18–32 shows, God's wrath means a process willed by God – the outworking of the destructive consequences of sin, destructive for the wholeness of man in his relationships.[2] Jesus' death therefore does not propitiate God's wrath in the sense that it turns an angry God into one who forgives; all are agreed on that. But in addition, it is not possible to say, as some do, that Jesus' death propitiates God's wrath in the sense of turning it away. The destructive consequences of sin do not suddenly evaporate. On the contrary, they are focused in fuller intensity on the sin – that is, on fallen humanity in Jesus. In Jesus on the cross was focused not only man's sin, but the wrath which follows upon that sin. The destructive consequences of sin are such that if they were allowed to work themselves out fully in man himself they would destroy him as a spiritual being. This process of destruction is speeded up in the case of Jesus, the representative man, the ἱλαστήριον, and destroys him. The wrath of God destroys the sin by letting the full destructive consequences of sin work themselves out and exhaust themselves in Jesus.

This means also that we must be careful in describing Jesus' death as penal, as a suffering the penalty for sin. If we have understood Paul's theology of sacrifice aright the primary thought is the *destruction* of the malignant, poisonous organism of sin. Any thought of *punishment* is secondary. The wrath of God in the case of Jesus' death is not so much retributive as preventative.[3] A closer parallel is perhaps vaccination. In vaccination germs are introduced into a healthy body in order that by destroying these germs the body will build up its strength. So we might say the germ of sin was introduced into Jesus, the only one "healthy"/ whole enough to let that sin run its full course. The "vaccination" seemed to fail, because Jesus died. But it did not fail, for he rose again; and his new humanity is "germ-resistant", sin resistant. It is this new humanity in the power of the Spirit which he offers to share with men.

(*b*) *Substitution.* As we have to seek a sharper definition of ἱλαστήριον than "propitiation" affords, so that of the two words "expiation" seems more able to bear that fuller meaning, so we must examine "substitution" to check whether it is the best word to describe Paul's theology of the death of Christ. For many "substitution" is perhaps the key word in any attempt to sum up Paul's thought at this point. It is significant that D. E.

---

[1] Barrett, *Romans*, p. 78.
[2] I refer particularly to the unpublished doctoral dissertation of S. H. Travis, *Divine Retribution in the Thought of Paul* (Cambridge University, 1970). See also Morris, *Apostolic Preaching*, pp. 161–66; Whiteley, *The Theology of St. Paul* (Oxford, 1964), pp. 61–72.
[3] For broader considerations on this issue see H. H. Farmer, "The Notion of Desert Bad and Good", *HJ*, 41 (1943), pp. 347–54; C. F. D. Moule, "The Christian Understanding of Forgiveness", *Theology* 71 (1968), pp. 435–43.

H. Whiteley's whole discussion of the death of Christ in Paul's theology is framed with reference to this question (with chiefly negative conclusions).[1] Both Dr Morris and D. Hill argue from 4 Macc. 6:29; 17:21 that the idea of "substitution" is involved in the thought of Rom. 3:24 f. – that for Paul Jesus' death was substitutionary.[2] And W. Pannenberg gives the word "substitution" a central role in his exposition of the meaning of Jesus' death.[3] So too for Dr Morris 2 Cor. 5:14, 21 can hardly be understood except in substitutionary terms – "the death of the One took the place of the death of the many".[4] This is a very arguable case, and it certainly gains strength from the theology of sacrifice outlined above – for there it would be quite appropriate to speak of the death of the sacrifice as a substitutionary death.

Nevertheless, although "substitution" expresses an important aspect of Paul's theology of the atonement, I am not sure that Paul would have been happy with it or that it is the best single word to serve as the key definition of that theology. The trouble is that "substitution" has two failings as a definition: it is too one-sided a concept; and it is too narrow in its connotation.

"Substitution" is too *one-sided* because it depicts Jesus as substituting for man in the face of God's wrath. But we do no justice to Paul's view of Jesus' death unless we emphasize with *equal or greater weight* that in his death Jesus also "substituted" *for God* in the face of man's sin – "God was in Christ reconciling the world to himself" (2 Cor. 5:19). In other words, "substitution" shares the defects of "propitiation" as a description of Jesus' death. It still tends to conjure up pagan ideas of Jesus' standing in man's place and pleading with an angry God (and it must be said that the usual illustrations of popular evangelism only confirm that picture). "Substitution" does not give sufficient prominence to the point of primary significance – that God was the subject:[5] God provided Jesus as the ἱλαστήριον; God sent his Son as a sin-offering; God passed judgement on sin in the flesh; God was in Christ reconciling the world to himself. Our earlier exposition of Paul's theology of Jesus as Man suggests that a much more appropriate word is "representation": in his death Jesus represented not just man to God but also God to man. And while "substitution" is an appropriate description of Paul's theology of sacrifice, it is perhaps more definite than our knowledge of Paul's thought and of the sacrificial ritual permits. Whereas, in discussing Paul's view of sacrifice, "representation",

---

[1] Whiteley, *Paul*, pp. 130–48.

[2] Morris, *Apostolic Preaching*, p. 173; Hill, *op. cit.*, pp. 75 f. J. Jeremias, *The Central Message of the New Testament* (London, 1965), p. 36, also uses the word "substitution" to describe Paul's theology.

[3] W. Pannenberg, *Jesus, God and Man* (1964, ET London, 1968), pp. 258–69.

[4] Morris, *Cross*, p. 220.

[5] Cf. Taylor, *op. cit.*, p. 75: "*God in Christ.* No thought is more fundamental than this to St. Paul's thinking".

the identification of the offerer with his sacrifice, was a word we could hardly avoid. So here, "representation" gives all the positive sense of "substitution" (a positive sense I by no means deny) which the context requires, while at the same time bringing in the other side of the equation which "substitution" tends to exclude.

"Substitution" is also too *narrow* a word. It smacks too much of individualism to represent Paul's thought adequately. It is true, of course, that Paul can and does say, Christ "loved me and gave himself for me" (Gal. 2:20). But his more typical thought is wider. For as we have seen, in Paul's theology Jesus represents *man*, not just a man, on the cross. Christ died as man, representative man. As Adam represents man so that his fallenness is theirs, so Jesus represents fallen men so that his death is theirs. The point is that he died not *instead of* men, but *as* man; "he died for all, therefore all have died" (2 Cor. 5:14). That is to say, fallen men do not escape death – any more than they escape wrath; they die. Either they die their own death without identifying themselves with Christ; or else they identify themselves with Christ so that they die in his death – his death works out in their flesh. And only insofar as it does so do they live (Rom. 7:24 f.; 8:10–13, 17; 2 Cor. 4:10–12; Phil. 3:10 f.; Col. 1:24).[1] Either way fallen humanity cannot escape death – resurrection life, the life of the Spirit, lies on the other side of death, his death. Jesus' death was the death of the old humanity, in order that his resurrection might be the beginning of a new humanity, no longer contaminated by sin and no longer subject to death. In short, Jesus dies not so much as substitute in place of men, but as man, representative man.

As we implied at the beginning of the second section, an emphasis on Paul's theology of Jesus as representative man and of his death as sacrifice for sin increases the strangeness of Paul's gospel to 20th century man. But if we can only do justice to Paul's theology by highlighting these aspects of it, then this is unavoidable. Indeed it is necessary to face up squarely to this strangeness and not baulk at it, for only by following out the warp and woof of Paul's thought will we begin to understand its overall pattern; and only by thinking through his mind, so far as we can, will we be able to reinterpret his thought to modern man without distorting its character and central emphases.[2] I do not suggest that that reinterpretation is easy, and to do so at this point requires a much fuller investigation of the other side of Jesus' death – the life of the Spirit (Rom. 8:1 ff.), the lifegiving Spirit (I Cor. 15:45). But that is another story.

[1] Cf. Delling, *op. cit.*, pp. 91 f.; R. C. Tannehill, *Dying and Rising with Christ* (Berlin, 1966).
[2] For examples of such an attempt see J. Knox, *The Death of Christ* (London, 1959), chapter 7, and Moule (p. 139, n. 3).

CHAPTER IX

THE OBEDIENCE OF CHRIST IN THE THEOLOGY OF THE EARLY CHURCH

RICHARD N. LONGENECKER

A CARDINAL FEATURE IN THE CHRISTIAN DOCTRINE OF RECONCILIATION is the theme of the obedience of Christ. Many passages in the canonical Gospels and Epistles depict or allude to our Lord's obedient response to the Father's will. The Fourth Gospel, for example, portrays him as at every turn able to say, "I always do those things that please him";[1] and the writer to the Hebrews picks up the Psalmist's confession and writes it large over Jesus' entire ministry, "Lo, I come . . . to do your will, O God".[2] Yet the nouns "obedience" (ὑπακοή) and "obedient" (ὑπήκοος) in description of Christ appear only three times in the New Testament and a mere handful of times in the extant literature of the earlier Fathers.[3]

It is the thesis of this brief article that by tracing out the occurrences of the nouns ὑπακοή and ὑπήκοος with reference to Jesus Christ in the NT and the patristic materials of the first four centuries, interpreting them with regard to their respective contexts, and relating them to cognate expressions within their respective bodies of material, two matters in regard to the theme of the obedience of Christ in the theology of the early Church come to the fore. In the first place, the fulness of the Church's thought as to Christ's redemptive activity and person is better able to be appreciated. Secondly, something of the development of revelational and speculative understanding as to this theme within the early Church is exhibited: developing, I suggest, from an almost exclusive stress on Christ's "passive obedience" to a treatment that includes an emphasis upon his "active obedience" as well, then to considerations of his perfected filial obedience, and finally to discussions of the obedience of Christ which are set in contexts that are dominantly ontological in character. This is not to propose that the later developments entirely displaced the earlier stages. It is only to point out that there can be noted distinctive emphases as one

---

[1] Jn. 8:29; cf. 4:34, 5:30, 6:38.
[2] Heb. 10:7, quoting Ps. 40:7 f. (MT = 40:8 f.; LXX = 39:8 f.).
[3] The nouns are also, of course, used with respect to Christians being obedient to God e.g. Rom. 6:16 ff.; Acts 7:39), obedient to Christ (e.g., II Cor. 10:5), obedient to an apostle (II Cor. 2:9; Phlm. 21), and in a state of obedience (e.g., Rom. 15:18, 16:19; II Cor. 7:15, 10:6 I Pet. 1:2, 14). Likewise, the verb ὑπακούω appears a number of times in injunctions as to the proper response of believers.

ioves through the various discussions of the obedience of Christ in the
IT and the early patristic writings – emphases which serve to express
omething of the fulness of the early Church's understanding of the re-
emptive ministry of Christ, and which exhibit to some extent a development of thought from the more functional to the more ontological
eatment of his work and person.

I   His Passive Obedience

Possibly the earliest extant portion of Christian literature is the hymn
f Phil. 2:6–11, incorporated by Paul into his exhortation to converts
: Philippi.[1] Climaxing the first half of that hymn, and undoubtedly the
ocal point of its *katabasis* description, is the statement of 2:8: "He became
bedient unto death" ($\gamma\varepsilon\nu\acute{o}\mu\varepsilon\nu o\varsigma$ $\acute{\upsilon}\pi\acute{\eta}\kappa oo\varsigma$ $\mu\acute{\varepsilon}\chi\rho\iota$ $\theta\alpha\nu\acute{\alpha}\tau o\upsilon$) – which, it
:ems, Paul highlighted by his own emotive interjection, "even death on a
ross!" ($\theta\alpha\nu\acute{\alpha}\tau o\upsilon$ $\delta\grave{\varepsilon}$ $\sigma\tau\alpha\upsilon\rho o\tilde{\upsilon}$). The expression "did not snatch at equality
vith God" of v. 6 "contains a reminiscence of the First Adam, who, in
isobedience to the Almighty, yielded to the temptation to 'be as God'
3en. iii. 5)";[2] and the phrases "taking the form of a servant" of v. 7 and
unto death" of v. 8 set the hymn "in the context of the thought of
ilfilment orientated to Is. 53".[3] The recognition of such a context is
nportant for the full explication of the varied nuances inherent in the
:atement "became obedient unto death". Significant for our purpose
ere, however, is the elemental fact that the theme of the obedience of
Christ, in what is possibly the earliest extant portion of Christian litera-
ure, is expressed in terms of obedience "unto death" ($\mu\acute{\varepsilon}\chi\rho\iota$ $\theta\alpha\nu\acute{\alpha}\tau o\upsilon$).
"he hymn indeed begins by asserting that "the divine nature was his from
he first" (NEB), but its emphasis in at least the *katabasis* section is on the
unctional aspects of Christ's humiliation and obedience – and in detailing
hat obedience, it lays almost exclusive emphasis upon Christ's death.

It is Christ's death, of course, that is the prominent factor in all of the
VT discussions of man's redemption from sin and reconciliation to God.[4]
And throughout the New Testament, that death is portrayed both in
erms of God's love and in terms of Christ's willing obedience – never

[1] On Phil. 2:6–11 as an early Christian hymn, see the seminal article by E. Lohmeyer,
'Kyrios Jesus. Eine Untersuchung zu Phil. 2:5–11", *Sitzungsberichte der Heidelberger Akademie
'er Wissenschaften*, XVIII (1927–28), which was republished as a separate monograph in
961 by Heidelberg Universitätsverlag. The most recent and exhaustive treatment of Phil.
:6–11, with almost complete bibliographical data, can be found in the works of R. P.
Martin, *An Early Christian Confession: Philippians II, 5–11 in Recent Interpretation* (London,
960) and *Carmen Christi* (Cambridge, 1968).
[2] H. A. A. Kennedy, *The Theology of the Epistles* (London, 1919), p. 159.
[3] G. Kittel, *TDNT*, I, p. 225.
[4] Cf. J. Denney, *The Death of Christ* (London, 1902), *passim; idem, The Christian Doctrine
of Reconciliation* (London, 1917), pp. 233–85.

as an accident, a matter of logical necessity, or the culmination of some arbitrarily arranged plan. The Fourth Evangelist, for example, commenting on Jesus' words that the Son of Man must be "lifted up", explains: "For God so loved the world that he gave his one and only Son";[1] and Paul declared that "God shows his love for us in that while we were yet sinners Christ died for us".[2] It was the Father's great love that motivated the sacrifice of Christ on the cross. But it was no less love on the part of the Son, as Paul, for example, points out in a number of intensely personal expressions: "Christ loved us and gave himself for us";[3] "Christ loved the church and gave himself for her";[4] "the Son of God loved me and gave himself for me".[5] Likewise, that redemptive death was rooted in the willing obedience of Christ himself. He knew, at least from Caesarea Philippi on, what lay ahead in his earthly ministry,[6] and he resolutely moved toward that climactic act with a willingness to accomplish the divine purpose.[7] This is clearly intimated in such affirmations as: "I have a baptism to be baptized with, and how I am constrained until it is accomplished!"[8] and, "I lay down my life that I may take it again. No one takes it from me, but I lay it down of my own accord. I have power to lay it down, and I have power to take it again. This charge I received from my Father".[9] There is never any suggestion in the NT accounts that the Father and the Son were in any way in opposition to each other in this regard, either in that the Son was wresting forgiveness from an unloving Father or that the Father was demanding a sacrifice from an unwilling Son. Divine love and willing obedience have been nowhere more in evidence than on that horrendous day at Calvary.

But love and obedience, apart from an existing need and an objective purpose, are concepts devoid of content. It is therefore necessary to ask regarding the need upon which that divine love was focused and the purpose for which Christ's obedience was expressed. One clue is supplied by Gal. 3:10–14, where Paul speaks of men being under condemnation and Christ having become a curse for us (γενόμενος ὑπὲρ ἡμῶν κατάρα). Another is in Rom. 3:21–31, where the apostle portrays all men as sinners who fall short of God's glory and Jesus Christ as the "atoning sacrifice" (ἱλαστήριον) that fully satisfies the just demands of a holy and righteous God.[10] In both passages, the dual features of man's desperate need and God's righteous justice come to the fore. In these passages, in fact, Paul has put his finger on two additional factors that motivated our Lord's crucifixion, and therefore it can be said that at the cross there was the convergence of (1) divine love, (2) divine justice, (3) Christ's willing and sacrificial obedience, and (4) man's desperate need.

[1] Jn. 3:16.   [2] Rom. 5:8.   [3] Eph. 5:2.   [4] Eph. 5:25.   [5] Gal. 2:20.
[6] Mk. 8:31 par., 10:45 par.; cf. 2:20 par.
[7] Note the expression "he offered himself" of Heb. 9:14.
[8] Lk. 12:50.   [9] Jn. 10:17 f.
[10] Cf. L. L. Morris, *The Apostolic Preaching of the Cross* (London, ³1965), pp. 144–213.

This is what has been called by older theologians the "passive obedience" of Christ. In that act, God was proclaimed both "just and justifier" ($\delta i\kappa\alpha\iota\sigma\nu$ $\kappa\alpha i$ $\delta\iota\kappa\alpha\iota\sigma\tilde{\nu}\nu\tau\alpha$),[1] Christ expressed the epitome of filial obedience and culminated the work of redemption,[2] and the believer was declared free from condemnation and reconciled to God.[3] It was the supreme act of love and obedience, which calls for – as Paul points out in his application of the Church's hymn in Philippians 2 – a similar response in the daily lives of those who have been so redeemed and reconciled.

II   His Active Obedience

The theme of the obedience of Christ, however, while epitomized in our Lord's sacrificial death, is not exhausted in a consideration of that act. The declared purpose of Jesus included a fulfilling of all the obligations and demands of the Mosaic law.[4] And Paul suggests this aspect of the redemptive ministry in Rom. 5:19, contrasting the disobedience of Adam with the obedience of Christ. Not only was "one man's trespass" countered by "one man's act of righteousness", as Rom. 5:18 declares with reference to his passive obedience, but "one man's disobedience" was rectified by "one man's obedience," as v. 19 goes on to say in regard to what theologians have called his "active obedience".[5] In that active obedience, Christ stood in the place of humble submission to the Mosaic law and fulfilled all of its obligations, thereby presenting before the Father a positive righteousnes for all who by faith take their stand "in him". "He was", as Karl Barth expressed it, "the only one who completely and genuinely stood in that place; he was *the* Jew".[6] Or, as the apostle Paul

---

[1] Rom. 3:26.

[2] Note Jesus' cry, "It is finished!" (Jn. 19:30).

[3] See Gal. 3:13 f.; II Cor. 5:21; Col. 1:20–22, 2:14 f.; Heb. 2:14 f.

[4] Mt. 5:17 f.; cf. also 3:15. On $\pi\lambda\eta\rho\tilde{\omega}\sigma\alpha\iota$ in Mt. 5:17 as meaning "to consummate" or "fulfil by bearing the obligation of" the law, rather than "to confirm the validity of" the law (for which Paul used $i\sigma\tau\acute{\alpha}\nu\sigma\mu\epsilon\nu$ in Rom. 3:31), see J. Jocz, *The Jewish People and Jesus Christ* (London, 1949), p. 26; D. Daube, *The New Testament and Rabbinic Judaism* (London, 1956), pp. 60 f.; C. F. D. Moule, "Fulfilment-Words in the New Testament: Use and Abuse", *NTS*, 14 (1968), pp. 293–320. G. Vos was somewhat overly optimistic, but nonetheless quite right, when in 1926 he wrote: "It may now be considered as settled that the words 'not to destroy the law or the prophets' speak not of an idealizing perfection, but of an actual realization of the law in conduct. The context allows of no other exegesis" (*The Self-Disclosure of Jesus* (Grand Rapids, 1956 repr.), p. 19).

[5] Paul also suggests a broader understanding of Christ's redemptive activity in Rom. 5:10 – just nine verses earlier – when he says: "For if being enemies we were reconciled to God through the death of his son, much more being reconciled we shall be saved by his life" ($\sigma\omega\theta\eta\sigma\acute{\sigma}\mu\epsilon\theta\alpha$ $\dot{\epsilon}\nu$ $\tau\tilde{\eta}$ $\zeta\omega\tilde{\eta}$ $\alpha\dot{\upsilon}\tau\sigma\tilde{\upsilon}$). The phrase "by his life" certainly has reference to our Lord's risen life upon which the new life of the believer depends, as most commentators are quick to point out; but it may also include an allusion to his earthly life of obedience, which is presented to the Father on behalf of all who are Christ's and upon which the believer's positive righteousness before God depends.

[6] K. Barth, *Christ and Adam* (Edinburgh, 1956), p. 33.

himself put it, he was "born of a woman, born under the law" – that is, truly human and bearing both the obligations and the curse of the law – "in order to redeem those under the law, that we might receive the full rights of sons".[1]

Paul's thought also seems to run along this line in his use of the expression ἐκ or διὰ πίστεως Ἰησοῦ Χριστοῦ, which is usually taken as an objective genitive and translated "through faith in Jesus Christ". Of late, however, some interpreters have sought to understand Paul's thought here by reference to the usage of the Hebrew word 'emunah in the OT and to suggest that just as 'emunah meant both "faithfulness" and "faith", the former when ascribed to God and the latter with reference to man, so Paul employed πίστις and its adjective πιστός for both the divine faithfulness and man's response of faith.[2] While it is true that the apostle spoke and wrote Greek, his words were always coloured by their Hebrew associations. It is therefore likely that in certain instances in his letters the phrase πίστεως Ἰησοῦ Χριστοῦ should be understood as "the faithfulness of Jesus Christ", the God-man. And if this be true, it means that Paul thought of the believer's justification, righteousness and access before God as based upon Christ's perfect obedience during his earthly life to the will of God expressed in the Mosaic law, as well as his sacrifice on the cross.

This is not to say that in every Pauline instance of πίστις the idea of divine faithfulness is to be understood, for certainly πίστις, its adjective πιστός, and especially its verb πιστεύω often signify human trust and commitment.[3] But it is to advocate that in the following verses, at least, the expression πίστεως Ἰησοῦ Χριστοῦ is best understood as "the faithfulness of Jesus Christ" through which comes righteousness and justification to all who respond by faith:

1. Rom. 3:22, "the righteousness of God [is manifested] through the faithfulness of Jesus Christ (διὰ πίστεως Ἰησοῦ Χριστοῦ) to all who believe."

---

[1] Gal. 4:4 f. While Christ's bearing the curse of the law in his death is stressed in Gal. 3:10–14, in the context of Gal. 3:22–4:5 the expression "born under the law" suggests a broader reference: Christ's bearing the full obligation of the law, in life as well as in death, so that men may live as sons of God without being under that παιδαγωγός (3:24 f.) or subject to what Paul calls τὰ στοιχεῖα τοῦ κόσμου (4:3).

[2] Cf. A. G. Hebert, "'Faithfulness' and 'Faith'", Theology, 58 (1955), pp. 373–79; T. F. Torrance, "One Aspect of the Biblical Conception of Faith", ExpT, 68 (1957), pp. 111–14; R. N. Longenecker, Paul, Apostle of Liberty (New York, 1964), pp. 149–152. Conversely, see C. F. D. Moule, "The Biblical Conception of 'Faith'", ExpT, 68 (1957), p. 157. Note, however, the pattern in Paul in this regard with reference to God: Rom. 3:3, "the faithfulness of God" (τὴν πίστιν τοῦ θεοῦ); I Cor. 1:9, 10:13, "God is faithful" (πιστὸς ὁ θεός); I Thess. 5:24, "faithful is the one who calls you" (πιστὸς ὁ καλῶν ὑμᾶς); and II Thess. 3:3, "the Lord is faithful" (πιστὸς δέ ἐστιν ὁ κύριος) – which pattern holds true as well in the LXX, the rest of the NT, and the writings of the Greek Fathers.

[3] E.g., Rom. 4:14, 16; I Cor. 15:14, 17; II Cor. 1:24.

2. Gal. 2:16, "knowing that a man is not justified by the works of the law but by the faithfulness of Christ Jesus (διὰ πίστεως Χριστοῦ Ἰησοῦ), even we have believed in Jesus Christ in order to justified by the faithfulness of Christ" (ἐκ πίστεως Χριστοῦ).

3. Gal. 3:22, "the scripture has consigned all things under sin in order that the promise which is based upon the faithfulness of Jesus Christ (ἐκ πίστεως Ἰησοῦ Χριστοῦ) might be given to those who believe."

4. Phil. 3:9, "not having a righteousness of my own which is based on the law but that which is through the faithfulness of Christ (διὰ πίστεως Χριστοῦ), the righteousness of God that depends on faith".[1]

5. Eph. 3:12, "in whom we have boldness and confidence of access through his faithfulness" (διὰ τῆς πίστεως αὐτοῦ).

And this may be the case as well in those very enigmatic expressions ἐκ πίστεως εἰς πίστιν of Rom. 1:17 and διὰ πίστεως τῆς ἐν Χριστῷ Ἰησοῦ of II Tim. 3:15.

In II Cor. 1:20, the apostle presents Christ not only as the "Yes" from God but also as the believer's "Amen" to God: "For all the promises of God find their Yes in him. That is why we utter the Amen through him, to the glory of God". In so saying, Paul suggests that Christ offered unto God the perfect response required of all men, but on behalf of all men. He accepted unto himself and completely fulfilled all that the law demanded in its requirements for righteousness. He stood for all men offering to a holy God the perfect righteousness required in the law, so that all who take their place "in Christ" stand before the Father clothed in his righteousness and not in their sins. It is his faithfulness to the will of God expressed in the Mosaic law that is accepted and that makes men righteous before the Father, not our own attempts to be righteous by means of some type of legal observance. As James Denney so aptly said: "It is the voice of God, no less than of the sinner, which says, 'Thou, O Christ, art all I want; more than all in Thee I find'."[2]

The Christian, therefore, stands before God as the beneficiary of both Christ's passive obedience and Christ's active obedience. He is redeemed, uncondemned and reconciled because of the former; he is the possessor of a positive righteousness, justified and has access before the Father because of the latter. And because Christ has both redeemed from the curse of the law and perfectly met the obligations of the law for all who respond to him by faith, Paul can affirm that "Christ is the end (τέλος) of the law in its connexion with righteousness (εἰς δικαιοσύνην) to everyone who

---

[1] Note the redundancy that is set up in these first four verses when πίστεως Ἰησοῦ Χριστοῦ is treated as an objective genitive. When, however, the expression is understood as a subjective genitive with reference to our Lord's faithfulness in life to the will of God expressed in the Mosaic law, the dual factors of Christ's perfect obedience and man's response of faith are set forth.

[2] J. Denney, *Christian Doctrine of Reconciliation*, pp. 162, 235, 301.

believes".[1] The obedience of Christ in his death and the obedience of Christ in his life are corollaries that can never truly be separated, for by means of both Christ has achieved man's complete reconciliation to a holy, righteous and loving God.

III *His Obedience Perfected*

The fact and effects of Christ's obedience are deeply rooted in the earliest strata of the Church's theology, both, as we have seen, in the hymnodic confession of Phil. 2:6–11 and in Paul's missionary preaching. And the themes enunciated in these more functional presentations of the redemptive message were carried on throughout the succeeding stages of Christian witness. Joined with this, however, is the more speculative approach to the subject that was inaugurated by the writer to the Hebrews in his declaration of Heb. 5:8–10: "Although he was a son, he learned obedience from what he suffered (ἔμαθεν ἀφ' ὧν ἔπαθεν τὴν ὑπακοήν), and once perfected (τελειωθείς), he became the source of eternal salvation for all who obey him and was designated by God to be high priest, just like (κατὰ τὴν τάξιν) Melchizedek". That this reference to Christ's obedience being perfected during his earthly life is no inadvertence on the part of the author is evidenced by the fact that the same point appears in briefer form in Heb. 2:10, where it is said that "in bringing many sons to glory it was fitting that God . . . should make the Pioneer of their salvation perfect through suffering" (διὰ παθημάτων τελειῶσαι), and Heb. 7:28, which speaks of "the Son, who has been made perfect forever" (υἱὸν εἰς τὸν αἰῶνα τετελειωμένον).

It may be rather startling at first to find in Hebrews such an emphasis upon Christ having "learned obedience" and become "perfected through suffering", particularly when one recalls the very high Christology expressed throughout the letter – even, perhaps, contradictory that "the Son" of Heb. 1:1–14 should have to learn obedience and become perfected. Yet however difficult it may be for us to comprehend the relationships between being and becoming in the life and ministry of our Lord, the writer to the Hebrews evidently felt no uneasiness about portraying Christ in terms of both status and process.[2] And we must not ignore either factor in seeking to protect the other.

The presentation in Hebrews of Christ's perfected obedience can hardly be taken to mean that our Lord's personal relation to the Father or his sonship were brought about by the things that he suffered, for chapter

[1] Rom. 10:4.
[2] Another explicit expression of this phenomenon is in Luke 1–2, where the loftiness of the Saviour's being is portrayed in many ways and yet the chapters conclude on a note of process and becoming: "And Jesus increased in wisdom and stature, and in favour with God and man" (2:52).

ne takes great pains to argue that Jesus is inherently and intrinsically the
ion – even the One to whom the created works of God can rightly be
iscribed.[1] And on its opening concessive clause ("although he was a son"),
Heb. 5:8–10 begins on the premise that Christ's sonship is a fact apart
from his sufferings. Nor can it be argued that Hebrews is teaching that
n some manner our Lord gained by his experiences a moral perfection
that was not his before. The letter introduces the Son as "the effulgence
of God's glory and the express image of his being" ($\dot{\alpha}\pi\alpha\dot{\nu}\gamma\alpha\sigma\mu\alpha$ $\tau\tilde{\eta}\varsigma$
$\delta\dot{o}\xi\eta\varsigma$ $\kappa\alpha\dot{\iota}$ $\chi\alpha\rho\alpha\kappa\tau\dot{\eta}\rho$ $\tau\tilde{\eta}\varsigma$ $\dot{\upsilon}\pi\sigma\sigma\tau\dot{\alpha}\sigma\varepsilon\omega\varsigma$ $\alpha\dot{\upsilon}\tau\sigma\tilde{\upsilon}$),[2] and elsewhere speaks of
esus being "without sin" ($\chi\omega\rho\dot{\iota}\varsigma$ $\dot{\alpha}\mu\alpha\rho\tau\dot{\iota}\alpha\varsigma$)[3] and without the need to
offer sacrifices for his own sins in that he was "separate from sinners"
$\kappa\varepsilon\chi\omega\rho\iota\sigma\mu\dot{\varepsilon}\nu\sigma\varsigma$ $\dot{\alpha}\pi\dot{o}$ $\tau\tilde{\omega}\nu$ $\dot{\alpha}\mu\alpha\rho\tau\omega\lambda\tilde{\omega}\nu$).[4]

What Hebrews has in mind when it speaks of process in our Lord's life
and ministry concerns, evidently, not his relationship to the Father or his
moral qualities but his redemptive capacity and work. Just as Peter
proclaimed that God made ($\dot{\varepsilon}\pi\sigma\dot{\iota}\eta\sigma\varepsilon\nu$) Jesus both Lord and Messiah
because of his resurrection,[5] and Paul reported that Jesus was declared to be
$\tau\sigma\tilde{\upsilon}$ $\dot{o}\rho\iota\sigma\theta\dot{\varepsilon}\nu\tau\sigma\varsigma$) the Son of God by the resurrection from the dead,[6] the
writer to the Hebrews affirms that God designated him ($\pi\rho\sigma\sigma\alpha\gamma\sigma\rho\varepsilon\upsilon\theta\varepsilon\dot{\iota}\varsigma$
$\dot{\upsilon}\pi\dot{o}$ $\tau\sigma\tilde{\upsilon}$ $\theta\varepsilon\sigma\tilde{\upsilon}$) to be High Priest because of his sufferings. Likewise, because he was truly man and suffered as a man, he is able to empathise
with men in their afflictions and "help those who are tempted" – evidently
n a manner such as would not have been possible apart from his incarnation and human experiences.[7] In view of the fact, therefore, that he is a
high priest who by nature is the sinless Son of God and by experience is
empathetic, the writer exhorts: "Let us approach the throne of grace with
confidence, that we may receive mercy and find grace to help us in our
tine of need".[8]

The discussion of the obedience of Christ in the Letter to the Hebrews
s set in the context of ontological affirmations regarding Jesus' sonship and
sinlessness as well as in the matrix of a functional portrayal of his priestly
activities on behalf of men. Hebrews is not to be contrasted with earlier
canonical writings in this interweaving of ontological and functional
motifs, though it is distinctive in the emphasis it gives to the ontological
and in its developed high priestly theme. Hebrews is unique, however, in
ts embryonic speculations about the relations between the ontological and
the functional in the redemptive ministry of Christ, which come to
expression in its speaking of a perfected obedience in the experience of
Jesus. And it is this type of thought that became prominent in the writings
of the Church Fathers, and has been dominant in dogmatic theology ever
since.

---

[1] Heb. 1:4–14.   [2] Heb. 1:3.   [3] Heb. 4:15.   [4] Heb. 7:26 f.
[5] Acts 2:36; cf. the similar emphasis in the *anabasis* section of the hymn of Phil. 2 (vv. 9–11).
[6] Rom. 1:4.   [7] Heb. 2:14–18.   [8] Heb. 4:14–16.

IV   Obedience and Ontology

The theme of the obedience of Christ, interestingly, does not come to explicit expression in the Church Fathers until the fourth century. And then it is associated very closely with the Christological debates that gave rise to and stemmed from the Council of Nicea in A.D. 325. Clement of Alexandria in *The Educator* (*c.* A.D. 190) spoke of the Christian's obedience to ὁ παιδαγωγὸς ἡμῶν Λόγος (i.e., Christ) as follows:

> First He persuades men to form habits of life, then He encourages them to fulfil their duties by laying down clear-cut counsels and by holding up, for us to follow, examples of those who have erred in the past. Both are most useful the advice, that it may be obeyed; the other, given in the form of example has a twofold object – either that we may choose the good and imitate it or condemn and avoid the bad.[1]

And he further argued that "the inspired Word exists because of both obedience and disobedience: that we may be saved by obeying it, and educated because we have disobeyed".[2] But Clement of Alexandria seems not to have spoken explicitly regarding Christ's own obedience, whether "passive", "active", or "perfected". And while the Fathers who preceded and followed him in the Ante-Nicene period proclaimed, of course, the redemptive work of Christ, their extant writings give no indication that they expressed themselves in terms of the obedience of Christ.

It was Eusebius of Caesarea (died *c.* A.D.370) who was the first patristic writer to refer explicitly to Christ's own obedience and to set the discussion in a thoroughly ontological context, speaking, as he did in the Ecclesiastical Theology (*c.* A.D. 336), of Christ's "voluntary and freely-given obedience" (τὴν ἐξ αὐθεκουσίου προαιρέσεως ὑπακοήν) which he will give to the Father.[3] But it was with Eusebius' successor at Caesarea, the noble Cappadocian bishop Basil (died *c.* A.D. 379), and Basil's younger brother, Gregory of Nyssa (died *c.* A.D. 394), that this theme in its ontological setting came most prominently to the fore. In opposition to Eunomius, who asserted in rather static fashion that his nature inevitably bound our Lord to a life of obedience, Basil of Caesarea argued that "by the incarnation, through his obedience (μετὰ τὴν ἐνανθρώπησιν, διὰ τὴν ὑπακοήν), the Father has bestowed upon the Son the name that is above all";[4] and, also opposed to Eunomius, Gregory of Nyssa insisted on the basis of the expression "became obedient" (ὑπήκοος ἐγένετο) of Phil. 2:8 that Christ was not compelled by his sonship to be obedient but

[1] Paidagogos I. 2.
[2] *Ibid.*, I. 5.
[3] Eccl. Theol. III. (on I Cor. 15:28).
[4] Contra Eunomium IV. 3

THE OBEDIENCE OF CHRIST
that his obedience sprang from a willing desire at a specific time in redemptive history.[1] The terms of reference in this debate as to whether
Christ's obedience stemmed from his sonship and generation as "the Only-
begotten God" (so Eunomius) or from his love, will and redemptive
activity (so Basil and Gregory) may seem at times considerably confused.
But the debate was fervent. And in its development, the theme of the
That this discussion of the ontological significance of Christ's obedience
was no local matter among a certain select few is suggested by a Lenten
Lecture on I Cor. 15:25–28 delivered by Cyril of Jerusalem (died *c.* A.D.
387). To those who argued from the statement, "he must reign until he
has put all his enemies under his feet" (I Cor. 15:25), that Christ will reign
no longer once his enemies have been subdued, Cyril responded: "For
surely He who is King before He has subdued His enemies will be King
after He has overcome them"; and to those who concluded from the
statement, "when all things are made subject to him then the Son himself
will also be made subject to him who subjected all things to him" (I Cor.
15:28), that the Son will be absorbed into the Father, Cyril argued: "Will
all else that is subject to the Son abide, but the Son, subject to the Father
not abide? He will be subject, not as though beginning to obey the Father
'for from all eternity 'he does always the things that please him' [Jn. 8:29],
but because then too He will tender not a forced obedience, but a self-
αὐτοπροαίρετον εὐπείθειαν). "For He is not a servant subject to necessity,
but a Son, obeying from choice and affection".[2] In addition, the longer
Greek version of Ignatius' letter to the Ephesians, which in its spurious
interpolations probably is to be dated in the latter part of the fourth

> I have taken upon me first to exhort you that you run together in accordance
> with the will of God. For even Jesus Christ does all things according to the
> will of the Father, as He himself declares in a certain place, "I do always those
> things that please Him" (Jn. 8:29). Wherefore it behoves us also to live accord-
> ing to the will of God in Christ, and to imitate Him as Paul did. For, says he,
> "Be followers of me, even as I also am of Christ" (I Cor. 11:1).[3]

Admittedly, neither ὑπακοή or ὑπήκοος appear in the wording of the
passage, yet certainly something of the fourth-century discussion on the
obedience of Christ is reflected in its expressions. So much so, in fact, did
the fourth-century Fathers think and write of the obedience of Christ in
an ontological context that Epiphanius of Constantia (i.e., Salamis) in
Cyprus (died *c.* A.D. 403) employed the term almost as a Christological

---

[1] Contra Eunomium II. 11. and *passim;* cf. also Bk. I *passim.*
[2] Catechesis XV. 29 f. These sermons may have been given as early as A.D. 349. Cyril was
resisted by Nicean theologians and is not often mentioned by the Fathers.
[3] Ad Eph. 3.

title in declaring that "through the Virgin was begotten the obedience of grace" (διὰ τῆς παρθένου γέγονεν ἡ ὑπακοὴ τῆς χάριτος).[1]

On the theme of the obedience of Christ, therefore, patristic writers of the fourth century picked up the embryonic ontological materials of the NT, but neglected in this particular form of expression the more functional features. The ontological developments were inevitable, and can only be judged on the basis of their continuity with the biblical data. The neglect of the more functional aspects – even though incorporated in other ways elsewhere in their respective systems of theology – may be viewed as regrettable, for fulness of doctrine is only attained as there is an explication that is both in continuity with the biblical data and in contact with all of the biblical data. In bringing together all of the biblical data on this one theme, however, and in tracing that theme through its various stages of discussion, something of both the fulness of doctrine on the obedience of Christ and its unfolding development in Christian understanding can be seen, which may serve to inform our more systematic theologies and our proclamation in regard to the redemptive work of Christ.

[1] Adver. Haer. LXXVIII. 18.

CHAPTER X

THE DEVELOPMENT OF THE CONCEPT OF REDEMPTION IN THE NEW TESTAMENT

I. Howard Marshall

POSTERITY MAY WELL RECKON THAT THE MOST IMPORTANT CONTRIBU-
TION of Leon Morris to New Testament scholarship is his study of
the vocabulary of atonement. His careful linguistic scholarship
provides the exegetical foundation for a systematic statement of the
meaning of the death of Christ, and the work of subsequent scholars has
shown that the foundation is essentially secure. For example, his discussion
of the meaning of the ἱλάσκομαι word group, in which he demonstrated
that it refers to propitiation rather than to expiation,[1] has been confirmed
by the work of R. Nicole and D. Hill.[2] Similarly, his interpretation of the
terminology of redemption,[3] though open to some correction, is essentially sound, and there is not much more to be said on the matter.[4] Since,

[1] L. L. Morris, *The Apostolic Preaching of the Cross* (London, 1955), pp. 125–85; ³1965,
pp. 144–213, incorporates his article "The Meaning of 'Ἱλαστήριον in Romans iii. 25",
TS 2 (1955–56), pp. 33–43.
[2] R. Nicole, "C. H. Dodd and the Doctrine of Propitiation", *WTJ* 17 (1954–55), pp.
17–57; D. Hill, *Greek Words and Hebrew Meanings* (Cambridge, 1967), pp. 23–48. The
opposite view was defended by C. H. Dodd, "'Ἱλάσκεσθαι, its cognates, derivatives and
synonyms in the Septuagint", *JTS* 32 (1931), pp. 352–60, reprinted in *The Bible and the
Greeks* (London, 1935), pp. 82–95.
[3] L. Morris, *op. cit.*, pp. 9–59 (3rd. edition references are added in brackets, here 11–64);
"The Vocabulary of Atonement 1. Redemption", *Themelios* 1:1 (1962), pp. 24–30.
[4] Following the example of B. B. Warfield ("'Redeemer' and 'Redemption'", *PTR* 14
(1916), pp. 177–201; "The New Testament Terminology of Redemption", *PTR* 15 (1917),
pp. 201–49 (both essays reprinted in *The Person and Work of Christ* (Philadelphia, 1950),
pp. 325–48, 429–75; the latter also in *Biblical Foundations* (London, 1958) 199–245); art.
"Redemption" in *HDAC* II, 302–309), Morris is particularly concerned to show that the
terminology of redemption invariably conveys the idea of release on payment of a price or
ransom. He concludes: "Both inside and outside the New Testament writings the payment of
a price is a necessary component of the redemption idea. When the New Testament speaks
of redemption, then, unless our linguistics are at fault, it means that Christ has paid the
price of our redemption." (*The Apostolic Preaching of the Cross*, p. 58 (61).)
    While this view of the extra-biblical evidence is correct (cf. D. Hill, *op. cit.*, p. 52; E. K.
Simpson, *Words worth weighing in the Greek New Testament* (London, 1946), pp. 8 f.), it is not
quite true for the OT. Although the meaning of *koper* (and of λύτρον) is uniformly that of a
payment which secures release, this is not always the case with the verbs *ga'al* and *padah*.
D. Hill (*op. cit.*, pp. 62 f.) has rightly observed that they are sometimes rendered into Greek
by words which simply indicate release and deliverance (e.g., ῥύομαι). This is particularly
the case when Yahweh is the subject and the theme is the deliverance of His people. Here
there is often reference to the mighty power which Yahweh displays in order to deliver His
people, but this is in no sense a price.
    We would suggest that the discussion has been befogged by a failure to define terms.
Morris implies that "price" and "cost" are synonymous: "there is reference to price in the

however, his treatment is concerned mainly with the *linguistics* of the word group, there is room for a consideration of the *concept* of redemption in the New Testament, tracing its origins and development.[1] Our aim will be to discover how the concept is used by Luke, by Paul and other writers, by the writer to the Hebrews and by Jesus, and then to frame a hypothesis regarding the development of the usage.

I

Like many other terms in New Testament theology the concept of redemption has its roots in the Old Testament. The divine act of deliverance from Egypt became the "type" for understanding God's future acts of salvation for his people. In Luke 24:21 the disciples "clearly are using 'redeem' in the typically Jewish manner of the long awaited intervention by Almighty God when his power would free his people from all their enemies and bring in a period of blessing and prosperity".[2] This Jewish hope finds further expression in Lk. 1:68 where God redeems his people by delivering them from the hand of their enemies, a thought which is not purely material in content, for in the same context there is reference to the forgiveness of sins (Lk. 1:77). Similarly, in Lk. 2:38 the author himself speaks of those who were awaiting deliverance for Jerusalem; the phrase should be taken with Lk. 2:25 where Simeon is said to be waiting for the

[1] Cf. D. Daube, *The New Testament and Rabbinic Judaism* (London, 1956), pp. 268–84; J. D. M. Derrett, *Law in the New Testament* (London, 1970), pp. 389–460 (with bibliography).
[2] L. Morris, *op. cit.*, p. 35 (38).

insistence that Yahweh's redemption is at the cost of the exertion of His mighty power" (*op. cit.*, p. 19 (26)). It would be more precise to use the term "price" for those cases where some *payment* or exchange is *received* by the person from whom the captive is delivered, and to use the term "cost" for whatever *expenditure* of money, life and effort is *demanded* on the part of the redeemer; obviously "price" and "cost" will often coincide, but it is possible to have "cost" without payment of a "price".

One should perhaps also distinguish more clearly between the meanings of words and of concepts. Thus Is. 52:3 expressly states that Israel will be ransomed without money (cf. Is. 45:13). Here the word "ransom" is used in a context which denies that Yahweh pays any kind of price for the deliverance of his people from their enemies; rather he forcibly sets them free by the exercise of his power.

It may be failure to make this distinction clearly which leads to Morris's strange comment on Lk. 24:21, where he admits in effect that there was a Jewish expectation of divine deliverance which did not lay any stress on the payment of a price; but, he goes on, "the passage is not of first importance for our purposes; for clearly a redemption rendered impossible by the cross can tell us little about the redemption effected by the cross" (*op. cit.*, p. 35 (38 f.)). D. Hill rightly objects that the consideration adduced here is irrelevant to the meaning of the word as used here (*op. cit.*, pp. 67 f.). The passage may say nothing about the cross, but it does show that the word "redeem" may be used without the idea of price being present. In fact, however, the passage does say something about the cross, for so far from the text showing that the expected redemption was "rendered impossible by the cross" it indicates that it was rendered possible precisely by the suffering of the Messiah (Lk. 24:26). The cross and resurrection are the means of redemption, although the ideas of "price" and "cost" do not appear to be present or to receive any stress.

comfort of Israel, and behind both phrases should be seen Isa. 52:9: "For the Lord has comforted his people, he has redeemed Jerusalem".[1] What is of significance is that this redemption is linked to the coming of the Messiah, the "horn of salvation . . . in the house of his servant David" (Lk. 1:69). Deliverance requires a deliverer; just as Moses was called a deliverer (Acts 7:35),[2] so Jesus is the deliverer, and the role ascribed to God in the OT is transferred to him.[3] For Luke this hope of deliverance has been actually fulfilled in the coming of Jesus.[4]

Elements of future redemption are also to be found. In Acts 3:19–21 there is a reference to future times of refreshing and the establishment of "all that God spoke by the mouth of his holy prophets from of old", a phrase which gives a verbal link with Lk. 1:70. Thus the future completion of salvation is tied to the person of Christ who is to come again. The link between past and future redemption is to be found in the person of Christ rather than in an implicit reference to the cross.[5]

This leaves Lk. 21:28 for consideration. The verse has no parallels in the other versions of the apocalyptic discourse, and the vocabulary and style are distinctively Lucan.[6] Although, therefore, the verse may be based on a source other than Mark, it appears to be a Lucan formulation,[7] and the idea of redemption here should be discussed against the background of Luke's thought. The reference is to the deliverance of God's people from the tribulation and distress of the last days by the coming of the Son of man (cf. 1 En. 51:2). It is noteworthy that Luke here uses the compound $\dot{\alpha}\pi o\lambda\acute{u}\tau\rho\omega\sigma\iota\varsigma$, whereas in his other references he uses the simple forms. The compound form is found only once in the LXX (Dn. 4:32, with no Hebrew equivalent). It seems likely that normally Luke has used the common LXX terminology, but here he has used a word which was in fairly common Christian use.[8] The difference in terminology may simply

---

[1] Cf. H. Schürmann, *Das Lukasevangelium* I (Freiburg, 1969), p. 131.

[2] Moses is so described in the Samaritan *Memar Marqah* 1:4 and in rabbinic sources from A.D. 300 onwards; parallelism between Moses and the Messiah is found earlier. Cf. J. Jeremias, *TDNT* IV, p. 860.

[3] In the OT the redemption of Israel is always ascribed to Yahweh and not to any other figure.

[4] The aorist in Lk. 1:68 f. should be taken literally and not as equivalent to a prophetic perfect (H. Schürmann, *op. cit.*, pp. 86 f.).

[5] Cf. F. Büchsel's comment on Luke's use of $\lambda\acute{u}\tau\rho\omega\sigma\iota\varsigma$: "The reference is not to a ransom but to a redeemer". (*TDNT* IV, p. 351).

[6] Note the use of the genitive absolute (H. Schürmann, *Der Paschamahlbericht* (Münster, 1953), p. 94); $\dot{\alpha}\nu\alpha\kappa\acute{u}\pi\tau\omega$ is found elsewhere in the NT only in Lk. 13:11 (narrative) and Jn. 8:7, 10; $\dot{\epsilon}\pi\alpha\acute{\iota}\rho\omega$ occurs 6 times in Lk. and 5 times in Acts; $\delta\iota\acute{o}\tau\iota$ occurs 3 times in Lk. and 5 times in Acts, never in the other Gospels; $\dot{\epsilon}\gamma\gamma\acute{\iota}\zeta\omega$ occurs 18 times in Lk., 6 times in Acts, 7 times in Mt. and 3 times in Mk.

[7] The verse is regarded as belonging to a non-Marcan source by L. Gaston, "Sondergut und Markusstoff in Lk. 21", *ThZ* 16 (1960), pp. 161–72; T. Schramm, *Der Markus-stoff bei Lukas* (Cambridge, 1971), pp. 180 f. The linguistic considerations above, however, show that any source has been revised by Luke, and it must remain open whether the use of $\dot{\alpha}\pi o\lambda\acute{u}\tau\rho\omega\sigma\iota\varsigma$ is due to the source or to Luke himself.

[8] In Paul the use of $\dot{\alpha}\pi o\lambda\acute{u}\tau\rho\omega\sigma\iota\varsigma$ appears to be traditional; see below.

be due to Luke's source (if he had one), but it may also be intended to reflect a distinction between the redemption inaugurated and achieved by the first coming of Christ and the final redemption consummated by his second coming.[1]

To sum up: Luke takes up the OT idea of deliverance from tribulation by Yahweh and finds it fulfilled typologically in Jesus Christ who fulfilled Jewish hopes by his incarnation, suffering and entry into glory and who will bring about final redemption and "times of refreshing" at his second coming. The language is that of OT piety, and there is little reflection over the means of redemption.

II

A much more concrete use of the terminology is found elsewhere in the NT, especially in Paul. There are some grounds for thinking that Galatians is the earliest of the Pauline Epistles.[2] In 3:13 and 4:5 Paul uses $\dot{\epsilon}\xi\alpha\gamma o\rho\dot{\alpha}\zeta\omega$ to describe the action of Christ in redeeming believers. The word is found with this sense only here in the NT, and it has no background in LXX usage. The fact that the usual terminology of redemption has an OT background makes the choice of word here all the more significant, and suggests that Paul had some definite reason for it.

The picture is one of release from a state of slavery under the law or the "elements" (Gal. 4:3 f.), as a result of which men are under the curse of the law (Gal. 3:13). The curse is pronounced upon those who fail to keep the law (Gal. 3:10) and consists in the sentence of death. But Christ has delivered men from the curse by himself being crucified, since to be crucified is a sign of standing under the curse of the law (Dt. 21:23). The verb used indicates that a purchase has taken place, leading to the release of slaves. The idea of "cost" is definitely present. So also is the idea that a ransom or "price" has been paid. A background may be sought in OT ideas of the redemption of a life that is forfeit by a payment of money,[3] but in this case it is the life of another man that is the ransom. If we are right in seeing the notion of "price" here, there remains the problem of the recipient, and there can be no doubt that it is God, if anybody, who receives the ransom.[4]

---

[1] Elsewhere in the NT, however, the same word is used for both aspects of redemption.

[2] F. F. Bruce, "Galatian Problems. 4: The Date of the Epistle", *BJRL* 54 (1971–1972), pp. 250–67. Even if this dating is questionable, Galatians should certainly be placed before Romans; it may be dated after 1 Corinthians, but this point does not greatly affect our argument.

[3] The first-born of men were redeemed (Ex. 13:13; 34:19 f.) by the consecration of the Levites to God and the payment of a ransom price (Num. 3:44–51; cf. 8:16–19); a ransom was payable by all Israelites at a census (Ex. 30:11–16).

[4] It is improbable that the elements are the recipients of the ransom, since Paul's thought is basically related to the law rather than to the elements.

As a result of this act, men are justified (Gal. 3:8, 11); they receive the gift of the Spirit (Gal. 3:14; 4:6), and they are set free from slavery to become the free sons of God (Gal. 4:5–7; cf. 5:1).[1] Thus the accent lies on the deliverance of sinners and their entry into freedom, and the metaphor used is that of the ransoming of slaves.[2]

In 1 Cor. 1:30 Paul uses the same kind of abstract language as in Gal. 3:13 (Christ becoming "a curse", i.e. accursed) by speaking of Christ becoming "our wisdom, our righteousness and sanctification and redemption". The use of "wisdom" arises from the context (1 Cor. 1:18 ff.), but the reason for the introduction of the other terms is less obvious.[3] It seems probable that Paul has utilised a set of familiar concepts in order to make the meaning of wisdom clearer. For Paul true wisdom is associated with the cross and its effects. It is significant that righteousness and redemption occur together in Gal. 3[4] and also in Rom 3:24. Paul does not give any further explanation of these terms, and hence it may be concluded that they were familiar to his readers from his preaching. They all clearly refer to what Christ means in the present time to his people (cf. the use of ἐγενήθη). A redemption achieved by the cross is clearly indicated, although the precise content attaching to the word is no longer clear to us.

A fresh term is used in 1 Cor. 6:20; 7:23 in what is evidently another stereotyped phrase, no doubt so familiar to the readers that this brief allusion was an adequate means of expression:[5] ἠγοράσθητε τιμῆς. The implication is that previously believers served themselves and men. Now they have been bought for a price, a word which suggests that an irrevocable transaction has taken place,[6] and which can refer only to the death of Christ. Consequently, they belong to God, so that paradoxically they are God's slaves and yet at the same time his freedmen (1 Cor. 7:22).[7] The emphasis, however, is not on deliverance leading to freedom, but on purchase leading to slavery.[8]

---

[1] At this point the terminology of redemption is linked to that of liberation and freedom: cf. Rom. 8:21; 1 Cor. 7:22 f.; Gal. 5:1, 13; Rom. 6:18, 22; 8:2; Jn. 8:32, 36 (H. Schlier, TDNT II, pp. 487–502).

[2] Cf. Diodorus Siculus 36:2:2: ἐξηγόρασεν αὐτήν . . . ταλάντων Ἀττικῶν ἑπτά.

[3] J. Bohatec has claimed that the four terms in v. 30 correspond to those in vs. 27 f. ("Inhalt und Reihenfolge der 'Schlagwörte der Erlösungsreligion' in 1 Kor. 1, 26–31", ThZ 4 (1948), 252 ff., as reported in H. Lietzmann and W. G. Kümmel, An die Korinther I, II (Tübingen, 1949), p. 169).

[4] It is curious that words associated with the third member of the set (ἁγιασμός) are entirely absent from Galatians.

[5] T. Holtz, Die Christologie der Apokalypse des Johannes, TU 85 (Berlin, 1962), p. 67.

[6] A. Deissmann, Light from the Ancient East (London, 1910), p. 329, notes how in sacral manumission it is expressly forbidden that the enfranchised may be re-enslaved.

[7] Although Paul is here speaking of two groups of people who have their status reversed when they become Christians, both groups are simultaneously free and slaves on a spiritual level, since the ἀπελεύθερος owes a certain duty to the κύριος (cf. C. K. Barrett, The First Epistle to the Corinthians (London, 1968), p. 171).

[8] Thus ἀγοράζω is used of simple purchase, ἐξαγοράζω of a purchase that leads to freedom.

The concept of redemption here is found in the OT and Judaism[1] but also stands close to secular analogies. A. Deissmann compared the process to sacral manumission whereby a slave was purchased from his earthly master by a god and thus became the fictitious property of the god.[2] The analogy is highly suggestive, but it has come under attack. In the commercial sphere the price was actually paid by the slave himself to the god who then used it to buy the slave from his master, but in Paul it is Christ who pays the price; moreover, the slave was only in a fictitious sense the property of the god – the point of the transaction being that he no longer had an earthly master – but the Christian is the slave of God in a real sense. These differences may be readily admitted, but they are in no way a decisive objection to the use of this metaphor.[3] A preacher would surely have delighted to point out the differences between sacral manumission and Christian redemption, and especially to contrast the price paid by the slave in the secular world with the free gift of God in Christ.[4]

W. Elert has proposed that a different idea may be present, namely *redemptio ab hostibus*.[5] In the ancient world the normal fate of prisoners of war was to become slaves, but it was possible for them to be released and returned to their native land on payment of a ransom by a fellow-citizen. The freedman stood under certain obligations to the person who had redeemed him, as a *libertus* to his *patronus*, until he had paid back the cost of his ransom.[6] So the Christian has been delivered from bondage to an enemy by Christ and now stands under obligation to him.

It is difficult to make an exclusive choice between these two possible backgrounds. Nor, in the present case, should one rule out the further possibilities of ordinary (non-sacral) manumission or even of simple sale of a slave from one master to another.[7] Thus it may be wrong to look for one specialized background to the NT concept of redemption;

[1] Is. 43:1; cf. D. Daube, *op. cit.*, pp. 272–84.

[2] A. Deissmann, *op. cit.*, pp. 322–34.

[3] Cf. H. Lietzmann, *Die Briefe des Paulus I* (Tübingen, 1910), p. 257.

[4] A number of further details form evidence that sacral manumission helps to provide the background to the NT statements. Deissmann (*ibid.*) notes: 1. The association of a sacrifice with the act of manumission; 2. the phrase ἐπ᾽ ἐλευθερίᾳ (Gal. 5:13, cf. 1) in the records of manumission; 3. the fact that slavery could be for debt shows the affinity between redemption and remission or forgiveness.

[5] W. Elert, "Redemptio ab Hostibus", *ThLZ* 72 (1947), pp. 265–70.

[6] F. Lyall, "Roman Law in the Writings of Paul – The Slave and the Freedman", *NTS* 17 (1970–71), pp. 73–79, also notes the duties of a freed slave to his *patronus*, but states that the slave's former master was his *patronus*. But it seems unlikely that this Roman practice provides the background to Paul's thought, since the believer's duty is to the new *patronus* who has bought him, not to the old master from whom he has been released; Paul's point is that the old relationship has entirely ceased.

The term ἀπελεύθερος may be understood as equivalent to the Latin *libertus* (or *libertinus*), a "freedman" owing service to his manumitter as his *patronus*. Lyall is thinking of a process in Roman law whereby a master might release his slaves. It is more likely that sacral manumission or *redemptio ab hostibus* is in Paul's mind.

[7] However, simple sale from one master to another is unlikely, because the new status is one of freedom and not simply of a change of master.

ather, the general concept of manumission forms the background, and different aspects of it contribute to the detailed understanding of the various NT passages. What is important is that along with the OT background this secular background is certainly present, so that redemption in these passages is to be thought of in terms of change of ownership as a result of payment of a price. Whereas in Galatians the rationale of the price in relation to the former state of the Christian is clear, in 1 Corinthians the former state of the Christian has retreated into the background, and the stress is now on the payment of the price as a sign that the Christian now belongs to a new master.

This stress on redemption as a change of ownership rather than as simply the setting free of slaves lived on. It is present in 2 Pet. 2:1 where Christ is described as the slave-master ($\delta\epsilon\sigma\pi\acute{o}\tau\eta\varsigma$; cf. Jude 4) who has purchased Christians for himself.[1] But the most important development is in Revelation where a series of references (1:5; 5:9; 14:3 f.) take up the idea. The verb $\dot{\alpha}\gamma o\rho\acute{a}\zeta\omega$ is used in 5:9 to describe the act of Christ in purchasing Christians from every race[2] for God. Here again the thought of service to God is expressed, notably in the idea of men as priests (Rev. 1:6; 5:10) and as an offering of first-fruits to God (Rev. 14:4).[3] At the same time, however, the release of Christians from sin (Rev. 1:5)[4] and their privilege of reigning (Rev. 1:6; 5:10) are stressed.

The association here of redemption with release from sin is based on Ps. 130:8: "And he will redeem Israel from all his iniquities".[5] The means is the death of Christ. The verb used, $\sigma\varphi\acute{a}\zeta\omega$, conveys the sense of a sacrificial offering (cf. Rev. 6:9 with reference to the martyrs),[6] especially since Jesus is presented as the lamb who is slain (Rev. 5:6, 12; 13:8). This introduces us to the fundamental point that redemption is accomplished by the offering of a sacrifice.

At first sight the collocation of redemption and sacrifice appears to indicate a confusion of imagery. In fact it is strongly rooted in the OT and Judaism. The following three factors are relevant: 1. The death of the

---

[1] The background of $\delta\epsilon\sigma\pi\acute{o}\tau\eta\varsigma$ as a master of slaves is described clearly enough by K. H. Rengstorf (*TDNT* II, pp. 44–49), but he fails to make use of it in explaining the present text, and hence finds the association of $\dot{\alpha}\gamma o\rho\acute{a}\zeta\omega$ with $\delta\epsilon\sigma\pi\acute{o}\tau\eta\varsigma$ surprising.

[2] The $\dot{\epsilon}\kappa$ is partitive, and does not indicate the owner from whom Christians have been delivered.

[3] In the OT the first-fruits are specially dedicated to God for use in his service; hence the thought of dedication to his service is probably present here also.

[4] In a paper read at the meeting of the Catholic Biblical Association in Los Angeles in 1972 Miss E. Fiorenza defended the view that Rev. 1:5 represented a traditional formula and Rev. 5:9 the seer's reworking of it. If this view is correct, it shows that the use of $\lambda\acute{u}\omega$ to express release from sin is early.

[5] $\lambda\acute{u}\omega$ is also used with reference to sin in Job 42:9; Is. 40:2 and Sir. 28:2, but in these cases it is the sin which is "released", i.e., pardoned, and not the person who is released from the sin; F. Büchsel, *TDNT* IV, p. 336, n. 8.

[6] It can be used non-sacrificially of murder or the slaughter of animals. In Rev. 6:9 the death of the martyrs is compared with the slaughter of sacrificial animals whose blood flows from the altar (O. Michel, *TDNT* VII, pp. 934 f.).

passover lambs was seen as an element in the redemption of Israel from Egypt: "May we eat there of the sacrifices and of the Passover-offerings whose blood has reached with acceptance the wall of thy Altar, and let us praise thee for our redemption and for the ransoming of our soul" (Pesahim 10:6).[1] Hence J. Jeremias comments: "As once the blood of the Passover lambs played a part in the redemption from Egypt, so by the atoning power of His blood He has accomplished redemption . . . from the bondage of sin . . ."[2] 2. L. Morris claims that the Hebrew verb *kipper* often has the denominative sense "to offer a *koper*". Atonement is thus made by the payment of a ransom or the offering of a gift to Yahweh.[3] Admittedly the way in which atonement and ransom are here brought together is not the same thing as the idea of redemption by the offering of a sacrifice, but it shows that the two ideas were closely associated in the Hebrew mind. 3. The thought of the deliverance of Israel from its sin and its consequences by the death of the martyrs, conceived as a propitiatory offering to God, developed in Judaism and is to be seen in 4 Macc. 17:22.

This complex of ideas lies behind the imagery in Revelation. Jesus is the slain lamb, and we should probably think of Him as specifically the passover lamb.[4] He is also described as "the faithful witness" (Rev. 1:5), a phrase which implies his death as well as his testimony by word of mouth.[5] Hence the comparison of Jesus' death to that of a martyr and its understanding in sacrificial terms has already taken place. We have moved beyond the simple idea of a commercial ransom price to the Jewish concept of redemption by means of a sacrificial offering to God.

It follows that the phrase "by his blood" in Rev. 1:5; 5:9 must be understood in sacrificial terms, just as in 4 Macc. 17:22. It expresses the "cost" of redemption[6] in terms of laying down of life, and the "price" is paid to God, if to anybody.

We are moving in the same circle of ideas when we turn to 1 Pet. 1:18 where the readers are told that they were redeemed from their former (sinful) way of life not with silver and gold but with the precious blood of

[1] Even if the annual passover offering was not regarded as atoning in effect, the origina Exodus passover offering and the eschatological passover were so regarded (J. Jeremias, *The Eucharistic Words of Jesus* (London, 1966), pp. 225 f.; E. Lohse, *Märtyrer und Gottesknecht* (Göttingen, ²1963), p. 142). However, it is possible that by NT times all sacrifices were regarded as having expiatory power to some extent (L. L. Morris, *op. cit.* (3rd ed.), pp. 131 f.).

[2] J. Jeremias, *TDNT* I, p. 340.

[3] L. L. Morris, *op. cit.*, pp. 143–52 (161–70); cf. BDB s.v.; D. Hill, *op. cit.*, p. 32. F. Büchsel (*TDNT* IV, p. 341) shows that in rabbinic thought a ransom is an expiation for sin (see b.Bab.Kamm. 40a, cited in Strack–Billerbeck III, 644).

[4] Paul regards Jesus as the passover (lamb) (1 Cor. 5:7) and 1 Pet. 1:18 should be interpreted in the same way; the same allusion may also be meant in the Johannine tradition (Jn. 1:29, 36), although L. L. Morris, *op. cit.* (3rd ed.), pp. 129–43, points out the weaknesses of this interpretation. Other ideas may well have been drawn into the concept in Rev., but this one alone seems sufficient to explain the sacrificial imagery.

[5] T. Holtz, *op. cit.*, pp. 55–57.

[6] T. Holtz, *op. cit.*, p. 64; L. L. Morris, *op. cit.*, p. 51 n. (55 n.).

Christ, as of a lamb without blemish or spot. Again the thought of deliverance from a past state of captivity and entry into sonship is linked to that of belonging to God (1 Pet. 2:9) and rendering him service. Martyrological ideas are not explicitly present here, and Christ's death is compared directly to that of a sacrificial lamb. In all probability the passover lamb is meant,[1] and this is confirmed by the presence of other Exodus terminology in the Epistle.[2] The verb λυτρόω takes us into the realm of OT ideas, especially the deliverance from Egypt.[3] The greatness of the sacrifice thus rendered by Christ ought to move the readers to godly fear (1 Pet. 1:17), and the contrast with silver and gold[4] shows that the idea of a ransom "price" is well to the fore.

The same thought of believers becoming the possession of God through redemption is found in Acts 20:28 where we read of the church of God which he obtained (περιποιέομαι) with the blood of his own One.[5] The verb is found in the LXX, but it translates a variety of Hebrew words, one of which is closely connected with redemption.[6] But the corresponding noun, περιποίησις, is used in stereotyped phraseology to signify Israel as Yahweh's special possession.[7] As Israel became God's special people at the Exodus, so he has acquired the church to be his people. That this is indeed the background may be deduced from the use of the noun in 1 Pet. 2:9; in both passages we may see the influence of Is. 43:20, and its seems that a piece of imagery traditional in the church is being used (cf. Tit. 2:14). J. B. Bauer has linked the concept of redemption here with that of the covenant whereby God made Israel his people.[8]

Eph. 1:14 now claims our attention. There are two main ways of understanding the passage. Some hold that it speaks of the way in which believers have received the Spirit as an earnest or foretaste (v. 14a) of the inheritance which will become fully their possession at the future day of

---

[1] The description of the lamb as "unblemished" (ἄμωμος) and "spotless" (ἄσπιλος) is, however, not sufficient to identify it as the passover lamb, since the former adjective is used freely of various offerings.

[2] See the references to the sprinkling of blood in 1:2 and to loins girt in 1:12. Paschal imagery has been found more widely by F. L. Cross, *1 Peter: a Paschal Liturgy* (London, 1954), but the picture has been over-drawn.

[3] Ex. 6:6; 15:13; Ps. 76 (77):15; 105 (106):10; Is. 63:9; Dt. 7:8; 9:26 and frequently.

[4] Observe the same contrast between money and divine provision in Acts 3:6.

[5] The text is uncertain. Some MSS have "the church of the Lord" (i.e. Christ), but this looks like an attempt to avoid the difficulty. There is in fact no difficulty about taking τοῦ ἰδίου to mean "of his own One" (MH I, pp. 90 f.); alternatively, one may supply ὁ Χριστός as the subject of περιεποιήσατο (E. Lohse, *op. cit.*, p. 180 n.).

[6] περιποιέομαι most frequently translates *ḥayah* with the meaning "to preserve alive" (10 times) and *ḥamal* "to have compassion on". It also translates 8 other roots, including the noun *segullah* "property", 1 Chr. 29:3.

[7] περιποίησις is found 3 times; it translates *segullah* at Mal. 3:17. This Hebrew word is more frequently rendered in the LXX by the adjective περιούσιος (Ex. 19:5; Dt. 7:6; 14:2; 26:18; Ps. 135:4; Ecc. 2:8).

[8] J. B. Bauer, *Encyclopaedia of Biblical Theology* (London, 1969), II, pp. 738–41. Note the link with the idea of the covenant in Heb. 9:15, and the association of Moses with redemption in Acts 7:35.

full redemption (Eph. 4:30).[1] Others argue that it refers to the way in which believers have been sealed with the Spirit (v. 13) as the sign that God will one day enter upon full possession of the property which has already become his. There is little doubt that this second view is better. It alone does justice to the background of the term περιποίησις; it fits in neatly with the idea of the saints being God's portion (Eph. 1:11) whom he purposes to make holy (Eph. 1:4) in order that his glory may be praised (Eph. 1:14).[2] There will thus be a day of final redemption when God enters into full possession of his people.

It must be noted, however, that this future sense is not the primary one in Pauline thought. The idea is of the completion of an act already begun by God's sealing of believers with the Spirit; the same is true in Rom. 8:23 where it is those who already possess the first-fruits of the Spirit who look forward to the redemption of the body. The point is strengthened by the fact that here the promised redemption is equated with divine sonship which, as we have already seen, was the gift of God to believers when they were justified and redeemed from the curse of the law (Gal. 4:5–7). For the believer future redemption means the deliverance of the body from the corruption and pain of the world into the glorious freedom of the children of God (Rom. 8:18–22); for God it means the completion of the process whereby believers become his possession.

In none of the passages just discussed is redemption directly related to the death of Christ; the thought is primarily of deliverance, and neither the agent nor the means is stated. Nevertheless, the use of the term forces us back to a consideration of that which is primary in Pauline thought, namely the redemption already wrought by Christ and received by believers.

We come finally in this section to the passages in which Paul uses the term ἀπολύτρωσις in connexion with the cross. We have already seen that 1 Cor. 1:30 should be interpreted of the redemption already achieved by Christ, although the meaning of the term is not spelled out in any detail. In Rom. 3:24 Paul explicitly applies it to the cross in a context which is so closely similar to Gal. 3 that we are justified in considering the one passage in the light of the other, and hence seeing ἀπολύτρωσις here as in some sense equivalent to ἐξαγοράζω in the earlier passage. The context in Rom. 3 is one of universal sinfulness and liability to judgement, inability to keep the law, and the impossibility of being saved by the law anyhow. The thought of being in bondage under the law is not expressed

---

[1] RSV; T. K. Abbott, *Ephesians and Colossians* (Edinburgh, [4]1922), pp. 23 f.; M. Dibelius and H. Greeven, *An die Kolosser, Epheser an Philemon* (Tübingen, [3]1953), pp. 62 f.; H. Schlier, *Der Brief an die Epheser* (Düsseldorf, 1957), p. 39; cf. F. Büchsel, *TDNT* IV, p. 353.

[2] NEB; L. L. Morris, *op. cit.*, p. 57 (60); J. A. Robinson, *The Epistle to the Ephesians* (London, [2]1922), pp. 147–49; J. Gnilka, *Der Epheserbrief* (Freiburg, 1971), pp. 86 f.; cf. Arndt s.v. ἀπολύτρωσις. Gnilka observes that the former view requires that something be read into the text.

here (see, however, Rom. 6:15), and it is the idea of slavery to sin which is to the fore; men are under bondage to sin (Rom. 7:14; cf. 6:16-23) and hence to death.[1] Their need is justification, and this is made possible, as in Gal. 3, by means of an act of redemption. Justification is provided freely by divine grace; there is nothing for us to pay ($\delta\omega\rho\epsilon\acute{a}\nu$), from which we may conclude that the cost has been borne by God. Redemption is secured "in Christ", i.e. by God's action in Him, and the means is his being offered as a propitiation by his blood. The language here is close to the martyrological terminology in 4 Macc. 17:21, which D. Hill thinks may have directly influenced Paul.[2] Hence the death of Christ, viewed as that of a martyr, is expounded in sacrificial terms,[3] redemption being secured by means of the offering of a sacrifice through which sin is forgiven and men are delivered from its power.[4] The "cost" of redemption is thus the death of Christ, seen as the gift of divine grace, and the "price" of it is the sacrificial offering made to God. Thus we find again the paradox that the redemption terminology can be used to express a "cost" borne by God and an offering or "price" made to God.

The question arises whether Paul is here using a traditional formulation upon which he has superimposed his own comments.[5] Opinions vary

[1] O. Michel, *Der Brief an die Römer* (Göttingen, [11]1957), pp. 91 f.

[2] D. Hill, *op. cit.*, pp. 41-48.

[3] F. Hahn (*Der urchristliche Gottesdienst* (Stuttgart, 1970), p. 53, n. 29) has argued that the concept of sacrifice is applied to the death of Jesus only in Eph. 5:2; 1 Pet. 1:19 and Hebrews: "the presentation as an atoning death ('for us') must not be equated with this, since it is based on a non-cultic atonement tradition". Even, however, if the death of Jesus is understood in terms of the atoning effects of the martyr's death, the theology of martyrdom had already applied the terminology of sacrifice to the death of the martyr. Hence Hahn's conclusion is erroneous.

[4] H. Lietzmann, *Die Briefe des Paulus* I (Tübingen, 1910), p. 19, emphasises that $\dot{a}\pi o\lambda\acute{v}\tau\rho\omega\sigma\iota\varsigma$ should be taken here in its full sense to signify "loskaufen", and should not be weakened to mean simply $\sigma\omega\tau\eta\rho\acute{\iota}a$. K. Kertelge ("*Rechtfertigung*" *bei Paulus* (Munster, [2]1971), pp. 48 f.), claims that the passage is to be understood against the background of the covenant and the OT usage of "redemption" which signifies the eschatological deliverance wrought by God for his people in order that the covenant may be restored; Paul has taken over this concept from a traditional formulation and widened its meaning in order to indicate the free justification of all men by grace. It is unnecessary to bring in Hellenistic ideas of manumission in order to explain a biblical concept. Similarly, F. Büchsel (*TDNT* IV, pp. 354 f.) holds that no real idea of ransom is present here. This view is to be rejected: 1. $\dot{a}\pi o\lambda\acute{v}\tau\rho\omega\sigma\iota\varsigma$ is hardly a biblical term, since it occurs only in Dan. 4:34 LXX. 2. The biblical idea of redemption itself retains the metaphorical sense of deliverance *from slavery* in Egypt. 3. In the present context the notion of the cost of deliverance is present in the use of $\delta\omega\rho\epsilon\acute{a}\nu$. 4. Whatever be the traditional formula which Paul is using (see next note), the present passage must be understood against the background of Gal. 3:13 and 2 Cor. 5:14-21; in the former of these passages the idea of redemption at the cost of the death of the redeemer is clearly present, and it is quite impossible that this idea should be absent from the parallel passage in Romans (cf. Paul's use of $a\hat{\iota}\mu a$!). Kertelge has failed to take the significance of this earlier, parallel passage into account.

[5] See especially the discussion in K. Kertelge, *op. cit.*, pp. 48-62, 71-84; also R. Bultmann, *Theology of the New Testament* I (London, 1952), p. 46; E. Käsemann, "Zum Verständnis von Römer 3, 24-26", *ZNTW* 43 (1950-51), pp. 150-54; K. Wegenast, *Das Verständnis der Tradition bei Paulus und in den Deuteropaulinen* (Neukirchen, 1962), pp. 76-80; P. Stuhlmacher, *Gerechtigkeit Gottes bei Paulus* (Göttingen, [2]1966), pp. 86-91; H. Thyen, *Studien zur Sündenvergebung* (Göttingen, 1970), pp. 163-72. There is general agreement that one may isolate a

regarding the precise content of such a formulation. As we have seen, similar ideas are expressed by Paul himself in Gal. 3, but the fact that here he uses the term ἀπολύτρωσις rather than ἐξαγοράζω suggests that he is using a piece of traditional terminology; again the fact that he does not need to explain the meaning of ἀπολύτρωσις in 1 Cor. 1:30 indicates that a familiar idea is being used. There is, however, no good reason for believing that the term "redemption" had a different meaning in its pre-Pauline use from that which Paul himself assigns to it; the use of the word here fits in with the general pattern of thought which we have already discovered in 1 Peter and Revelation, as well as with Paul's own usage in Gal. 3. Hence, if traditional formulations are being used here, this is evidence for the early currency of the idea of redemption, but not for the existence of a concept different in content from the Pauline one.[1]

Two Pauline passages remain for consideration, Col. 1:14 and Eph. 1:7 In Col. 1:14 redemption is linked with deliverance from the power of darkness into the kingdom of God's Son,[2] but it is stressed that redemption is to be equated with the forgiveness of sins.[3] It is thus a present possession

[1] See p. 163 n. 4.

[2] Here the verb ῥύομαι becomes associated with the concept of redemption, although the association is not very close. The verb is used in a very similar way to the words at present under consideration to express various forms of deliverance. There is no suggestion of cost or price in the usage; the accent falls on the dangers from which God delivers men in order that they may enter into salvation. Cf. W. Kasch, *TDNT* VI, pp. 998–1003.

[3] The question arises as to why "redemption" is glossed by "forgiveness of sins". J. B. Lightfoot (*Colossians and Philemon* (London, ³1886), p. 141) drew attention to later Gnostic perversions of the concept so that it was equated with initiation into mystical secrets; he suggested that some similar perversion at Colossae may have made it necessary for Paul to define the term more closely. C. F. D. Moule (*Colossians and Philemon* (Cambridge, 1957), p. 58) suggests that the Colossians may have held "fancies about 'escape' into immortality without a corresponding change of character." This view might be supported by reference to the pregnostic heresy reflected in 1 Cor., 1 Jn. and 2 Pet., according to which the practice of sin and immorality was thought to be compatible with claims to the possession of the Holy Spirit and the experience of salvation.

pre-Pauline formula more or less as follows: "being justified by the redemption which is in Christ Jesus, whom God set forth as a propitiation by his blood to show his righteousness through the remission of past sins in the forbearance of God." On this view the terms "justified", "redemption", "propitiation" and "blood" are from pre-Pauline tradition. "Redemption" is then understood as in the previous note.

It seems doubtful to me whether we can delineate the content of the pre-Pauline formula so precisely, and whether we can indeed speak of a formula at all. For some proponents of this view "justified" is a pre-Pauline concept; thus P. Stuhlmacher (*op. cit.*, p. 219) claims – without offering any evidence – that δικαιόω is pre-Pauline in Rom. 3:24; 5:9; 6:7; 8:30 and 1 Cor. 6:11. The indications are rather that "to justify" in the sense of "to forgive" was introduced into Christian theology by Paul (cf. H. Thyen, *op. cit.*, p. 164). At most we can speak of a use of pre-Pauline phraseology in which some important concepts were beginning to be brought together.

It is noteworthy that "blood" appears frequently in the context of redemption (Acts 20:28; Eph. 1:7; Heb. 9:12; 1 Pet. 1:18; Rev. 1:5; 5:9). It has been argued that the term "blood" found its way into Christian theology through the influence of the Lord's Supper formulae; covenant associations are also present there. Hence it has been suggested (E. Käsemann, *op. cit.*) that the present formula is to be traced back to the Lord's Supper. The association of blood and covenant may well have led to a further link with the idea of redemption as part of an Exodus typology; see below.

of believers (ἔχομεν), and it is linked to a concept which is closely related to justification. But, as in Rom. 3:24, the thought of redemption is mentioned in passing, and Paul moves on to the idea of reconciliation by means of the blood of the cross. If vs. 15–20 form part of a pre-Pauline hymn,[1] then Paul's introduction of the reference to the blood of the cross in v. 20 may be more closely related to the idea of redemption – as is certainly the case in Eph. 1:7 where redemption is directly linked to the blood of Christ. The parallels elsewhere justify us in regarding the blood as a reference to the sacrificial death of Jesus; it indicates the cost of redemption, especially since the grace of God is also mentioned in the context (cf. Rom. 3:24), and it also indicates the "price" paid to God in terms of sacrifice.[2] It is against this background that the idea of future redemption in Eph. 1:14 should be seen; it refers to the consummation of what has already been achieved.

III

The Epistle to the Hebrews uses the concept in two passages. In 11:35 we read of the martyrs who refused to accept deliverance for themselves in order that they might attain to a better resurrection. The word thus relates to deliverance from death and the captivity which was associated with it at the "cost" or "price" of denying their faith. Here the elements of "cost" and "price" are clearly present, although the use is obviously metaphorical.

The other passage is 9:11 ff. Christ entered into the "holy place" above, like the high priest on the day of atonement, not with the blood of animals but with his own blood and "found" eternal redemption.[3] Similarly, the writer says that a death has taken place for the redemption of sins (9:15). Here redemption is closely associated with the forgiveness of sins; believers are delivered from their sins, i.e. from their penal effects.[4] The

---

[1] Most reconstructions of the hymn assumed to underlie this section of Colossians start from v. 15 and do not include v. 14 (see E. Lohmeyer and W. Schmauch, *Die Briefe an die Philipper, Kolosser und an Philemon* (Göttingen, 1964), pp. 47–55; E. Lohse, *Colossians and Philemon* (Philadelphia, 1971), pp. 41–46). If vs. 15–20 are based on such a hymn, then Paul's thought of redemption in v. 14 and his addition to the hymn of the words "by his blood" in v. 20 may perhaps be linked more closely to each other. Further, the concepts of redemption and reconciliation are brought together, being linked by the common idea of the means involved, namely the death of Christ viewed sacrificially.

[2] D. Hill (*op. cit.*, pp. 73 f.) has objected that the phrase διὰ τοῦ αἵματος αὐτοῦ can hardly refer to a price paid for redemption, since "the shedding of blood is hardly to be regarded as the price paid for the release from sins." He is no doubt correct in asserting that the phrase indicates "means" rather than "price", but the objection seems pedantic: the NT evidence as a whole shows a close association between the ideas of redemption and sacrifice, just as in the OT atonement and "ransom-price" are closely linked. We, therefore, prefer the exegesis of F. F. Bruce (*The Epistle to the Ephesians* (London, 1962), p. 31) at this point.

[3] M. McNamara *Targum and Testament* (Shannon, 1972), p. 139 draws attention to a parallel to the phrase "eternal redemption" in Ps.Jon. (Gen. 49:18).

[4] The genitive is one of separation.

means of deliverance is the death of Christ, "blood" being clearly used in a
sacrificial sense. As in 1 Pet. 1:18, any thoughts of martyrdom have passed
completely into the background, and the idea of redemption has been fully
assimilated into the author's sacrificial thinking. The influence of other
ideas traditionally associated with redemption may be seen in the
references to the covenant and inheritance (9:15). The idea of the
"mediator" may also form part of this traditional complex in view of
its reappearance in 1 Tim. 2:6.

Hebrews shows us an individual development of the idea of redemption
in which it is closely linked with the sacrificial ritual of the tabernacle
(rather than with the passover sacrifice, as in Rev. and 1 Pet.). It shows the
continuing strength of the idea, although to some extent it has lost its
original force.

IV

The "ransom" saying of Jesus (Mk. 10:45)[1] reappears in 1 Tim. 2:6 in a
text which has been demonstrated to be a less Semitic form of expression.[2]
It has become one of the fixed formulae used by the author of the Pastoral
Epistles, and he offers us his own further interpretation of the text in Tit.
2:14. In 1 Tim. 2:6 Christ acts as mediator between God and man,[3] and
performs his task by giving himself as a ransom for the lives of all. His
death is an offering to God and serves as a ransom payment to free all
men from death and so to reconcile them to God. The author's understanding of this is made clearer in Tit. 2:14 where the word ἀντίλυτρον is
replaced by ἵνα λυτρώσηται, using language based on Ps. 129 (130): 8 LXX
(cf. Rev. 1:5). Men are thus delivered from lawlessness, i.e. they receive
forgiveness and deliverance from the power and penalty of sin, and they
are cleansed in order to become God's special people (λαὸς περιούσιος)
hence the redemption has the effect of purchasing men to be the property
of God. All this is achieved by Christ who is described as "Saviour", thus

[1] The wording in Mt. 20:28 is identical, with ὥσπερ replacing καὶ γάρ.
[2] J. Jeremias, "Das Lösegeld für Viele (Mk. 10:45)", in Abba (Göttingen, 1966), pp. 216–29,
especially pp. 225 f. H. Thyen (op. cit., p. 158) admits the Semitic colouring, but claims
that it does not establish the priority of Mk. 10:45 over against 1 Tim 2:6. On the contrary,
the secondary use of "Son of man" and the use of ἦλθεν, which presupposes the Hellenistic
μεσίτης concept, indicate that Mk. 10:45 is the later form. These arguments are to be rejected.
The first rests on a blanket rejection of the Son of man sayings (op. cit., p. 156) which is totally
unjustified; it is possible in any case to argue for the authenticity of Mk. 10:45b as a saying
of Jesus as an independent logion separate from v. 45a. Nor does the use of ἦλθεν speak
against authenticity: cf. J. Jeremias, New Testament Theology I (London, 1971), p. 293, n. 6;
"Die älteste Schicht der Menschensohn-Logien", ZNTW 58 (1967), pp. 159–72, especially
pp. 166 f.
[3] The verse should perhaps be taken as an expression of the divinity and humanity of Christ
(rather than as a two-member credal statement): "There is one who is God, one who is also
(καί) the mediator between God and man, the man Christ Jesus." Thus the mediatorial
office of Christ depends on his double qualification as God and man. In favour of this view is
the way in which in the parallel passage Tit. 2:13 f. the writer can speak of "the glory of our
great God and Saviour, Jesus Christ" (not "the great God and our Saviour Jesus Christ").

linking the concept of deliverance with the closely associated one of salvation.[1] The further linking of redemption with cleansing suggests that behind the author's thought lies the idea of the sacrificial blood of Christ which liberates and cleanses men (cf. Heb. 9:12-14).

Behind these developments lies the simpler wording in Mk. 10:45 in which Jesus serves men by giving his life as a ransom for many. Mark no doubt intends the saying to be seen against the background of 8:37 where the question is raised whether a man can give any exchange for his life. Behind the question lies Ps. 49 (48):7-9: "Truly no man can ransom himself, or give to God the price of his life, for the ransom of his life is costly, and can never suffice, that he should continue to live on for ever, and never see the Pit". What man cannot do has been done by Christ. We are surely justified in discerning here the thought of human mortality as the result of human sin, and in seeing in the death of Christ the ransom "price" paid to God[2] for the redemption of mankind from death.[3] We may also see here a reference to the death of the suffering Servant which benefits the "many" when he makes himself an offering for sin.[4] The saying may thus contain a sacrificial idea, since the ransom is an offering to God for the lives of others, and the intermediate link may be found in the idea of martyrdom.[5]

V

It is time to draw together the threads of our discussion and see whether we can sketch the development of the idea of redemption more precisely.

In his book on the atonement in the NT, E. Lohse has argued that the theology of the earliest church regarding the death of Christ is to be found in the kerygma in I Cor. 15:3-5; the "sayings of the Lord" in Mk. 10:45 and 14:24; the formal statements based on these; the use of the term "blood" and the comparison of Jesus with the passover lamb. Behind these various uses Lohse finds the influence of Is. 53. He claims that the oldest form of the cup-saying omitted the reference to the covenant and spoke of the death of Jesus in terms of Is. 53 as the giving of his life many. Originally the thought was not sacrificial, but referred to the atoning death of the Servant. Then at a very early stage the thought of the

[1] See especially Rom. 5:9; Phil. 1:19; Heb. 5:7; Jas. 5:20; 1 Pet. 4:18; Jude 5; W. Foerster and G. Föhrer, *TDNT* VII, pp. 965-1024.
[2] F. Büchsel, *TDNT* IV, p. 344. The arguments of E. Lohse (*op. cit.*, p. 121, n. 3) to the contrary fail to convince.
[3] F. Büchsel (*TDNT* IV, p. 343) stresses that the deliverance is from sin rather than merely from death.
[4] The influence of Is. 53 is rejected by H. Thyen, *op. cit.*, pp. 158-60, but he is unable to demonstrate that it is impossible. On the other side see R. T. France, "The Servant of the Lord in the Teaching of Jesus", *Tyndale Bulletin*, 19 (1968), pp. 26-52, summarised in *Jesus and the Old Testament* (London, 1971), pp. 116-21.
[5] We have utilised Mk. 8:37 to help elucidate the meaning of Mk. 10:45 in its Marcan context. Some such background must be presupposed for the saying in its original setting.

covenant was attached to the saying, and hence the blood of Jesus was interpreted in terms of the covenant sacrifice.[1]

Whatever be the truth regarding the details of this description, there is sufficient substance in it for us to build upon it and to claim that in this material available to the early church we have the necessary and sufficient presuppositions for the development of the concept of redemption. The decisive point is the association of Mk. 10:45 with 14:24, an association that lay easily to hand in their common dependence on Is. 53. This association would be all the easier if Mk. 10:45 were also linked with the Lord's Supper.[2]

From Mk. 10:45b a direct line leads to the formal expressions in the Pastoral Epistles. The saying itself speaks of the martyr death of the Servant, and hence gave rise to a. sayings which speak of Christ giving himself or handing himself over (Jn. 6:51; Gal. 1:4; 2:20; Eph. 5:2, 25; cf. "laying down one's life", Jn. 10:11, 15, 17 f.); b. sayings which interpret the death of Jesus as having the atoning power of a martyr's death (Rom. 3:24).

The association with Mk. 14:24 brings in the idea of the blood of Christ, again taken in a martyrological sense. Again two lines of thought develop: a. Paul uses the idea of manumission to express the idea of redemption in a more tangible form, perhaps especially for Christians in the Hellenistic world. The same idea is found in Rev. and 1 Pet. b. Once the martyr death of Jesus has been seen to have atoning power, the way lies open for a further understanding of it in terms of the Jewish sacrificial system. This operated in three ways: i. Sacrificial ideas ($i\lambda\alpha\sigma\tau\eta\rho\iota o\nu$) were already bound up with the idea of martyrdom (4 Macc.; Rom. 3:24); ii. The concept of the covenant, already associated with the cup-saying, led to the understanding of the death of Jesus in terms of the sacrifices associated with the Exodus, namely the sacrifice of the passover, which in Jewish thought wrought redemption for Israel, and also the covenant sacrifice (1 Pet. 1:2); iii. The death of Jesus was associated with the sacrificial ritual of the tabernacle on the day of atonement, and this sacrifice was thus regarded as a means of redemption.

The motif which does not fit into this development is the concept of a still future redemption (Lk. 21:28; Rom. 8:23; Eph. 1:14; 4:30). This may serve as a warning against trying to force the evidence into one rigid pattern.[3] It is best to see here a development from the Jewish idea of

---

[1] E. Lohse, op. cit. Pt. 2.

[2] In its present context Mk. 10:45 appears in an ethical context unconnected with the Lord's Supper. But the parallel tradition in Lk. 22:24–27 does appear in a Supper tradition, and hence it is possible that the tradition in Mk. 10:42–45 was originally linked to the Supper. On the other hand, some scholars regard Mk. 10:45b as an isolated saying, about whose origin it is difficult to be certain.

[3] This warning also holds good for the attempt to see the element of "price" in every, or almost every, use of the phraseology. We have been able to observe in the course of our study that this element is not universally present. In a number of cases the idea is that of

eschatological redemption, quite distinct from the Christian idea based on the theology of the cross. It takes two forms. In Luke the eschatology is seen to be essentially "realised" in the coming of Jesus, and hence this idea of redemption can be easily linked to the main line of development. But the thought of a future redemption also persisted, though in a specialized sense, and it plays a modest part in NT thought; again, however, the terminology leads to the future redemption being seen to some extent in the light of the past redemption at the cross.

On this view Mk. 10:45 represents the simplest form of the concept and lies at the base of the development. The saying is free from ideas of blood, covenant, sacrifice and manumission, but depends on Is. 53, a text which is not taken up elsewhere in the development. Again, the saying undoubtedly comes from the earliest tradition of the church, as is shown by its Semitic form and the fact that it has been handed down as a Son of man saying; there is in fact good reason to argue that it is an authentic saying of Jesus.[1]

It may be objected that the influence of Mk. 10:45 is attested only in the Pastorals, and that Paul's terminology is different. In fact, however, Paul's choice of ἀπολύτρωσις, a word with no significant precedent in the LXX, and other associated words, suggests that the λύτρον saying lies at the root of the development. Paul's vocabulary expresses the result of Christ's death rather than its character, and this fits in with NT thought in general, which is more concerned with the nature of salvation than the precise way in which it has been achieved. Moreover, if ἀπολύτρωσις is a traditional term in Paul, this pushes the date of the entry of the idea into Christian theology still earlier.[2]

Thus the concept of redemption is to be traced back to the teaching of Jesus[3] and has undergone a rich development, leading to its use with various shades of meaning and in different associations of thought. It is one of the most frequently used categories of interpretation of the death of Jesus in the NT and excellently expresses its meaning. We may cordially agree with L. Morris: "In the Scripture we see the price paid, the curse borne, in order that those who are redeemed should be brought into the liberty of the sons of God, a liberty which may paradoxically be called slavery to God. The whole point of this redemption is that sin no longer has dominion; the redeemed are those saved to do the will of their Master."[4]

[1] See R. T. France, op. cit.
[2] The other formative element in the redemption tradition, namely the cup-word at the Last Supper, is also of early date, as is seen in its attestation by Paul in 1 Cor. 11:25.
[3] So also W. Mundle (with J. Schneider and L. Coenen), TBNT I, pp. 258–72, especially p. 263.
[4] L. L. Morris, op. cit., p. 59 (62).

"cost" rather than "price". Nevertheless, when this caveat has been observed, it remains true that in about half of the texts the element of "cost" or "price" is fairly explicit. No less than seven times is redemption associated with the blood of Christ, and in a further four cases with his death.

PART TWO:

HOPE

CHAPTER XI

THE ESCHATOLOGICAL ROLE OF LAW IN PRE- AND POST-CHRISTIAN JEWISH THOUGHT

ROBERT BANKS

IN RECENT YEARS, A RENEWED INTEREST HAS BEEN DEMONSTRATED IN THE centrality and character of the Law in Apocryphal, Pseudepigraphal and Rabbinic eschatological speculations.[1] To a large extent this has been undertaken in the hope that such conclusions as can be reached will illuminate the eschatological preoccupations of various NT writers, both of a "realized" and "futuristic" nature. In particular, connexions between the outlook of Matthew, John and Paul and contemporary Jewish eschatological expectations concerning Moses and the Law, have come in for close consideration. As as result of these investigations, there has been a revival of interest in the view that the arrival of a new Torah in the Messianic Age and/or Age to Come was a well defined and accepted hope within Judaism. In the main, however, this has been restated in a qualified form i.e., that there were at least elements within Judaism expecting the modification or substitution of various parts of the Mosaic legislation. Without contravening the old, these were sufficiently comprehensive to justify the description "new".[2] It is the adequacy of this interpretation of the evidence, and by implication the conclusions that have been drawn from it for NT, particularly Matthaean, perspectives, that forms the theme of this study.

I

In the OT, it is only in the priestly and prophetic writings that there is any explicit reference to the future role of Law. The wisdom literature, with its exclusive concentration on the *torah* of the wise and its lack of eschatological concern, is quite silent on the matter. Throughout P,

[1] The most exhaustive treatment of the New Torah theme occurs in W. D. Davies, *The Setting of the Sermon on the Mount* (Cambridge, 1964), pp. 109-90 which incorporates, with minor alterations, his earlier monograph on *Torah in the Messianic Age and/or in the Age to Come* (Philadelphia, 1952). On pp. 109-10 of the former work he lists previous investigations of the subject. The more recent contributions of H. M. Teeple, J. Jocz, G. Barth, E. Bammel, H. J. Schoeps and R. N. Longenecker are detailed in the following pages.
[2] This is the view of Davies himself, as also of Teeple and Longenecker after him. The stronger view had been expounded by Edersheim, Dalman, Köhler and, in part, Aptowitzer in the earlier years of this century. More recently it has been reiterated by Jocz and Schoeps.

however, for the first time in OT legal material, individual statutes are described as having been given "forever" or as being "everlasting" in character. Though such statements are accompanied by occasional warnings against disobedience, the possibility of a dissolution of the covenant, together with its legal contents, does not seem to have been seriously entertained.[1]

It was the prophets who faced up most realistically to the inevitability of just such a dissolution. In so doing they not only predicted the certainty of the coming judgement but presented visionary glimpses of what lay beyond it. Along with the promise of a new Exodus and a new Covenant, in several passages there is reference to the role of the Law in the future as well viz., Is. 2:1–5 (cf. Mic. 4:1–5); Is. 42:1–4; Is. 51:4; Jer. 31:31–34; Ezek. 36:24–28.

In view of the equation of *torah* with the prophetic message throughout First Isaiah (Is. 1:10; 8:16, 20; 30:9), the term should almost certainly be interpreted in a similar sense in Is. 2:3. It would then refer to something far wider than the Law, particularly those fundamental ethical principles which are constantly re-iterated in the work, and would be equivalent to the phrase "word of the Lord" with which it appears to stand in parallelism.[2] In Is. 42:1 f. the servant is described as one who will give *torah* (v. 4), and here, taking into account the total setting of the passage, the word has almost the sense of "revelation". This is also surely the case in Is. 51:4–5 where *torah* is linked with such conceptions as "righteousness" and "salvation".[3]

Although *torah* is used in Jeremiah with reference to the traditional Law, in several contexts it appears in conjunction with the "word" of the prophet, indicating that it cannot be fulfilled properly unless the prophetic word is also heeded (2:8; 9:12–13; 16:10–12) while in others it is equated with that prophetic word itself (6:19; 26:4–5; 44:18).[4] The same conjunction of ideas occurs in 31:33–34 where the "law" (v. 33) written in the heart is linked with "knowledge" (v. 34) of the Lord. It is clear from Jer. 2:8; 3:15; 5:1–4; 8:7; 11:18; 24:7; 32:8 and 44:29 that knowledge of Yahweh embraces much more than obedience to the Law, and this is reinforced in the present passage by the phrase "they shall teach no more every man his neighbour" (v. 34). It seems probable then that *torah* in v. 33, as in the

[1] *'olam* often means quite simply "for a long time" but in these passages it should probably be given its strongest connotation. See Köhler-Baumgartner, pp. 688–89.
[2] The commentators do, in fact, generally interpret the word in terms of "instruction". By dating the passage in the post-exilic age, W. D. Davies, *Setting*, pp. 138 f. nevertheless seeks to give the word a stronger legal connotation. According to the detailed investigation of these verses by H. Wildberger, *Jesaja* (1965), pp. 78–80, however, such a dating is unnecessary.
[3] On Is. 42:4 cf. C. R. North, *Second Isaiah* (Oxford, 1964), pp. 108–109 and C. Westermann *Das Buch Jesaja: Kapitel 40–66* (Göttingen, 1966), p. 81. On Is. 51:4–5 see J. L. McKenzie *Second Isaiah* (New York, 1968), pp. 36–38.
[4] On the close relationship between traditional Law and prophetic word in Jeremiah see further J. Bright, *Jeremiah* (New York, 1965), pp. 63–64 (on 8:8).

Isaianic passages, refers primarily to the survival of Yahweh's prophetic instruction beyond the disintegration of the present covenantal framework.[1]

At first sight only the Law seems to be in view in Ezek. 36:24–28. In this prophecy, Yahweh speaks of a "new spirit" and a "new heart" which will bring with it obedience to "my statutes". It is significant, however, that Ezek. 40–48 contains items which have no parallel in the Mosaic Law, while Ezek. 43:11–12 and 44:5 explicitly refer to the presence of prophetic *torah*. One should be careful, therefore, in reading too traditional a meaning into the "statutes" referred to in 36:27.

In all these passages, then, the presence of *torah* in the new age of Israel's history is affirmed. Such *torah*, however, refers primarily to the prophetic instruction. This should not be separated from, indeed it includes, the traditional Law, but it is not that Law which is here primarily in view. It is most strongly in view in the Ezekiel passage and though in Jeremiah the emphasis is principally upon its ethical requirements, in view of 33:18 it must also have contained ritual stipulations. This would also certainly be the case in the Isaianic passages as well.

II

In the post-biblical literature a significant shift in attitude can be detected, one associated with the coalescence of each of the major Israelite traditions more closely around the Law. In material of a legal character this leads to a strengthening of the tendency in P to insist upon the everlasting character of many of the Law's requirements, though now eschatological considerations begin to come into view. This may not be so in Tob. 1:6 but such are certainly present in the so-called "Formulary of Blessings" at Qumran. Though reference to it does not appear as frequently as one might expect, the rabbinic writings clearly presuppose the eternal validity of the Law throughout.[2] Not only of Torah as a whole is the idea expressed (Ex. R. 33:7), but even of the words, the very jots and tittles, that make it up (Ex. R. 6:1; Lev. R. 19:2). Both these emphases

[1] W. D. Davies, *Setting*, pp. 127 f. places the emphasis here upon the Mosaic Law, citing in support the somewhat similar terminology to Jer. 33:33 in Ps. 37:31; 40:8; Dt. 11:18 and 10:14. In light of Jeremiah's use of *torah* elsewhere, and the tenor of the present passage, I do not find these comparisons compelling.

[2] Cf. Strack-Billerbeck, I, pp. 244–47. In later rabbinic writings a clear distinction is drawn between the "Messianic Age" and the "Age to Come". This is already present in the statement of R. Johanan in b. Ber. 34b (and pars.) and in the discussion centring on the length of the Messianic time (b. Sanh. 99a *et al.*) as in the late apocalyptic writings (2 Bar. 40:3; 2 Esd. 7:28–31 and Rev. 20:4 f.). A rigid separation does not seem to occur in the sayings of the earlier teachers recorded in the Mishnah e.g., those of Eliezer, Hillel and Shammai, nor in the remainder of the apocryphal and pseudepigraphal literature. The period following upon the destruction of Jerusalem is therefore usually considered to be the decisive point from which the distinction became more apparent. See further on this point M. Löwy, "Messiaszeit und zukünftige Welt" *MGWJ*, 5 (1897), p. 401 and K. Schubert, *Die Religion des nachbiblischen Judentums* (Freiburg, 1955), p. 49.

exhibit a more comprehensive and stricter attitude than in P. Closer in mood to the latter is the statement in Yoma 5b that the sacrificial laws will be particularly observed in the time to come. An interesting tendency is noticeable in j. Meg. 1.70d where it is only of the Pentateuch that eternal duration is predicted, the Prophets and Writings having ceased in the Messianic time. No doubt this is based on the view expressed in b. Shabb 104a, Ex. R. 42:8 and elsewhere that the prophets brought nothing additional to the Law but only reinstituted commandments that had originally been formulated by Moses. For most rabbis, however, the other Scripture also possessed eternal status, however inferior to the Pentateuch they may have been considered. Parallel to this, at the other end of the time-scale is the affirmation of Torah's pre-existence in such passages as Ab. 3:15 Sif. Dt. 11:10 and Gen. R. 1:1.

A similar attitude to the Law is displayed in the apocalyptic tradition. In the book of Jubilees the eternal character of the Law is ceaselessly reiterated. Its enactments, written on heavenly tablets (3:31; 6:17) and mediated by angels to man (1:27) are considered to be the complete expression of Yahweh's will. Ritual laws are given special prominence especially those dealing with the Sabbath (2:26 ff.), circumcision (15:26 f.) festivals (6:17; 16:29) and tithing (32:10). To all these is ascribed eternal validity. In the other apocalypses it is rather the Torah as a whole which is in view (1 Bar. 4:1; 1 En. 99:2, 14; 2 Esd. 9:37; 2 Bar. 77:15 cf. Ps. Sol. 17:37). In these, with the exception of 1 Enoch, the Law is also identified with Wisdom. This is indicated in 1 Bar. 3:9 f.; 2 Bar. 77:16 and 2 Esd 8:52 f.; 13:54–55. In 1 Enoch, however, the identification is not explicitly made, indeed in 42:1 f. it appears to have been decisively rejected. It is interesting, therefore, that in this work, it is not Torah but wisdom and righteousness which are chiefly associated with the activity of the Elect One who is to come (39:6; 42:1 f.; 43:6; 48:1; 49:1; 53:7; 71:14, 16 91:10). Thus here too we have testimony to the persistence of the prophetic tradition in which the Law, however highly it may be valued, is not in the Coming Age the only, or even central, factor. Even in the other apocalypses, however, the content of that Law has been considerably amplified.[1]

---

[1] The assertion of A. Schweitzer, *The Mysticism of Paul the Apostle* (London, 1956), pp. 191–92 (cf. also H. J. Schoeps, *Paul. The Theology of the Apostle in the Light of Jewish Religious History* (London, 1961), p. 172), that late Jewish apocalypses, while not expressing the idea that Law is of no further importance in the time to come are so dominated by the idea that they nowhere assert that Law will be in operation nor describe life in terms of perfect obedience to it, goes too far beyond the evidence. While it is true that in the Psalms of Solomon 2 Baruch and 2 Esdras the term "Law" is not emphasised in passages dealing with the Messianic period, ideas of "wisdom" and "righteousness" which elsewhere in these works are equated with the Law do appear (cf. Ps. Sol. 14:1–2; 2 Bar. 67:6 and passages cited above). While as we have seen, this does not occur in 1 Enoch, there is mention in this work of the eternal duration of the Law (1 En. 99:14). His attempt to bypass this with the statement "that the Law is eternal does not mean it is of eternal application", picturing its position in the Messianic Age as of the same order as its pre-existent state, is not particularly satisfying.

The Old Testament wisdom literature, geared as it is to the present world is silent as to the duration of its *torah*. In the apocryphal wisdom literature, however, the everlasting character of the Law does find expression in Ecclus. 24:9, 33 and most probably in Wisd. 18:4. Neverthe-less it is implied that Wisdom, which though equated with the Law is also more comprehensive than it, can be spoken of in similar terms.[1]

Comparison with the later Old Testament writings, therefore, shows that in each of these traditions there is a heightened though not exclusive emphasis upon the future importance of the Law.

III

We must now turn to those passages which allegedly testify to the occurrence of changes in the Law in the days to come.[2] In the first place, brief mention may be made of those texts in which certain difficulties and obscurities in the Torah are mentioned as being clarified in the Messianic era. It is above all Elijah who will return at that time to explain the significance of points in the Law that had perplexed the Rabbis. How-ever, the solution of difficulties and apparent contradictions that was to take place through his activity only served to highlight the unity and per-petuity of the Law.[3]

Other passages seem to suggest that there will be an annulment of particular provisions in the Law. So according to Lev. R. 9:7, this will be the fate of all sacrifices and prayers but that of Thanksgiving. Such

[1] On the latter see W. J. Deane, *The Book of Wisdom* (Oxford, 1881), p. 209. Ecclus. 1:15 speaks of Wisdom as an "eternal foundation", a description which at first sight appears to be a direct statement of its everlasting character. The verse, however, is full of difficulties and has been amended by G. H. Box and W. O. E. Oesterley, *Apocrypha*, ed. R. H. Charles, I, p. 319, to read "established for ever" i.e., from eternity. There is a similar thought in Wisd. 7:26 where Wisdom is described as an "effulgence from everlasting light". In these verses, therefore, the theme of Wisdom's pre-existence, already affirmed in Prov. 8:1 f., is taken up anew (see further Wisd. 9:1 f.; Ecclus. 1:4 f.; 24:9). The implication is probably present, however, that it is eternal in the other direction as well and Ecclus. 24:9 illustrates just how closely the two thoughts are bound together. There is a further clear testimony to the eternal character of the Law in Philo De Vita Mos. 11.44.
[2] R. Longenecker, *Paul: Apostle of Liberty* (New York, 1964), pp. 128–29 has rightly warned that in taking up such a survey the concepts "abrogation of the Law" and "establish-ment of a new Law" are not, as is commonly assumed, complementary and that they must be treated as quite separate questions. A further clarification is provided by H. M. Teeple, *The Mosaic Eschatological Prophet* (Philadelphia, 1957), pp. 15 f., who states that there was a considerable variety of opinion concerning the degree of observance of the Law in the time immediately preceding the Messianic period (e.g., Tos. Eduy. 1:1; Cant. R.2:9) and to what extent the Law should be binding upon Gentiles (e.g., Gen. R.98:9). None of these discussions, however, were intended to "involve any change in the Law itself but merely a change in the degree of observance of it".
[3] Cf. Sh. Spiegel, "Ezekiel or pseudo-Esekiel", *HTR*, 24 (1931), pp. 260–61. See also H. Danby, *The Mishnah* (Oxford, 1933), p. 436, n. 19 and G. Barth, "Matthew's Understanding of the Law", in *Tradition and Interpretation in Matthew* (London, 1963), p. 156, n. 4 on Eduy.8:7 against M. Löwy, *MGWJ* (1904), p. 324.

an attitude probably springs from the conviction that since in that period sin would not exist these sacrifices would be unnecessary. However, the passage is late and cannot be dated before the latter half of the second-century.[1] Yalkut on Prov. 9:2, probably to be dated earlier in the second century, speaks of Purim and the Day of Atonement as the only Festivals which will be celebrated in the Messianic time. One should reckon with the possibility, however, that both passages are more concerned to emphasise the importance of the activities mentioned than to deny the continuance of others.[2] One of the views expressed in Midrash Tehillim on Ps. 146:7 insists on the abrogation of the distinction between clean and unclean animals in this future period but this is immediately followed by two contradictory opinions.[3] A change in Torah also seems to be implied in Sif. Dt. 17:18. However, the parallel passage in Tos. Sanh. 4:4 f., which is most likely earlier, specifically defines the change as concerning only the script of Torah, not its contents.[4]

A more important passage is b. Shabb. 151b in which R. Simeon b. Eleazar (c. 165–200 A.D.) draws a comparison between the state of the dead and the Messianic era. In the latter, contrary to the present, "there is neither merit nor guilt" and W. D. Davies, comparing this text with the freedom of the dead from the Law mentioned in b. Nid. 61b, suggests this means that "the Torah no longer holds in the Messianic Age". H. J. Schoeps interprets b. Shabb. 30a and j. Kil. 9.4 in the same way. Freedom of the dead from the Law, however, need not involve any limitation of its validity. It is merely the case that such are now, by the nature of the case, no longer able to observe it.[5] Similarly, cessation of the *yetzer ha-ra'* in the Messianic time, the conception that appears to underlie the statement in b. Shabb. 151b, does not invalidate Torah but merely the possibility of acquiring merit or guilt through it. A prediction of the complete abrogation of Torah has been derived from b. Sanh. 97b and Ab. Zar. 9a: "The world is to exist six thousand years. In the first two thousand years

---

[1] So H. Loewe, *A Rabbinic Anthology* (London, 1938), p. 350 though J. Israelstam, *Midrash Rabbah: Leviticus* (London, 1939), p. 114 disputes his attributing it to Menahem of Galilee.

[2] Cf. J. Klausner, *From Jesus to Paul* (London, 1944), p. 321, n. 13.

[3] W. D. Davies, *Setting*, p. 165 makes the suggestion that the greater strictness of the Law's demands in the future reflected in the second contradictory opinion testifies to the possibility of a change in the Torah. However, though the statement does refer to an increased strictness in marital relations such are not regulated on the whole by statutes in the Old Testament, and it is God's presence, not Torah, which alters the situation here. It should be noted that some Jewish scholars are doubtful about the authenticity of these and related passages in the Midrash (cf. Davies, *op. cit.*, 164, n. 1).

[4] Against J. Bonsirven, *Le Judaïsme palestinien* (Paris, 1934–35), I, p. 453, n. 9.

[5] Against W. D. Davies, *Setting*, p. 170 and H. J. Schoeps, *"ΧΡΙΣΤΟΣ ΤΕΛΟΣ ΝΟΜΟΥ"*, *Aus frühchristlicher Zeit: religionsgeschichtliche Untersuchungen* (Tübingen, 1950), p. 223. On b. Nid. 61b see also H. Silver, *A History of Messianic Speculation in Israel* (New York, 1927), p. 9; J. Jocz, *The Jewish People and Jesus Christ* (London, 1949), p. 155; R. N. Longenecker, *Paul*, pp. 130–31. W. Bächer, *Die Agada der babylonischen Amoräer* (Strassburg, ²1967), p. 105, n. 23, however, limited this abrogation to the ceremonial commandments alone.

there was desolation, two thousand years the Torah flourished; and the next two thousand years is the Messianic era . . .". However, such schematizations, which are typically third century in outlook and not relevant for earlier periods, are aimed at fixing the date of the Messiah rather than limiting the validity of Torah.[1]

Thus the view that within the framework of a doctrine of the immutability of Torah expectations of its partial modification or abrogation are occasionally to be found, exceeds the evidence adduced in its support.

IV

We turn next to those passages in which, it has been alleged, a new Torah is explicitly indicated. Just as we commenced the previous set of texts with an examination of the future activity of Elijah and its possible connection with changes in Torah, so it is necessary here to enquire into the hope surrounding the return of Moses, or of a figure like him, and their bearing on the question of a new Torah. There is reference to a return of Moses in several rabbinic passages. These state that his death and burial in the wilderness took place so that in the future he might lead that generation into the promised land. All these, however, are later than the first century A.D. The earliest is probably Sif. Dt. 33.21 which is said to come from the school of R. Ishmael (120–140 A.D.) though the Midrash is not dated until the seventh century or later.[2] The return of Moses and Elijah together is mentioned in Dt. R. 3:17. Despite the later redaction of the Midrash it has been suggested that since the tradition is presented by Johanan ben Zakkai it is most probably early. However, this view has been strongly contested.[3] We must conclude that the idea of a reappearance of Moses at the beginning of the Messianic Kingdom is a later innovation.[4] Moreover, in none of these passages is his supposed return associated with any legislative activity.

[1] Cf. E. Bammel, "Νόμος χριστοῦ", St.Ev., III (1964), p. 122 and H. Freedman, Sanhedrin (London, 1939), ch. 11, p. 657, n. 9.
[2] The most comprehensive discussion of these, and other, rabbinic passages is probably that in R. Bloch, "Die Gestalt des Moses in der rabbinischen Tradition", Moses in Schrift und Überlieferung (Düsseldorf, 1963), pp. 95–171.
[3] Thus against I. Abrahams, Studies in Pharisaism and the Gospels (Cambridge, 1924), II, p. 53; H. J. Schoeps, Theologie und Geschichte des Judentums (Tübingen, 1949), p. 96; H. M. Teeple, Prophet, p. 45 and T. F. Glasson, Moses in the Fourth Gospel (London, 1963), p. 27, n. 2 see J. Jeremias, TDNT, IV, p. 855, n. 96; G. H. Boobyer, "St. Mark and the Transfiguration", JTS, 41 (1940), p. 130 and J. Giblet, "Prophétisme et attente d'un messie prophète dans l'AT", L'Attente du Messie (Paris, 1954), pp. 102–103.
[4] Cf. P. Volz, Die Eschatologie der jüdischen Gemeinde im neutestamentlichen Zeitalter (Hildesheim, 1966 ed.), especially p. 195. It is also significant that no account of the assumption of Moses occurs in the apocalyptic work of that name. The earliest references appear to be postchristian (2 Esd. 14:9; 2 Bar. 59:3–4), but rabbinic sources indicate that alongside it the biblical view also prevailed. See the discussion in H. M. Teeple, Prophet, pp. 41–43.

A further group of passages speak not of a return of Moses but of a figure who possesses Mosaic characteristics. In this connexion, references to the prediction in Dt. 18:15-18 of a "prophet like Moses" are first to be considered. It is rather surprising to find only three occurrences of this prophecy in the rabbinic literature, each of which relates the promise to one of the past prophets (Pesik. 112a; Sif. Dt. 18:15, 16).[1] In 1 Macc. 4:46 and 14:41 mention is made of the expectation of "a (faithful) prophet".[2] Even if Dt. 18:15-18 lies behind the passage, something that is by no means certain due to the general nature of the prediction, it is more likely that it does so only in the sense of prophesying the coming of a figure who, like Moses, will stand as a representative between God and the people, not in terms of any detailed similarity with the actual role of Moses. In fact, his task does not appear to be that of giving new legislation in an eschatological context, but of settling certain disputed points not covered by Torah.[3]

On the basis of CDC 6:8 f., and certain other passages, it has been maintained that the Teacher of Righteousness is also described in terms of Dt. 18:15-18.[4] Whether this is so or not, CDC 1:10-12 suggests that his task is that of setting out instructions for the life of the community rather than making alterations in the Mosaic Law or giving utterance to new Torah. CDC 6:14 implies that these were to be regarded as an interim-ethic, valid only until the dawn of the Messianic era.[5] A fragment of the Testimonies Scroll cites Dt. 18:15-18 in connexion with the further figure – the Prophet to come – and from 1 QS 6:14 it has been inferred that he also engages in legislative activity. Again it must be stressed that

---

[1] Cf. also Philo De Spec. Leg., I, 65. A further parallel in Ass.Mos. 10:15, despite R. H. Charles, *Pseudepigrapha*, II, p. 412, is uncertain, as J. Jeremias, *TDNT*, IV, p. 857, n. 114 points out. Test.Lev. 8:14 f. cannot credibly be derived from Dt. 18:15-18, as some have surmised.

[2] The similar reference in Test. Benj.9:2 sometimes alluded to in this connection, is probably a christian interpolation. Cf. R. H. Charles, *Pseudepigrapha*, II, p. 358 against R. E. Brown, "The Messianism of Qumran", *CBQ* 19 (1957), p. 59, n. 35.

[3] So P. Volz, *Eschatologie*, pp. 193–94; J. Giblet, "Prophétisme", p. 105 and W. D. Davies, *Setting*, pp. 143–45. A stronger link with Dt. 18:15-18 is insisted upon by R. Schnackenburg, "Die Erwartung des 'Propheten' nach dem NT und dem Qumran-Texten", *St. Ev.* I (1959), pp. 631–32 and F. Gils, *Jésus, Prophète d'après les Évangiles Synoptiques* (Louvain, 1957), pp. 30–31. However, if any figure is to be associated with the expectation of the prophet it is more likely to be Elijah, especially in view of the Torah ministry later connected with his return. Cf. J. Klausner, *The Messianic Idea in Israel* (London, 1960), p. 260.

[4] See, apart from the writings of Jeremias, Gils, Schoeps and Giblet already mentioned, especially N. Wieder, "The Law-Interpreter" of the Sect of the DSS: A Second Moses", *JJS*, 4 (1953), pp. 158–75; G. Vermès, "Die Gestalt des Moses an der Wende der beiden Testamenten", *Moses in Schrift und Überlieferung*, pp. 85 f. and O. Betz, *Offenbarung und Schriftforschung in der Qumransekte* (Tübingen, 1960), pp. 62 f. Other titles and descriptions are applied to both Moses and the Teacher – e.g. 'star', 'vessel', 'craftsman' – but since these were applied to other figures as well they are less relevant here. Cf. J. Morgenstern, *Some Significant Antecedents of Christianity* (Leiden, 1966), pp. 1 ff.

[5] In view of this, the translation "lawgiver" in these passages is better rendered "searcher of the law" (Ch. Rabin, *The Zadokite Documents* (Oxford, ²1958, p. 22) or "law-interpreter" (N. Wieder, *JJS*, 4 (1953), p. 159).

is only the Rule of the community, not at all the Mosaic Law, which is involved. It should be noted here that the identification of these two figures, despite some support, is highly questionable, as is the attaching of any Messianic significance to their activity.[1] Moreover, despite the appearance of some Mosaic traits in the Teacher, and the reference of the Deuteronomic passage to the prophet, if any one figure is to be associated with either it would again seem to be that of Elijah, especially in view of his dual role as preparer for the Messianic era and interpreter of uncertain aspects of the Law.

Samaritan expectations, centred around the coming of the Ta'eb, appear to have awaited a figure with similarities to Moses. In fact, Dt. 18:15-18 seems to form the basis of their eschatological speculation and was even regarded by them as the tenth commandment.[2] In view of their recognition of the Pentateuch alone this is scarcely surprising, and it is precisely this limitation which advises caution in arguing for a corresponding concept in orthodox Jewish thought at the same time, quite apart from the lateness of the sources which refer to this expectation. In any case, the Samaritans did not look for the Ta'eb to bring a new Law or make alterations in the old, but principally to instruct non-Samaritans in the existing Torah.[3]

In the New Testament several passages reflect popular expectations of a coming prophet (Mk. 6:15; 8:28; Mt. 11:9, 14; 17:12; Jn. 1:21, 25; 6:14; 7:40). The variety of figures put forward in these texts shows just how little uniformity there was in the popular hope and it is apparent that even if Dt. 18:15-18 played some part in the expectation, it was by no means the dominant category. The figure of Elijah is once again prominent.[4] It has also been claimed that the revolutionary prophets mentioned in Jos. Ant.

---

[1] Consult the detailed discussion in H. Braun, *Qumran und das NT* (Tübingen, 1966), I, p. 149-50; II, pp. 67-68. The suggestion of W. D. Davies, *Setting*, pp. 149-50 that the future "making new" in 1 QS 4:18-26 included refashioning of the Law is highly conjectural.

[2] See M. Gaster, *The Samaritans* (London, 1925), p. 91; W. A. Meeks, *The Prophet-King* (Leiden, 1967), pp. 205 f.

[3] It is extremely doubtful whether the term "Messiah" should be ascribed to the Ta'eb expectation. Against S. Mowinckel, *He That Cometh* (Oxford, 1956), p. 293; J. Jeremias, *TDNT*, IV, p. 858 and H. M. Teeple, *Prophet*, p. 108, it must be noted that the term is never applied to him in the Samaritan writings. Since his function is only one of restoration, and he possesses no royal lineage, the description is probably inappropriate. Cf. J. MacDonald, *The Theology of the Samaritans* (London, 1964), p. 361. Indeed his inferiority to Moses has been emphasised by J. E. H. Thompson, *The Samaritans* (London, 1919), pp. 194-95 and A. Merx, *Der Messias oder Ta'eb der Samaritaner* (1909), p. 43. The description in Jn. 4:25, therefore, has its basis in christian terminology. Cf. P. Volz, *Eschatologie*, p. 200.

[4] See further E. Fascher, *ΠΡΟΦΗΤΗΣ* (Giessen, 1927), p. 208; R. Meyer, *Der Prophet aus Galiläa* (Leipzig, 1940), p. 98 and R. E. Brown, *The Gospel According to John* (New York, 1966), pp. 234-35 and note on 1:27. For all these passages but Jn. 6:14 it is generally agreed that a Messianic identification of the prophet is out of the question. This is true for Jn. 6:14 as well, see W. Baldensperger, *Das Selbstbewusstsein Jesu* (Strassburg, 1888), 114-15; R. Bultmann, *Das Johannesevangelium* (Göttingen, ¹¹1950), p. 61; J. H. Bernard, *The Gospel according to St. John* (Edinburgh, 1942), I, p. 37; H. Strathmann, *Das Evangelium nach Johannes* (Göttingen, 1955), p. 114.

XX, 97–99; 167–172; War II, 261 (cf. Ant. XX, 188; War VII, 438; Ac 21:38) held both Mosaic and Messianic pretensions. It is more likel however, that parallels with Elijah and Elisha (for Theudos), and Josh (for the prophet from Egypt) lie behind their activities. If Dt. 18:15– does, at least in part, lie behind such expectations, it cannot be said involve any notion of lawgiving.[1]

There remain certain other passages which allegedly depict the Messia as a second Moses even though there is no reference to Deuteronomy 1 These have as their basis the doctrine that the deliverance from Egypt is type of Messianic redemption. While the two periods are typologicall linked in the Old Testament, Apocrypha and Pseudepigrapha, n reference is made in these works to the later rabbinic principle "as the fir redeemer (Moses), so the final redeemer (Messiah)". It has been suggeste that earlier traces of this idea can be detected in the deliberate echoes Mosaic times in the Qumran writings (CDC 1:7 f.; 4:3; 6:5; 8:14 f. et al. the desert prophets mentioned by Josephus (supra) and certain oth passages in the New Testament (Mk. 1:4 f.; Mt. 24:23 f.; Acts 21:38 However, the association with the wilderness is based less on the pa *appearance* of Moses or the expected appearance of the Mosaic Messia than on the fulfilment of prophetic pronouncements as to the *place* of th eschatological drama. There is also the strong possibility that quite oth considerations, such as secrecy and convenience, played their part in th locations chosen.[2] In addition, the rabbinic examples are not only la but are scarcely representative.[3]

We must conclude, then, that there is no evidence for pre-christia speculation on the return of Moses, or of a figure fashioned in his likene and given his functions. Where the expectation of a "prophet like Moses does occur the emphasis is laid more on God's action in raising up prophetic spokesman than on any specific similarity to the ministry

---

[1] Cf. E. Meyer, *Ursprung und Anfänge des Christentums* (Stuttgart, 1925), II, pp. 402–40 and O. Betz, *Offenbarung*, pp. 99–109 against W. Staerk, *Soter* (Gütersloh, 1933), I, p. 60 J. Jeremias, *TDNT*, IV, p. 859; G. Vermès, "Moses", p. 85; U. Mauser, *Christ in the Wilderne* (London, 1963), pp. 56–57. Messianic designations are denied these prophets by F. J. Foake Jackson and K. Lake, *BC*, IV, p. 276 and R. Schnackenburg, *St. Ev.*, I (1959), p. 628.

[2] For John the Baptist see C. C. McCown, "The Scene of John's Ministry . . .", *JBL*, (1940), p. 130 and for Josephus especially F. J. Foakes-Jackson and K. Lake, *BC*, IV, p. 27 The contrary view is put by J. Jeremias, *TDNT*, IV, pp. 861–62 and H. M. Teeple, *Prophe* p. 113.

[3] See Qoh.R.1:9 in the name of R. Jiçchaq II (*c.* 300). The parallel in Midrash Samuel 14: ascribes it to R. Levi (cf. Num.R.11:2 and Ruth R.5:6) who is to be dated about the same tim The theme is developed in a number of detailed comparisons between Moses and the Messia elsewhere. See further R. Bloch, "Moses", pp. 159–64. The reference in Tanchuma *eqeb* 7 ascribed to R. Akiba, which is claimed by Jeremias and Teeple (supra) to be the earlie occurrence, is a comparison with Mosaic times not Moses himself, and the scriptural referenc is to Job 30:4 not Dt. 8:3 as in the later examples. Moreover, R. Akiba seems to have though of the Messiah in Davidic rather than Mosaic terms. In any case his view is immediate contradicted. Again it must be emphasised that, in all these examples, reference to a new La is nowhere in view.

Moses himself. This is, in fact, the purport of both Hebrew and Greek renditions of the passage from Deuteronomy, a point that is often overlooked in this whole discussion.[1] It has been too readily assumed that Moses is predicting the future appearance of an alter ego. In the later references, as we have seen, whatever Mosaic characteristics may be present, the dominant type seems rather to have been Elijah. Certainly Messianic identifications cannot be sustained for in our period those seem first to have taken place in Christian exegesis.[2] In no single instance is any legislative activity vis-à-vis the Mosaic Law associated with these expectations. Indeed in Dt. R. 8:6, whether it be a case of anti-christian polemic or not, such activity is expressly prohibited. "Moses said to them: So that you may not say 'another Moses will rise and bring us another Torah from heaven', I have long made known to you: the Torah is not (any longer) in heaven". The Messiah when he comes will rather be the great teacher of Torah.[3]

V

Quite apart from the expectation surrounding Moses there are four other places in which the idea of a "new Law" is said to be present. Tg. n. on Is. 12:3, based on first century traditions, states that in the Messianic time "ye shall receive 'ulpan ha-dat with joy from the mabhire ṣaddiqayya'. D. Daube, equating 'ulpan with torah, understands from this that Israel will be given a better Law, a new and final revelation. mabhire ṣaddiqayya' must, however, refer to a group rather than a single individual, and in this case it becomes difficult to see how 'ulpan could refer to new Torah.[4] Qoh. R. 11:8 maintains that "the torah which a man learns in this world is vanity compared with the torato shel Mashiah. The similar, and earlier, saying in Qoh. R. 2:1 (in the name of R. Simon b. Zabdai c. 300 A.D.) makes it clear, however, that it is not Torah itself which will be subject to change, but man's study and knowledge of it.[5] In Lev. R. 13:3 R. Abin b. Kahana

[1] As well as the commentaries on Deuteronomy of S. R. Driver, G. A. Smith, H. Wheeler Robinson and J. Reider ad loc, see also H. J. Cadbury, BC, I, 5, p. 372, n. 2 and F. F. Bruce, The Acts of the Apostles (London, ²1952), p. 113.

[2] Even so the emphasis is upon the raising up of a prophetic spokesman as such, not on any particular likeness to Moses. See further F. Hahn, Christologische Hoheitstitel (Göttingen, 1963), pp. 353–54. Cf. also W. A. Meeks, Prophet-King, p. 29 who nevertheless places too much weight on the importance of Moses with respect to the expectation of a prophet and O. Cullman, The Christology of the New Testament (London, 1959), p. 23 who, however, admits the fusion of the two at some points in the New Testament. H. M. Teeple, Prophet, p. 102 f. also recognizes the distinction but confuses the issue by referring to a "Prophet-King Messiah" when the latter is rather to be regarded as a "Prophet-King" in lieu of the Messiah.

[3] See especially P. Seidelin, "Der Ebed Jahwe und die Messiasgestalt im Jesajatargum," NTW, 35 (1936), pp. 194 ff. and the passages cited by W. Gutbrod, TDNT, IV, p. 1057.

[4] W. D. Davies, Setting, p. 174 admits that what is meant by the plural is not clear. But see D. Daube, "ἐξουσία in Mark 1.22 and 27", JTS, 39 (1938), p. 55.

[5] Cf. A. Cohen, Midrash Rabbah: Ecclesiastes, p. 51.

(fourth century A.D.) provides a solution to the problem raised by the ill
gal procedure involved in the slaying of Behemoth by Leviathan in tl
Messianic Age by quoting Is. 51:4 "(new) instruction shall go forth fro
me" (only some MSS read "new"). Quite apart from the variation in tl
manuscripts, it would be more in line with rabbinic processes to think he
in terms of a new interpretation of the Law by which the contradiction w
be abolished.[1] A more fundamental passage is Yalkut on Is. 26:2 whi
states that "God will sit and expound *torah ḥadashah* which he will, o
day, give by the Messiah's hand". It is, however, grammatically possib
to interpret the phrase *ṭaʿame torah ḥadashah* if it read *ṭaʿame torah ḥadashi*
i.e., "new grounds of Torah". Moreover, the compilation to which
belongs is extremely late, not earlier than the thirteenth century. It
doubtful, therefore, whether the passage is sufficiently early to warra
serious attention.[2]

In this discussion we have observed the basis for the view that the La
is eternal in the priestly writings of the Old Testament. The prophets al
spoke of the permanence of Torah but in different terms, laying great
stress on the presence of prophetic revelation, within which the Mosa
Law was encompassed, in the days to come. With only one exceptio
however, the inter-testamentary writings, including for the first time tl
wisdom literature, spoke only of the traditional Law in this fashion an
this was further elaborated upon in later rabbinic teaching. On investig
tion, no adequate basis was found for the view that within the framewo
of a doctrine of the immutability of Torah occasional expectations of i
modification or partial abrogation were to be found. Such alterations
were to take place only enhanced its authority and indicated that in tl
future it would be understood more accurately and observed more closel

It would be unwarranted to infer from the presence of an untypic
opinion to the contrary (viz. Midr. Tehillim on Ps. 146:7) or from tl
occasional anti-christian polemical utterance on the subject (e.g. Dt. I
8:6) that there was a more widely-held minority belief in the coming of
new Torah within pre-Jamnian Judaism. So far as the first is concerned, tl

---

[1] Thus J. Israelstam, *Midrash Rabbah: Leviticus*, p. 167 against K. Köhler, *JE*, V, p. 21
H. J. Schoeps, *Paul*, p. 172, n. 4 and W. D. Davies, *Setting*, p. 167. See also the similar ide
mentioned in the passage Tg.Cant.5:10 W. Bächer, *Die exegetische Terminologie der jüdisch
Traditionsliteratur* (Leipzig, 1965), I, p. 56; II, p. 64 claims that *ḥadash* and *ḥadosh*, in bo
Tannaitic and Amoraean periods, were technical terms for the outlining of a new halakah
a legitimate interpretation of Torah.

[2] On the grammatical point see Gesenius-Kautsch, p. 492 comparing 1 Sam 2:4; 1 Kng
1:41; Is. 2:11 *et al*. That a new Torah is implied here is the view of G. Friedländer, *T
Jewish Sources of the Sermon on the Mount* (London, 1911), p. 57; K. Köhler, *JE*, V. p. 21
H. J. Schoeps, *Zeit*, p. 224, n. 4; H. M. Teeple, *Prophet*, p. 26 and W. D. Davies, *Settin
p. 177. The references in Sib.Or.3.373–74 and 3.757–58 which do seem to advocate
new Torah owe too much to the Greek ideal of a universal law of nature to be releva
here. The passages in Justin Martyr referring to Is. 51:4–5 and Jer. 31:31 ff. ought not I
regarded as evidence for the attitude of contemporary Judaism to the question (see Just.Dia
11:4; 13:3; 18:3).

veneration with which the Law was held within all Jewish groups during this period, however differently this may have been expressed, and the centrality it possessed in their outlook and conduct, including their views on the future, makes any such possibility extremely unlikely.[1] With respect to the second, it is highly improbable, despite recent suggestions to the contrary, that the earliest christian writers, notably Matthew, thought in terms of Jesus as the new Lawgiver at all.[2] In addition to these factors, when in the later centuries flexibility was once again allowed to rabbinic eschatological speculations, no such view of Torah re-emerged. Had it done so, the possibility of its temporary suppression due to the ascendancy of rabbinic elements opposed to apocalyptic speculation would carry more weight, but this is not the case.

It is for this reason that the very circumstantial case built up by W. D. Davies for the presence of such a belief in the earlier period, relying as it does almost entirely on his interpretation of the later rabbinic speculations, loses most of its plausibility when a different construction is placed upon them. Thus against those who claim that the idea of a new Torah was widely held in rabbinic literature or that there were at least elements in Judaism which thought in such terms, it must be insisted that all such passages belong to a considerably later period than the first century A.D. and that insofar as more is meant than a new interpretation of the old Torah one cannot speak of such an expectation in the later period either.[3]

[1] See G. F. Moore, *Judaism in the First Centuries of the Christian Era* (Cambridge, Mass., 1932), I, p. 273.

[2] See further, R. Banks, *Jesus and the Law in the Synoptic Tradition* (Diss: Cambridge, 1969), pp. 231–96. There is, in any case, a difficulty with this line of reasoning reluctantly acknowledged by Davies himself. Having hesitantly agreed with the thesis of J. Klausner, *Messianic Idea*, pp. 466–69 that the New Torah doctrine arose when relations between Church and Synagogue had become less antagonistic and speculation along similar lines less unthinkable, he admits that he is "not quite sure that he (i.e. Klausner) is correct in thinking that it would be easier for later Judaism to contemplate a New Torah than it would have been for first-century Judaism. The antipathy to Christianity had become greater, not less". He sidesteps the problem raised by such an admission by proposing that "the concept of a new Torah might perhaps have been indigenous and not merely the result of Christian influences". In distinction from Davies, Klausner, of course, argued that it was *only* in the later post-apostolic period that belief in a new Torah arose.

[3] For similar judgements based on a less comprehensive survey of the material, see E. Bammel, *St. Ev.*, III (1964), p. 123 and G. Barth, "Law", pp. 154–56.

CHAPTER XII

THE FUNCTION OF THE SON OF MAN IN THE GOSPEL OF JOHN

Robert Maddox

RECONCILIATION AND HOPE, SOTERIOLOGY AND ESCHATOLOGY, MAY perhaps be discussed separately as themes or motives within the New Testament's theology, but they are not distinctly separable realities. God's action which sets reconciliation in motion points to the hope of complete reconciliation in a renewed creation. This can be illustrated by many examples in the New Testament, but nowhere more clearly than by the fact that Jesus is called, or rather calls himself, the Son of Man. And since Dr Morris has devoted a considerable part of his labours, especially in the last few years, to studies in the Gospel of John, it seemed that to explore the meaning of the title Son of Man in the Gospel of John would be a fitting way to contribute to the purpose of the present volume.

I

People observe from time to time[1] that little research is directed to the Son of Man theme in John, at least by comparison with the flood of studies on the Son of Man in the synoptic gospels. The topic has of course not been entirely neglected.[2] In order to justify another examination of it, one must offer some comment not only on the conclusions, but, perhaps even more, on the aims and methods of recent investigators. For essays simply headed "The Son of Man in the Fourth Gospel" (or the like) can in fact have widely differing aims, which are too seldom explicitly stated.

One possible aim is the historical: to see whether, and how, the Gospel of John takes us back to the actual words of Jesus, or at least to the general

---

[1] R. Schnackenburg, "Der Menschensohn im Johannesevangelium", NTS, 11 (1964–65), p. 123; S. S. Smalley, "The Johannine Son of Man Sayings", NTS, 15 (1968–69), p. 278.

[2] In addition to the works mentioned in n. 1, see S. Schulz, Untersuchungen zur Menschen-sohn-Christologie im Johannesevangelium. Zugleich ein Beitrag zur Methodengeschichte der Auslegung des 4. Evangeliums (1957); E. D. Freed, "The Son of Man in the Fourth Gospel", JBL, 86 (1967), pp. 402–409; and relevant chapters in E. M. Sidebottom, The Christ of the Fourth Gospel (1961); A. J. B. Higgins, Jesus and the Son of Man (1964); F. H. Borsch, The Son of Man in Myth and History (1967) and C. Colpe, ὁ υἱὸς τοῦ ἀνθρώπου, TWNT, VIII (1967). See also R. Schnackenburg, The Gospel according to St. John, I (1965, E.T. 1968), Excursus V, pp. 529–42, which is similar to though not identical with his article mentioned in n. 1.

intent of his teaching. Several of the works mentioned in notes 1 and 2 (especially those of Higgins, Freed and Smalley) are mainly concerned with this aim. To many it seems the most obvious reason for studying the subject. Indeed, in the opinion of Schnackenburg[1] it is just because of the wide-spread recognition that John is less likely to take us back to the authentic words of Jesus that studies on the Son of Man have for the most part been concerned only with the synoptic gospels. Another, related aim would be to ask how the Son of Man texts in John came to be so formulated: to what extent, and how, the evangelist was influenced by earlier Christian tradition or by language about the Son of Man in the wider religious environment. It is with such questions that the studies of Schulz, Sidebottom, Schnackenburg, Borsch and (naturally) Colpe are largely concerned.

All such questions are of course important, and anyone who seeks to contribute to the general topic will have to take proper account of them. But in the meantime the point is to be made that enquiry can also profitably be directed to another set of questions, which in the case of the Son of Man passages in John have not received adequate attention. How are we to read rightly the phenomenon of the designation of Jesus as Son of Man in John? What connotations does the term carry? Are they recognizably the same connotations in all Johannine instances? Are they similar connotations to those carried by the term in the synoptic gospels? How are the connotations of the term Son of Man related to those of other Christological titles in John? Was "Son of Man" a "live" Christological formula in the circles in which John was written? These questions form the centre of interest of the present study. But before tackling them directly it will be necessary to state briefly some conclusions on the historical questions which others have explored.

To identify the authentic sayings of Jesus about the Son of Man is notoriously difficult in the case of the synoptic gospels.[2] In the case of John our scepticism about arriving at clear-cut answers must be still greater. Although in recent years, through the work of C. H. Dodd and others, the case has been strengthened for accepting sound historical traditions behind John, our confidence is properly directed towards the mention of persons, places and events, but not towards precise formulations of the teaching of Jesus, for this has been refracted through the vigorous theological response of the Johannine church, on the one hand to the original Gospel events, on the other hand to the questions, challenges and opportunities of new circumstances in a new generation.[3] Therefore

[1] *Loc. cit.* (n. 1).
[2] See I. H. Marshall, "The Synoptic Son of Man Sayings in Recent Discussion", *NTS*, 12 (1965–66), pp. 327–51, and my comment on Marshall's results in "The Function of the Son of Man according to the Synoptic Gospels", *NTS*, 15 (1968–69), pp. 45 f.
[3] See C. K. Barrett, "The Dialectical Theology of St. John", ch. 4 in his *New Testament Essays* (1972), esp. p. 68.

S. S. Smalley (*op. cit.*) seems to me to be straining too hard to establish connexions between details of the Son of Man sayings in John and the original words of Jesus.[1] On the other hand, A. J. B. Higgins is also over-confident in his conclusion that the tradition used in the Fourth Gospel "(does not shed) any fresh light on the problem of Jesus and the Son of man, (but) does support the view that the Son of man was the basic Christology of the early church", and that the Johannine tradition "provides no sure evidence that Jesus spoke of himself as Son of man, either in his involvement in his earthly ministry, or in regard to his approaching passion".[2] Higgins' view on John is influenced by his conclusion that even in the synoptic gospels there is no authentic teaching of Jesus in which he identifies himself with the Son of Man;[3] then the point on which his interpretation of the Johannine material turns is the understanding of John 9:35, "Do you believe in the Son of Man?", as a Christological confession of the Johannine church, which "points to the Son of man as the evangelist's fundamental and principal Christology". This is a dubious conclusion, and the weighty arguments against it will be referred to later.

There are in fact no convincing arguments either for Smalley's assertion of the general authenticity of the Son of Man sayings in John or for Higgins' denial of it. Rather we should extend to John the important principle laid down by M. D. Hooker concerning the Son of Man sayings in Mark: "It is comparatively easy to argue against the authenticity of any one particular saying considered in isolation; the arguments look less convincing when they are weighed against the total evidence of all the Son of man sayings . . . It may well be, in fact, that *all* our 'Son of man' sayings are, to a lesser or greater degree, distorted; and that, conversely, all together are needed to contain the whole truth about the Son of man".[4] The way in which this principle is applied will not of course be quite the same for John as for Mark. We must take account, first, of the possibility that some Son of Man sayings of Jesus himself have been preserved, to

---

[1] In particular, two tendencies seem to me to lead in wrong directions: (a) Johannine sentences mentioning the Son of Man are treated in isolation as "logia", implying that the sentences have come down from early tradition in solid form as they appear in the text, whereas most of them are closely interwoven with their contexts and therefore may be supposed to have been formulated by the evangelist. (b) It is repeatedly said that "vindicated suffering" is an integral part of the Son of Man theme, even in pre-Christian sources. Such an understanding of Daniel 7 is possible though not certain (depending on whether 7:9 f., 13 f. was written as one piece with the rest of the chapter, or had an independent, prior existence in oral tradition, as many hold). But it is wrong for 1 Enoch. It is likely that Isa. 52:13 (LXX) has influenced the terminology of $\dot{v}\psi\omega\theta\tilde{\eta}\nu\alpha\iota/\delta o\xi\alpha\sigma\theta\tilde{\eta}\nu\alpha\iota$ relating to the Son of Man in John 3:14, 8:28, 12:23–34 and 13:31 f., but even that does not mean that the whole pattern of the Suffering Servant in Isaiah was associated by John with the Son of Man (cf. J. W. Doeve, *Jewish Hermeneutics in the Synoptic Gospels and Acts* (1954), pp. 133 f.): still less persuasive is Smalley's detection of a note of suffering in John 1:51 because Gen. Rabbah 68:16, which some have adduced as a "parallel" to John 1:51, alludes to Isa. 49:3.

[2] *Op. cit.*, pp. 182 f.

[3] On this, see my review of Higgins's book in *ABR*, 13 (1965), pp. 64 ff.

[4] M. D. Hooker, *The Son of Man in Mark* (1967), p. 79.

nerge in John, by a stream of oral tradition that did not contribute to the noptic gospels; secondly, of active, formative influences within that eam; and thirdly, of the theological purposes of the evangelist. Once e point is granted, as I think it must (against Higgins and others, such as Vielhauer and N. Perrin), that the designation of Jesus as Son of Man is e historically to Jesus' own initiative,[1] the point of the principle that ll (the sayings) together are needed to contain the whole truth about the on of Man" is that it is *a priori* unlikely that the carriers of the early tradin, when modifying and extending the corpus of Son of Man sayings, ould have done so in such a way as to give the title a radically different nse from that in which Jesus used it.[2]

Concerning the religious background and the relation of John to the rlier tradition of the sayings of Jesus about the Son of Man, it will ffice here to indicate general agreement with the statement of the matter Schnackenburg; one or two questions on which I take a different view ll be indicated below, as they arise. From this starting-point we can oceed to do the exegesis of the Johannine Son of Man sayings, taking em not only individually but also as a group, and regarding them not ly in isolation but also in relation to their respective contexts. The reting picture will certainly not take us back to the very words of Jesus nself, but it will show us how Jesus' teaching about himself as Son of an looked from John's perspective. This question is worth asking for its vn sake, but is usually obscured by pre-occupation either with the estion of "genuineness" or with the tracing of the religious background. hen the answer to this inquiry concerning John is compared with the sults of a similar investigation concerning the synoptic gospels,[3] we all have a way of approach, indirect but still useful, to the shape and eaning of Jesus' own teaching. Where a similar significance shines

[1] There is neither space nor need to take up this question here. I have discussed it in some tail in my article "The Quest for Valid Methods in 'Son of Man' Research", *ABR*, 19 971), pp. 36–51, reprinted in *TSF Bulletin* 61 (1971), pp. 14–21, and as "Methodenfragen der Menschensohnforschung", *Ev. Th.*, 32 (1972), pp. 143–60.

[2] It is true that the Church Fathers, from Ignatius and pseudo-Barnabas on, show a distinct eak from the earlier tradition when they take "Son of Man" as referring to the incarnation: Colpe, *op. cit.*, pp. 480 f. They are, however, not primarily concerned with the gospel dition but with opposing Gnosticism, for which purpose the traditional title, taken literally, s a convenient weapon. That they could do this weighs heavily against Higgins's contention t "Son of Man" was a living form of Christological confession in the Johannine church, ce Ignatius, at least, cannot be separated very far from John in time or place.

[3] This was undertaken in my article "The Function of the Son of Man according to the noptic Gospels" (p. 187, n. 2) to which the present study is a sequel. My conclusion there s that through all three of the traditional groupings of the Son of Man sayings (earthly , passion and ressurrection, future coming) there is a constant theme: the Son of Man he who carries out ultimate judgement; those whom he saves are those who stand in a cial relationship to him; those who resist his claim for obedience and for allegiance to his ct community he condemns to destruction. In the synoptic gospels it is declared not only t the Son of Man will soon hold his universal assize (which is what we find already in the nilitudes of 1 Enoch) but that he has appeared on the stage of human history, and that the ocess of eschatological judgement has therefore already begun.

through different forms of expression, we may have reasonable confiden
that the different streams are carrying water from the same well-sprin

II

John 1:51, "Truly, truly I tell you, you will see the heaven opened a
the angels of God ascending and descending upon the Son of Man". Th
saying, in which the Son of Man is mentioned for the first time in Joh
rings with echoes of so many biblical passages that its interpretation is
subtle matter. On the one hand, it has affinities with sayings in the syno
tic gospels about the future coming in glory of the Son of Man as univers
judge; cf. Mark 14:62/Matt. 26:64 (" you will see", and the association
the Son of Man with heaven), and Mark 8:38 pars. (the heavenly Son
Man associated with angels). On the other hand, the clear allusion to Ge
28:12[1] seems to set the Son of Man in the place of Jacob, i.e., on the eart
he is the "Bethel" – the place of God's revelation, which is promised n
as an eschatological prediction but as a gift for faith.[2] Again, "the heav
opened" is taken by some to be reminiscent of the scene at Jesus' baptis
(Mark 1:10 f.), which would support the interpretation that true discipl
along with Nathanael, are here promised a revelation of the identity of th
earthly Jesus as God's Son. (That "Son" or "Son of God" and "Son
Man" are fully interchangeable terms in John has often been asserted:
this question we shall return later.) However, the further parallel in Ac
7:56 (Stephen, as he dies, says "I see the heavens opened and the Son
Man standing at God's right hand") seems to me to be more significa
than most commentators allow, and to tip the scales in favour of unde
standing the Son of Man in John 1:51 to be at the heavenly, not th
earthly end of the ladder. In its context the saying identifies the "great
things" that Nathanael will see. That this refers to the Son of Man e
throned in his heavenly glory is made probable not only by the passag
in the synoptic material telling how people "will see" the Son of Man, b
also by John 6:62, where Jesus says to his disciples, "What then if you s
the Son of Man ascending where he was before?" To take 1:51 otherwi
would be to make it too much *sui generis*, by comparison not only with th
Son of Man tradition as a whole, but also with the conceptions of th
Gospel of John. (That the angels first ascend and then descend does n
help to locate the Son of Man, but is wording due to Gen. 28:12.) In th
context, the saying must be taken as pointing to an understanding of Jesu
status and function superior to that which has just been mentioned, "th
King of Israel" (1:49). In all the gospels, that greater status and functio

[1] That it is Genesis itself and not the story referred to in Gen. Rabbah 68:18 is the vie
expressed, probably rightly, by several recent commentators.
[2] So Schnackenburg, *Commentary, ad loc.*

e those of the Son of Man, who will be exalted to heaven to be enthroned judge of the world and saviour of the community of his disciples. ere nothing is said explicitly about these mutually complementary nctions, but the function of saving his elect is hinted at by the picture of e angels ascending and descending (cf. Mark 13:27/Matt. 24:31). though the Son of Man will be exalted high in heaven, he will not be t of touch with his people on earth. It is not Jesus but Nathanael, the e who is "truly an Israelite" (1:47) who corresponds to Jacob in Gen. :12: it is he, and those who share his faith, who will not only be re-ured by the sight of their Saviour in heaven, as Stephen was, but also ve the aid of the divine messengers to maintain lively contact with him. The next two Son of Man sayings come together. John 3:13 f., "No e has gone up into heaven except the one who came down from heaven, e Son of Man. And as Moses lifted up the serpent in the desert, so must e Son of Man be lifted up, in order that everyone who believes in him ay have eternal life." In his commentary, Schnackenburg argues with me force that in this chapter vv. 31–36 were originally intended to nd between vv. 12 and 13. Since that passage has to do with salvation d judgement, it would follow that the reference to the Son of Man in 13 would have to be read in the context of soteriology rather than of velation (v. 12). If this could be accepted with confidence, it would ean that the Son of Man occurs in the same sort of setting familiar from e synoptic gospels, I Enoch 37–71 and Daniel 7: he ascends to heaven to ceive from God the authority to judge and save. Yet hypotheses about e rearrangement of the text of John are notoriously tricky. Many such oposals have been made, and while any given one may seem plausible d attractive from one point of view, it then usually turns out to be ubtful from another. This same passage has been carved up in other ays: for example, G. H. C. Macgregor (*The Gospel of John*, Moffatt .T. Commentary (1928), *ad loc.*) proposed to put vv. 31–36 after, not fore, v. 13, and to take off vv. 14–21 to be woven into 12:33–35. These ntradictory theories do not disprove the possibility that the text of hn has suffered some displacement, but in the absence of more sub-ntial evidence it is safer to deal with the text as we have it. This means at the mention of the Son of Man in 3:13 is not introduced by any plicit reference to the theme of salvation and judgement. But it is teworthy that what is said of the Son of Man fits harmoniously with hat is said in 1:51, as we have interpreted it. And this mention of the cension of the Son of Man to heaven leads naturally to a discussion of e means whereby this exaltation takes place (the crucifixion, 3:14) and its nsequences (the imparting of life to believers and the judgement of believers, 3:15 ff.). The reference to Jesus as Son of Man is therefore ndamental to the pericope: it is when this title has been introduced that e discussion of salvation/judgement is elaborated.

However, the introduction of the title "Son of Man" in 3:13 has further important significance. We have argued that in 1:51 the ascending and descending angels indicate the continuing, lively relationship between the Son of Man in heaven and his disciples on earth; and this is consonant with the synoptic and pre-Christian concepts of the Son of Man, in which he is always associated with an earthly community that looks to him for vindication. Now v. 13 forms the transition to vv. 14–21, which are about judgement and salvation, from vv. 1–12, which are about the new life that must be entered by rebirth through water and spirit. Looked at in a certain light, the Gospel of John seems to have an individualistic conception of judgement and salvation.[1] On the other hand, it seems to me undeniable that John has an interest in the sacraments, which comes to expression here in relation to baptism and in ch. 6 in relation to the eucharist, and that this points to an interest in the church as the gathered community of those who owe their salvation to the Son of Man. Those who receive the new life made available by the death and heavenly exaltation of the Son of Man do so by being incorporated within the Son of Man's earthly community. In this respect, too, John turns out to be in the same line of interpretation of the Son of Man theme as the synoptic evangelists. The church is the eschatological community, and it is the faithful members of the church whom the Son of Man rescues from the destruction of the final judgement.[2] This communal aspect of salvation and judgement is further indicated in vv. 19–21, where men are divided, in the fashion of Qumran, into those who love the light and those who love the darkness. The same note is struck still more distinctly later, at the end of the most emphatic Johannine discussion of the judgement of the Son of Man: 12:36, "While you have the light, believe in the light, that you may become sons of light". At Qumran "the sons of light" are the members of the community destined for salvation; and the same seems to be implied in these Johannine passages too.

In interpreting the function of the Son of Man in 3:14 ff., we encounter a problem, which will recur later in relation to 5:27. In vv. 14 f. it is "the Son of Man" whose "lifting up" will enable every believer to have eternal life; but in vv. 16 ff., it is "the (only) Son (of God)". This change of title is not matched by any change of function; in fact what is predicated of the Son of Man in v. 15 is repeated verbatim as a predicate of "the only Son" in v. 16: that is, the function is the same no matter what the title, and to that extent the titles are synonymous.[3] E. D. Freed underlines the

[1] So C. F. D. Moule, "The Individualism of the Fourth Gospel", *Nov. Test.*, 5 (1962) pp. 171–90.
[2] Cf. A. Corell, *Consummatum Est* (1950, ET, 1958), pp. 162–65.
[3] R. Bultmann, *The Gospel of John: A Commentary* (1966, ET, 1971), pp. 153 f., n. 3, says that for the evangelist the identity of the two figures is a matter of course, but that in v. 16 "the Son" only becomes "the Son of Man" "as a result of his mission". This seems a rather forced interpretation, especially in view of v. 13, ". . . he who came down from heaven, the Son of Man".

oint, not only in relation to this passage but generally throughout John.
Ie shows that "the Son of Man" usually occurs in passages where Jesus
 also spoken of by name, or by another title or metaphor, and that
ierefore there is a fluid interchange of connotations, and no connotations
re exclusively reserved for any one title. This leads him to conclude: "The
vidence indicates that the title Son of man is only a variation for at least
vo other titles, namely, the Son of God and the Son. And this means,
ierefore, that there is no separate Son of man christology in the fourth
ospel".[1] By this he apparently means that various traditional titles for
:sus are introduced by John merely for the sake of literary variation, and
vithout regard for any special connotations the respective titles originally
arried. On any reading, of course, John is in this respect quite different
om the synoptic gospels, where "the Son of Man" almost never (only
Iark 14:61 f., pars., and Matt. 16:13–16) occurs in the same context as
the Son" or "the Son of God", and the titles have quite distinct mean-
igs.[2] The matter is more correctly explained by Schnackenburg,[3] who
tys that in the Johannine Christology the central concept is "the Son",
) which the theme of "the Son of Man" has been assimilated. But the
rocess of assimilation is not, I think, complete. The following difference
an still be observed. When Jesus is described as acting more or less
idependently, on his own initiative, in his function of judging/imparting
fe, he is called "the Son of Man"; when he is seen as the earthly repre-
:ntative and manifestation of the action of God, he is called "the Son"
r "the Son of God". At least this explanation suits the transition from
:14 f. to vv. 16 ff. We shall need to test it further in relation to 5:19–30,
elow. In 3:14–21 the primary concern is Jesus' role as saviour and judge,
id so he is called the Son of Man. And the comparison of the "lifting up"
f the Son of Man with that of the serpent in the desert indicates (what
ihn discusses more specifically in 12:20–36) that it is by his death and
eavenly exaltation that the Son of Man carries out this function. But
ien it is recalled that this is also the work of the Father, and so Jesus is
:condarily referred to as "the Son".

John 5:27, "And he has given him authority to carry out judgement,
ecause he is the Son of Man". Here we find the most striking expression
 John, and indeed in the whole NT, of the essential function of the Son
f Man as Judge. Without broaching here the question of the history of
ie tradition behind this passage (since such discussion is not the main
oncern of this paper), we may observe some striking points of corres-
ondence between John 5 and Mark 2. The statement that it is because he
Son of Man that Jesus has been given authority to carry out judgement

[1] Op. cit., p. 403.
[2] See F. Hahn, The Titles of Jesus in Christology (1963, ET. 1969), chs. 1 and 5.
[3] "Der Menschensohn . . .", p. 136, cf. Colpe, op. cit., p. 469. The view of Schulz, op. cit.,
irt II B, that the "Son" sayings are really "Son of Man" sayings in a more advanced stage
: interpretation, has been rightly rejected by later writers.

is of the same order as Mark 2:10, "The Son of Man has authority t
forgive sins on the earth". In each case the setting is the healing of a sic
man whom Jesus commands to rise, take up his bed and walk (John 5:8
is identical in wording with Mark 2:9c). As usual, the Johannine pericop
is more extended and complex than its immediate synoptic equivalen
In this case, the immediate sequel to the healing miracle, in John 5:9c–1
is a controversy between Jesus and "the Jews" arising from the fact tha
Jesus had performed the cure on the Sabbath: and this recalls a simila
incident in Mark 3:1–6, which follows immediately upon Jesus' sayin
that "the Son of Man is lord even of the Sabbath". To this saying there
an approximate equivalent in John 5:17, "My Father is working unt
now, and I am working (i.e. even on the Sabbath)". The context of idea
in which this saying is to be understood is, I think, eschatological: th
Sabbath as observed by the Jews is only a shadow of the true Sabbath c
of the Age to Come, of which the Epistle to the Hebrews speaks.[1] Thu
before the judgement exercised by the Son of Man is mentioned ther
seem to be oblique allusions to his authority to forgive sins and to h
eschatological "lordship". It seems, then, that this fourth Johannine So
of Man saying is also consistent with the general pattern of ideas concern
ing the Son of Man.

However, it has sometimes been suggested[2] that John 5:27–29 is
foreign body intruded into the text by a late redaction. Bultmann ob
serves that here we have futuristic eschatology drawing heavily on th
language of Dan. 12:2, in contrast to the "realized" eschatology typical c
John.[3] To make John "consistent" in this regard would require the settin
aside also of similar passages in 6:39, 40, 54; 12:48 – and Bultmann i
fact regards these too as interpolations. This exegesis is, however, some
what Procrustean. The evangelist works in terms not of logical consis
tency but of poetic paradox: there is a paradoxical oscillation betwee
future-mythological and present-historicized eschatology, just as there
between physical event and spiritual meaning in the Johannine miracle

---

[1] I have discussed this question in "The Function of the Son of Man according to the Synop
tic Gospels" (p. 187, n. 2), pp. 66 f., with reference to H. Riesenfeld's important stud
"Sabbat et jour du Seigneur", in A. J. B. Higgins (ed.), N.T. Essays in Memory of T. W
Manson (1959), pp. 210–17. This line of approach is more fruitful than that taken by R. E
Brown, The Gospel according to John (Anchor Bible), I (1966), ad loc., where Rabbinic evidenc
is cited to show that the Jews held that God did, after all, work on the Sabbath. Brown
view accounts for the reaction of the Jews that Jesus was making himself God's equal, bu
does not explain the striking time-phrase ἕως ἄρτι.

[2] Notably by Bultmann, Commentary, ad loc.

[3] In his review of C. H. Dodd's The Interpretation of the Fourth Gospel (NTS, 1 (1954–55
pp. 77–91, ET in Harvard Divinity Bulletin 27, 2 (1963), pp. 9–22) Bultmann complains (pp. 1
18 f., 22) of Dodd's refusal to take seriously the question of a source-analysis of John. Th
difficulty is that Bultmann's only proof of his source-analysis is his own conception of th
consistency of thought to be expected of the evangelist, together with his conviction that th
Christology and soteriology of John have a gnostic rather than Jewish background – an ide
which does not have much support in contemporary research.

The other ground of objection is that in the immediate context (vv. 19–30) the main title by which Jesus speaks of himself is not "the Son of Man" which occurs only once, v. 27) but "the Son" (eight times; in v. 25, "the Son of God"), and yet his double function of imparting life and judging receives concentrated discussion from v. 21 to v. 30. The question thus arises again, as in 3:14–21, whether for John "the Son" is not a fully appropriate title under which to present Jesus in his work of salvation and judgement. If so, then the suspicion arises that vv. 27–29 may have been inserted by a redactor influenced by the older tradition, in which these functions were specifically associated with the title Son of Man. Closer examination shows, however, that the change of title from "the Son (of God)" in vv. 19–26 to "the Son of Man" in v. 27 is due to a shift in the emphasis of the argument. The same thing is happening as in 3:14–21, except that this time the progression of thought is in the opposite direction. The three references to "the Son" in vv. 19 f. refer not to judgement but to the unity of action of the Son with the Father. This theme, introduced in v. 17, is really the main theme of the whole chapter. And it is to this theme that the title "the Son" is appropriate in the over-all usage of John.[1] Now when Jesus says in v. 17 "the Father is working until now, and I am working", and in v. 20 "for the Father loves the Son and shows him everything which he himself is doing", it is natural for the author to give some indication of what work it is that the Father and the Son are both doing. The answer is, as throughout the book, that Jesus, representing the Father, imparts life to those who believe in him and judges those who do not. So in vv. 21 ff. the nature of the work which the Son does in company with the Father is explained; but the emphasis still is not on the work itself but on the Son's unity with the Father: "He has given all the judgement to the Son, *in order that* all may honour the Son as they honour the Father who sent him" (vv. 22 f.). In v. 24 more deliberate attention is given to the process whereby life is received and judgement avoided, but Jesus speaks of himself in the simple first person. In v. 25 the words have an apocalyptic ring, like v. 28, and so "Son of Man" might have been expected – as indeed some MSS read. But v. 26, which supplies the basis and explanation of v. 25, shows that once more what is meant is the unity of the Son with the Father. Now that this point has been so firmly established, attention is allowed to return for the time to the reality of the judgement, and therewith the Son, who acts only and always in unity with the Father, is identified as the Son of Man, the eschatological judge and saviour.

John 6:26–65, "(27) Work for ... the food which lasts to produce eternal life, which the Son of Man will give you ...(53) If you do not eat the flesh of the Son of Man and drink his blood you do not have life within yourselves. ... (62) What then if you see the Son of Man going up

[1] Cf. C. H. Dodd, *The Interpretation of the Fourth Gospel* (1953), pp. 257 ff.

where he was before? . . ." In this discourse the title "Son of Man"
mentioned these three times and "the Son" once, in v. 40. Again, the u
of the latter title is intended to emphasize Jesus' unity of action with tl
Father, "This is the will of my Father, that everyone who sees the Sc
and believes should have eternal life." That the title "Son of Man
is intended to be a prominent element in the discourse is shown not onl
by its use explicitly at the beginning and end and once in the middle, bt
also by the repeated use of the idea of "coming down from heaven" (vv
33, 38, 42, 50, 51, 58), cf. 3:13, and the statement that those who receiv
life will be "raised up at the last day" (vv. 39, 40, 44, 54), cf. 5:28 f. Her
only the positive aspect of the work of the Son of Man is emphasized, th;
of imparting life. This work is connected with both the death and th
heavenly exaltation of the Son of Man, as in 3:13 ff. Again the concept c
the eschatological community is introduced by way of reference to th
sacramental life of the church, this time in the eucharist.[1] In its eucharisti
worship (though not because of it in any mechanical way)[2] the churc
receives from the Son of Man the gift of life. V. 27, "Work not for th
food that perishes, but for the food that lasts, and produces eternal lift
which the Son of Man will give to you", is close in its essential thougl
to 4:14 ". . . But the water which I shall give him will be a spring c
welling water which produces eternal life". But in the whole of ch.
the title "Son of Man" is not used. Several reasons can be suggested wh
it was used in ch. 6. First, the life-producing bread spoken of by Jesus ;
compared with the manna of the desert, which "came down from heaven'
and in John one of the chief predicates of the Son of Man is that he "cam

[1] That there is indeed reference to the eucharist here is the view of most commentator
and seems to me unavoidable. The wording of vv. 53–56 could hardly be more explicit, give
the setting in which this discourse is delivered. Bultmann, who holds that the evangelist is a
anti-sacramentalist, regards vv. 51b–58 as an interpolation, but the unity of the chapter ha
been demonstrated by P. Borgen, *Bread from Heaven* (1965), cf. C. K. Barrett, "The Dialectic;
Theology of St. John", in his *N.T. Essays* (1972). The discussion becomes *explicitly* sacramenta
only in these verses, but a sacramental concern is implicit from the beginning. Other inter
preters regard the language about eating Jesus' flesh and drinking his blood as metaphorica
rather than sacramental. Among these is Dr Leon Morris, who says (*Commentary*, on v. 53)
"Both 'eat' and 'drink' are aorists, denoting once-for-all action. It is not a repeated eating an
drinking, such as would be appropriate to the sacrament. . . . Eating and drinking thus appea
to be a very graphic way of saying that men must take Christ into their innermost being.'
This linguistic argument is not conclusive. Blass-Debrunner 373:3: in the N.T. ἐάν is used
in the overwhelming majority of cases, with the aorist subjunctive, whether the reference i
general or to a specific case in the future. It may also be observed that eating and drinking ar
referred to with present participles in vv. 54 and 56, which suggests a general or repeated action
[2] Cf. Barrett, *op. cit.*, p. 67: "He who eats the flesh and drinks the blood of the Son of mar
has life, but he does not have it as a personal possession which he holds in his own right
he will never cease to need what is expressed in the words 'I will raise him up at the last day'
There is thus a radical difference between this Johannine paragraph and the Ignatian φάρμακο
ἀθανασίας, the ἀντίδοτος τοῦ μὴ ἀποθανεῖν. The Lord's Supper is thus neither a bar
historical commemoration of an interesting and impressive event in the life of Jesus, nor a
independent automatic means of conveying spiritual substance. It is part of the dialectic o
time and eternity, of matter and spirit (cf. verse 63), in which the 'night in which he wa
betrayed' and the 'last day' each play their significant roles."

down from heaven" (3:13, cf. 6:62, 9:39).[1] Second, like the first part of ch. 3, where also the Son of Man is mentioned, but unlike ch. 4, ch. 6 has a sacramental interest. In the sacraments the communal life of the church is held in view, and it is an essential part of the pre-Johannine tradition about the Son of Man that he forms and saves the eschatological community. Third, in ch. 6 there is reference to the death of Jesus, as there is in ch. 3 but not in ch 4. The Son of Man, then, is a heavenly being who enters the world in order to impart to men the gift of eternal life. Men receive this gift when they "believe in him", which includes obeying his call for allegiance to his teaching and to the life of his community. After his death his power to win men to his allegiance is immeasurably increased, since his presence is no longer physically limited, but his Spirit is wherever his community is (6:62 f., cf. 7:38 f., 16:7). That those who are saved by the Son of Man are thought of as a community rather than as isolated individuals is clear in the synoptic gospels, as in 1 Enoch. In John this is stated in different terms, relating specifically to the church's worship in obedience to the command of Jesus (1 Cor. 11:24 f.): "If you do not eat the flesh of the Son of Man and drink his blood, you do not have life within yourselves" – if you do not participate in the worshipping life of the church you are not among those who receive his life: extra ecclesiam nulla salus.

The next of John's Son of Man sayings is perhaps the most obscure: 8:28, "When you lift up the Son of Man, then you will know that I am." The obscurity is due partly to the epigrammatic, even enigmatic, style of the surrounding discourse, and partly to textual and grammatical problems, of which the most difficult, in the immediate context, is in v. 25b. In the interpretation of R. E. Brown (*Commentary*, *ad loc.*), when the Jews ask Jesus, "Who are you?" he answers, "What I have been telling you from the beginning". It is unfortunately not certain whether τὴν ἀρχήν has a temporal force, or, if it has, whether it modifies εἰμί (understood), meaning "I am from the beginning (of creation)" or λαλῶ, meaning

---

[1] It may be that Daniel 7:13 is the background of this idea. "Came down from heaven" sounds like a paraphrase of "coming with the clouds of heaven", once the latter was interpreted of descent rather than ascent or, perhaps, lateral movement. This reinterpretation may already have been known to Luke and have been the reason for his omission (at 22:69) of the words (from Mark 14:62) "and coming with the clouds of heaven". It occurs in Joshua ben Levi's statement (*c.* 250 A.D.) that if Israel is unworthy the Messiah will come riding on an ass and if Israel is worthy he will come with the clouds of heaven (bT Sanhedrin 98a); and in the traditional Christian interpretation. But the relating of this coming of the Son of Man from heaven to the past event of the life of Jesus rather than to a future event is a peculiarity of John's. Here John seems to be under the influence not only of the fundamental teaching found in the synoptic gospels, that Jesus was in his lifetime the Son of Man, but also of the idea of the Son of Man's pre-existence, found in the Similitudes of 1 Enoch, where it is said that the Son of Man had been hidden with God in heaven since before the foundation of the world, and that "the wisdom of the Lord of Spirits has revealed him to the holy and righteous . . . For in his name they are saved, and according to his good pleasure has it been in regard to their life" (48:6 f.) .This passage recalls both the incarnational Christology of John and also John's soteriological theme, that salvation is achieved when God reveals the Son of Man to men.

(with Brown) "I have been telling you from the beginning". If the latter is right, Jesus' answer presumably refers to his first statement about himself in this gospel, which is 1:51, "You will see . . . the angels ascending and descending upon the Son of Man". That is, when the Jews ask him about his identity, Jesus answers, in effect, "I am the Son of Man". Such a downright statement identifying Jesus with the Son of Man never occurs in any of the gospels: the nearest approach to it is, perhaps, John 8:28 itself, but here we come upon our next problem. At first reading, the verse might appear to mean that when the Jews "lift up" the Son of Man, then they will know that that is who Jesus is – the Son of Man. However, the phrase ἐγώ εἰμι may be intended here, as in several other places in John, not to imply a specific predicate, but in a mysterious way, echoing God's speech about himself in the Old Testament (e.g. Isa. 43:10, LXX), to hint at Jesus' divine status. At all events, what is plain is that after the Jews ask about Jesus' identity (v. 25) he speaks about his coming death and exaltation as the Son of Man. As F. H. Borsch has well observed,[1] this sequence in the dialogue is somewhat reminiscent of two scenes in Mark: 8:27 ff. (at Caesarea Philippi) and 14:61 ff. (at the trial before the High Priest): "A 'Who is Jesus?' question leads to a statement about the Son of Man". To this we can add the further observation, that both in John 8:25 ff. and in the dialogue following the question at Caesarea Philippi in Mark there is a reference to the Son of Man's right to judge those who do not hear the words that he speaks into the world (John 8:26) or who are ashamed of him and his words in an adulterous and sinful generation (Mark 8:38).

In 9:35 Jesus asks the man whom he had healed of his congenital blindness, and whom the Jews had now excluded from the synagogue, "Do you believe in the Son of Man?" Several scholars regard this saying as standing apart from the general pattern of Son of Man sayings in John, on the ground that, whereas the others seem to have deep roots in tradition (whether or not those roots are thought to reach back to Jesus), this one looks like a confessional formula that may have been taken over from the baptismal practice of the church to which John belonged,[2] and as pointing "to the Son of Man as the evangelist's fundamental and principal Christology".[3] These suggestions are unconvincing. This saying on its own is far too flimsy a basis for assuming that it represents a baptismal confession, especially in view of the remarkable fact (and how remarkable it is, is perhaps too easy to forget) that "the Son of Man" never occurs as a title for Jesus in the NT outside the gospels, except for Acts 7:56,[4] and

[1] Op. cit., p. 304, n. 1.

[2] On this point, Smalley, op. cit., pp. 296, 297, agrees with Higgins, Jesus and the Son of Man, p. 155.

[3] Higgins, loc. cit.

[4] Heb. 2:6–9; Rev. 1:13; 14:14 are not real exceptions, since there OT passages in which "Son of Man" occurs are applied to Jesus.

hat, again with the sole exception of Acts 7:56, the title is always spoken by Jesus himself.[1] If we are looking in John for a confessional formula of the church, we would do better to think of 20:28, where Thomas calls Jesus "my Lord and my God".[2] Against the view that the title Son of Man expresses "the evangelist's fundamental and principal Christology" we may cite not only Thomas' confession but also the original ending of the gospel: 20:31, "These things have been written so that you may believe that Jesus is the *Christ*, the *Son of God* . . ." In John's day the living talk about Jesus was in terms of Lord, Christ and Son of God: Borsch and Colpe are right in thinking that the prominence of the title Son of Man in John is due entirely to the strength of the tradition that in his life-time Jesus had used this title of himself.[3]

Far from being an oddity among the Son of Man sayings, John 9:35 has, when its context is taken into account, interesting lines of connexion with other Son of Man passages in John, and even in Mark. First, the theme of judgement, so prominent in association with the Son of Man in the synoptics and 1 Enoch, occurs here too: 9:39, "For judgement I came into this world, so that those who do not see may see and those who see may become blind".[4] The disclosure that Jesus is the Son of Man is only properly complete when he has declared the function of the Son of Man as the one who brings judgement into the world. This connexion of the Son of Man with judgement comes, as we have seen, in John 3:14 ff., 5:27 and 8:25–28, and it will come once more, in 12:31–35. But there are also points of more specific literary contact with some of these passages. It is as the light-bearer that the Son of Man brings judgement into the world: so 3:19 ff., following 3:14 f., and 12:31–35; in ch. 9, judgement is carried out by the bestowal or deprivation of sight (vv. 39–41), and this harks back to v. 5, "When I am in the world, I am the light of the world". Then in 9:39 there is an allusion to Isa. 6:9, and the same passage is quoted in 12:39 f., where the line of thought is still continuing from 12:31–35. Second, like 5:27, 9:35 makes a good parallel to Mark 2:10.[5] That the Son of Man has authority to forgive sins is only another way of

---

[1] John 12:34 is of course not an exception, since the crowd takes up a statement Jesus has, we are meant to assume, made about himself.

[2] Indeed, even in the present passage, according to most MSS, when Jesus has revealed his identity as the Son of Man the response of the formerly blind man is to worship him *as Lord* (v. 38), though since the discovery of P75 the case for excluding this verse as an interpolation has been made quite strong. See R. E. Brown, *Commentary, ad loc.*; B. Lindars, *New Century Bible: The Gospel of John* (1972), *ad loc.*

[3] Borsch, *op. cit.*, pp. 304 f., Colpe, *op. cit.*, p. 468:9–14.

[4] I cannot see what reason Smalley has for saying that "even the theme of judgement which follows closely (39) is not really connected (with the Son of Man saying in v. 35)", *op. cit.*, p. 296. The connexion is all the closer if vv. 38, 39a are to be excised.

[5] Against Schnackenburg, "Der Menschensohn . . .", p. 131, "Unbestreitbar wird der joh. Jesus schon in seiner gegenwärtigen Befindlichkeit auf Erden als der 'Menschensohn' betrachtet. . .; aber sprachlich und inhaltlich fehlt in den joh. Logien jeglicher Kontakt mit jenen synoptischen Sprüchen, die davon künden, dass der Menschensohn macht hat, auf Erden Sünden zu vergeben (Mark. 2:10). . ."

saying that he has authority to judge. Though certainly John's terminology
is different from Mark's, the two gospels (indeed all four) share the
proclamation that the Son of Man is not only a superhuman figure of the
future but is present on earth in the person of Jesus, already exercising
eschatological judgement. Third, it is interesting for the present discussion
that Jesus finds the man whose sight he has restored and reveals himself
to him as the Son of Man only after he hears that the man has been excommunicated.[1] The man has been thrown out of the religious community
of Israel, but he is offered the chance to "believe in the Son of Man", i.e., to
become a member of the new eschatological community.[2] Those who do
not believe are thereby "judged": their sins are retained, and they mark
themselves out as "sons of darkness" rather than "sons of light" (cf. vv.
40 f.).

John 12:20–36, "(23b) The hour has come for the Son of Man to be
glorified . . . (31 ff.) Now is the judgement of this world; now will the
ruler of this world be thrown out; and I, when I am lifted up from the
earth, will draw all men to myself. (In saying this, he was indicating the
kind of death by which he would die.) . . . (34) Why do you say that the
Son of Man must be lifted up? . . ." Jesus himself mentions the title "Son
of Man" only once in this pericope (v. 23). The glorification of the Son
of Man is related to the death of Jesus through which life is made available
for men (cf. 7:39; 12:16; 17:1 f.). But when Jesus speaks (without using a
title) of his ὑψωθῆναι (v. 32) the crowd understands this as a reference to
the death of the Son of Man.[3] In this pericope Jesus begins his speech
about the Son of Man's glorification through death in "answer" to
Andrew and Philip, when they report to him that there are some Greeks
who wish to see him. This means that the Gentile mission is made possible
only by the death and glorification of the Son of Man. The same point is
repeated in v. 32, "And I, when I am lifted up from the earth, will draw
all men to myself". "All men" does not, however, include the Jews, who
refuse to believe in Jesus and thus remain "sons of darkness" (vv. 35–41),
though the possibility of course remains for individual Jews to align

[1] V. 34, cf. v. 22. The precise nature of this excommunication is not important for the
present discussion; cf. Barrett, *Commentary*, on v. 22.

[2] On the baptismal associations of John 9 see R. E. Brown, *op. cit.*, pp. 380 f., cf. A. Corell,
op. cit., pp. 67–69.

[3] The connexions of this passage with the Marcan tradition have been explored by others,
and require no comment here: see esp. Borsch, *op. cit.*, pp. 305–12. It is wrong to take the
question of the crowd, as some have done, to be evidence that the concept "Son of Man"
was unknown in first-century Judaism. G. H. P. Thompson, "The Son of Man – Some
Further Considerations", *JTS*, 12 (1961), pp. 203–209, has rightly pointed out that the
question of the crowd is provoked not by Jesus' use of the title Son of Man but by his saying
that he must be lifted up. The identity of Jesus and the Son of Man is to be assumed from the
context (cf. v. 23). The Jewish interlocutors of Jesus must be assumed to be familiar with the
concept of a heavenly Son of Man such as is set out in 1 Enoch 37–71. The problem for them
is not the expression Son of Man in itself, but the idea of a Son of Man who must be "lifted
up", for the Son of Man is supposed to be in heaven already.

emselves with the new rather than the old community of salvation (v.
). Like many of Jesus' interlocutors in the Johannine dialogues (e.g. 4:19
5:18, 6:41 f., 7:27, etc.) the crowd want to argue about the interpre-
tion of traditional religious teachings (v. 34). But as usual Jesus refuses
be drawn into such a dispute (cf. 4:20 f., 7:41 f.). The important thing to
cognize is that in the coming of Jesus men are faced with the moment of
cision, which is also the moment of judgement; and since his crucifixion,
hich seals the doom of Israel, is already imminent, the time for making
is decision is very short (vv. 35 f.). The very fact of asking questions
stead of making the decision of allegiance to Jesus marks men out as
fit for the eternal life which he offered them. This is true not only of
ndom individuals but of the Jews as a nation, as is indicated by the use,
 this concluding report of Jesus' public ministry (v. 40), of the same
otation from Isa. 6:9 f. with which Luke ends the book of Acts (cf.
so Matt. 13:15). But since John has less interest in historical movements
an Luke has, and confines his interest to theology, he makes quite
plicit, what Luke also would not have denied, that in spite of the rection of the Jews as a whole each man can of his own initiative "come to
e light" so that he will not "remain in darkness" (v. 46): i.e., can accept
e "words" of Jesus, which are his "commandment", which is the gift
 eternal life, and thus escape the judgement that inevitably falls on those
ho reject him (vv. 47–50).
The last occurrence of the title "the Son of Man" in John is in 13:31,
Now the Son of Man has been glorified, and God has been glorified in
m". Jesus speaks these words as soon as Judas (a "son of darkness", cf. v.
b, into whom Satan has entered, v. 27) has left the supper; and since
das is going out in order to arrange Jesus' arrest there is a hint that when
sus speaks of the "glorification" of the Son of Man he is again referring
 his death (cf. 12:23 ff.). It is perhaps surprising that this title, which has
en rather prominent in the section of John dealing with Jesus' public
inistry, occurs only this once in the farewell discourse, and will not be
sed again in the remainder of the book. Several factors may combine to
rovide an explanation. First, it is also true that "Christ" and "Son of
od" or "Son" are less frequent from now on; only "Lord" remains
irly frequent, especially after the resurrection: thus the change of scene
ems to influence the general usage of the titles. Second, since the title
Son of Man" owes its prominence in the gospels to the force of the
emory that Jesus spoke of himself thus (though not all Son of Man
yings are to be regarded as verbatim quotations of Jesus), we might
xpect it to be less prominent in those passages, such as the farewell dis-
ourse in John, where the tradition of the teaching of Jesus plays a smaller
ole and Christian meditation on the person and work of Jesus a larger.
hird, we must reckon with the probability, to which reference has
lready been made, that the general theme of the Son of Man continues

to have an influence even where the title has been allowed to dro
out.[1]

13:31 is the beginning of the farewell discourse, and perhaps is to b
regarded as a kind of heading to it, so that the significance of the title
to be understood as underlying the whole discourse. The salvation of Jesu
disciples is soon discussed (14:1–6), and indeed is spoken of repeatedly an
at length throughout chs. 14–17. The judgement of the world is hinted
in 14:17 ff., but is not properly resumed until 15:18–27; 16:7–11. In the
passages judgement is not associated with any title of Jesus but rath
with the Paraclete whom Jesus will send (15:26; 16:7 f.). But there is th
closest possible connexion between the Paraclete and Jesus,[2] and indee
Jesus as the Son of Man.[3] It is beyond the scope of this paper to discuss th
background of the term "Paraclete" as used in John, and its possibl
connexions with the Son of Man theme. But it may be observed tha
some of the vocabulary associated with the Son of Man theme can b
traced in the farewell discourse, including passages concerning the Para
clete. The disciples are those whom Jesus has "elected" (15:19);[4] they ar
closely bound to Jesus, and with him are sharply distinguished from "th
world" (15:18–21, cf. Matt. 10:22–25 – a "Son of Man" passage). Th
theme of the judgement of the Paraclete is "sin, righteousness an
judgement" (16:8). Sin consists in not believing in Jesus – and in th
synoptic gospels, as in 1 Enoch, the judgement of the Son of Man falls o
those who oppose the Son of Man or his elect community.[5] "With respec
to righteousness, because I am going to the Father" perhaps means tha
Jesus' heavenly exaltation will be followed by the judgement in which i
will be revealed who really are "the righteous", i.e., those who are linke
by faith and obedience with the Son of Man (so Matt. 13:37–43; 25:31

---

[1] Examples in the synoptic gospels that come readily to mind are the narrative of the trans
figuration, Mark 9:2–8 pars., cf. v. 9, and the ending of the Gospel of Matthew, Matt
28:16–20. Here we come upon the large question, why "the Son of Man" is missing from th
NT epistles, and whether there are nevertheless indirect echoes of the Son of Man theme i
them; but there is not the space to pursue that question here.

[2] Cf. N. Johansson, Parakletoi (1960), pp. 256–70. Without explanation, the Paraclete i
said to be another Paraclete. In 1 John 2:1 Jesus himself is called a Paraclete. The connexion
between Jesus and the Paraclete in John 14–16 is evidently intended to amount almost t
identity.

[3] So Schulz, op. cit., pp. 153–57.

[4] In 1 Enoch 37–71 "the Elect One" is an alternative title for "the Son of Man", and th
earthly group which looks to him for salvation is called "the elect" or "holy" or "righteous"
or some combination of these adjectives. "Elect" is used a number of times in the synopti
gospels to designate the members of the community associated with the Son of Man (Mark
13:20, 22, 27 pars.; Luke 18:7; cf. Matt. 22:14): more rarely, Jesus himself is called "elect'
(Luke 9:35; 23:35; and, according to a perhaps correct variant reading, John 1:34). Correspondingly, in the epistles and Revelation Christians are not infrequently called "elect", but this
term is used for Jesus only in 1 Pet. 2:4, and that in dependence on Isa. 28:16 (LXX) – but it i
in keeping with the "elect" terminology of 1 Enoch that there is a parallelism between
Jesus as the Elect One (1 Pet. 2:4, 6) and his community as an "elect race" (v. 9).

[5] That this is the meaning of the "unforgivable sin" in Matt. 12:32, I have argued in "The
Function of the Son of Man according to the Synoptic Gospels", pp. 58 ff.

37 etc.).[1] "Concerning judgement, because the ruler of this world has been judged" is reminiscent of 12:31, "Now will the ruler of this world be thrown out", which is linked with the "lifting up" of the Son of Man. There are also other indications that the whole farewell discourse is to be read in the light of the Son of Man theme. The long discourse at the supper recalls 1 Enoch 62:14, "And with that Son of Man shall they eat and lie down and rise up for ever and ever". Still more strikingly, the "mansions" or "resting-places" in "the house of my Father" recall 1 Enoch 41:2, 45:3.[2] The farewell discourse plays in John a dramatic function remarkably similar to that played in Matthew by the last part of the eschatological discourse (Matt. 24:45 – 25:46), for in John the Son of Man gives his disciples the new commandment, that they should love one another (13:34 f., repeated 15:11–17 and 17:11–23), and in the Matthew passage emphasis is laid on the responsibility of the leaders of the church to maintain the unity and fellowship of Jesus' disciples, who are the eschatological community of the Son of Man.[3] (Similarly, John 12:20–50 may be taken as approximately equivalent to Matt. 24:1–44, for in both passages the theme is the judgement of the world by the Son of Man.)

III

That Jesus was conscious of a special filial relationship to God has left its mark on the synoptic tradition (Mark 14:36; Matt. 11:25 ff.; Luke 10:21 f.), but in John has become so prominent as virtually to have become the organizing principle of John's presentation of the whole career of Jesus. Therefore "the Son" is the most frequently used of the Christological titles in John. Two other titles, which in the synoptic gospels have meanings quite different both from each other and from "the Son", namely "the Son of God" and "the Son of Man", have been assimilated in meaning to it. But our exegesis has shown that in the case of "the Son of Man" this assimilation is far from complete. In spite of considerable differences of vocabulary and imagery, the fundamental significance of the title "the Son of Man" in John is not different from that which it has in the synoptic gospels. As already in the Similitudes of 1 Enoch, the Son of Man is the eschatological judge who stands in intimate relationship to those who look to him for vindication and salvation and who will save them at the end. The closest approach to the synoptic imagery in which the judgement of the Son of Man is described comes in

[1] Cf. A. Descamps, Les justes et la justice dans les évangiles et dans le christianisme primitif (1950): there is a sectarian-eschatological significance in NT statements about "the righteous ones" (see esp. pp. 305 f.).

[2] So B. Aebert, Die Eschatologie des Johannesevangeliums (1936), pp. 33 f.

[3] On this, see my article, "Who are the 'Sheep' and the 'Goats'?", ABR, 13 (1965), pp. 9–28.

John 5:27 ff.: judgement will take place at the end of the world, thoug]
in the case of John it is the general resurrection rather than the "parousia'
of the Son of Man which is emphasized. As in the synoptics, the eschato·
logical judgement exercised by the Son of Man has already begun with th(
earthly ministry of Jesus, the Son of Man, and indeed this aspect of th(
matter is insisted on by John almost to the exclusion of the future aspect
Like Matthew and Luke, John sees eschatological significance in the life o:
the church, which is brought into being by the Son of Man and lives ir
close spiritual unity with him. As in Matthew, it is emphasized that th(
church is the earthly locus of salvation (3:1–21; 6:26–65; 9:35–41) and
that the unity and fellowship within this community of the Son of Man
are of great importance (13:31 ff.). In common with Luke, John sees the
ministry of Jesus, the Son of Man, as a great turning-point in the world's
history, which results in the rejection of the Jews because of their rejection
of Jesus, and the reception into the community of salvation of men of all
nations (12:20–36). The idea, which in the synoptic gospels is only hinted
at (Mark 10:45 pars.), that the death of the Son of Man not only precedes
his exaltation but also effects the salvation of his elect community, has a
prominent part in John (especially ch. 12, but also chs. 3, 6 and 13): for
the death of the Son of Man is seen as identical with his heavenly exaltation, and the heavenly exaltation of the Son of Man has made possible
the activity of the "other Paraclete", the Holy Spirit, by whose power the
church in fact "receives life" while the world remains in death, and by
whose agency the judgement of the world is carried out. For John the
important fact, already foreshadowed in the synoptic gospels (and in the
teaching of Jesus, though we cannot with any confidence reconstruct the
details), is that eschatological salvation and its negative counterpart
of condemnation and punishment are in all essential features already
accomplished.

CHAPTER XIII

THE RESURRECTION OF JESUS AND THE MISSION OF THE CHURCH

DARRYL PALMER

CONSIDERATION OF THE FORM AND FUNCTION OF RESURRECTION appearances in early Christian gospels must begin with the work of C. H. Dodd, *The Appearances of the Risen Christ: an Essay in Form-Criticism of the Gospels*.[1] Dodd perceived two classes of resurrection narrative, concise and circumstantial, with a common pattern:

A. The situation: Christ's followers bereft of their Lord.
B. The appearance of the Lord.
C. The Greeting.
D. The Recognition.
E. The Word of Command.[2]

Here a wider range of material will be surveyed[3] and a more precise analysis attempted.

I *Form*

The relevant material may be classified as follows.[4]

A. Epiphanies

(a) Fuller form
  Mt. 28: 1–8
  Mk. 16:1–8
  GN 13:1

(b) Shorter form
  Lk. 24:1–9
  Mt. 28:8–11
  GP 50–57

B. Commissions

(a) Fuller form
  Jn. 20:19–23
  Jn. 20:26–29

(b) Shorter form
  Mt. 28:16–20
  Mk. 16:14–18
  GN 14:1

---

[1] In D. E. Nineham (ed.), *Studies in the Gospels* (1955), 9–35; reprinted in C. H. Dodd, *More NT Studies*(1968), pp. 102 ff.

[2] *Studies in the Gospels*, p. 11. Concise narrative: Mt. 28:8–10; Mt. 28:16–20; Jn. 20:19–21; Jn. 20:26–29; Mk. 16:14–15. Circumstantial narrative: Lk. 24:13–35; Jn. 21:1–14; Gospel of the Hebrews. Mixed type: Lk. 24:36–49; Jn. 20:11–17.

[3] From outside the NT, Dodd considers only Gospel of the Hebrews and Gospel of Peter.

[4] Abbreviations for apocryphal works: Ep. Ap. = Epistle of the Apostles; GH = Gospel of the Hebrews; GN = Gospel of Nicodemus; GP = Gospel of Peter.

C. *Recognition Scenes*
    Lk. 24:13–32
    Jn. 20:14–16
    Jn. 21:1–14

D. *Other*
    GN 15:6
    Lk. 24:33–53
    GH
    Ep. Ap. 9–12
    GP 35–44

This list includes appearances not only of the risen Jesus but also of angels, since, formally, there is no distinction between angelophanies and Christophanies.[1] However, narratives sometimes regarded as pre-dated resurrection appearances, such as the Transfiguration, feeding miracles, and the miraculous catch of fish in Lk. 5 corresponding to Jn. 21, are excluded from consideration, because, functionally, the evangelists have not used them as resurrection narratives, and, formally, they do not have the characteristics of resurrection appearances.[2]

A. *Epiphanies*

	Lk. 2:8–14	Rev. 1:10–19	Mt. 28:1–8	Mk. 16:1–8	Dan. 10–12
(i) Introduction of situation	8	10–11	1	1–4	10:2–4
(ii) Messenger and his appearance	9a	12–16	2–3	5a	10:5–6
(iii) Terror of viewers	9b	17a	(4)	5b	10:7,8,9
(iv) Command: "Fear not"	10a	17b	5a	6a	10:12a
(v) Reason	10b	18	5b	—	10:12b
(vi) News	11	—	6	6b	10:13–15; 10:20–12:3
(vii) Charge	(12)	19	7	7	12:4,9–13
(viii) Response	15	—	8	8	—

[1] While *ministering* angels occasionally appear in the gospels, as at the Temptation (Mk. 1:13 and parallel Mt. 4:11) and in Gethsemane (Lk. 22:43), such active and *interpretative* angels as appear in the resurrection narratives have not been in evidence since the infancy narratives of Mt. and Lk.

[2] For more detailed treatment of these passages, see Dodd in *Studies in the Gospels*, 22–26. On Lk. 5:1–11 Dodd comments, "practically every *formal* feature of post-resurrection narratives has been eliminated. . . . The features which are common to Lk. 5 and Jn. 21 . . . are those which, even as they occur in John, are not characteristic of post-resurrection appearances" (p. 23).

It is notable that the fuller Epiphany form not only occurs in resurrection narratives, but is also used with the appearance of the angel to the shepherds in Lk. 2:8–14 and with the appearance of one "like a Son of Man" in Rev. 1:10–19. The appearance to Daniel (Dan. 10–12) also contains all the elements in the appropriate order, though in a diffuse and elaborated form. Characteristic of the messenger's appearance (ii) is the brightness of his face and clothing (Rev. 1:16b; Mt. 28:2; Mk. 16:5; Dan. 10:6). The terrified response of the viewers (iii) is exhibited particularly by their becoming feeble (Dan. 10:8) or sleepy (Dan. 10:9) or as if dead (Rev. 1:17a; Mt. 28:4). In Mt. the fearful response is reported only for the tomb-guards, who otherwise play no part in this pericope, and not for the women, who are properly the receivers of the epiphany. Of course, that the women too showed fear, is implied by the μὴ φοβεῖσθε and especially by the additional ὑμεῖς (Mt. 28:5, expanding Mk. 16:6). The heavenly messenger regularly supports his command not to fear (iv) with some good reason (v), which may be introduced by γάρ (Lk. 2:10b; Mt. 28:5b) or ὅτι (Dan. 10:12b; Hebrew: ki). Although Mt. 28:5 and Mk. 16:6 are parallel at this point, Mark lacks the Matthaean introductory phrase, "for I know that", before "you seek the crucified Jesus (of Nazareth)". Thus, despite the parallel, there is no reason given in Mark. GN 13:1 follows Mt. closely. But whereas Mt. has only a trace of his tomb-guard material in this pericope (at Mt. 28:4) and tells the story entirely from the point of view of the women, GN has quite reversed the situation and tells the story as a report from the guards to the Jewish authorities. GN thus has all the elements of the epiphany form except the final Response, but while (i), (ii) and (iii) refer, properly, to the guards, the latter simply overhear elements (iv), (v), (vi) and (vii), which are directed only to the women. (The final response of the guards, though not a literary element of the narrative, consists in their coming to make their report about what has happened.)

The shorter version of this Epiphany form differs only in that the angelic announcement cannot readily be subdivided into the elements (iv), (v), (vi) and (vii) of the fuller form.

	Lk. 24:1–9	GP 50–57	Mt. 28:8–10
(i) Introduction of of situation	1–3	50–54	8
(ii) Messenger and his appearance	4	55	9a
(iii) Terror of viewers	5a	—	(9b)
(iv) Message	5b–7	56	10
(v) Response	8–9	57	(11a)

As will be seen later, Luke's special proclivity for the motif of prophecy fulfilled is the reason why in Lk. 24:1-9, although like Matthew he is following Mk. 16:1-8, he has nevertheless departed from the fuller form of Epiphany. There is no command to refrain from fear, and hence no reason given for doing so. Nor is there any charge to pass on the news of the resurrection; but the women depart to report to the other followers of Jesus in any case. In GP 50-54, more convoluted than its Marcan parallel (Mk. 16:1-4), a dominant motif is the women's fear of the Jews. And that is perhaps why the author has not made further use of the element of fear in response to the appearance of the angel. Like Lk., GP has no charge to the women to inform the disciples. And the final response of the women is reported even more abruptly than in Mk. – they simply "fled in fear." Matthew goes beyond the Synoptic and Petrine empty tomb pericopes in adding an appearance of Jesus himself, who meets the women on their way to tell their news to the disciples. This Christophany is a doublet of the angelophany which immediately precedes it; and that may be the reason why the second epiphany not only is of the shorter form, but also has a much less detailed presentation of the individual elements. First, Mt. 28:8 does double service as the conclusion to the preceding angelophany and the introduction for the Christophany. Then, unlike the angel, Jesus' appearance does not have the apocalyptic accompaniment of an earthquake. And since there is no description of his face or clothing, there is no reason to assume the usual dazzling brightness in this instance. In keeping with this difference, the women respond not with fear but with a more positive obeisance (προσελθοῦσαι, Mt. 28:9). The final response of the women appears only briefly in the Genitive Absolute which begins the following paragraph: they went their way (πορευομένων δὲ αὐτῶν, Mt. 28:11).

B. Commissions

While the Message or Charge was no doubt the most important element in the Epiphanies, this element attains even greater prominence in the Commissions. The Johannine examples form a distinctive sub-type.

		Jn. 20	
(i)	Situation	19a	26a
(ii)	Arrival of Jesus	19b	26b
(iii)	Greeting	19c	26c
(iv)	Showing of wounds	20a	27
(v)	Response of disciple(s)	20b	28
(vi)	Commission	21-23	29

these two passages items (i), (ii), (iii) and (iv) are virtually identical.
hen to the disciples' response of joy (v. 20b) corresponds Thomas'
onfession of faith (v. 28). And in place of the apostolic commission (vv.
1-22), Jesus addresses through Thomas a blessing on all actual and po-
ntial believers (v. 29). The prominence of the commission and the
lessing is emphasized in that these elements are left standing as the cul-
inating points of their pericopes without any further response re-
orded.

In the remaining Commissions, the charge achieves its prominence by
eing the only considerable element; there is otherwise a minimum of
troduction. Mt. 28:16-20 ends with Jesus' commission and promise,
vithout recorded response. In Mk. 16:14-19 the commission is followed
y Jesus' ascension. GN 14:1 quotes Mk. 16:15-18 verbatim, and also
oncludes with the ascension, but in terms as much reminiscent of Acts
:9 as of Mk. 16:19.

C. Recognition Scenes

In a third group of appearances the distinctive feature is not the un-
olding of an epiphany according to an orderly pattern, nor the emphasis
n a climatic commission, but the recognition of Jesus by his followers.
a some accounts the risen Jesus is at first mistaken for a ghost and only
absequently recognized as the crucified and risen master, but this feature
not definitive for the appearances here classed as Recognition Scenes.
.ather the designation is applied to scenes in which Jesus appears without
pocalyptic accompaniments as a perfectly normal human being and
ather unobtrusively, but where he is not immediately recognized as
imself. So in Lk. 24:13-32 as the two disciples walk to Emmaus Jesus
oins them as an unknown stranger – οἱ δὲ ὀφθαλμοὶ αὐτῶν ἐκρατοῦντο
οῦ μὴ ἐπιγνῶναι αὐτόν, Luke explains (v. 16). Only at the end of the
cene as he breaks bread is Jesus recognized: αὐτῶν δὲ διηνοίχθησαν οἱ
φθαλμοί, καὶ ἐπέγνωσαν αὐτόν (v. 31). Thereupon Jesus' disappearance
 reported in technical epiphanic terminology (καὶ αὐτὸς ἄφαντος
γένετο ἀπ' αὐτῶν, v. 31) which dispels the impression of a normal human
eing. In Jn. 20:14-18 Jesus is at first unrecognizable to Mary, but his
ppearance is ordinary enough for Mary to mistake him for the gardener.
lowever, after he has been recognized in the simple address "Mary", the
ommand "Touch me not" again indicates the abnormality of this person.
.ikewise in Jn. 21 Jesus at first appears unrecognized on the shore (v. 4);
he miraculous catch of fish convinces the Beloved Disciple that "it is the
.ord" (v. 7); and, though Jesus remains on the scene, the mystery of his
oresence is now indicated in the attitude of the disciples, none of whom
lared ask him who he was, knowing it was the Lord (v. 12).

D. Other

The appearance to Joseph of Arimathea at GN 15:6 might also have been classed as a Recognition Scene, were it not for an equal preponderance of apocalyptic and magical elements along with the recognition motif. At the beginning Joseph's house is magically raised by its four corners, and at the end Joseph is magically replaced in his house after visiting the tomb. The account includes the usual auditory and visual elements of an epiphany, and the fearful response. But besides sight and sound, this account also has the elements of touch and smell. Here Jesus is first mistaken for a ghost. Once that impression is dispelled, he is mistaken for Elijah. Then Jesus proceeds to prove his true identity by recalling his burial by Joseph, and by taking Joseph to the tomb and showing him the burial cloths.

Lk. 24:33–53 contains remnants of the usual epiphanic elements: introduction of the situation (vv. 33–35), arrival of Jesus (v. 36), fearful response (v. 37). But the whole account, and especially the address of Jesus, is elaborated in line with Luke's special interests. First, to counter the disciples' impression (v. 37b), it is shown that Jesus is not a ghost (vv. 38–43). Luke divides the process of convincing into two stages. First Jesus shows his hands and feet and invites the disciples to touch him and see that, unlike a ghost, he has flesh and bones (v. 39). The disciples cannot believe their eyes for joy and wonder (v. 41a). Their reaction is to be distinguished from the disbelief motif of Jn. 20:24–29, Mk. 16:9–20 and Ep. Ap. 9–12. In Lk. 24:41 the idea is not "It cannot be true" but "It is almost too good to be true": Luke here presents not disbelief, but a stage on the way to full acknowledgement. The second part of Jesus' proof that he is not a ghost consists in his asking for something to eat and eating "before their eyes" (vv. 41b–43).[1] Luke now proceeds to the second major theme of this appearance, the fulfilment of prophecy (Lk. 24:44–48), which he had also employed in his two preceding pericopes. The motif occurred in relation to Jesus' own prediction of his passion and resurrection, as recalled by the angels to the women at Lk. 24:6b–7; then Jesus expounded the scriptures concerning himself to the Emmaus disciples (Lk. 24:25–27) and this exposition is now repeated for the benefit of the Eleven and their associates. This lengthy appearance concludes with the promise of an apostolic commission (v. 49), and the departure of Jesus (vv. 50–51), to which is added a notice of the interim activity of the disciples.

---

[1] Later occurrences of the ghost motif add variety to the proofs offered. In Ep. Ap. 1 Jesus invites Andrew to check his footprints, since the foot of a ghost or demon does not touch the ground (Coptic), or at least leaves no print (Ethiopic). In GN 15:6 Joseph recites the Commandments to scare away the supposed ghost. But the latter joins in the recitation "Now as you well know, a phantom immediately flees if it meets anyone and hears the Commandments." So it could not be a ghost.

GH is unique in portraying the fulfilment of a vow of abstinence.[1] One suspects that the author has constructed the whole incident by letting his imagination play on the traditions that appear in Mk. 10:38 (cf. Mt. 20:22) and especially Mk. 14:25 (cf. Mt. 26:29). If GH has used the latter tradition, then it has transferred the vow from Jesus to James, and has substituted bread for wine, and the resurrection of Jesus for the coming of the Kingdom of God as the limit of the vow. At any rate, Jerome's reporting shows that Jesus appeared to James, that there were others present (*adferte*, plural), and that Jesus dramatically released James from his vow. The fragments hint at a skilful creation of suspense, with the appearance of Jesus, his command to bring table and bread, his taking the bread, giving thanks and giving the bread to James, and finally his telling pronouncement: *frater mi, comede panem tuum, quia resurrexit filius hominis a dormientibus.*

In Ep. Ap. 9–12 Jesus appears first to the women at the tomb. He sends two of them in turn to take news of the resurrection to the disciples. But the disbelieving response of the disciples brings it about that finally Jesus himself goes to convince them. The persistent disbelief of the disciples recalls Mk. 16:9–20, where they first reject Mary's report (v. 11), then the report of the Two (v. 13), and are finally rebuked by the appearance of Jesus himself (v. 14). The two passages thus correspond not only as to the motif of disbelief, but also in the threefold pattern of witnesses, of whom the last is Jesus. Such triplicity is probably a folk-literary device, which may be compared with its different uses in the Synoptic parables of the Wicked Husbandmen (Mk. 12:1–12 and pars.).

Only the addition to Mk. 16:3 in the Old Latin version k and GP attempt to portray the resurrection itself. The editor of the addition to Mk., while manifestly desiring to provide an explicit account of the resurrection, has failed to integrate it into the Marcan record. For the insertion merely interrupts the progress of the women to the tomb without having any effect on them; the time designation *ad horam tertiam* does not correspond well with Mark's λίαν πρωΐ (Mk. 16:2); and there is nothing in the Marcan pericope to evoke the description of sudden and universal darkness and the subsequent return of light.[2] Such features suggest that the insertion was not specially composed for this context but had an independent existence elsewhere. Because of the common elements of attendant angels and the visible resurrection-ascension, it is natural to think of GP 35–42. But the time and the change of light–darkness–light fit

---

[1] It is not easy to assess this isolated pericope, nor even to determine the boundary between Jerome's quotation of GH and his own explanatory comment. Editors vary in assigning the sentence *iurauerat enim. . .resurgentem a dormientibus* to the present context of GH, or to Jerome's explanation of an earlier context therein. If the sentence belongs to the present context of GH, the fulness of its explanation almost precludes the possibility that GH contained a pre-passion scene in which James took his vow. But it is perhaps more likely that such scene was described by GH, and that Jerome now refers back to it in an explanatory note.
[2] *subito. . .tenebrae diei factae sunt per totum orbem terrae. . ., et continuo lux facta est.*

no better with GP than with the Marcan context. Moreover, k lack
characteristic details of GP: the presence of the cross, the great height o
the figures, and the support of Jesus by the angels. On the other hand, a
regards the actual description of the ascension from the tomb in th
manner of k and GP, the lack of further examples is striking.[1]

The Old Latin insertion at Mk. 16:3 is scarcely an appearance in th
strict sense, since it is not clear that anyone actually sees the event. Th
same is true of GP 35–44, if to a lesser degree. For it is of the essence of a
appearance that it includes communication with those who witness i
Here, however, the Jews and Roman soldiers are mere onlookers.[2] Th
structure of the pericope is determined not by the formal requirements o
an epiphany, but by the angelic descent and ascent. In addition to th
descent of the two angels and their implied return with Jesus, GP ha
another angel descend to the tomb in preparation for the meeting with th
women. Because GP excludes communication between the angeli
figures and the soldiers, the account readily falls into two sets of materia
linked by adverbial phrases at most of the joints: what the soldiers sav
(GP 35–37; 39–42; 44), and what the soldiers did (GP 38; 43).

Finally, mention may be made of Jn. 20:4–9, which develops the empt
tomb in the direction of an appearance. Elsewhere the empty tomb a
such is scarcely allowed any positive significance; and where it is, i
occurs in relation to an angelic appearance. Thus in Mk. the women do
not find an *empty* tomb, but an open tomb with an angel, whose message
to be sure, includes the empty tomb. This is also the pattern of Mt., G
and GN. Luke differs only in making the empty tomb set up the situatio
for the appearance of the angels: καὶ ἐγένετο ἐν τῷ ἀπορεῖσθαι αὐτὰ
περὶ τούτου καὶ ἰδοὺ ἄνδρες δύο ἐπέστησαν αὐταῖς (Lk. 24:4). Th
empty tomb does not accomplish anything in itself. Its lack of significanc
is most pronounced in Ep. Ap. 9–10. On their way to the tomb the womer
are "mourning and weeping over what had happened" (i.e. the passion)
They inspect the tomb and fail to find Jesus' body. And they continu
"mourning and weeping" as before, with no apparent reaction to th
empty tomb. Indeed the author builds up the motif of mourning ove

---

[1] Even in the Ascension of Isaiah 3:16–17, while two angels support Jesus as he emerge
from the tomb, there is no reference to Jesus' ascent to heaven but only to his sending out o
the twelve disciples etc. The ascensions or assumptions of OT figures do not seem to provide
literary models for the accounts in k and GP. What the OT itself and the apocryphal writing
provide is either a mere notice that a figure was taken up; or a description such that as of the
taking up of Elijah (2 Kings 2:1–12); or a description of a journey around the heavenly realms

[2] The amount of apocalyptic imagery in this passage of GP makes it worth asking whether
it might be classed as an apocalyptic vision. The apocalyptic elements are as follows. Loud
voice in heaven: μεγάλη φωνή occurs twenty times in Rev. which in turn reflects OT
revelation passages; cf. also Mk. 1:11 and pars. (baptism of Jesus) and Mk. 9:7 and pars.
(Transfiguration). Heavens opened (GP 36, 44): Is. 64:1; Ez. 1:1; Mk. 1:10 and pars; Ac
10:11; Rev. 4:1; 6:14; 19:11. Descent of angels (GP 36, 44): Rev. 10:1; 18:1; 20:1. Brightness
(GP 36): Rev. 1:16; 15:6; 19:8; 22:16. Extreme height of figures (GP 40): Rev. 10:1–6;
Herm. *sim.* 9:6; 4 Esr. 2:43; Book of Elchasai, fr. 1 (= Hipp. *Ref.* 9.13.1–3).

the passion as a foil to the imminent appearance of Jesus himself. As a result the empty tomb has become rather superfluous, though that in itself shows that the empty tomb was by now such an established piece of tradition that it could not be omitted.

Jn. 20 makes considerably more out of the empty tomb. In Jn. 20:1 it is not actually said that Mary Magdalene inspected the tomb, only that she saw the stone removed. But in the light of v. 2, John probably intends the reader to assume that Mary actually found the body missing. Moreover, her statement, "We do not know where they have put him", is already a development beyond other empty tomb passages. And this in turn prompts the visit of the two disciples to the tomb. John is the only evangelist to make explicit mention of the grave cloths in the tomb. Peter sees them; the Beloved Disciple saw and *believed*. The grave cloths constitute a sort of negative appearance. It might be objected that the empty tomb already does this; but that is not true for John. And therein is seen the artificiality of his scheme: John *could* not mention the interior of the tomb in v. 1, because he was reserving the impact of the grave cloths for the Beloved Disciple in v. 8.

In summary, the Epiphanies have the most detailed formal structure; they occur within the Synoptic empty tomb pericopes, and the equivalent passages of GN and GP; thus the one who appears is an angel (or angels), except for the appearance of Jesus himself in the Matthaean doublet (Mt. 28:8-11). In the Commissions, Jesus appears, and the absence of epiphanic appurtenances throws the emphasis more forcibly on the message itself, especially in the shorter form. One would expect the Commissions, because of their content, to be the final appearance in any writing. This is the case in Mt. and it becomes the case for the longer ending of Mk. GN, however, extends some way beyond the report of the Commission, though it can no longer go on quoting canonical gospel material, except by further retrospects to the life of Jesus before his passion. As for John, it is somewhat problematical that he has two appearances of the Commission type – they cannot both be last. The Recognition Scenes show a less rigid form, though, so long as the risen Jesus is appearing to disciples, the presence of certain basic structural elements is inevitable. Any clearer understanding of the literary purpose of the appearances will only be achieved by seeing how the various types of appearance are used in each writing.

II *Function*

Mark

If Mk. 16:8 is taken as the end of the gospel, a very heavy burden is placed on the sole appearance, that of the angel. Nevertheless, this is a burden which the appearance is able to bear. For the message with which the angel entrusts the women includes the promise of an appearance of Jesus himself. The nature of this message suggests that Mark envisages a single appearance, not a series of them. Moreover, it is not clear that the appearance of Jesus is to be a resurrection appearance in the sense of proving the resurrection. The resurrection is in any case already established, from Mark's point of view, by the angel's announcement and his interpretation of the empty tomb (Mk. 16:6). The content of the angel's charge confirms Jesus' own prediction to the Twelve at Mk. 14:28. But neither Mk. 14:28 nor its recapitulation at Mk. 16:7 provides a clear interpretation of the promised appearance of Jesus. Much depends on the significance of Galilee for Mark. Certainly the emphasis on Galilee throughout the gospel is Mark's own work. C. F. Evans sees Mark's Galilee as "the land of the Gentiles, which is symbolic of the world-wide mission".[1] But that is rather a Matthaean emphasis: "Galilee of the Gentiles" in Mt. 4:15, quoting Is. 8:23, is a Matthaean addition to the Marcan source; and the world-wide mission appears in Mt. 28:19 without Marcan basis. The odd thing about Galilee in Mk. is that, although its presence is redactional, nothing much is made of it. This gives plausibility to Marxsen's view that Galilee is where the Marcan community now is. Moreover, if

> Mark inserts 16:7 into an already existing context, then we are dealing with the latest stratum reflecting the evangelist's own situation. *But then this redactional note cannot deal with an appearance of the Risen Lord awaited in Galilee; in Mark's context this passage can only refer to the expected parousia.*[2]

This understanding may be supported by tying Mk. 14:62 in with Mk. 14:28 and Mk. 16:7. It is notable that Mk. 16:7 adds to Mk. 14:28: ἐκεῖ αὐτὸν ὄψεσθε, καθὼς εἶπεν ὑμῖν. But Jesus did not tell the disciples that. However, in response to the High Priest's question, σὺ εἶ ὁ χριστὸς ὁ υἱὸς τοῦ εὐλογητοῦ; he did say, ἐγώ εἰμι, καὶ ὄψεσθε τὸν υἱὸν τοῦ ἀνθρώπου ἐκ δεξιῶν καθήμενον τῆς δυνάμεως καὶ ἐρχόμενον μετὰ τῶν νεφελῶν τοῦ οὐρανοῦ (Mk. 14:62). ἐγώ εἰμι is a proper form of reply to the question; the rest is not. Moreover, the plural ὄψεσθε seems uncalled for in addressing the High Priest (singular). It may be suggested that ὄψεσθε κ.τ.λ. is secondary to the context, and that the plural ὄψεσθε once applied to the disciples; and that Mark betrays awareness of this in Mk. 16:7.

On this interpretation, what Mark envisages as happening in Galilee is not merely a resurrection appearance, nor even the one and only resurrection appearance, but the coming of Jesus as Son of Man on clouds of

[1] *Resurrection in the NT* (London, 1970), p. 81.
[2] W. Marxsen, *Mark the Evangelist* (ET Nashville, 1969), p. 85.

lory to preside at the last judgement. That would be enough to frighten
nyone, even the faithful (Mk. 16:8).[1]

The longer ending of Mk. has been added to supply what was felt to
e a lack. The extremely awkward relation of Mk. 16:9 to Mk. 16:8,
oth grammatically (ἀναστάς, with Jesus as subject) and in content
virtual doublet of Mary Magdalene at the tomb), shows that vv. 9–20
rere not composed specially for the "completion" of the gospel. At the
ame time, the addition as a whole is held together at least by the motif of
isbelief.[2] Thus the first function of the appearance of Jesus in vv. 14–18
, to dispel the disbelief of the disciples. The second and main function,
or which the disbelief has served as a foil, is the mission charge. The
ropagators of the longer ending must have felt that Mark had been too
ecretive about this important motif, and desired to make it quite explicit.
'his desire is shown by the fact that Jesus' words in vv. 15–18 are not
onfined to a charge proper, but spill over into propaganda. The emphasis
, maintained in the final verse (Mk. 16:20), where the carrying out of the
harge is recorded.[3]

Matthew

After the angelophany of Mt. 28:2–7, Matthew introduces a Christo-
hany (Mt. 28:9–10), whose function is not immediately obvious. That
ne women have already accepted the fact of the resurrection on the basis
f the angel's announcement is clear from v. 8, where they run in fear and
by to tell the disciples. Moreover, the angel's charge already contained
ne promise of an appearance of Jesus in Galilee. Consequently in the
Christophany in vv. 9–10 neither Jesus' presence nor his message adds
nything to what is already known and believed. It might almost be said
nat he merely interrupts the women in the task which they are already
astening to perform. However, the appearance at least confirms the
ews of the angel; and the women's worship of the risen Jesus is an
ppropriate gradation beyond the angelophany. Moreover, Jesus'
epetition of the charge concerning Galilee serves a multiple purpose: it
nrows greater emphasis on to the Galilean appearance; it plays down the
resent appearance as subordinate to the later one; and it relativizes the
gnificance of the empty tomb as such – the actual presence of Jesus in
Mt. supersedes the Marcan argument from silence.[4]

---

[1] Whatever its prehistory, the account of Mk. 16:1–8 as it now stands cannot mean that
ne women disobeyed the angel's charge. The clause, καὶ οὐδενὶ οὐδὲν εἶπαν, in v. 8 means
nat they ran away in a fright "without saying a word to anybody", not that they failed to
eliver the message to the disciples.
[2] Besides the disbelief of the disciples afforded to Mary Magdalene at v. 11 and to the Two
t v. 13, and rebuked by Jesus at v. 14, the issue of belief is also prominent within the mission
harge, v. 16 and v. 17.
[3] After Mk. 16:14 the Washington Codex inserts a short conversation between Jesus and
ne disciples concerning eschatological problems. By this means Mk. 16:9–20 is transformed
nto a miniature gnostic gospel.
[4] "He is not here," Mk. 16:6 (= Mt. 28:6).

Mt. 28:16–20 gives an explicit description of a Galilean appearance to fulfil the promise of Mt. 28:7 (parallel to Mk. 16:7). In making this appearance of outstanding importance, Matthew still adheres to the gist of his Marcan source. Thus apart from Matthew's special tomb guard material (Mt. 28:4, 11–15), Mt. 28 as a whole is closely related to Mk. 16:1–8. While it would be going too far to take Mt. 28:16–20 as an account of the parousia of the Son of Man, yet the appearance is oriented in that direction. For Matthew has merely acknowledged that the parousia is not so imminent as Mark had thought, and has made corresponding adjustments. Thus, while the parallel to Mk. 14:28 is maintained verbatim at Mt. 26:32, the parallel to Mk. 14:62 at Mt. 26:64 is modified by the addition of ἀπ' ἄρτι to the prediction ὄψεσθε τὸν υἱὸν τοῦ ἀνθρώπου. Matthew has thereby transformed the parousia from the strictly future event, which it is in Mk., into an eschatological process beginning right now. This is Matthew's way of dealing with the "delay" of the parousia. Mt. 28:16–20 is, however, precisely a preview of the parousia in its fulness: it exhibits to the faithful the sovereign position, which Jesus already occupies (Mt. 28:18), but which will not be fully revealed until the last day. συντέλεια τοῦ αἰῶνος is a common Matthaean phrase (Mt. 13:39, 40, 49; 24:3) with clear judgemental implications. So in Jesus' promise to be with his disciples (Mt. 28:20) the phrase indicates not a blissful indefiniteness, but a critical limit. Meantime the disciples are commissioned to win over "all peoples everywhere", so that they will be on the right side when the judgment comes (vv. 19–20).

The three appearances in Matthew's narrative thus build towards a climax. The preparatory appearances of the angel (Mt. 28:2–7) and of Jesus (Mt. 28:9–10) have served to reconstitute the band of the disciples. In the final appearance (Mt. 28:16–20) Jesus commissions them for their task as missionaries to the whole world.

Luke

Luke begins his resurrection narrative with the shorter form of Epiphany, despite the fact that he is following Mark, who has the fuller form. The reason for this alteration seems to hinge on the mention of Galilee. Luke had already omitted the pre-passion prediction of a Galilean appearance at Mk. 14:28 (and the parallel Mt. 26:32). That is consistent with the fact that Luke wants to confine appearances of the risen Jesus to the vicinity of Jerusalem. Thus, although Luke is clearly aware of the reference to Galilee at Mk. 16:7, he radically changes its application. Instead of the message, προάγει ὑμᾶς εἰς τὴν Γαλιλαίαν· ἐκεῖ αὐτὸν ὄψεσθε, καθὼς εἶπεν ὑμῖν (Mk. 16:7), Luke has: μνήσθητε ὡς ἐλάλησεν ὑμῖν ἔτι ὢν ἐν τῇ Γαλιλαίᾳ, λέγων τὸν υἱὸν τοῦ ἀνθρώπου ὅτι δεῖ παραδοθῆναι εἰς χεῖρας ἀνθρώπων ἁμαρτωλῶν καὶ σταυρωθῆναι καὶ τῇ τρίτῃ ἡμέρᾳ ἀναστῆναι (Lk. 24:6–7). This altered message now picks up Jesus' prediction of his passion and resurrection at Lk. 9:22 (cf. Mk. 8:31, Mt. 16:21). In keeping with the alteration the angel's opening words are not the usual μὴ φοβεῖσθε (or its equivalent, μὴ ἐκθαμβεῖσθε, Mk. 16:6), but the slightly censorious question: τί ζητεῖτε τὸν ζῶντα μετὰ τῶν νεκρῶν (Lk. 24:5). They should have known better!

In Lk. the women report the resurrection to the disciples without being commanded to do so, but the disciples do not believe them (Lk. 24:11). The motif of disbelief opens the way for further appearances. First comes the Emmaus appearance to the Two (Lk. 24:13–32). In the passion and resurrection prediction at Lk. 18:31–34,[1] Luke has added both to the previous Lucan prediction (Lk. 9:22) and to the Marcan source at this point (Mk. 10:33) the notion that these events are to take place as the fulfilment of scriptural prophecy. Within the Emmaus appearance the prophecy-fulfilment motif is picked up at Lk. 24:25–27, where Jesus is said to have rebuked the slowness of wit of the Two, and to have expounded at length the scriptural prophecy concerning himself. The same motif is stressed again at the end of this appearance, where the Two reflect on their experience (v. 32). The disciples' slowness of wit allows Luke to fill out the appearance with kerygmatic expansion: introductory device (Jesus' assumed ignorance), vv. 17–18; kerygmatic content, vv. 19–24. Luke's own literary activity is prominent here. The risen Jesus and his disciples become a pedagogical device for the instruction of Luke's readers.

Lk. 24:33–35 is a single appearance, but it readily falls into three parts: the ghostly appearance of Jesus (vv. 33–43); the scriptural basis for the current stage of divinely directed history (vv. 44–49); and Jesus' departure and the disciples' response.[2] It is difficult to account for the first part. Why does Jesus create such a ghostly impression at first (v. 37), when in the previous pericope (Lk. 24:13–32) he had appeared as a normal human being (until his departure)? How is the ghostly impression to be reconciled with the solid flesh-and-bone state which Jesus claims (Lk. 24:39)? Conversely, if the risen Jesus behaves in a physiologically normal way, how is one to account for his mysterious disappearance at Emmaus (Lk. 24:31), and his mysterious arrival and departure at Jerusalem (Lk. 24:36, 51)? Moreover the nature of Jesus' resurrection body does not otherwise seem of interest to Luke. We must suppose an apologetic, anti-docetic concern, which was nevertheless not an issue for the main line of Luke's treatment of the resurrection.

[1] If the phrase, ἔτι ὢν ἐν τῇ Γαλιλαίᾳ (Lk. 24:6), is taken strictly, it cannot refer to Lk. 18:31–34, since by that stage Jesus was well on his way to Jerusalem according to the Lucan arrangement (almost to Jericho, in view of the following pericope, Lk. 18:35 ff.).

[2] Lk. 24:50–53 is taken as belonging to the gospel, except for the last clause of v. 51 ("and was taken up into heaven") and the phrase at the beginning of v. 52 ("having worshipped him").

The second part (Lk. 24:44–49) of this appearance takes up again the theme of fulfilment of scriptural prophecy. One aim of the theme is to make the resurrection more acceptable. But it is more important that Luke's emphasis on scriptural prophecy sets the resurrection of Jesus in the context of divinely ordered history. Thus in the final Lucan appearance, Jesus' exposition of scripture goes beyond his own passion and resurrection to include the apostolic preaching of repentance and forgiveness in a universal mission beginning from Jerusalem (Lk. 24:27). This aspect of the appearance corresponds closely to the Commission of Mt. 28:16–20. But there are radical differences. In the Matthaean appearance there is both a finality in relation to what has gone before and a sense of imminence in the mention of the "end of the age". Luke, on the other hand, only indicates that there will be an apostolic commissioning (Lk. 24:49), without recording it in his gospel. And for Luke the commissioning does not include Jesus' promise to be with his disciples in their teaching ministry until the end comes. Instead Jesus' earthly work, now complete, gives way to a new era of the Spirit and the church.[1] The prophecy-fulfilment motif in the Lucan resurrection appearances is intended to bring the disciples, and Luke's readers, to understand that, while Jesus' work is now completed and confirmed, there remains the mission of the church, in which the disciples, empowered by the Spirit, must play their part.

John

In Jn. 20:1–18 there are spliced together an empty tomb story involving the two disciples, which is now represented in vv. 3–10, and an appearance to Mary Magdalene, which is now represented in vv. 1 and 11–18, v. 2 being an editorial joint. The result of this literary workmanship is an ascending movement: the empty tomb is a mere puzzle to Mary (vv. 1–2); but the grave cloths lead to faith for the Beloved Disciple (v. 8); the angels challenge Mary's sorrow (v. 13); and the appearance of Jesus himself confirms his resurrection (vv. 15–16). Then follows the gift of the Spirit and the apostolic commission (vv. 19–23). According to a Matthaean or Lucan pattern, this should be the climax of the resurrection appearances and of the gospel. But John now adds the story of Thomas. The purpose of the story is not to prove the real bodily resurrection of Jesus, a tendency perceptible in Lk. 24:36–43. Any correspondence with Lk. exists rather in relation to Luke's limitation of the resurrection appearances to a short period. According to John the gap between the later church and Jesus is bridged not by resurrection appearances but by faith. The appearance to Thomas is thus scarcely on a level with the other Johannine appearances. It is rather a piece of theological apologetic, conveyed by means of an

---

[1] Ac. 1:4–5 and 2:38–39 identify "the promise of my Father" (Lk. 24:49) as the gift of the Spirit; cf. Ac. 1:8; 2:17 (quoting Jl. 2:28); 2:33; 5:32.

ppearance, but which precisely limits the function and value of such ppearances.

Jn. 21 is an appendix from a different hand. There are problems of ternal construction, which suggest the combination of separate strands f tradition concerning a miraculous catch of fish, an appearance to Peter, nd a meal at which the risen Jesus officiates. Particularly vv. 1–14 are narked off as appearance by the editorial terminology: μετὰ ταῦτα ϕανέρωσεν ἑαυτὸν πάλιν ᾽Ιησοῦς τοῖς μαθηταῖς . . . · ἐϕανέρωσεν δὲ ὕτως (v. 1); τοῦτο ἤδη τρίτον ἐϕανερώθη ᾽Ιησοῦς τοῖς μαθηταῖς νερθεὶς ἐκ νεκρῶν (v. 14). Such language, especially πάλιν (v. 1) and δη τρίτον (v. 14), shows that appearances are thought of as proofs of ne resurrection, and value is assigned to the mere number of appearances. Iowever this appearance is mainly a vehicle for the apologetic motifs of ne restoration of Peter and his apostolic authority both in general and specially in relation to the Beloved Disciple.

pocryphal Writings

The appearance in GH must have had as a major function the proof of ne resurrection. This is indicated by the fact that the account is clearly narked at the beginning as an appearance,[1] by the wording of James' ow,[2] and by Jesus' words releasing him from it,[3] as by the very notion of vow of abstinence.[4]

The mention of Jesus' contact with the priest's servant in GH is a hint hat in that gospel the "enemies" were among the first witnesses of the esurrection. Such a motif is fully developed in GP, where the resurrection akes place before the Roman soldiers and the Jews. The aim is to produce ncontrovertible testimony in favour of the resurrection. For the Roman uthorities are depicted as notably fair and impartial throughout GP, ust as the Jewish authorities are hostile. When both these sources admit the esurrection, who can deny it? In contrast to an Epiphany proper, the ;uards register no fear at these astounding events, but calmly take note f what happens. If the Jewish observers[5] are very worried (ἀγωνιῶντες ιεγάλως, GP 45), that is not the reaction of a believer granted an

---

[1] *iit ad Iacobum et apparuit ei.*

[2] *donec uideret eum resurgentem a dormientibus.*

[3] *quia resurrexit filius hominis a dormientibus.*

[4] Since the James fragment begins with the words, *dominus autem cum dedisset sindonem ;ruo sacerdotis*, it is possible that the preceding pericope in GH also functioned as a proof of the esurrection. Of course the presence of Jesus himself should be enough to carry conviction. But, as with James there was the token of the bread, so with the priest's servant there is the inen cloth.

[5] That οἱ περὶ τὸν κεντυρίωνα (GP 45) are not the στρατιῶται (GP 35, 38) but the ;ρεσβύτεροι (παρῆσαν γὰρ καὶ αὐτοὶ ϕυλάσσοντες) (GP 38), is shown by Pilate's response o their report: ἐγὼ καθαρεύω τοῦ αἵματος τοῦ υἱοῦ τοῦ θεοῦ ὑμῖν δὲ τοῦτο ἔδοξεν GP 46).

epiphany, but the result of rational reflection on the implications of th
scene: ἀληθῶς υἱὸς ἦν θεοῦ (GP 45).

In the next pericope (the women's visit to the tomb, GP 50–57), th
fear of the Jews (50, 52, 54) and the women's purpose in going to the tom
(rites and lamentation for the dead, 50, 52, 53, 54) are peculiar to GP. Y
these motifs yield no result in what follows. The angel informs the wome
of the resurrection, draws attention to the absence of the body, an
announces the departure of Jesus for his place of origin, which, in view
the preceding pericope, means heaven. Then the women flee in fea
Thus GP 50–57 does not carry the action any further, but merely create
suspense.[1] This interpretation is supported by the condition with whic
the angel prefaces his invitation to inspect the place where the body ha
lain: εἰ δὲ μὴ πιστεύετε (GP 56; not in Synoptics). Thus doubt is throw
on the women's credulity. This motif then ties in with the visible occur
rence of the resurrection before impartial and hostile witnesses: what eve
the followers of Jesus find hard to believe, really did happen!

The angel's message lacks any charge to tell the disciples that Jesus wi
appear to them in Galilee, or even that he is risen. Nevertheless, in th
following pericope, the disciples do return to Galilee; and the scene is s
for an appearance, when the manuscript breaks off (GP 58–60). GP ha
its own means of getting the disciples to the new location: they simpl
return home at the end of the festival of unleavened bread. Thus if th
disciples are to be convinced of the resurrection, it will not be because o
the empty tomb or the angel's announcement to the women. The simi
larity of GP 58–60 to Jn 21:1 ff. tempts one to postulate a parallel appear
ance, in which Peter would now predominate without any competitio
from the Beloved Disciple. But detailed speculation is idle. Even the sig
nificance of a concluding apostolic commission would be modified b
the structure of GP, where the Romans and the Jews have already seen th
light. The arrangement of the appearances in GP is thus drastically differen
from that of the canonical gospels. For GP begins with what in Mt., Lk
or Jn. could only be the envisaged result of a Christian mission not re
corded in the gospels themselves: the conversion of the Gentiles and of th
unbelieving Jews.

The Pilate literature in general exhibits a developed form of the desire
evident in GP, to establish the certainty of the resurrection by appeal to
the most impartial or even hostile witnesses. In GN, which draws on th
earlier Pilate literature, the unimpeachable evidence of the Roma
investigations is played off against the consistently stubborn unbelief of th
Jewish authorities. Because of this approach the appearances are neve

---

[1] This motif occurs briefly at Lk. 24:3–4, where the women, failing to find the body o
Jesus, are in a state of ἀπορεῖσθαι; and in Jn. 20:2, 11–15, where Mary's discovery of th
empty tomb causes her puzzlement and tears. In GP the angel's message has a correspondin
effect.

lated in simple narrative but are always the subject of a report by wit-
sses. So the tomb guards report to the "synagogue" the appearance of
e angel to the women, largely according to Mt. 28:1–8. Similarly a
iest, a teacher and a Levite report from Galilee an apostolic commission
the words of Mk. 16:15–18. GN provides a new setting for the Marcan
mmission. Mk. 16:14 gives no specification of place, but has the Eleven
clining (at table) – a detail which is reminiscent of Lk. 24:34, and there-
re suggests Jerusalem. GN has the disciples sitting on a mountain in
alilee. That is an adjustment to Mt. 28:16. But GN has not used the
atthaean commission, perhaps only because Mark gives a more detailed
scription of what the mission will involve. At any rate, by taking these
pearances out of their original context and making them the subject of
second-hand report, GN has transformed their function. Their purpose
now generalized, so that regardless of their own peculiarities of form
d content, they are merely proofs of the resurrection offered by reliable
itnesses to the Jewish authorities. The tendency is thus exactly opposite
that of Jn. 20:24–29.

The appearance to Joseph of Arimathea (GN 15:6) makes no use of
nonical material. It seeks to establish the reality of Jesus' bodily resurrec-
on and to show that it really is Jesus and not someone else. The main
urpose, however, from the point of view of the Jewish interrogation, is
e proof that the resurrection really did happen. There is no attempt to
umb the meaning of the resurrection; it is a brute fact which is the
lcrum for a contest over its truth or falsity.

In Ep. Ap. the women's observation of the empty tomb has no apparent
fect on them, since their mourning and weeping is not a response to the
sence of the body (as in Jn. 20:13), but a continuation of their previously
ported response to the passion (Ep. Ap. 9). The initial function of Jesus'
pearance is as a general assurance to the women that he is indeed risen:
Do not weep; I am he whom you seek" (Ep. Ap. 10). To this assurance is
nmediately added the command that one of the women should pass on
e news to the disciples. The elaboration of this motif plays up the dis-
elief of the disciples: repeated visits of the women do not convince
em. The theme of disbelief is apologetic: yes, it is hard to believe that
sus rose from the dead; even the disciples did not believe it at first; (but
is true!) Even Jesus' own presence (Ep. Ap. 11) does not immediately
nvince the disciples. In proving his resurrection, Jesus interweaves the
vo aspects found separately in GN 15:6: it is Jesus and not a ghost; it is
sus and not somebody else. Finally (Ep. Ap. 12) the disciples are con-
nced that it is really Jesus, truly risen, in the flesh.[1]

[1] At this point Jesus commences the teaching section, which aligns Ep. Ap. with the gnostic
spel form. Within this section Ep. Ap. retains one further common function of appearances:
e apostolic commission. This occurs at several points, either in the form of a command by
sus (Ep. Ap. 19, 30, 41, 46; cf. 31), or in the form of a spontaneous undertaking by the
sciples (Ep. Ap. 40).

III   *Conclusion*

In conclusion, it is possible to make a distinction between the canonical and the apocryphal appearances. The form of the canonical resurrection appearances gives primary emphasis to the heavenly message which they convey. The function of the appearances depends on the content of the message, and on the way in which the appearances fit into the structure of the resurrection narrative as a whole in each gospel.

Among the canonical additions, the longer ending of Mark attempts to assimilate Mark to the other canonical gospels, with prime emphasis on the missionary motif; Jn. 21 is mainly the vehicle of apologetic concerning apostolic authority. As for the canonical gospels in their original form, since each has its own particular theological emphasis, the resurrection appearances are in each case subordinated to a wider theology of history in which Jesus' ministry, passion and resurrection play a part. Neither the Christophanies nor the angelophanies are intended to prove the resurrection. In the Marcan and Matthaean empty tomb pericopes, the angel's announcement makes clear that the resurrection itself is a mere preliminary to the further eschatological action of Jesus. Mark ends with that ominous promise. Matthew confirms the angelic pronouncement by an ancillary appearance of Jesus himself, and then moves on to the main appearance of Jesus, which is both a mission charge and a proleptic manifestation of the exalted Son of Man. In the Lucan empty tomb pericope the angel announces not just the fact of the resurrection, but the necessity of the resurrection in keeping with Jesus' earlier prediction. This theme is developed in the subsequent appearances of Jesus himself. Jesus brings home to the disciples not the mere fact of his resurrection, but its necessary place in the order of history ordained by God. Indeed the function of the resurrection appearances in Luke is to prevent the disciples from looking backwards at the resurrection itself, and to require them to look forward to the coming of the Holy Spirit and the part which they themselves must now play in God's history.

John has attempted to interpret the resurrection in more clearly defined stages. He presents in order the empty tomb as theologically mute (Mary); the grave cloths as a sign to faith (Beloved Disciple); an appearance which takes the puzzlement and distress out of the empty tomb and focuses on the positive aspect of the risen Jesus (for Mary); an apostolic commission to the assembled disciples; and a final blessing on the individual believer. Here are two distinctive features: John does in a sense attempt to prove the resurrection (Beloved Disciple at the tomb, and appearance to Mary); and he is unwilling to end with the apostolic commission. There is probably a connexion between these two features. For "proving the resurrection by appearances" cannot mean the same for John as it would for the Synoptics. In the Synoptics, Jesus predicts his own resurrection in

e body of the gospels, though the disciples do not understand what he is
lking about. In John, Jesus already in the body of the gospel interprets the
eaning of the resurrection as – himself! – "I am the resurrection and the
e" (Jn. 11:25). So already resurrection has been de-eschatologized and
terpreted in terms of the individual's relation in faith to Jesus. This may
lp to explain why John ends not with the apostolic commission but with
. appearance which seeks out an individual and demands and receives
s faith. The retention of the apostolic commission shows that for John
ere still is a Christian missionary commission. But it does not have the
me eschatological focus as in the Synoptics. In the Synoptics, the Chris-
n church is a community of eschatological prophets; in John it is a
oup of Christian existentialists.

The apocryphal material has a common emphasis on the attempt to
ove the resurrection. This is particularly clear in the tribunal atmos-
ere of GN, and in relation to the disbelief motif in Ep. Ap. GH too
ems to have proof of the resurrection as its major concern. And in GP
e visible resurrection before the non-Christian witnesses has the aim of
tablishing the resurrection beyond all doubt.

This apocryphal material thus exhibits two striking and contradictory
atures: it is credally correct, and theologically dead. It certainly pro-
iims the passion and resurrection of Jesus, and thus correctly continues
e apostolic preaching. But it is so concerned for the correctness of its
rygma, that is has lost the concern for its meaning. In defending the
ith of the fact that Jesus really did rise from the dead, this literature has
st sight of what it was about Jesus that made his earliest followers believe
 his resurrection in the first place – which has been preserved in the
iity and diversity of the canonical gospels.

CHAPTER XIV

SOME OBSERVATIONS ON ROMANS 8:19-21

C. E. B. CRANFIELD

IN ROMANS 8 (THE FOURTH SECTION OF THE MAIN DIVISION OF THE EPISTL in which the life promised for the man who is righteous by faith described) Paul is concerned with the fact that the life promised for th man who is righteous by faith is a life characterized by the indwelling c the Holy Spirit. In vv. 1–11 the basic statement of the section is mad Paul then goes on in vv. 12–16 to affirm that to be indwelt by God's Spiri is to be a child of God, having the freedom to call God "Father". Th implication of v. 15 understood in its context would seem to be that it i in the believer's calling God "Father" that God's holy law is establishe and its righteous requirement (v. 4) fulfilled. (To tell him that he has bee given the freedom to call God "Father" and to bid him exercise his free dom is to say *in principle* all that there is to be said in the way of Christia ethics; for nothing more is required of him than that he should do ju this – should do it with full understanding of what it means, with fu seriousness and with full sincerity. For to address the true God by th name of Father intelligently, seriously, sincerely, will, of course, involv seeking wholeheartedly to be and think and say and do what is pleasin to him and to avoid being or thinking or saying or doing what displease him.) Verse 17 makes the transition from the subject of obedience (callin God "Father") to that of Christian hope (that to be indwelt by the Hol Spirit is to be possessed of the gift of hope is the theme of vv. 17–30) b way of the connexion between sonship and heirship. The words εἴπε κ.τ.λ. (RV: "if so be that", etc.) are added in confirmation of what ha already been said in the earlier part of the verse, the sense being that th fact that believers are now suffering as a result of their loyalty to Christ so far from calling the reality of their heirship in question, is in truth pledge of their being glorified with him hereafter. Verse 18 explain (hence the "for") how the sufferings and the glory, to which v. 17 ha referred, stand in relation to each other: in the light of his understandin of the gospel Paul can see that the sufferings of the present are but a ver little thing compared with the transcendent greatness and splendour o that glory which is the object of the Christian hope.

Such is the context of the verses with which we are specially concerned The first of them is introduced as support ("for") for what has been said in v. 18, and is then itself clarified by vv. 20 and 21.

About the meaning of ἡ κτίσις (RV: "the creation") there has been much controversy. It has been variously interpreted down the centuries as signifying the whole creation including mankind both believing and unbelieving and also the angels; all mankind; unbelieving mankind only; believers only; the angels only; sub-human nature together with the angels; sub-human nature together with unbelieving mankind; sub-human nature only.[1] But believers must almost certainly be excluded, since in v. 23 they are contrasted with ἡ κτίσις. Moreover, οὐχ ἑκοῦσα (RV: "not of its own will") in v. 20, if it is understood in the sense in which in the context it seems natural to understand it, namely, as indicating that it was not as a result of its own choice that the κτίσις was subjected to vanity, would seem to exclude mankind generally; for, if Paul intended to include mankind, he could scarcely have meant to exclude Adam, the created man *par excellence*, and Adam clearly cannot be said to have been so subjected otherwise than as a result of his own choice. The suggestion that the reference is only to unbelieving mankind is unlikely, since, while it is true that κόσμος (RV: "world") is sometimes used of unbelievers in contrast with believers, it is unlikely that a New Testament writer would use in this way a term which expresses a relation to God in which Christians stand equally with non-Christians and in which, moreover, they above all men must rejoice. That angels are referred to seems also unlikely, no really convincing suggestion being forthcoming as to what v. 20 could mean with reference to them. The only interpretation of ἡ κτίσις in these verses which is really probable is surely that which takes it to refer to the sum-total of sub-human nature both animate and inanimate.

The objection to this interpretation that it is inconsonant with Paul's use of personal language here is not to be sustained. Paul's use with reference to irrational nature of ἀποκαραδοκία, ἀπεκδέχεται, οὐχ ἑκοῦσα, ἐφ' ἐλπίδι, συστενάζει (RV: "earnest expectation", "waiteth for", "not of its own will", "in hope", 'groaneth ... together") is, as John Chrysostom recognized,[2] an example of personification such as is quite often to be found in the OT.[3] There is a poetic quality in parts of Romans, and especially in vv. 19–22, which must be recognized, if Paul's meaning is properly to be understood. What we refer to is not a matter of the things which belong to the outward form of poetry so much as of those things which belong to its inner essence – such things as imaginative power, feeling for the evocative word, deep sensitivity, universality of sympathy, and a true generosity of vision and conception. It is this poetic quality which is to be discerned in the personal language of these verses. With poetic boldness Paul speaks of the earnest anticipation, the neck-

[1] For details of the history of exegesis reference may be made to volume 1 of my forthcoming commentary on Romans in The International Critical Commentary.
[2] PG, 60, col. 529.
[3] Cf., e.g., Ps. 65:12 f; Isa. 24:4, 7; Jer. 4:28; 12:4.

craning expectancy,[1] of the whole splendid theatre of the universe and of
all the manifold sub-human life within it as eagerly awaiting the revelation of the sons of God. By "the revealing of the sons of God" Paul means
that revelation by which those who now are truly sons of God (cf. the
present tenses of the verb "to be" in vv. 14 and 16) but whose sonship is
veiled and imperceptible except to faith, will at last be made manifest in
their true glory, that public and open proclamation of their adoption
which – rather than their adoption as such – is what is meant by *υἱοθεσία*
(RV: "*our* adoption") in v. 23. Until that time, in the words of the Scottish
paraphrase,

> "Concealed as yet this honour lies,
> By this dark world unknown".[2]

The "For" at the beginning of v. 20 indicates that what follows
explains why it is that the creation awaits so eagerly the manifestation of
the sons of God. The explanation consists of vv. 20 and 21 together as a
whole; but it is necessary to consider it piecemeal before we can hope to
understand it as a whole.

We take first the words *τῇ ... ματαιότητι ἡ κτίσις ὑπετάγη* (RV: "the
creation was subjected to vanity"). The aorist tense shows that the reference is to a particular event, and the passive voice is no doubt to be understood as an indirect reference to a divine action.[3] Paul probably had in
mind the divine judgement recorded in Gen. 3:17–19 (note especially the
words in Gen. 3:17: "cursed is the ground for thy sake"). The position of
τῇ ... ματαιότητι at the beginning of the sentence gives it special emphasis. In view of the parallelism between *τῇ ... ματαιότητι ... ὑπετάγη*
and *τῆς δουλείας τῆς φθορᾶς* (RV: "the bondage of corruption")
some interpreters have assumed that *ματαιότης* must here be used as a
synonym of *φθορά* and others that the two words are intended to signify
respectively the mutability and the mortality which characterize creaturely
existence as we know it. Some have taken *τῇ ματαιότητι* to be an example
of the abstract used for the concrete, and have understood Paul's meaning
to be that the creation was subjected to vain men. Others have thought that
the clue to the meaning of *ματαιότης* here was to be found in the way the
cognate verb is used in 1:21 (RV: "became vain"): they have therefore
suggested that Paul had in mind the subjection of the creation to man's
idolatry which exploits the sub-human creation for its own base and
futile purposes (cf. 1:23, 25), and have gone on to explain *φθορά* as
signifying the moral corruption resulting from idolatry (cf. 1:24, 26–32

---

[1] The basic idea expressed by *ἀποκαραδοκία* (also *ἀποκαραδοκεῖν, καραδοκία,
καραδοκεῖν*) is that of stretching the neck, craning forward to see something which is
approaching (*κάρα* is a poetical equivalent of *κεφαλή*): the *ἀπο-* is intensive, as also in
ἀπεκδέχεσθαι.
[2] *The Church Hymnary*, rev. ed., Oxford, 1938, no. 483.
[3] Cf. below on *διὰ τὸν ὑποτάξαντα.*

nd the δουλεία τῆς φθορᾶς as signifying the sub-human creation's ondage to man's corrupt and futile abuse of it. Others have suggested hat, since ματαιότης could be used to denote a god of the heathen, Paul nay have meant by subjection to ματαιότης subjection to various cele- tial powers, and Gal. 4:9 with its reference to bondage to the weak and eggarly στοιχεῖα (RV: "rudiments") has been adduced in support of this iew. Yet others have maintained that it is along the lines of the sense vhich it has in Ecclesiastes, where the majority of its occurrences in the eptuagint are to be found and where it denotes the futility, the disorder, he sheer absurdity, of things, that ματαιότης is to be interpreted here. But he most natural and straighforward interpretation is surely that which nderstands it in its basic sense as denoting the ineffectiveness of that vhich fails to attain its goal (cf. the adverb μάτην which means "in vain"), nd so takes Paul's meaning to be that the sub-human creation has been ubjected to the frustration of not being able properly to fulfil the pur- ose of its existence.

And, if the question is asked, "What sense can there be in saying that the ub-human creation – the Jungfrau, for example, or the Matterhorn, or he planet Venus – suffers frustration by being prevented from properly ulfilling the purpose of its existence?", the answer must surely be that he whole magnificent theatre of the universe, together with all its plendid properties and all the varied chorus of sub-human life, created or God's glory, is cheated of its true fulfilment so long as man, the chief ctor in the great drama of God's praise, fails to contribute his rational art. The Jungfrau and the Matterhorn and the planet Venus and all iving things too, man alone excepted, do indeed glorify God in their own vays; but, since their praise is destined to be not a collection of indepen- lent offerings but part of a magnificent whole, the united praise of the vhole creation, they are prevented from being fully that which they were reated to be, so long as man's part is missing, just as all the other players n a concerto would be frustrated of their purpose if the soloist were to ail to play his part.

On the assumption that "the creation" signifies the sub-human creation enerally, οὐχ ἑκοῦσα (RV: "not of its own will") is naturally understood s meaning "not through its own fault".[1] It is man, not the sub-human reation, which is to blame for the frustration of the latter. Contrasted ἀλλά) with ἑκοῦσα is διὰ τὸν ὑποτάξαντα (RV: "by reason of him who ubjected it"). There is no doubt that ὁ ὑποτάξας must be God, not Adam, or man in general, nor Satan; for it would be intolerably harsh to take he participle to refer to anyone other than the agent implied by the assive ὑπετάγη ("was subjected") in the earlier part of the verse, who

---

[1] If "the creation" were understood to mean or to include mankind, οὐχ ἑκοῦσα would ave to be understood along the lines of Augustine's interpretation of it as referring to the nvoluntariness of the creation's submission to the penalty imposed upon it.

must surely be God, since no one other than God could be said to have subjected the creation ἐφ᾽ ἐλπίδι ("in hope"), and, moreover, "subject" clearly denotes here an authoritative action such as neither Adam nor man in general nor Satan could have effected.[1] It is significant that Paul opposes to ἑκοῦσα not a mere reference to man's responsibility but a reference to the judicial decision pronounced by God on account of man's sin; for by keeping God's part firmly in view he preserves the thoroughly evangelical quality of what he is saying.

The words ἐφ᾽ ἐλπίδι (RV: "in hope") are more naturally connected with ὑπετάγη ("was subjected") than with ὑποτάξαντα ("who subjected it"). The sub-human creation was not subjected to frustration without any hope: on the contrary, the divine judgement consequent on man's disobedience included the promise of a better future, when at last that judgement would be removed. It is possible that Paul may have thought of the promise in Gen. 3:15 that the woman's seed should bruise the serpent's head (cf. Rom. 16:20: "And the God of peace shall bruise Satan under your feet shortly"). Hope for the sub-human creation was included in the hope for man. The reading διότι is probably to be preferred to the variant ὅτι and, in view of Pauline usage, διότι should probably be understood as meaning, not "that", but "because" or "for" – that is, as introducing a statement explaining why the creation was subjected to frustration "in hope" (the subjection was "in hope", because the sub-human creation itself is going to be set free . . .). In καὶ αὐτὴ ἡ κτίσις (RV: "the creation itself also") there is an implied contrast with the children of God (cf. vv. 1 and 17, and also the "us" in v. 18 and "of the sons of God" in v. 19). That Paul's main interest in these verses is in the certainty of the coming glory of believers is no doubt true (cf. the εἰς ἡμᾶς (RV: "to us-ward") of v. 18) but to state categorically, as one commentator does, that Paul "is not concerned with creation for its own sake"[2] is to do him a grave injustice (there is nothing in this context to warrant such a statement, and to cite 1 Cor. 9:9 in support of it would surely be unfair). The implication of these verses is surely rather that, with a noble breadth and generosity of vision and sympathy such as may be expected of one who truly believes in God as Creator,[3] Paul sees the future glory of believers not by itself but accompanied by the glorious liberation of the whole sub-human creation. This liberation (ἐλευθερωθήσεται is more accurately translated "shall be

[1] Karl Barth's suggestion (*A Shorter Commentary on Romans*, London, 1959, pp. 99 f.) that Paul was thinking of Jesus Christ as having subjected "man, and with him the whole creation to vanity" by the judgment pronounced and executed on Golgotha, is surely a forced interpretation of τὸν ὑποτάξαντα – though it is, of course, thoroughly true that the Cross was the final revelation of the ματαιότης to which the creation was subjected on account of man's sin, just as it was the final revelation of the wrath of God (cf. Rom. 1:18).

[2] C. K. Barrett, *A Commentary on the Epistle to the Romans*, London, 1957, p. 165.

[3] Suggestive in this connexion is the way in which in Genesis 1 God's approval of his whole creation including man (v. 31) is preceded by the often-repeated refrain of his approval of his sub-human creation (vv. 4, 10, 12, 18, 21, 25).

et free" than, as in the RV, "shall be delivered") is liberation from the
condition of slavery to decay, death, corruption, transitoriness, into
he condition of freedom (ἀπὸ τῆς δουλείας τῆς φθορᾶς εἰς τὴν
λευθερίαν). The words which follow, τῆς δόξης τῶν τέκνων τοῦ
)εοῦ (RV: "of the glory of the children of God"), define this condition
)f freedom. The first of the three genitives has often been taken to be
.djectival to the preceding τὴν ἐλευθερίαν (so the AV has "the glorious
iberty"); but it is more consonant with the structure of the sentence and
with the thought of the passage to take it to have a sense corresponding
o that of τῆς φθορᾶς. As the δουλεία τῆς φθορᾶς is a bondage to
:orruption, the bondage which corruption may be said to impose, so the
λευθερία τῆς δόξης τῶν τέκνων τοῦ θεοῦ is the liberty which results
rom, is the necessary accompaniment of, the (revelation of the) glory of
he children of God. (The meaning is, presumably, not that the creation
will possess the same liberty resulting from glory as the children of God
will possess, but that it will possess its own proper liberty as a result of the
;lorification of the children of God.) And this liberty which will come
o the sub-human creation when at last the children of God are made
nanifest will surely be the liberty of each several part of that creation,
whether animate or inanimate, fully and perfectly to fulfil its Creator's
)urpose for it – the liberty which it cannot have so long as man is unready
o play his role in the great drama of God's praise.

What then may be said in conclusion about the significance of these
hree verses?

It is true that their function in their context is to underline the greatness
)f the believers' hope (the fulfilment of that hope is even longed for with
:ager anticipation by the sub-human creation, since it will mean its
leliverance from its present bondage); but this does not mean that Paul
was not interested in the sub-human creation for its own sake.

That the sub-human creation's subjection to ματαιότης is ἐφ' ἐλπίδι,
hat it is destined to be liberated in the way indicated in v. 21, this clearly
ias an important bearing on the Christian's relation to the sub-human
:reation and – more generally – on the whole subject of "the environ-
nent" about which there is now such widely felt concern. It is of course
rue that the debt of love which we owe our fellow men includes the
)bligation not to spoil or destroy their environment but to cherish it for
heir sake. We have an obligation to the sub-human creation for men's
:ake, for the sake of our living fellow men and also for the sake of those
10t yet born. Of this truth we must not for a moment lose sight. But these
rerses indicate that this truth is by no means the whole truth of the matter
ind that to value the sub-human creation solely as man's habitat, man's
:nvironment, man's amenities – even if we do think of "man's" as
neaning "our neighbour's" rather than "our own" – is to be guilty of
dolatry. If the sub-human creation is part of God's creation, if to it also

he is faithful, and if he is going to bring it also (as well as believing men, to a goal which is worthy of himself, then it too has a dignity of its own and an inalienable, since divinely-appointed, right to be treated by us with reverence and sensitiveness. And our duty to it is not only a part of our duty to love our neighbour as ourselves, but also an integral part of our duty to love God with all our heart, and with all our soul, and with all our mind, and with all our strength. Since God has not created the sub-human creation solely for man's use and comfort but also with the intention of bringing it in the end to that liberty of which v. 21 speaks, true love to him must involve not only loving our fellow men as ourselves, but also treating with respect and with a proper sense of responsibility his humbler creation, whether animate or inanimate.

As well as indicating indirectly our obligation to the sub-human crea-tion, these verses show us the hopefulness with which we should set about trying to fulfil that obligation; for they reveal to us the fact that over that groaning and travailing creation stands the promise: ἐλευθερωθήσεται ἀπὸ τῆς δουλείας τῆς φθορᾶς εἰς τὴν ἐλευθερίαν τῆς δόξης τῶν τέκνων τοῦ θεοῦ. And those who believe in God know that in the end, in spite of the worst that polluters, spoilers and destroyers, that insatiable greed and mindless cruelty, can do, God's word "shall have its course".

And these verses remind us too that the Christian hope is something far more wonderful and more generous than at most times our preoccupation with ourselves and the feebleness of our concern for God's glory allow us to conceive.

CHAPTER XV

THE PRIESTHOOD OF PAUL IN THE GOSPEL OF HOPE

D. W. B. ROBINSON

I

THE ONLY EXPLICIT STATEMENT OF PAUL'S PURPOSE IN WRITING THE Epistle to the Romans is in 15:15, 16, which the RSV renders as follows:

> On some points I have written to you very boldly by way of reminder, because of the grace given me by God to be a minister of Christ Jesus to the Gentiles in the priestly service of the gospel of God, so that the offering of the Gentiles may be acceptable, sanctified by the Holy Spirit.

In other words, the matters Paul writes about spring from the nature of his special apostleship to the Gentiles. He describes this in the metaphor of a priestly cult. In this cult the god is Jesus Christ, and Paul is his λειτουργός i.e., the priest. The worshippers are the Gentiles, and the priest's responsibility is to ensure that their προσφορά or offering is presentable (εὐπρόσδεκτος, ἡγιασμένη) according to the requirements of the cult. This image is probably drawn from cultic religion in general, rather than from the levitical system in particular. It is not meant as a picture of the Christian religion as a whole; it merely illustrates the dependence of the Gentiles on Paul in making a right response to the gospel. Thus, in his metaphor Paul calls the cult itself "the gospel of God". It is in preaching and expounding it that Paul acts as a priest (ἱερουργοῦντα τὸ εὐαγγέλιον τοῦ θεοῦ).[1] It is unnecessary to suppose that the Gentiles are themselves the προσφορά[2] and that Paul offers them up. The better sense is that the προσφορά is what the Gentiles offer to Christ, namely their own glorifying of God (15:9), or their obedience (15:18). Paul has the same operation in view when he speaks of "what Christ has wrought through me

---

[1] This remarkable metaphor is perhaps foreshadowed in the expressions which Paul employs at the beginning of the epistle: "servant (δοῦλος) of Jesus Christ, set apart for the gospel of God . . . whom I serve (λατρεύω) with my spirit in the gospel of his Son" (1:1, 9).

[2] The idea is not in itself inappropriate, but seems unnecessary here. Some who support it quote Is. 66:20; but there the people offered are diaspora Jews being brought back to Jerusalem by their Gentile lords as a gift to the God of Israel. For an interesting discussion see J. Munck, *Paul and the Salvation of Mankind* (E.T. London, 1959), pp. 49–51, and Keith F. Nickle, *The Collection* (London, 1966), p. 129 ff.

to win obedience from the Gentiles" by "fully preaching the gospel" (15:19).

This statement of Paul's purpose should be taken with full seriousness as explaining the intention of Romans.[1] It occurs in the epilogue of the epistle, where Paul resumes the intimate and personal tone of the prologue. More importantly, it follows hard on the climax of the body of the epistle where Paul summarized his thesis in these words:

> Christ became a servant to the circumcised to show God's truthfulness, in order to confirm the promises given to the patriarchs, and in order that the Gentiles might glorify God for his mercy (15:8, 9).

This summary was followed by a catena of scriptures supporting the thesis, and then by the benediction:

> May the God of hope fill you with all joy and peace in believing, so that by the power of the Holy Spirit you may abound in hope (15:13).

The operative word is "hope". The last of the scriptures quoted is "The root of Jesse shall come, he who rises to rule the Gentiles; in him shall the Gentiles hope". We may say that the aim of Romans is to show the Gentiles how their hope rests on Israel's Messiah: how that through the prior fulfilment of the promises to Israel a stepping stone is made for the Gentiles. The gospel is the gospel of hope – not of judgement only – and the Gentiles are to embrace this hope. But it is the hope of Israel in the first instance, and if the Gentiles are to respond adequately to the gospel – if they are to glorify God acceptably and make their offering in true holiness – they must comprehend what their relation is to the Jew, to Israel, and in particular to the Israelite Paul, by whom in God's design the benefits of salvation have been ministered to them.

Paul cannot separate his own role from the operation of the gospel which he thus expounds to his Gentile readers in Rome. Romans is both an exposition of the gospel of hope and at the same time Paul's *apologia* for his "priesthood" in that gospel.

II

To understand Romans one must first come to terms with its eschatology. The subject of "justification" looms large in this epistle, not merely because Paul may be "replying to a legalistic type of religion",[2]

---

[1] Paul S. Minear, *The Obedience of Faith* (London, 1971), rightly sees that the purpose of Romans is related to the actual situation there, and that relations between Jewish and Gentile believers are integral to that situation, though his suggestion that Paul addresses five separate groups in turn is doubtful. For the situation in Rome see E. A. Judge and G. R. S. Thomas, "The Origin of the Church at Rome: a New Solution", in *RTR*, 25 (1966), pp. 1-14.

[2] C. F. D. Moule, *What Theologians Do*, ed. F. G. Healey (Grand Rapids, 1971) p. 40.

ut because as Paul understands "the gospel" it is, in the first place, a proclamation from God that his judgement is imminent.[1] It declares the coming
of "the day when . . . God judges the secrets of men by Christ Jesus" (2:16);
not, however, as merely giving prior notice of the event, but as fixing the
eschatological reference point for God's present and immediate overture
to mankind. Paul will have much to draw out from his initial statement
that by the gospel God's justice or righteousness is revealed (1:17), but
it takes its immediate relevance from the basic and common Christian
conviction that "the Judge is standing at the doors" (James 5:9) and that
"the kingdom of God is at hand" (Mark 1:15).

The vital question for the serious hearer of this message was whether
the revelation of the divine justice meant doom only – the entail of the
divine wrath – or whether there was a hiding place from the storm, some
hope of glory in the light of the graciousness of God. How does Paul
approach this question?

In his greeting (1:1–7), "the gospel of God" is the announcement that
the kingdom is at hand, as promised through the prophets. Already the
"Son of God" i.e., the Messiah, has been revealed and enthroned, and
awaits only the "obedience" of the nations. To the promulgation of this
gospel Paul has been assigned. He is thus himself an eschatological figure.
A hint of the impending consummation may be seen in the first verse of
the prologue (1:8–17), when Paul says that "your faith is proclaimed in
all the world". The terms here used are those which belong to the gospel
itself, and suggest that Paul may see in the success of the gospel at Rome
a sign that the end is near.[2]

The first major stage of Paul's argument (1:18–3:20) depends on the
theme of the impending day of judgement. The wrath of God already
hangs over mankind. The judgement itself is asserted in terms derived
from the Old Testament picture of God's just assize based on the deeds
of men (2:1–16), and, as we have seen, the gospel is, in part, the proclamation of its certainty (2:16). As Paul turns to address the Jew (2:17–3:20)
the theme of judgement-day continues. It is the universal judgement of all
nations (3:4–6, 19, 20), but especially now of Israel "under the law".[3]

[1] The context of coming judgement is evident in Mark 1:14, 15; 2 Thess. 1:8; 1 Pet. 4:17;
Rev. 14:6, to take representative examples from the few writers who seem to employ
εὐαγγέλιον in an independent way. The concept of an authoritative proclamation (e.g., of
coming judgement) is the predominant element in the use of this word in the NT, rather than
the alleged etymological sense of "good news". Although εὐαγγέλιον has a long history in
Greek literature, it should be noted that there is no instance in the singular known to us
before the NT of its meaning "good news" simply, or an announcement of any kind; that it
does not occur in the LXX except in its classical sense of "reward"; that its current first
century use outside the NT is generally in connection with the political imperial cult
(announcements regarding the emperor's activities or intentions); and that within the NT it
is a specialized term designating a specific message from God. In no case in the NT is
there any linguistic justification for translating εὐαγγέλιον simply as "good news". A term
with connotations of authority, like "proclamation", is generally to be preferred.
[2] Cf. 1 Thess. 3:6; Col. 1:6, 23.
[3] Cf. the judgement theme in Matt. 25:31–46.

Thus, Paul's exposition of justification is set against the background of standard scriptural eschatology regarding the *dies irae*. The gospel first endorses this judgement of God, but reveals also, in the very heart of it, an output of divine power by which justification of both Jew and Gentile is provided. This positive prospect is described as "the glory of God" and is the other side of the picture from "the wrath of God". Forfeited through sin (3:23), this glory is now the "hope" which follows justification (5:2). The precise connotations of this ("we rejoice in the hope of the glory of God", RVm) are not at first clear, but it means in some sense to be admitted to the sphere of God's favour and blessing. It is to attain and enjoy eternal life (6:8, 22, 23), and the term "reign" is used in 5:17, 21. This divine beneficence has its ground, of course, in the death and resurrection of Jesus Christ (6:1–11; 8:11, 17).

This "hope of glory" is amplified in 8:17–30, where it is seen as the glory of God transmitted to, or shining upon, his sons. They are "glorified". This glorification is profoundly based on the election and predestination of the children of God, and is related to the ultimate purposes of creation.

It is important to notice that "the glory of God" and "the glory of the children of God" is as much part of the general scriptural eschatology accepted by Paul as is the day of judgement itself. In the day when "the Lord GOD comes with might, and his arm rules for him", his glory is revealed (Isa. 40:1–11) and shines on his ransomed Israel (Isa. 55:5). In particular, for Paul, this glory is the inheritance of those who belong to Messiah and is the fruition of their "sonship" (8:15–17). This "sonship" is the chief prerogative of Israel among the nations (9:4), and indeed Paul's whole understanding is based on the "type" of Israel's experience of God's covenant, as it passed from the bondage of Egypt, through the redemption of the exodus, to the possession of the land of inheritance as God's son under the kingship of David. Paul further relates the final redemption of God's sons to the fulfilment of the purpose of creation and the removal of the curse (8:19–21), which is also part of the prophetic expectation. Paradise would be restored in a new heaven and new earth when God fulfilled his covenant to redeem and glorify Israel and establish it for ever in his holy mountain (e.g., Isa. 60:1–3; 65:17–25).

All this compels an observation of major significance for this study. No Jew, least of all St Paul, could have written or read Romans 8 without being aware that what was being rehearsed, and embraced in hope, was the glory which God had promised would finally shine on his people Israel. The language in this chapter – of election, of calling, of justification, of glorification, of the saints, of God's foreknowledge, of his purpose, of redemption, of sonship, of inheritance – all belonged to the theology, and specifically to the eschatology, of Israel.

This is the explanation of the pathos with which Paul goes on at once to speak of "my brethren, my kinsmen according to the flesh, forasmuch as they are Israelites" (9:1-5). No one recognizes more keenly than Paul that the sonship, the glory, the covenants, the promises, the patriarchs and Messiah himself, belong inalienably to Israel (9:4, 5). In proclaiming the hope of glory (the fruit of righteousness) and the anticipated liberty of the sons of God, how could Paul fail to relate them to his "kinsmen according to the flesh"? A little earlier, in discussing the grounds of justification, he was under similar constraint to explain what "Abraham our forefather according to the flesh" had found in this regard (4:1).

For all the mystery of its unbelieving members, there is, for Paul, only one Israel.[1] What, then, is the connection between the destiny of Israel as adumbrated in Romans 8 on the one hand, and in Romans 9–11 on the other? What Paul says explicitly in Romans 9–11 is clear enough. There has been, and could be, no change of intention on God's part, for God does not change his mind about his gifts and calling (11:29). All Israel will be redeemed and saved, according to promise (11:26, 27). Of this outcome, the present believing remnant (including Paul himself) is a guarantee any earnest (9:27; 11:1-5, 16). The salvation of the Gentiles is mysteriousld intertwined with the temporary and partial hardening of Israel, but the very pattern of salvation remains part of the heritage of Israel, and can only be learned by the Gentiles from Israel. The olive tree, which has as its root God's promise of blessing to Abraham, is Israel, and Gentiles can partake of that rich root only as wild branches grafted on to the stem, in among natural Israelite branches (11:17-24).

How does this relate to Romans 8? Many commentators assume that there is little or no connexion between the salvation of chapter 8 and the salvation of 9-11, or that Paul only begins to relate salvation to Israel when he commences chapter 9.[2] This is a serious misunderstanding. In chapters 9–11 Paul grieves, not for all Israelites, nor, strictly speaking, for Israel, but for those of his kinsmen who do not believe. His grief is precisely because they are Israelites (οἵτινές εἰσιν Ἰσραηλεῖται) and as such possess all the prerogatives of God's salvation (9:3-5). But the poignancy of this resides in the fact that Paul has just been exulting in the hope of glory which awaits those Jews whose patriarchal heritage has been confirmed to them (4:12), whose law has been therein established (3:31), and who lack nothing of all that God had promised them. The justification and glorification which Paul has been expounding in chapters 3-8 are the justification and glorification primarily of the *Israel that will be saved*, and it is from his own experience of salvation as a member of the remnant of Israel according to the election of grace that Paul is able to speak with such assurance and joy, and is able to hold out the hope of glory to the

---

[1] See D. W. B. Robinson, "The Salvation of Israel in Romans 9–11", in *RTR*, 26 (1967), pp. 81-96.
[2] But R. M. Grant rightly observes that Paul "has in mind the specific problem of the relations between Jews and Gentiles (not only in Rom. 9–11 but throughout the letter)", *A Historical Introduction to the New Testament* (London, 1963), p. 189.

Gentiles. The rest of this essay will examine more closely the proposition that, throughout Romans 1–8, Paul is conscious of the distinction between Jew and Gentile in the economy of salvation, and is describing justification and its results as he, an Israelite, had experienced it, this being his qualification to be the teacher of the Gentiles, bringing them to trust and hope in the Saviour of Israel.

III

No one has any difficulty in seeing a personal and apologetic element on Paul's part in both the prologue and epilogue of Romans. He claims to occupy a vital and unique role in the bringing of God's gospel to the Gentiles, and he is required to justify himself in this role even to the Romans whom he has not seen. It is our belief that this apologetic element pervades the intervening chapters as well, and that Paul expounds his gospel throughout from the point of view of one who was both a Jew – born under the law but justified freely through faith in the promise – and also Messiah's designated servant for the extension of God's salvation to the Gentiles. Our suggestion is that Paul's use of "we", "us" and "our" is generally in accord with this apologetic standpoint, and that although he frequently engages in direct address to his readers ("you"), only rarely does he identify himself with them on the ground of a common position. When Paul says "I", he naturally is referring to himself, either personally, or, when he adopts the diatribe style, as a representative figure for the purposes of his argument. But he also can employ "we" in the same way to refer to himself. In the prologue and epilogue he often speaks of his apostolic role in the first person singular e.g., "I am not ashamed of the gospel" (1:16); but the first person plural also occurs with no apparent difference in standpoint e.g., "through whom we have received grace and apostleship" (1:5). We wish to argue that this apostolic standpoint, rather than one inclusive of his readers, is also regularly implied in the use of "we" etc. in the body of the letter.[1] This apostolic viewpoint reflects Paul's Jewishness (and therefore the representative or "standard" character of his Christian experience) and also his defensive attitude (since he has the task of commending this experience to Gentiles).

The proposition on which Paul bases his whole exposition is that the gospel to which he is committed as an apostle is "the power of God for

---

[1] For Paul's inclusion of others, such as Barnabas, Apollos, Silvanus and Timothy, within the scope and nomenclature of apostleship, see D. W. B. Robinson, "Apostleship and Apostolic Succession" in *RTR*, 13 (1954). See also A. T. Hanson, *The Pioneer Ministry* (London, 1961), especially chapter 4, "Paul and His Fellow Workers". Dr Hanson examines Paul's use of "we", though not in Romans except for the opinion that Rom. 1:5 is the "only clear instance of the epistolary 'we'" outside the Thessalonian and Corinthian epistles. Dr Hanson's general thesis is at many points relevant to the subject of this essay.

salvation . . . to the Jew first and also to the Greek" (1:16). This is a priority for the Jew not merely in hearing the gospel, but in believing and in being saved by believing. Paul relates the questions of sin, condemnation, and justification to the same formula: "the Jew first and also the Greek" (2:9, 10). So Paul is not a disinterested party: he is a Jew! He discusses the depravity of the Gentile world in an objective and conventional manner, but when the condition of the Jew comes into view, in chapter 2, he quickly loses his detachment and starts constructing a vivid, personalized case, a form of interrogation. Now prosecutor, now defendant, he exposes the mystery of being a Jew from a wide range of experience. Under cover of the diatribe, Paul is himself the Jew who is first condemned for his failure, and then first justified by faith. His Roman audience have little part in this debate. But they could hardly fail to see that the Jew, notwithstanding his falling short of the glory of God like the rest of mankind, still stands at the centre of God's work of salvation for the world.

A second apologetic and personal motif appears quite early in Paul's approach. This emerges as a reply to a charge against the apostle that he supports the policy "Let us do evil that good may come". It is not clear who is making this charge, but Paul uses it as a yardstick to examine the kind of behaviour produced in himself and his kind by the power of the gospel. The influence of this charge may be more extensive in Romans 1–8 than is commonly noticed, producing a distinct apologetic note. Paul cites the accusation explicitly in 3:8, and it determines the form of his argument as he begins the discussion of sanctification in chapters 6–8.

Thus, not only in the prologue of Romans but in the body of the letter have we reason to expect Paul to speak from his own position. The gospel is for the Jew first, and Paul is among those Jews who "first hoped in Christ" (Eph. 1:12); also a serious charge has been made against the principles of his conduct, which is most relevant to the subject of righteousness which he has under review. While Paul is not easily confined to strict consistency, we think that the majority of his "we"s etc. refer to himself in one or other of these situations. If he wishes to include his readers, or Christians generally, with himself, he makes this clear by the argument, often with the addition of "all".

IV

A. Argument on Justification: 1:18–5:21

This long section begins in a formal and objective manner. A strictly personal element appears in 2:16, "my gospel", and 3:8, "as some charge us with saying". But other references to the first person are either the generalizing "I" of 3:7 ("if through my falsehood God's truthfulness

abounds to his glory, why am I still being condemned as a sinner?"), or are
otherwise part of the rhetorical idiom, e.g., 2:2; 3:5; 3:19; 3:28; 3:31
4:1; 4:9. Some, if not all, of these instances are appropriate in argument
only from a Jewish point of view e.g., the "we know" verses. A comparison of the whole section with Gal. 2:15–18 confirms the inference of a
Jewish standpoint, for this closely parallel passage on the nature of justification explicitly identifies the "we" who are justified by faith as "ourselves who are Jews by birth and not Gentile sinners". Other "we"
passages even more clearly demand a Jewish point of view, e.g., 3:5
("our wickedness"), 3:9; 4:1 ("our forefather"); 4:12. When Paul wishes
to include Gentiles as well as Jews in the seed of Abraham, he does so by
means of a careful argument (4:11 f.), and then designates Abraham as
"the father of *all* who believe". With this "all", reinforced by Gen. 17:5
"the father of many nations", Paul, for the first time in his argument, can
include his readers with himself in the "us" of 4:16, "Abraham . . . the
father of *us all*".

The crucial statement on justification, 3:21–26, is in general terms, with
no personal pronouns at all. It establishes the one basis of salvation for all
following the condemnation of the "whole world" in 3:19. But then at
once the viewpoint narrows in 3:27: "Then what becomes of ἡ καύχησις?"
which the RSV rightly interprets as "*our* boasting" i.e., the vaunted
Jewish confidence. Although this Jewish boast is excluded as a ground of
justification, Paul affirms that God is still the God of the Jews (though
not exclusively), that he justifies the circumcision by faith (though not
the circumcision alone), that the law is upheld through faith (though it
does not justify), and that Abraham is the father of circumcision to those
of the circumcision who believe (though not their father alone). The
distinction in identity between Jews and Gentiles is kept in view throughout this section.

The short passage which concludes the chapter on the faith of Abraham
4:22–25, is ambiguous in its pronouns:

> But the words, "it was reckoned to him", were written not for his sake alone
> but for ours also. It will be reckoned to us who believe in him that raised from
> the dead Jesus our Lord, who was put to death for our trespasses and raised
> for our justification.

Does "us" and "our" here mean all believers, or is Paul narrowing his
platform again to that of the justified Jew, as he prepares for another
aspect of his *apologia* in chapter 5? A general, inclusive "us" would be
appropriate here, following the discussion about "all who believe" in
4:11. On the other hand, "all" is not repeated in 4:24, and the passage can
be regarded as consistent with a limited Jewish point of view. The reference to the scripture "written . . . for our sake . . . who believe" may indicate Jews to whom the oracles of God had been committed and who,

nlike the "some" of 3:1-3, had *not* been unfaithful. The credal formula of
:25, "who was put to death for our trespasses and raised for our justi-
cation", is also patient of a Jewish interpretation. If Acts 13:26-39 can
e relied on – and Paul's kerygma there is strikingly parallel to that
ontained in 1 Cor. 15:1-5 – Paul was quite capable of expressing the
octrine of justification through the death and resurrection of Christ
ccording to the scriptures in terms peculiarly applicable to Jews; and if
aiah 53 is the basis for the formula in 4:25, this would be a further
round for limiting the application to Israelites, for theirs was the solidarity
ith the Servant in that passage.

What is the place of chapter 5 of Romans in the progress of Paul's
rgument, and what evidence does it yield to support the view that Paul
defending his experience as a Jew who believes?

Clearly Paul is rounding off the discussion of justification by describing
s fruition in the hope of glory. There are two parts to the chapter. The
rst part, 5:1-11, follows logically the end of chapter 4 ("Therefore, since
e are justified by faith..."), and supports its assertion of the hope of
lory with the argument: "for if while we were enemies we were
econciled to God by the death of his Son, much more, now that we are
econciled, shall we be saved by his life". The second part, 5:12-21, is an
xposition of the principle on which this "much more" argument is
ased. Throughout the chapter stress is laid on the ultimate "life" in which
ustification issues, and thus Paul concludes his discussion of justification
hich began in 1:17 with the text, "He who through faith is righteous *shall
ve*".

There is a marked difference of tone and style, however, between the
wo parts of this chapter. The second part, dealing with the Adam/Christ
nalogy, is couched in entirely impersonal terms; no personal pronoun is
sed. The distinctive position of the Jew is alluded to, however, by reason
f the attention paid to the role of the law. Death, it is claimed, is due, not
) the law, but to sin which is much older in man's experience. The reign
f death was established long before Moses. Within the total area affected
y Adam's sin, the law merely caused an "abounding" of sin in the
xperience of a limited group. This, however, had its counterpart in the
vork of Christ, in the "abounding" of grace. Again, then, there is an
mplied distinction between the Jew and the Gentile, though only one of
egree. The Jew under the law is actually worse off than the Gentile,
ecause he has an "abundance" of sin. On the other hand, he finds in
Christ an "abundance" of grace to offset his former disability.

In contrast to the objective style of this second part of chapter 5, the
rst part, 5:1-11, is highly personal in style. Practically every verse is in the
rst person plural. What is the force of this "we"?

The answer is bound up with the question of whether ἔχωμεν or
χομεν is the correct reading in 5:1. The manuscript evidence is such that

intrinsic probability must decide the matter. But which reading is intrinsically more probable? If the subjunctive ("let us have peace with God") is original there can be no doubt that "us" is the inclusive pronoun, the same "we all' of 4:16. It would follow that 4:24, 25 – the passage discussed above – must be taken in the same way, for an exhortation at this point could only be intended by Paul for his readers as well as himself. On the other hand, most commentators have preferred the indicative reading here ("we have peace with God"), and, if this be original, the possibility is open that Paul is using the narrower Jewish "we" with which he began the discussion of justification, which certainly prevailed from 3:1 to 4:12, and which he possibly resumed in the credal formula of 4:25. Such an interpretation would mean that in 5:1–11 Paul is summarizing the benefits of justification from his own experience as a believing Jew.

In support of the narrower reference here is the subjective character of the experience Paul describes: "we have peace", "we rejoice", "we rejoice in our sufferings", "God's love has been poured into our hearts". This is different from describing the *status* of believers as children of Abraham, which Paul is able to predicate of his Gentile readers in 4:16, even though he has never met them, for at least he knew they were believers. But is Paul here asserting that all believers, including his readers, *do* experience this peace, joy and love? If the point is what *ought* to follow justification, it would be better to accept the (better attested) subjunctive reading, and interpret the passage as an exhortation. If, however, Paul is asserting the *actual* fruit of justification, the better sense is yielded by taking the whole of 5:1–11 as autobiographical. For consider how concrete the description is. "Peace" is not merely a status, but the experience of harmony which follows from acceptance. "This grace in which we stand", could, it is true, describe the status of all justified persons (3:24; 4:16), but it could equally well refer to Paul's position as a Jew who believed (11:5) or as an apostle (1:5; 12:3; 15:15; 1 Cor. 15:10). "Joy" is an emotion kindled by the hope of glory. "Our sufferings", in which Paul says "we rejoice", are most likely those which he constantly endured as an apostle. Paul might easily assume that all believers would encounter suffering, but it is less likely he would assert that all were rejoicing in it. Finally, the pouring of God's love into one's heart through the Spirit seems to describe a subjective experience of a palpable kind.

In all, it is reasonable to see here a description of the actual experience which, for Paul and his circle, had followed justification. Of course he wants this to be understood as the model for his Gentile friends. But he also has a serious apologetic purpose: he is preparing the way for the next stage of his argument in which he finally refutes the charge that he, of all people, advocates continuance in sin, and in which he sets out at length the character of the new life in Christ.

V

B. *Argument on the New Life: 6:1–8:39*

Three features of Paul's approach in chapter 6 indicate that he is basing his argument on his own behaviour and experience. First, he reverts to the rhetorical style ("What shall we say then?") which he used earlier as a guise in which to present the speaker's own case. Secondly, he at once brings forward for consideration a proposition which, in 3:8, was explicitly (though falsely) alleged to have been his own point of view. There it was "Why not (... as some affirm that we say) 'Let us do evil that good may come'?". Now Paul says "What shall we say then? 'Let us continue in sin that grace may abound'?".[1] Thirdly, there is such a marked change of address at the conclusion of the first section in verse 11 ("So you also must consider yourselves dead to sin"), that the preceding verses, all in the first person plural, must be taken as not including the readers. Indeed, the argument requires this. The "we" of verses 1 to 9 have already reckoned themselves dead to sin and alive to God: it remains only to challenge those who hear the case ("you also") to do likewise.[2]

All the rest of chapter 6, from verse 11, is a continuation of Paul's direct exhortation to his readers: "Let not sin therefore reign in your mortal bodies ...". Only once, in verse 15, is there a reversion to "we": "What then, are we to sin, because we are not under law but under grace?". The explanation is simple.[3] The question being in the style of diatribe, and being completely surrounded by Paul's direct exhortations to his readers ("you"), it is put into the mouth of those readers. This is further required by the connexion with the preceding verse where Paul has just described his readers as "not under law but under grace".

Paul's apology for the law occupies chapter 7, although it is not entirely clear why he launches on such a discussion at such length at this point. Gentiles as Gentiles were never under the law. Had the Romans been

[1] I take ἐπιμένωμεν not as a deliberative question, but as a hortative subjunctive, as in the form of the earlier expression. This is suggested by Pallis, *To the Romans* (Liverpool, 1920), The point is not unimportant. Paul is citing an alleged or proposed attitude in both places.

[2] There is actually a double contrast implied by the καὶ ὑμεῖς of verse 11: with Christ who died and now lives (verse 10), and with Paul and co. who have already been baptized into Christ's death and now live in newness of life.

[3] If the similarity of this verse to 6:1 be taken to indicate a return to *Paul's* position – again taking the verb (ἁμαρτήσωμεν) as a deliberative subjunctive rather than as a question – the train of thought, somewhat elliptical, would be thus: "We teach *you* that sin should not rule you since you are not under law but under grace: do you suppose that *we* advocate 'Let *us* sin because *we* are not under law but under grace'? Absurd!". A similar argument, though not identical, would emerge if the Western reading of G *er* vg^w Ambrosiaster, ἡμαρτήσαμεν, were adopted: "Did *we* sin because we are not under law ...?" Could this indicative be original? It is not easy to explain as an alteration. Pallis, in his curious commentary, adopts it, but interprets the verb in the classical sense: "did we commit an error when we withdrew from the Law...?"

troubled as were the Galatians we could understand Paul explaining the role of the law to them. But there is no explicit warning to his readers to steer clear of the law. In fact, his readers rate no mention in the whole chapter, except in the rhetorical opening words "Do you not know...?" and in verse 4, "Likewise, my brethren, you have died to the law through the body of Christ, so that you may belong to another", which is a simple statement of fact. It is even possible, as Paul Minear has proposed,[1] that Paul is here turning to address his fellow Jews among his audience at Rome. There is no obvious Gentile interest in the whole passage.

In reality, Paul is doing two things in this chapter. First, he is clinching the argument that the law had been utterly superseded as a means of justification before God. Seldom has the state of the case been more succinctly put than in 7:6: "We are discharged from the law, dead to that which held us captive, so that we serve not under the old written code but in the new life of the Spirit". But secondly, having demoted the law, Paul offers a vigorous defence of it as "holy and just and good". Whatever inferences he may wish his Gentile readers to draw from all this, his point of view, *vis-à-vis* the law, is peculiar to the justified Jew.

The chapter is in two unequal sections. 7:1–6 discusses the life of obedience to Christ (already described in its Gentile context in 6:16–23) in terms of freedom from the Mosaic law. The illustration is used – clear to any who "know the law" – that the marriage law binds a woman to her husband only while he is alive. If he dies, the law is no longer binding, and the woman can freely marry someone else. Under this figure, Paul describes the position of the Jewish believer. He was bound to sin, and this bondage was reinforced, and given legal status, by the Mosaic law. But, through the death of Christ, sin itself, the "husband", died. The law, therefore, had done its work, and had no more power to make sin abound (cf. 5:20). The justified Jew was free to "marry" and obey the risen Christ.

For whose benefit is Paul saying this? In Galatians he uses similar teaching about the Jew being redeemed by Christ from the law as the basis for his powerful admonition to the Gentiles not on any account to allow themselves to fall into the slavery from which the Jews had been saved.[2] But there is no such admonition or exhortation here in chapter 7. A straightforward explanation of the allegory is given in verse 4, and, despite the "you" of the first half of the verse, Paul must be talking about, if not to, believing Jews. In any case, he reverts to "we" before the verse is finished, and goes on in verses 5 to 7 to describe a situation only applicable to a Jew, for he speaks of those passions of the flesh which were "aroused by the law" (cf. 7:9 ff.), and of the contrast between the old

[1] See p. 232, n 1.

[2] See D. W. B. Robinson, "The Distinction Between Jewish and Gentile Believers in Galatians" in *ABR*, 13 (1965), pp. 29–48; also "The Circumcision of Titus, and Paul's 'Liberty'", *ABR*, 12 (1964), pp. 24–42, and "'We are the Circumcision'", *ABR* 15 (1967), pp. 28–35.

service of the written code and the new service of the Spirit. The truth seems to be that Paul is more concerned with analysing the role of the law than with particular implications. This concern is heightened as the chapter proceeds.

Speaking about Romans 7:7–25, Krister Stendahl comments: "While much attention has been given to the question whether Paul speaks about a pre-Christian or Christian experience of his, or about man in general, little attention has been drawn to the fact that Paul here is involved in an argument about the Law; he is not primarily concerned about man's or his own cloven ego or predicament".[1] This is substantially correct. Paul, having greatly restricted the function of the law in 7:1–6, now addresses himself, in the manner of the diatribe, to two questions which any serious-minded Jew might ask following Paul's assessment. The first question is "Is the law sin?",[2] to which the answer is "Far from it; the law is holy, just and good". The second question is "Did something which is good (the law), then, become death to me?", and again the answer is "Far from it". But the explanation is more complicated and calls for an analysis of the three-cornered relationship between sin, the law, and the individual under the law. Paul says in effect: "The real villain is sin, which the law shows up for what it is, and which is at work in my members. Even when I am 'under the law' I recognize it as God's law, and as good, though with my flesh I serve the law of sin".

Throughout this section the law and its character are defined exclusively in relation to the speaker; "I should not have known sin" etc. Yet Paul is not speaking of the relation of the law to him specifically but to him characteristically as a Jew under the law. The "I" is the generalizing "I", recalling the style of 3:7, "if through my falsehood God's truthfulness abounds to his glory, why am I still being condemned as a sinner?". As Paul rebuts the suggestion that his teaching about freedom from the law makes the latter an instrument of sin and death, it becomes clear that the "I" whose relation to the law he defines for this purpose can only be the man who is still under the law and still under the dominion of the sin which works through his members. The experience no doubt had been Paul's, yet not his alone. The "I" is a conventional device by means of which Paul becomes "the type of the moral relation in which the as yet unregenerate Israelite stands to the divine law".[3] One of the pillars of Paul's position in Romans is that "Christ is the end of the law, that everyone who has faith may be justified" (10:4). But "the end of the law" has not yet come for the "wretched man" of 7:7–25.

---

[1] "The Apostle Paul and the Introspective Conscience of the West", *HTR*, 56 (1963), p. 211.
[2] In view of the introductory question τί οὖν ἐροῦμεν this may be a proposition which Paul is questioning, rather than a question he is asking i.e.: "What shall we say then? 'That the law is sin'?".
[3] H. A. W. Meyer on Romans (E.T. Edinburgh, 1876) II, p. 2.

Once more, then, though this time in retrospect, Paul has in consideration his own position, not that of his readers. In this apology for the law
he is chiefly concerned lest they should misjudge the law and its dignity.
At the same time, he paves the way for the last stage of his *apologia* for his
conduct. There was indeed a time when he was under sin's dominion, but
there can be no continuance in that. Even the law condemns no more.
"We are discharged from the law" (7:6), and "there is no condemnation
for those who are in Christ Jesus" (8:1). Further, the dominion of sin and
death – *its* law – is broken, and what the law of God required now finds
a true fulfilment in Paul's life (8:4). To continue in sin would be to have the
mind of the flesh, and this Paul repudiates. He sums up his position in
8:12: "So then, brethren, we are debtors, not to the flesh, to live according
to the flesh". This conclusion, relating as it does to the profounder realities
of flesh and Spirit, is in a form readily transferable to the Gentiles who are
Paul's special concern, but the conclusion has been reached along the path
of a Jewish experience.

Paul directly addresses his readers only briefly in chapter 8, in verses
9 to 15. It is significant that the confident note which characterizes the
transcript of his own experience is lacking here, and is replaced by a
series of conditional sentences:[1] "if the Spirit of God really dwells in
you"; "if Christ dwells in you"; "if the Spirit of him who raised Jesus
from the dead dwells in you"; "if by the Spirit you put to death the deeds
of the body . . .". Paul is certainly anxious for his readers to know that the
Spirit they have received is the same "spirit of sonship" which he and his
colleagues have received and which enables them to enjoy a true relationship with God as Father (8:15,16), but in general, the theme of chapter 8 is,
as we remarked at the beginning of this essay, the liberty of the Jew who
has entered his inheritance in Christ, and his hope of glory according to
promise and election.[2]

"We are fellow heirs with Christ, provided we suffer with him in order
that we may also be glorified with him", says Paul in 8:17, and this
proviso is the text for the exalted and deeply moving final testament of
hope. There is no address to readers here, only personal confession and
testimony. Earlier, in 5:1–5, there was a foreshadowing of the theme that
"we rejoice in our sufferings, knowing that . . . hope does not disappoint

[1] Only the first of these is actually indefinite (εἴπερ), but the string of conditionals following
this first usage is impressive nevertheless.

[2] A curious problem, in view of the thesis of this essay, lies in the textual variants of 8:2.
The best mss. and widest support is for "thee", but there is strong support for "me", and the
other alternatives, "us" and no pronoun, are not negligible. "Thee" is hard to explain in
terms of Paul's style here, for though he uses this style in e.g., 2:1 and 2:27, here the pronoun
slips in without warning. The situation is that σε is both the best attested reading and the
lectio difficilior! Pallis (*op. cit.*) suggests that the statement is addressed to the questioner of
τίς με ῥύσεται. This would mean either that the Spirit-led Paul addresses the unredeemed
Paul, or that God addresses Paul. For the latter, 2 Cor. 12:9 might be a parallel. There is no
"but he said to me" in Romans, but there is the initial question "Who will deliver me?"

us", and we suggested there that Paul's sufferings as an apostle of Christ were probably in view. The same may well be true in chapter 8. The closest parallel to this passage is 2 Cor. 3–6, which relates the sufferings of the apostle to the glory of God. In Romans 8, suffering is not a token of sin or of God's displeasure, but the opposite. It is a sign of hope and a pledge of glory. More than that, it is the suffering of the "servant" of the Lord, "Israel in whom I will be glorified" (Isa. 49:3). Paul elsewhere identifies himself with the servant of Isaiah 49, in Gal. 1:15 (cf. Acts 13:47), and his confident appeal to the servant song of Isa. 50:4–9 in vv. 31–34, together with his citation of the words of the righteous sufferer of Psalm 44, to interpret his experience, is a remarkable seal on his *apologia*.

Thus, both the positive Christian experience related in this chapter, and the expectation of final glory, are set forth deliberately as the experience of the justified Jew, indeed of Israel itself in the person of the servant and apostle of the Lord. The exposition of salvation in these terms, based on God's covenant with Israel, is part of the exercise of Paul's priesthood – which is his apostleship – in regard to the Gentiles, providing the way by which they, too, embrace the free gift of forgiveness, exchange the flesh for the Spirit, and find their hope in the root of Jesse.

CHAPTER XVI

THE DEATH OF DEATH
(I CORINTHIANS 15:26)

J. DAVIS McCAUGHEY

Paul's argument in I corinthians 15 has been called by Dr. Morris "the classical Christian discussion of the subject" (i.e. the Resurrection). The aim of this essay is to examine again the development of that argument in order to see what light can be cast upon some current presuppositions about death. Such a discussion is necessarily dialectical: it is impossible to come to the biblical text without certain questions either in mind or presupposed, and it is to be hoped that exegetical discoveries will in turn challenge our presuppositions. For present purposes it is not necessary (nor would space allow us) to mention every important point in this lengthy passage, or to go into detail on matters discussed fully in recent commentaries.[1]

I

We begin with the text, asking what it is that Paul is saying to whom, and (as far as we can reconstruct it) in what circumstances. When we look at the chapter as a whole we find what is at first sight a bewildering oscillation between different ways of writing. The language of the first paragraph (vv. 1–11) is that of the *kerygmatic tradition* of the Church: "so we preach and so you believed" (11). In the second paragraph (12–19 (22)) the argument becomes *ad hominem:* "how can some of you say that there is no resurrection of the dead?" The argument is predominantly of a negative or at least of an indirect kind: the reliability of the apostle and his message is impugned by this denial (v. 15); faith is meaningless and justification ineffective (v. 17); hope for those who have died in Christ is groundless (vv. 18 f.). The third paragraph (vv. 20–28) is introduced by the positive affirmation of the resurrection of Christ, with a use of the Adam-Christ parallelism which is to be developed later (vv. 45–49), language which owes something to the Jewish-Christian tradition but probably also something to Gnosticism. Then we move into the first use

---

[1] In addition to many older commentaries of value, the student of the New Testament is today well served by recent commentaries in French, English and German, by J. Héring (Delachaux et Niestlé, Neuchâtel and Paris, 1949), L. L. Morris (*TNTC*, London, 1958), C. K. Barrett (BNTC, London, 1968), and Hans Conzelmann (KNT, Göttingen, 1969).

of an *apocalyptic scheme* (vv. 23–28). The fourth paragraph (vv. 29–34) resumes the *ad hominem* style of argument: What do people mean . . . why am I in peril . . . what do I gain . . .? The fifth paragraph which may be subdivided into the introduction (v. 35) and three sections vv. 36–38; 39–44; 45–50, is introduced by the unmistakable sign of *a diatribe:* "Someone will ask . . .". Paul no doubt still has in mind the Corinthian reader but to a degree is now arguing with an imaginary opponent. If in the second and fourth paragraphs he can be assumed to be laying hold of phrases used and practices followed in the Corinthian Church, that assumption can be made with less assurance here. The third of the sub-sections certainly takes up the theme introduced in vv. 21–22: the whole paragraph may begin with general considerations arising out of the logic of the argument, it ends using the kind of language with which the Corinthians may well have been familiar. The sixth, and concluding paragraph (vv. 51–58) resumes *the use of apocalyptic terms,* lifting the whole to a climax in the citations from the Old Testament (vv. 54 and 55) and in thanks to God for the victory through Jesus Christ.

These, then, are the formal characteristics of the chapter. It moves from kerygma, to *ad hominem* argument, to apocalyptic discourse, to return to *ad hominem,* moving through diatribe to its conclusion in the language of apocalyptic and of praise. Is it possible to detect method in the apostle's changes of tone and manner, or do thoughts come tumbling into words in a random fashion? If it is possible, we may gain some insight into the nature of his controversy with the Corinthian Christians, or some of them. We may also gain some insight into Paul's distinctive attitude to death and resurrection, and may as a result wish to make some comments upon current attitudes.

I. *The kerygmatic opening: 1–11*

Two questions arise, relevant to our present purpose: first, if the question of resurrection was referred to Paul by letter (or messenger) why does he depart from his customary opening: Concerning this, that or the other (7:1, 25; 8:1; 12:1; 16:1)? The absence of the formula (along with other evidence) has led Schmithals to suggest that this section belongs to what he calls Letter A, which preceded that in which Paul deals with matters referred to him.[1] Schmithals supports his case for assigning this chapter to this earlier letter with a hypothesis that Paul had misunderstood the nature of the Corinthian contention that there is no resurrection of the dead. Schmithals' thesis will be confirmed if it can be shown that Paul's understanding of the situation in this case deviates from his understanding of it elsewhere (in Schmithals' Letter B); his contention will be weakened

[1] W. Schmithals *Die Gnosis in Korinth* (Göttingen, 1965), pp. 146–50 E.T. *Gnosticism in Corinth* (Nashville and New York, 1971), pp. 155–59.

if we can show that throughout Paul seems to be dealing with varied expressions of the same fundamental error. In fact it can be shown that throughout this letter, as we have it, Paul is contesting that enthusiasm which suggests that the eschatological conditions are already fulfilled (see 4:8 and note the superiority of the enlightened in the argument over food offered to idols, to take but two examples), so that there is no place left for a future resurrection.[1] Given this, it may be assumed that the Corinthian objection was too narrowly phrased to admit of direct answer. Paul begins his refutation of their error by reminding them of what it means to stand in a tradition of preaching and believing. The gospel of the death and resurrection of Christ begins with what happened to him in Palestine – he died, he was buried, he was raised, he appeared – and that has significance for men everywhere.

The second question is as good as answered already: why did Paul not base his case here, as to the Thessalonians (I Thess. 4:15) on a "word of the Lord" – presumably a prophetic revelation – but upon the kerygmatic tradition of the resurrection of Christ? Presumably because he was concerned to defuse the enthusiastic atmosphere of the Church in Corinth; Günther Bornkamm, in an essay "Faith and Reason in Paul",[2] contends that "Paul allots to reason, to the rationality of men, an exceedingly important role for the self-understanding of the Christian and for all areas of his life." He points out how Paul avoids wherever possible the "revelation-speech" type. He shows how in I Corinthians 14 (the section immediately preceding the passage under review) Paul places prophecy (speaking with the mind) and speaking with tongues (speaking with the spirit) in sharp contrast one to the other, and states his strong preference for the former. Intelligent and intelligible speech is always to be preferred to the inspirational, which exalts at the moment. Thus in introducing the discussion of the resurrection, Paul does not pit his experience against that of the Corinthians. Indeed the reference to himself in this opening section is to one to whom the Lord appeared, not (be it noted) to one who had shared in the risen life. He speaks not of what happened in himself, but of what happened to him: he was confronted by the living Lord, and then only "to one untimely born"; and his calling is to be an apostle, not a purveyor of the present experience of the resurrection, a preacher to whose message the appropriate response is not heightened experience but faith. "So we preach and so you believed."

2. The first argumentum ad hominem: 12–22

Verses 1–11 had demonstrated what it means to stand in the Christian tradition. It is valid for men everywhere; it means going back to the

---

[1] So Barrett, Conzelmann, Käsemann in several essays, and others.
[2] E.T. in *Early Christian Experience* (London, 1969), p. 35.

Church in Palestine; it means going back to Christ crucified and raised from the dead. Verse 12 brings the matter into the life of the Corinthian Church: Now if Christ is preached as raised from the dead (with the implication taken over from the previous verse that "you believed"), how can some of you say that there is no resurrection of the dead?

It is important to note that Paul does not write to the Corinthians as though they were not Christians. On the contrary he treats them as confused Christians. If the Corinthians had held (as has frequently been assumed) that there was a complete destruction of the personality through death and so resurrection was not a possibility, it is doubtful whether they could be called Christians. It is, of course, possible that the force of the ἐν ὑμῖν is that Paul is excepting from the Christian community those who denied the possibility of resurrection, as though to say that there are those among them who are not of them. This is probably reading too much into the words; and it is more likely that Paul is pointing to their failure to continue to look forward to a future resurrection. This error was (as we have already assumed) that of a presentative eschatology, everything was present for them, perhaps in the cult (hence the words added by Paul to the tradition concerning the Lord's Supper: "as often as you eat this bread and drink the cup, you proclaim the Lord's death until he comes", 11:26). In that case the words that follow, "if there is no resurrection of the dead, then Christ has not been raised" (v. 13), are not to be taken as an argument from the general to the particular. Rather, the denial of a future resurrection isolates the resurrection of Jesus in such a way as to deprive it of all meaning and substance. "Christ is indeed no historical private person, but according to verse 45 the last Adam, in whom the believers are enclosed, as they previously were in Adam."[1] So absolutely everything which flows from Christ's resurrection as preached among them is rendered null and void: faith is futile and hope is vain (vv. 14–19).

This reading of the argument explains the positive statement which follows in verses 20–22. Most editors of the Greek text, followed by most translators, complete the paragraph which began at verse 12, at the end of 19. It is noteworthy that C. K. Barrett makes the break between 22 and 23. Verses 20–22, being the positive statement, provide us with the essential clue to what has been in Paul's mind. Christ's resurrection is no isolated event. Using terminology which would be equally meaningful to the Jewish and gnostically minded, Paul draws out the Adam-Christ parallel but with the essential contrast in tenses: "as in Adam all die (present), so also in Christ shall all be made alive (future)" (v. 22). What is at stake then resides in this future tense.

[1] Gerhard Barth, "Erwägungen zu 1. Korinther 15:20–28", *EvTh* 30, [10](1970), an essay to which the present writer is deeply in debt. See too, Conzelmann *op. cit.*, pp. 313–14; and footnote 20 on p. 314, with the following sentence quoted from H. Braun: "if the resurrection of Christ is isolated to a single instance, it is no longer the Christ event."

Paul has, then, depended upon the argument that Christ's resurrection and that of Christians are integrally related. He has not yet, however, made clear why they must be separated by a time span. It is for this purpose that he introduces:

3. The first apocalyptic passage: 23–28

What is the effect of introducing this kind of language at this point? It is three-fold.

First it provides a time scheme within which the resurrection of Christ and of those who belong to him each has its proper place: Christ the first fruits at the time designated in the kerygmatic opening referred to above, those who belong to Christ at his parousia. Then, and only then, the end. In other words, what Paul does by the introduction of this language is to continue to restore the horizontal perspective to the Corinthians. This indeed had been the effect of the kerygmatic section: they had been placed in a tradition stretching back to Palestine, to the death of Jesus and his being raised on the third day. Now they are placed in a sequence of events which opens out before them into the future. The present derives its significance from its past and its future: it is "christologically the time of overcoming the Powers, anthropologically the time of the Church, of the proclamation of the death of Christ, of faith and of hope".[1] The conquest of death belongs to that future: it is the very last event of all, before the Son hands everything to the Father. Whatever else apocalyptic had been, it was an interpretation of history. This kind of historical thinking expressed in apocalyptic terms forces a separation between Christ's resurrection and that of believers, and attaches the latter to the end of the process: for those who think in such terms it is no longer possible to speak of resurrection, the risen life, as present possession.

Secondly, the strength of what Paul does here does not derive simply from the introduction of a new way of speaking, one which after all might have been alien to his readers, as it is strange to us. Jürgen Becker has recently warned us of the necessity, especially in dealing with Paul's apocalyptic passages, of asking "how and why and with what aim Paul in specific instances formulates exactly this way and not otherwise."[2] We must press the issue: how does he do it and with what aim? A careful reading of the passage suggests that what is at stake among the Corinthians is not simply a matter of a correct or incorrect reading of the time-clock of history. Apocalyptic discourse is not being introduced merely in order to correct the calendars of the Corinthian Christians. The passage is introduced to reassert the sovereignty of Christ and the sovereignty of God. What is at stake is not simply the anthropological question, the question

[1] Conzelmann op. cit., p. 329.
[2] "Erwägungen zur apokalyptischen Tradition in der paulinischer Theologie" EvTh 30, 11 (1970).

of the self-understanding of believers, but the Christological ("He must reign until he has put all his enemies under his feet") and the theological ("that God may be all in all").[1] The word πᾶς is used no fewer than ten times in the verses 24–28, frequently with great emphasis.[2] Christ will deliver the kingdom to the Father after destroying *every* rule and *every* authority and power. For he must reign till he has put *all* his enemies under his feet (a citation from Psalm 11:1 but with the adjective inserted by Paul). And so on, until it can be made effective that God is πάντα ἐν πᾶσιν. Hope for the future resurrection has now become, in G. Barth's phrase, "theologically necessary". The Corinthian Christians who in their enthusiasm claim that already they are filled with the Spirit, already they reign with Christ in heavenly places, are denying the sovereign work of Christ over history, over the contrary forces which beset men, over death itself. Moreover, a too exclusively risen-Jesus centred experience of the Christian faith, excludes God whose sovereign will and purpose Jesus was appointed to serve.

This leads to the third effect of the introduction of this language: faith in and hope for the resurrection is rescued not only from the subjective experience of the Corinthians, but also from preoccupation with the individuals on to a broader canvas. Death, the last enemy, is not merely a threat to personal survival. Death is the last of the contrary forces to be overcome by the Lord of life. Death calls in question the meaningfulness of life. Christ who was raised from the dead will bring meaning to the processes of history and of life. The insertion by Paul of the phrase, "Death is to be destroyed, the last enemy", between the two citations from scripture, between the two affirmations of Christ's completed work in handing over the kingdom to the Father, gives the statement a strange and decisive prominence. Christ's reign and death coexist in the meantime, until the end. Christian faith exists not only as *memoria passionis, mortis et resurrectionis Jesu Christi*, but also as hope based upon promise, a promise which encompasses the individual believer and the race. Indeed unless Christ's reign is triumphant over the contrary powers on the grand side, including death, it is difficult to see how it can be regarded as totally effective for the life of the individual. The death which must be overcome is not only my death but the death of my world.

4. *The second* argumentum ad hominem: *29–34*

This section is introduced abruptly: we are conscious of a sharp change in style and tone. First in a series of rhetorical questions, Paul points to the

---

[1] In his very instructive article referred to in the previous note, Professor Becker argues (against Käsemann) that Paul uses apocalyptic language to heighten the understanding of their present existence in faith on the part of his readers, and not for the extension of their understanding of Christ as Pantocrator. It is noteworthy, however, that Professor Becker never refers to this passage.

[2] See on this point Gerhard Barth, *op. cit.*, p. 523.

Corinthian Church's own practice (baptism on behalf of the dead, which
if we do not understand, Paul did, and to which he could appeal), and to
his own apostolic labours with the hazards involved, described either
literally or metaphorically as fighting with beasts in Ephesus. Then in a
series of brief sentences, Paul exhorts them to adopt the kind of behaviour
which would be expected of those who live in the period of Christ's
reign, of his conquest of the evil forces; the kind of behaviour which
would be appropriate among those who await the destruction of death in
the resurrection. Those who do not have such a hope have a corrupting effect
on their fellows: they live only for the present moment (v. 32b). They
have no knowledge of God (v. 34b), a phrase which must surely now be
understood in the light of the argument of the previous paragraph, that
hope for a future resurrection is a necessity if we are to believe that God is
God.

The paragraph need not detain us further, except to note that, as frequently with Paul, the great affirmations (in this case given in apocalyptic
language in what has preceded) must always be seen to have quite particular and precise implications for the attitudes, relationships and behaviour
of the Christian. The Corinthians are to wake up properly out of the
drunken stupor of their enthusiasm (v. 34: see Barrett *ad loc.*), and live
like sober Christians ready for what lies ahead of them. Paradoxically
enough, the awareness that resurrection – and therefore death – is still
in the future, should bring them to life now.[1]

5. The diatribe: 35–49

Having set the great (the vision of Christ reigning and of the ultimate
triumph of God's sovereignty) and the small (the behaviour of the Corinthian Christians and the activity of the apostle) in juxtaposition, Paul
can now proceed to occupy the middle ground. He has talked much
about resurrection, but what does it mean? If it is not simply the present
exalted experience of the Corinthians, what will the resurrection-life be?
This is the kind of question which Paul could imagine being raised, which
does not, of course, mean that it is speculative or unrelated to the views
held in Corinth. The passage calls for separate exegetical treatment; but
we must content ourselves here with a few observations which may be
relevant for our present purposes.

Verses 36–38 stress the necessity of death, and the discontinuity between
the present and the resurrection life. It is important to note this because
it has been said too often and too easily that to Paul the Jew the thought
of a naked soul is abhorrent, a bodiless life impossible. Before Paul speaks
about different kinds of body, he makes clear that there is real discontinuity: without death there is no possibility of resurrection (v. 36b). If

[1] See R. Bultmann, *Faith and Understanding* E.T. (London, 1969), I, p. 87.

we read into the analogy of the seed sown and the "body" subsequently given in the plant our knowledge of the processes of germination, we are reading into a metaphor something which would not have occurred to Paul or the Corinthians, any more than Jesus or his hearers would have seen in the mustard tree out of the smallest seed what we would call a natural development. The stress in verse 38 is on the subject of the sentence: *God* gives it a body, according to his choice. The matter is in his hands. The death is real, the miracle of the new life is no natural development as though the same entity can be clothed in two ways, as though (to quote Bultmann) "into the place of the body ($\sigma \tilde{\omega} \mu a$) has moved the Greek concept of form ($\varepsilon \tilde{\iota} \delta o \varsigma$), gained from the observation of nature."[1] To await the resurrection is genuinely to wait upon God for a new personal existence.

Verses 39–41 are best taken then as illustrations of the creative work of God, in all its variety. So too the dead are in the hands of the Creator God who takes "things that are not, to bring to nothing things that are." Once more, as in the previous (apocalyptic) paragraph, Paul points to the theological core of the matter. The kinds of flesh which characterize animals, birds and fish, the glory that belongs to heavenly and earthly bodies, to the sun and the moon, in all their infinite variety derive from God. So it is with the resurrection of the dead.

Verses 42–50 state in stark contrast the antitheses between death and life:

$\phi \theta o \rho \acute{a} / \grave{a} \phi \theta a \rho \sigma \acute{\iota} a$	the perishable/the imperishable
$\grave{a} \tau \iota \mu \acute{\iota} a / \delta \acute{o} \xi a$	dishonour/glory
$\grave{a} \sigma \theta \acute{\varepsilon} \nu \varepsilon \iota a / \delta \acute{\upsilon} \nu a \mu \iota \varsigma$	weakness/power
$\psi \upsilon \chi \iota \kappa \acute{o} \nu / \pi \nu \varepsilon \upsilon \mu a \tau \iota \kappa \acute{o} \nu$	psychic/spiritual
$\acute{o} \pi \rho \tilde{\omega} \tau o \varsigma \, \breve{a} \nu \theta \rho \omega \pi o \varsigma / \acute{o} \, \breve{\varepsilon} \sigma \chi a \tau o \varsigma$ $'A \delta \acute{a} \mu$	the first man/the last Adam
$\grave{\varepsilon} \kappa \, \gamma \tilde{\eta} \varsigma \, \chi o \ddot{\iota} \kappa \acute{o} \varsigma / \grave{\varepsilon} \xi \, o \grave{\upsilon} \rho a \nu o \tilde{\upsilon}$	from the earth, of dust/from heaven

The matter is summarized: living men (flesh and blood) in their perishable, unworthy, weak, psychic nature cannot inherit the kingdom of God. That entry can be effected only by God himself.

It is wise to assume that in the whole of this section Paul's thought is permeated and controlled by his customary understanding of $\sigma \tilde{\omega} \mu a$ the body. To repeat, it does not mean simply the vehicle for personal existence. Life in the body is personal existence, but it is more. Gerhard Barth invokes the recent studies of Käsemann and Schweizer in this regard.[2] Käsemann correctly stresses that Paul uses $\sigma \tilde{\omega} \mu a$ "to denote the corporeality of human life, organic to the creation, claimed by God as his own by right, yet threatened by the cosmic powers . . . . . . No New Testament writer stresses more than Paul that the resurrection of the body is

[1] *op. cit.*, p. 90. [2] *op. cit.*, pp. 526–27.

the goal of all the divine action and that therefore to this extent corporealit
is the end of all the ways of God. It is for this reason that when the Apostl
wants to portray the new aeon created and ruled by Christ, he goes fc
his terminology not to the gnostic myth of the world-soul but to th
myth of the Archetypal Man, who is also the Redeemer, with his immens
body." And again: "We must conclude that $\sigma\tilde{\omega}\mu\alpha$ does not mean for th
Apostle what it means for the modern idea of person or personality –
does not mean individuality . . . . In the anthropology of classical Greece
the essential characteristic of the body is that it experiences limitation an
individuation through its form and proportions. For Paul, on the othe
hand, it is the possibility of communication."[1]

So, far from reverting to individual hopes, let alone subjective exper
iences, Paul in this section sketches as the hope of the resurrection life
new life in community and in communication, in Christ and before God
a life which the unrighteous cannot inherit (6:9), nor can men in thei
weakness and mortality, but which can be received as a gift at the hand c
the Creator-Redeemer.

6. The concluding apocalypse: (50) 51–57

"At this point", writes Barrett, "Paul moves into specifically apocalyp
tic language"; and of that there is no doubt. The mystery is the reveale
truth about the end. Paul does not say how he became possessed of thi
knowledge: there is no stress on any special gift which he may have fo
discerning these things, no entry into competition with the enthusiasts c
Corinth. Just as in the previous apocalyptic passage Paul had used a tradi
tional scheme for his own purposes, so here Paul uses the material t
hand, with reserve. There is none of the detailed delineation of the fat
of the righteous and the unrighteous, or of the order of their appearin
at the end. Two points only are stressed; and they are the points centra
to Paul's controversy with the Corinthians. First, "the dead will be raised"
the resurrection is a future event, belonging to the End when the las
trumpet will sound. Secondly, "we (i.e. those still living) shall be changed"
in other words, we are not risen with Christ; not for us yet, until ou
mortal bodies have been changed, the life beyond death.

If we ask how Paul uses apocalyptic imagery in this concluding section
the answer must be: in such a way as to reinforce what he has said befor
He is not using it to introduce fresh ideas, but to emphasize – in languag
which has perhaps greater imaginative power, which certainly has it
peculiar eloquence – what he has been saying throughout.

[1] "The Pauline Doctrine of the Lord's Supper" E.T. in *Essays on New Testament Theme*
(London, 1964) pp. 129–130, 132–133. See too Eduard Schweizer, *TWNT*, VII, p. 1063.

In a further, most notable way, Paul concludes by taking up a point with which he had begun this discourse. He had said twice in his keryg-matic opening that the key events of Christ's death and resurrection were according to the scriptures". So too the final event: "then shall happen, come to effect, the Word that has been written: 'Death is swallowed up in victory' . . ." That future event is part of the great purpose of God unfolded in the kerygma about Christ. Indeed the meaning of the "he was raised on the third day according to the scripture" will then be disclosed: scripture, it will be shown, has pointed to the true meaning of Christ's resurrection, which is no single isolated event in itself but is a victory over death, of universal significance.

Not even in this thought, however, are the Corinthians allowed to rest. For Paul, men may not simply acquiesce in an assurance of future victory. This victory is over the dominating experiences of historical existence: in the here-and-now death, sin, and the law are the great forces contrary to us. In so far as we have a new attitude to them, we begin to share in the victory of Christ. Paul was to develop his exposition of this three-fold victory in Romans 6–8.[1] For present purposes the allusion to it, and the thanksgiving for it, are sufficient.

II

"The prime virtue of the historian", writes Käsemann, "and the beginning of all meaningful hermeneutic consists for me in so drilling ourselves to listen that we first of all allow the alien element in history its full validity and do not let the basic idea of involvement do violence to it".[2] It has been one of Dr. Leon Morris's great virtues as a scholar that he has again and again sought to expose his readers to the text, even if it brings them to an alien world. The fifteenth chapter of I Corinthians certainly introduces us to a strange world: its language is no longer our language, and the errors of the Church addressed are in important respects different from ours. The work of the interpreter is not finished, however, when he leaves the reader in that alien world. There remains the difficult but inescapable question: what can this text mean for us? The remaining paragraphs of this essay can do no more that suggests directions for further enquiry.

First, we might observe that a great deal of ink has been spilt in recent decades, especially in the heyday of Biblical Theology, on the issue Immortality of the Soul versus Resurrection of the Body. It seems clear

[1] See the great sequence: freedom from sin (chapter 6), freedom from the law (chapter 7), freedom from death (chapter 8); and note the particularly instructive treatment of these by A. Nygren in his *Commentary on Romans* (E.T. London, Philadelphia, 1949).

[2] "Zur Thema der urchristlichen Apokalyptik" *Exegetische Versuche und Besinnungen* (Göttingen, 1965) II, p. 107 n. 2. E.T. in *JTC* 6 (1969), p. 101.

that the issue in Corinth was nothing like as simple as that definition ⸗
the problem would suggest. It is true, however, that the consciousness ⸗
modern man has been deeply influenced by these two concepts. The que⸗
tion for us is not whether the argument between survival and resurrectio⸗
raged in Corinth, which it did not, but how far the two notions of deat⸗
therein embodied are retained in the imagination of our contemporaries⸗
and therefore in our own imaginations.

For us in the Western tradition, Greece gave the ways of thought an⸗
speech which views death as a transition from this to another life. Ther⸗
is, it is assumed, survival. This has given us some of our greatest poetry⸗
The survival is frequently of a shadowy character, which has contribute⸗
to the power of the verse through the melancholy which pervades it. S⸗
Odysseus at the entrance to the underworld:

> "Now the souls gathered, stirring out of Erebos,
> brides and young men, and men grown old in pain,
> and tender girls whose hearts were new to grief;
> many were there, too, torn by brazen lanceheads,
> battle-slain, bearing still their bloody gear."[1]

Through Homer and Virgil and Dante the pictures come and are part ⸗
the inherited imagination of those who today have not read the poe⸗
themselves, or even paused before the illustrations of Blake.

Plato first gave philosophical justification for belief in survival. Th⸗
Orphic-Pythagorean assertion of survival which Plato inherited came u⸗
against the objection that we have no knowledge of this. Plato provide⸗
the argument. For him sense-perception does not yield knowledge bu⸗
only opinion; to gain knowledge we have to transcend sense-perceptio⸗
although this can be suggestive in that it points to archetypes, the worl⸗
of Forms. The soul of man by coming into contact with the Forms ha⸗
contact with what is unchangeable. Death is the moment at which th⸗
soul is released from the body and so enters into the realm of pure idea⸗
or forms to which it properly belongs. Here is the root of the doctrine c⸗
the immortality of the soul.

It does not belong to early Christianity. It entered powerfully into late⸗
Christianity. It is with us still. Death as the separation of body and sou⸗
would be regarded as an essential Christian dogma by many Christian⸗
today.[2] Compared to the view put forward by Paul in I Corinthians⸗
most (perhaps all) statements about death in these terms fail to take th⸗
finality of death with a radical seriousness.

By way of contrast with this, the Biblical understandings of death ar⸗
pretty well united in being, as Eberhard Jüngel argues,[3] "two-dimensional"⸗

---

[1] *The Odyssey* XI. 38–42, tr. Robert Fitzgerald (New York, 1961).
[2] For a sophisticated discussion of this view by a leading Roman theologian, see Kar⸗
Rahner, *On the Theology of Death* (Herder, Freiburg, 1961), pp. 24–34.
[3] Eberhard Jüngel, *Tod* (Stuttgart, 1971), pp. 145 ff.

Certainly behind Paul's teaching lies on the one hand a conviction about the reality, the finality of death and on the other a hope, based upon a promise made by God to man in the resurrection of Jesus. The reality of death as the loss of all relationships, the destruction of the contacts of life between man and man, and between man and God, is certainly one that can be grasped by contemporary historians and natural scientists. Historical existence comes to an end, and historians cannot touch what (if anything) occurs subsequently to the individual concerned; biological death occurs when certain biochemical reactions are observed, there is a breakdown in organic processes and decomposition sets in.

From the time of Abraham and the promise that in his seed all the nations of the earth should be blessed, this view of death as the end of meaningful existence for the individual has been complemented by a hope which resides in the future of the race. One generation rises and passes away, but the hope is in posterity: before man lies the future. The race goes on, hopefully to a culmination, a realization of its full potentialities, its true end. Nothing could be further from Plato and the tradition which flows from him; but Christianity has oscillated between these two essentially incompatible views of death: one the moment of transition to another life or realm of existence, the other the end of the individual, only the race goes on. This latter view is one which is tolerably congenial to modern man, whether humanist or Christian. The humanist may think life well lived if he is contributing towards a better future. The Christian can point to much in the Biblical message which speaks of a future and hope: the eschatological perspective of the Christian faith keeps him looking forward.[1]

The contemporary awareness of death is, however, qualified by two other ways of talking about death: the existential and the ecological. The former finds its most eloquent expression in the imaginative literature of the 19th and 20th centuries. We might begin by observing the distinctive quality of the existential awareness in Dostoevsky. In a much quoted passage from *The Idiot*, Prince Myshkin tells the story of a man who was taken to a place of execution and at the last moment was reprieved. Dostoevsky himself had had this experience; and his description of a man facing death illuminates his attitude towards this phenomenon. Death is not simply that which gives a boundary to life, but is that which gives significance to what lies this side of the boundary. Whereas there has been a strong tendency in the Western tradition (and perhaps elsewhere) to speak and think of death in terms of what lies beyond it, this way of thought and speech lays stress on what the fact of death means for life this side of the event. Moreover, the passage from *The Idiot* suggests that such an awareness of the ever-present reality of death is not morbid, but

[1] Justly celebrated as an exposition of what this might mean for the believer is Jürgen Moltmann's *Theology of Hope* E.T. (London, 1967).

liberating. It is liberating because, through awareness of death, in
peculiarly decisive way, man becomes aware of himself. He becomes awa
of the fact that he is always more than he is, that his being is never co
plete at any given moment: man is possibility, as Heidegger would s
Above all, face to face with death man becomes aware of his ov
individual existence, his *Jemeinigkeit* as the Germans say – what belon
to me.

Man then not only knows about death, observes it from a number
points of view, he also is aware of his own death – and that awarenes
decisive for authentic existence, for a true and full life. I not only obser
the death of others, which I surround with ceremonies which take
individual event into a wider general context, I know that I must c
I shall not witness my own funeral, to borrow a phrase of Profes.
Antony Flew;[1] or, as one summary of the existentialist view has put
"death appears as my own present untransferable possibility of being
longer in the world".[2]

It goes without saying that such a view of death is not only liberatin
it is also a threat. The finality of death not only confers significance up
life, it also calls that significance into question. Contemporary "anxiety
not fear, being afraid of this or that definite object, but the uncan
feeling of being afraid of nothing at all".[3] Nothingness is the object
much contemporary anxiety. Edvard Munch's often reproduced painti
The Cry speaks not of an anguished spirit protesting against the univer
it articulates the anguish which is at the heart of things. In the paral
picture, *Anxiety* is dressed in respectable clothes, and the anxious figu
look not at some definable object but out of the canvas, at us, in
Nothing.

This imaginative awareness of the Nothingness with which he
surrounded, this awareness that in life we are in the midst of death,
given historical reality by the threat under which man lives, as he tal
hold of destructive weapons of hitherto unknown power and as he u
up the environment on which he depends to support life. The existent
awareness of death is now complemented by the predictions of t
scientists. Modern man faces not only his own individual death but a
that of the race. It is doubtful whether Christian preaching or pasto
care has yet appreciated to the full the effect on men's minds of t
disappearance of hope for the future of the human race.

One last note must be sounded in this brief survey of the modern re
ponse to death. We have suggested that this response is characterized
men seeing a new significance or lack of significance in life, through th
exposure to the fact of death. The possible effect of the loss of significan

[1] See Antony Flew: "Can a man witness his own funeral?", *HJ*, 54 (1956), pp. 242–25
[2] J. MacQuarrie, *An Existentialist Theology* (London, 1955), p. 118.
[3] William Barrett, *Irrational Man* (London, 1961), p. 128.

is well stated by Albert Camus in his novel *The Outsider*. There the author tests the validity of the detached objectivity of attitude of the central figure, Meursault, the young clerk in Algiers. The novel is written in the first person, as it were autobiographically from a prison cell, the cell of a man condemned for murder. Meursault can observe his mother's death, with which the novel opens, with detachment; he can sleep with his girl friend, without love or commitment, or equally agree to marry her, not because he wants to but simply because she asks him. He knows neither jealousy nor fear; and he seems to be free from hypocrisy also. For the murder in which he is involved he has feelings neither of guilt nor of self-justification. The frightening, Kafka-esque trial, with the manifest injustice, he can observe almost with calm. Only, at the end, the prison chaplain exasperates him: "As a condemned man himself, couldn't he grasp what I meant by that dark wind blowing from my future? ..." After this outburst he has a longish sleep and wakens just before dawn on the day of his execution; and the novel concludes:

> Then just on the edge of daybreak I heard a steamer's siren. People were starting on a voyage to a world that had ceased to concern me, for ever. Almost for the first time in many months I thought of my mother. And now, it seemed to me, I understood why at her life's end she had taken on a fiancé; why she'd played at making a fresh start. There too, in that Home (the old people's home where his mother had died) where lives were flickering out, the dusk came as a mournful solace. With death so near, Mother must have felt like someone on the brink of freedom, ready to start life all over again. No one, no one in this world had any right to weep for her. And I, too, felt ready to start life over again. It was as if that great rush of anger had washed me clean, emptied me of hope, and, gazing up at the dark sky spangled with its signs and stars, for the first time, the first, I laid my heart open to the benign indifference of the universe. To feel it so like myself, indeed so brotherly, made me realize that I'd been happy, and that I was happy still. For all to be accomplished, for me to feel less lonely, all that remained was to hope that on the day of my execution there should be a huge crowd of spectators and that they should greet me with howls of execration.[1]

The indifference and isolation of modern man, the outsider, is complete; and he knows it at the hour of death.

Man the outsider rejects life, when he sees it from the perspective of death. But this may happen to man the insider also. The insecurity of a future made possible by scientific and technical achievements is already leading many to a rejection not only of that civilization but of historical existence, life itself.

III

This then, briefly and crudely, suggests a strange new world in which

[1] A. Camus, *The Outsider*, Penguin ed. (London, 1961), pp. 119–20.

the Christian must try to make meaningful his talk about death, and about the victory over it. It is beyond the scope of the present essay to do more than raise the question; it is certainly beyond the powers of the writer to answer it. A few suggestions may, nonetheless, be in order.

Paul's starting point in the kerygmatic tradition suggests that for us, as for the Corinthians, an existential or experiential awareness of death is not enough. It is as inadequate to see and speak of death in itself without regard to both its antecedents and what comes after, as it was for the Corinthians so to speak of resurrection. We are creatures of time and history: we have a beginning, and the possibility of a new beginning in the death and resurrection of Jesus Christ. We also have a future in him, a historical future in which he reigns till *all* things are put under his feet. Paul's use of apocalyptic rescues us from the individual and private apprehension, to a forward look, to that which lies beyond our individual lives, to the future of the race. But since that future is in the hands of the crucified living one of the kerygmatic tradition it is one which genuinely encompasses us all: the miracle of resurrection, of life in Christ, is open to every man.

The Christian faith therefore certainly speaks of man as possibility, certainly not (as Heidegger stresses) simply as "a free-floating potentiality-for-Being",[1] but because of the miracle of Christ's resurrection, and the awaited miracle of our risen life. Death cannot for the Christian be the last word. It may be the last "station on the road to Freedom" (Bonhoeffer). It is a station always ahead of us. What has been traditionally regarded as being true for the individual must now be seen as operative also for the human race. It too lives under the threat of death, but also under the promise of a new life. Just as the Christian proclamation must begin with a backward look to the death and resurrection of Jesus Christ, so it must finish with a forward look, not indeed to a parallel death and resurrection for man, but to acts of God's sovereignty exercised through the reign of Christ. There is no reason to think that that reign is or will be exercised other than in the manner of the risen crucified one; but nor is there any reason for the Christian to forget the strange victory which was won in precisely this manner. The Christian looks to the future with hope, not because of anything inherent in the world but because of his faith in Jesus the Kyrios, who points to and makes effective the sovereignty of God.[2] In a day when the secular expectation looks to "the death of man", the Christian does not respond with a theology of "the death of God"; nor does he try, by induced mystical experience or the exercise of

---

[1] *Being and Time* E.T. (London, 1962), p. 144.
[2] Cf. J. Moltmann *Theology of Hope* E.T. (London, 1965), p. 162, n. 1, referring to "He must reign" of I Corinthians 15:25, "It is not a $\delta\epsilon\hat{\iota}$ ('must') in terms of salvation history, but one that discloses the future necessity and future tendency inherent in the event of the resurrection of Jesus. That is why it is linked not to the expectation of a fate, as in apocalyptic, but to the Kyrios title of Jesus."

psychic powers, to demonstrate the presence of God in the midst of life and death. He speaks rather of a future and a hope. The death of death depends not upon experience but on promise.

CHAPTER XVII

"SO THAT YOUR FAITH MAY ALSO BE YOUR HOPE IN GOD"
(I PETER 1:21)[1]

W. J. DALTON

THIS ARTICLE, BY WAY OF GENERAL INTRODUCTION, WILL FIRST discuss more recent scholarly writing on the authorship of 1 Peter. It will then be concerned with the understanding of one passage in this letter, 1:3–25. The structural analysis of this text will help to bring out its message of hope, which is happily summed up, it would seem, in the title of the article.

I

It is good to see in recent times[2] a continuing interest in what Selwyn called "a microcosm of Christian faith and duty".[3] In the English language alone, we have the work of Bo Reicke,[4] A. R. C. Leaney,[5] J. N. D. Kelly[6] and E. Best,[7] while F. W. Beare's original commentary of 1945 has been represented in its third edition.[8] A notable addition to the number of French commentaries is that of C. Spicq.[9] Among the more recent articles of special note, two may be mentioned, one by W. Trilling, "Zum Petrusamt im Neuen Testament: Traditionsgeschichtliche Überlegungen anhand von Matthäus, 1 Petrus und Johannes,"[10] and the other by M.-A. Chevallier, "1 Pierre 1/1 à 2-10: Structure littéraire et conséquences exégétiques."[11]

All these writers have something to say about the problem of the authorship of 1 Peter. Scholarly opinion has moved strongly in favour of

[1] This translation will be justified later in the course of the article.
[2] Without wishing to be exhaustive and, no doubt, with regrettable omissions, this brief review begins from the time of my own work on 1 Peter, *Christ's Proclamation to the Spirits* (Rome, 1965).
[3] *The First Epistle of St. Peter* (London, [2]1947), p. 1.
[4] *The Epistles of James, Peter and Jude* (New York, 1964).
[5] *The Letters of Peter and Jude* (Cambridge, 1967).
[6] *A Commentary on the Epistles of Peter and of Jude* (New York, 1969).
[7] *I Peter* (London, 1971).
[8] *The First Epistle of Peter* (Oxford, [3]1970).
[9] *Les Épîtres de saint Pierre* (Paris, 1966).
[10] ThQ 151 (1971), pp. 110–33.
[11] RHPR 51 (1971), pp. 129–42.

understanding the letter as a pseudepigraphical work. Beare can repeat in the third edition of his commentary in 1970: "Recent Continental writers, except for the Roman Catholics, seldom take the argument for authenticity – with or without the collaboration of Silvanus – at all seriously".[1] But opinion is also changing among Roman Catholics. As long ago as 1961, in the first edition of Schelkle's work, the question was left an open one.[2] In 1971, W. Trilling offers new arguments against authenticity and finds the Silvanus hypothesis unsatisfactory.[3] Can we therefore regard the question as closed? At least one strongly dissentient voice is heard in the person of C. Spicq, an exegete of no mean reputation. He maintains that the apostle Peter wrote the letter personally.[4]

Certainly some of the arguments against Petrine authenticity are rather tenuous. A reference to the term ἀγράμματος used of Peter in Acts 4:13 is not decisive. First of all, it is by no means sure that this is an indication that Peter "could neither read nor write his own native tongue (Aramaic)."[5] Further we may ask whether, in fact, it fits in with the picture of Peter which Luke provides in the early chapters of Acts: Peter is hardly presented as an illiterate fisherman.

One would have to do a lot more work on the Galilean background of Peter, the influence of Greek in this area, on Peter's social standing, his probable education, the influence of the synagogue, and on the level of education which Jesus, who was called "Rabbi", shared with his disciples, before one could with confidence dismiss Peter as a possible author of the first letter which goes under his name.

Actually we know more about the linguistic situation in Palestine in the time of the New Testament than would appear in most commentaries on 1 Peter. Josephus is a good example of what was possible at that time, an example which might well be meditated upon by scholars who are so quick to turn to pseudepigraphy as a solution. Born about A.D. 38 at Jerusalem, he was educated in the Jewish law and actually spent three years in the wilderness as a member of an ascetical group. Only at the age of twenty-six did he go to Rome. It was this Josephus who first wrote *The Jewish War* in Aramaic, and then, with some assistance, translated this work into the Greek version which we now have, a version which is remarkably free from semitisms. Surprising but true! Of course, there is no strict parallel here to a biblical work, and we do have the fact that the writer of 1 Peter cites from the LXX version of the Old Testament. But can we be so sure that, in the more Hellenized Galilee, the LXX was not in use among moderately educated Jews?[6]

---

[1] *Op. cit.*, p. 216.
[2] *Die Petrusbriefe. Der Judasbrief* (Freiburg-Basel-Wien, ²1964), pp. 11–15.
[3] *Art cit.*, pp. 120–125.
[4] *Op. cit.*, pp. 21–26.
[5] Beare, *op. cit.*, p. 28.
[6] See *Encyclopaedia Judaica*, X, pp. 251–65. For the use of Greek at Jerusalem in the first

Further, it is clear from the writings of Paul (quite apart from the evidence of Acts) that Paul could "dialogue" with Peter. Despite the angry tone of Galatians, Paul puts Peter side by side with himself: "I had been entrusted with the gospel for Gentiles, as surely as Peter had been entrusted with the gospel for Jews" (Gal. 2:8). We know a good deal about the intellectual capacity and education of Paul. It is possible that we could learn something about Peter too from this association.[1]

What complicates the issue is that competent scholars do not even agree on the level of 1 Peter's Greek style. C. Spicq, whose earlier work on Hebrews[2] marks him as one of the finest modern commentators in this area, strongly denies that the Greek of 1 Peter can be compared with that of Hebrews. He agrees with A. Charue: "L'allure générale est plutôt embarrassée et conventionelle, comme il arrive aux auteurs qui n'ont pas le style coulant ou qui n'ont pas la maîtrise d'une langue."[3] On the other hand, Chevallier believes that his investigations into the structure of 1 Peter indicate quite the contrary, thus providing a new argument against the authorship of Peter.[4]

Many scholars point to the heavy dependence of 1 Peter on the writings of Paul (or those associated with Paul) and so conclude that Peter could not have been its author. This is often done by listing ideas and expressions which are common to both. It is likely enough that Paul did not borrow from 1 Peter, but until we can sift out with some confidence what is specifically Pauline in the writings of Paul and what he shared with the Christian world of his time, we have really no clear idea of what the writer of 1 Peter actually borrowed from Paul.

[1] There is ample evidence to show that Galilee was far more influenced by Hellenism than Jerusalem. We know that Peter and Andrew were commercial fishermen associated with Zebedee, who had his "hired men." Since fish provided the main industry of the region, we have every reason to believe that this was a prosperous group with corresponding possibilities of education. We might allow some force to Peter's words: "We here have left everything to become your followers" (Mk. 10:28 par.). Nor should we underrate the organization and education associated with the synagogue in which, we may reasonably suppose, Peter and his companions, as devout Jews, fulfilled their responsibilities (See *Encyclopaedia Judaica*, XV, pp. 578–83). For all this, the conclusion of Spicq may be too absolute: "Par conséquent, la pseudo-ignorance du grec par Pierre ne devrait plus figurer dans les discussions sur l'authenticité de *Ia Petri*" (*op. cit.*, p. 23). It remains to be seen whether, in fact, the work which Chevallier has begun on the literary structure of 1 Peter establishes the fact that the author was a highly sophisticated writer.
[2] *L'Épître aux Hébreux*, Vols. 1, 2 (Paris, 1952 f.).
[3] *Les Épîtres Catholiques* (Paris, 1938), p. 441.
[4] *Art. cit.*, p. 138.

century B.C., see K. Galling, *RGG*[3], V, 24. Further evidence for the use of Greek in the last decades of the first century A.D. has appeared in the findings at Murabba'ãt. See Spicq, *op. cit.*, pp. 21–23, and also R. H. Gundry, "The Language Milieu of First-Century Palestine", *JBL* 83 (1964), pp. 404–408.

The Letter of James may provide a useful parallel to 1 Peter. F. Mussner, in *Der Jakobusbrief* (Freiburg, 1964), pp. 1–42, has taken up and answered the main arguments against the authorship of James, "the brother of the Lord". Yet the Greek of this letter is generally admitted to be good. James came from the same Palestinian background as Peter.

Best[1] has endeavoured to give a more balanced view of 1 Peter's apparent dependence on Romans and Ephesians, but even here it is difficult to assess such evidence, since criteria for firm conclusions are more easily supposed than established.

Selwyn gave his authority to the view that the Silvanus of Acts, who was also Paul's companion, composed 1 Peter under the authority of Peter himself. This view continues to be proposed with various degrees of approval,[2] but has been strongly, even sharply attacked by Beare.[3] It would still seem to be a hypothesis worth considering. One advantage that Silvanus could have over Peter himself in claiming credit for the composition of 1 Peter is the fact that he was associated with Paul in his evangelizing of Hellenistic towns and that, as delegate of the Council of Jerusalem (Acts 15), he took its decrees to the Gentile churches. Thus one might better account for the Hellenistic style of the letter (if one thought this necessary). The text of 1 Pet. 5:12 is open to this meaning, but by no means imposes it. On the other hand, Silvanus is not associated with Peter at the beginning of the letter (as he is with Paul in 1 and 2 Thess.), and, even in the case of 1 and 2 Thess., it is extremely doubtful if he had any part in their composition.[4] If Peter did need help in the composition of 1 Peter, then it might be better not to press the claim of Silvanus, but to leave this unknown cooperator in the obscurity of history.

Of course, the whole question is associated with the probable date of the letter. Beare asserts firmly that "the Epistle cannot be attributed to the time of Nero".[5] Yet the primitive theology of the letter,[6] the primitive church order, the impression that the recipients of the letter are first-generation Christians, the unspecified nature of the persecution facing them, all allow and even point to an early date. If indeed the letter does belong to the Neronian period, then it must have come from Peter, whether he personally composed it or not.[7]

So, despite the vigorous efforts to solve this problem once and for all, and despite the fluctuations of exegetical fashion, one is still justified in asking: How cultivated is the Greek of the letter?; How strong is the evidence that it was composed at a later date?; To what degree is it dependent upon other New Testament writings? And behind these questions we have a further one: What was the education and talent of

[1] *Op. cit.*, pp. 32–36.
[2] It is interesting to note that Bo Reicke, writing in 1964, defends the view that Silvanus composed the letter under the general direction of Peter (*op. cit.*, pp. 69–71). Kelly in 1969, inclines to an early date and to general Petrine authorship, but requires a more skilled Greek writer than Peter to explain the composition of the letter (*op. cit.*, pp. 30–33).
[3] *Op. cit.*, pp. 212–216.
[4] See B. Rigaux, *Saint Paul: Les Épîtres aux Thessaloniciens* (Paris, 1956), p. 107.
[5] *Op. cit.*, p. 30.
[6] Note the vast difference between the eschatological attitude of 1 Peter and that of 2 Peter, which can be accepted as a later pseudepigraphical work.
[7] To my mind, the best and most balanced discussion of this whole question is to be found in the introduction of Kelly's commentary, *op. cit.*, pp. 26–33.

Peter himself? And, in the complications of the arguments for and against, it might be good to remember that the letter does start: "From Peter, apostle of Jesus Christ ..." In the circumstances, it seems reasonable to accept the authorship of Peter as a working hypothesis until better evidence emerges to prove the contrary.[1]

II

Before we consider in some detail the structure of the section 1:3–25, it would be good to situate it in the context of the whole letter. In an earlier work, I have already argued for the literary unity of 1 Peter.[2] There is no need to discuss once more the various attempts to identify the letter as substantially a baptismal homily or liturgy. Actually, there is only one unmistakable reference to baptism in the whole letter, 3:21–22. Here the picture of baptism is given in terms which are legal in tone: "the pledge to God of a good conscience."[3]

It does not seem at all evident that, wherever in the letter there is reference to a "new birth" (1:3, 23; 2:2), baptism is directly referred to. The author himself explains this new birth in 1:23: "You have been born anew, not from corruptible seed but from incorruptible, through God's living and abiding word". And this is further explained in 1:24–25: the "word of God" which "abides for ever" brings the believing Christian to share in God's own eternal life (as opposed to the "corruptible seed" of 1:21); and "this word[4] is the good news which has been preached to you".[5]

If the letter is not primarily concerned with baptism can it be regarded as a message of Christian hope?[6] This description does justice to the spirit of the letter: it is addressed to Christians facing persecution as a message which exhorts and testifies that "this is the true grace of God" (5:12).

Persecution and hope go together,[7] and these ideas dominate the whole letter. The tone is set in the opening address: "To God's scattered people who lodge for a while in Pontus ..." They are God's pilgrim people who are on the way, in hope, to their real homeland. It is in this context

[1] This opinion is not presented from any confessional point of view: there are obviously canonical books of Scripture which are pseudepigraphical. It is a question of critical judgment. It is also a view which is excluded by a whole exegetical school. The representative work of Feine–Behm–Kümmel, *Einleitung in das Neue Testament* (Heidelberg, 1969), p. 309, provides the simple comment: "1 Pt. ist darum zweifellos eine pseudonyme Schrift."

[2] *Christ's Proclamation to the Spirits* (Rome, 1965) pp. 72–83.

[3] See Kelly, *op. cit.*, pp. 162–163.

[4] In the text ῥῆμα is used, not λόγος in fidelity to the LXX translation.

[5] See Chevallier, *art. cit.*, pp. 139–140.

[6] Beare, *op. cit.*, p. 56. "The impression, once widely held, that the writer is pre-eminently the 'Apostle of Hope', as if Hope received a disproportionate attention in this Epistle as compared with the rest of the New Testament, is quite false."

[7] Note that the rise of apocalyptic in Judaism was the response of hope in the face of severe persecution. We find a similar Christian response in the Book of Revelation.

that we find passages on the Christian vocation (1:3 – 2:10) and on the Christian life (2:11 – 3:12). Here a verse-by-verse exegesis does not do justice to the spirit and purpose of the letter. It is to be read as a living whole.

In this total setting of the letter, let us look at 1:3–25. After the opening verses (which announce the three themes of God's foreknowledge, the Spirit's sanctification, and obedience to Jesus Christ together with the sprinkling of his blood), the first large section of the letter is 1:3 – 2:10, which, in the context of persecution and hope, depicts, first of all, the nobility of the Christian vocation (1:3–25) and then its responsibilities in Christian living (2:1–10).[1]

Looking further at 1:3–25, we see that it too falls into two parts, 1:3–12, which is a doctrinal affirmation, and 1:13–25, which is an exhortation based on this, the whole passage being bound together by the inclusion: ἀναγεννήσας … ζῶσαν … ἄφθαρτον (1:3–4), ἀναγεγεννημένοι … ἀφθάρτου … ζῶντος (1:23). In addition, both these sections begin with similar words, ἐλπίδα (1:3) and ἐλπίσατε (1:13) and end with similar words ἀνηγγέλη, εὐαγγελισαμένων (1:12) and εὐαγγελισθέν (1:25). They are bound together by the link-words ἀπεκαλύφθη … ἐπιθυμοῦσιν (1:12) and ἀποκαλύψει … ἐπιθυμίαις (1:13, 14).

When we consider again the two sections 1:3–12 and 1:13–25, we find, in each case, that there is some form of inclusion indicating the unity of each section. Thus the οὐρανοῖς of 1:4 is echoed by the οὐρανοῦ of 1:12, while there is at least a verbal correspondence between the passive participles preceded by ἀνα- in 1:13 (ἀναζωσάμενοι) and in 1:23 (ἀναγεγεννημένοι).

In both sections, there is a remarkable community of cognate words: πίστις-πιστός-πιστεύω (1:5, 7, 8, 9 and 1:12) twice; ἔσχατος (1:5 and 1:20); τιμή-πολυτίμος-τίμιος (1:7, twice, and 1:19); χρυσίον (1:7 and 1:18); ἀγαπάω (1:8 and 1:22); ψυχαί (1:9 and 1:22).[2] Note also that the two sections are bound together by the chiastic use of expressions for time: 1:5 (καιρὸς ἔσχατος), 1:11 (καιρός), 1:17 (χρόνος), 1:20 (ἐπ᾽ ἐσχάτου τῶν χρόνων).

Let us look now at the development of the first section (1:3–12). We find that it is one long sentence which flows along by the multiplication of relative clauses beginning at 1:6, 8, 10, 12.[3] We have a blessing in 1:3–5,

---

[1] Justification of this division of the text is to be found in the writer's earlier work, pp. 72–83. This discussion of the plan of 1 Peter was a mere beginning, based largely on the work of A. Vanhoye, La structure littéraire de l'Épître aux Hébreux (Paris, 1963), In the article of Chevallier already referred to, this analysis is carried much further. The writer gratefully uses this research in what follows.

[2] Chevallier (art. cit., p. 133) adds two corresponding groups of words which begin with the following prefixes: ἀνα- (1:3, twice, and 1:13, 15, 17, 18, 23); ἀ- or ἀν- (1:4, three times; 1:8, and 1:14, 17, 19, 22, 23); προ- (1:11 and 1:20); ἐξ- (1.10, twice and 1:24).

[3] Note that the combination πίστεως … σωτηρίαν of 1:5 is echoed by exactly the same words (though in different grammatical arrangement) at the end of 1:9.

followed by a statement giving grounds for this blessing (1:6–9). The next sentence (1:10–12) is connected with 1:6–9 by the link-word, σωτηρία, and gives further grounds for the blessing with which the whole section begins. It is of interest to note that the three divisions of 1:3–12 have each a word derived from ἀποκαλύπτω: ἀποκαλυφθῆναι (1:5), ἀποκαλύψει (1:7), ἀπεκαλύφθη (1:12).

We come now to the passage which is the second section (1:13–25) of the total text we are considering (1:3–25). This is an exhortation sharply marked off from the preceding passage by διό. This exhortation is carried along by the four imperatives, ἐλπίσατε (1:13), γενήθητε (1:15), ἀναστράφητε (1:17), ἀγαπήσατε (1:22); and the section falls naturally into the four divisions indicated by these words. As usual, in keeping with the general style of 1 Peter, there is a considerable repetition of words,[1] but probably nothing specific about the structure of the passage can be derived from this. However the repetition of one word, in its noun and verb forms, stresses, by its meaning, the exhortative nature of the passage: ἀναστροφῇ (1:15), ἀναστράφητε (1:17), where it is one of the key imperatives of the whole section), ἀναστροφῆς (1:18).[2]

In the above analysis of 1:3–25, it is very difficult indeed to be sure of what is really significant in the over-all pattern of words. It is, above all, the cumulative effect of many different elements of pattern and arrangement which is impressive.

Two conclusions come to mind. First, to be fruitful, such a method should go hand in hand with an examination of the meaning and content of the passage. We have here a sort of control which could prevent the discussion of structure ending up in a sterile and illusory playing with words.[3] Secondly, it would seem to this writer to be an extremely difficult task to determine the difference between the structure resulting from conscious art and the structure which emerges spontaneously when a writer of some imagination and intelligence applies himself with feeling to develop some theme. It would be instructive, for example, to see the interplay of inclusions, link-words, announcement of themes, verbal echoes in a passage written spontaneously by an imaginative but untutored writer. In other words, what are the criteria which would establish

---

[1] 1:15, καλέσαντα, 1:17, ἐπικαλεῖσθε; 1:14, 22, ὑπακοή; 1:15, 16, ἅγιος, 1:22, ἠγνικότες; 1:21, πιστούς-πίστιν; 1:17, 20, χρόνος; 1:18, φθαρτοῖς, 1:23, φθαρτῆς-ἀφθάρτου; 1:21, 24, δόξα.

[2] Chevallier, art. cit., pp. 136–37, continues his analysis of 2:1–10, which at the moment does not concern us.

[3] In the attempt of the present writer to present a plan for 1 Peter (op. cit., pp. 72–83), elements of literary structure as well as other indications of meaning were combined. It is true that in the middle section of the letter there seem to be fewer verbal indications of structure, but these few, taken with other indications, have their own value. Thus, 2:11 – 3:12, with the emphatic ἀγαπητοί at the beginning and with the concluding τὸ δὲ τέλος of 3:8 followed by an extensive scriptural citation is clearly a unit. The last section, it is admitted, presents some difficulties, particularly the precise place of 4:7–11, but at least it is clear that the doxology of 4:11 marks the end of a section and that 4:12–5:11 is a clearly defined unit.

such conscious art, the sort of "art consommée" which Chevallier finds in 1 Peter 1:1–2:10? Here we move in a very subjective order, where, at least up to the present moment, a great deal of the evidence is tentative and hypothetical.[1]

III

Let us now consider the eschatological meaning of our text, 1:3–25. In this treatment we will attempt to take into account not merely the structure of the passage discussed above, but the ideas which appear in the text. Thus we hope to build up some impression of what the author was trying to say.

As we have seen, this passage is a unit, divided into two sections (1:3–12; 1:13–25), the whole being bound together in various ways, and, in particular, by the chiastic use of expressions for time (1:5, 11, 17, 20), where the play between the time of this earthly life and the last times provides an eschatological setting. This is in keeping with the description of the readers in the opening address: "God's scattered people settled temporarily in Pontus . . ." We are led to expect the pilgrim themes of persecution and hope.

Nor have we long to wait. In the blessing with which the body of the letter and the first section of our text begin, this note is heard loudly and clearly: εἰς ἐλπίδα ζῶσαν. It comes out with the same insistence in the first emphatic imperative of the second section, ἐλπίσατε (1:13) and in the eschatological climax at the end of 1:21. As the first section of our text (1:3–12) develops, this theme is taken up in the idea of "an inheritance kept for you in heaven" (1:4), which recalls the promises of the Old Testament: "the land which the Lord will give you for an inheritance" (Deut. 15:4; 19:10). The thought then turns to the readers of the letter themselves. While their inheritance is in heaven, they are on earth, but they, in turn, are being kept safe "for a salvation which is ready to be revealed in the end-time" (1:5).

After the blessing of 1:3–5, the first phrase of the new development is ἐν ᾧ ἀγαλλιᾶσθε, where the exultation is that of eschatological joy.[2] This little section, 1:6–9, powerfully presents the contrast between the inevitable present distress of Christians, which for a short time will try their faith, and the glory to come at the revelation of Jesus Christ. This is

---

[1] For this reason, further study of the literary structure of 1 Peter may indeed prove to be an argument against Petrine authorship, but the two ends of the comparison, Peter's ability and the conscious art of the writer, would seem, as yet, too vaguely discerned to constitute a convincing proof.

[2] See Kelly, *op. cit.*, p. 53: "The verb 'exult' (*agalliasthai*) belongs to the vocabulary of the LXX and NT, in both often having a strongly eschatological flavour; it connotes the joy of the created order, and especially of God's chosen people, when He is revealed as Judge and Saviour." The verb is repeated in 1:8.

the condition of the pilgrim community: it does not reach its goal in spite of suffering, but it is precisely *through* its suffering that it is able to meet and know its crucified Lord and to be recognized by him at his final coming. In the writer's image, pure gold can only be produced and recognized when it emerges from the fire. In 1:8–9, the writer turns to the Christians' present life of faith and love, but the note of hope remains strong. Although they do not see the Lord, they exult with eschatological joy. Already they receive "the end of the faith, the salvation of souls."[1] Here future glory and the present life of faith are bound together. Christian experience is not sheer waiting in a void: it possesses already, in the obscurity of hope, what it will later fully possess in the splendour of the Lord's revelation.

The next small section, 1:10–12, looks back to the searching of the Old Testament prophets[2] into the coming grace of God. Here, of course, the Old Testament is seen through Christian eyes. "The Spirit of Christ" (understood as the pre-existent Christ) guided the prophets to discover something of his future sufferings and resurrection; but in this they were merely servants of future Christian believers, in whose time these events were to be proclaimed by the ministers of the gospel.[3] These mysteries of the Christian faith stand at the very centre of the created universe: "on them the angels look down with rapt attention".[3]

The theme of hope still runs through 1:10–12, only this time it is transposed into the past. God's plan in Christ is seen as a vast movement, beginning with "the Spirit of Christ" in the Old Testament, realized then in two stages, the proclamation of the death and resurrection of Jesus, and his final coming. So closely are the two stages bound together that the same terms can be used of both of them: $\sigma\omega\tau\eta\rho\iota\alpha$ (1:5, 9), $\dot{\alpha}\pi o\kappa\alpha\lambda\dot{\upsilon}\pi\tau\omega$ (1:5, 12). We have already seen above the structural importance of these two words in the thought of 1:3–12

The second section (1:13–25) of our text is an exhortation flowing from the statements of the first section (1:3–12). We would naturally expect such an exhortation to be directed to the present needs of the community, yet the emphasis remains firmly on hope.

The section begins: "Gird up therefore the loins of your mind." While the expression is a common one denoting readiness for action, in the context it probably does recall the Exodus event, in which the people of Israel eat the Passover with loins girded at the beginning of their long pilgrim experience. As we have seen, this section is punctuated by emphatic imperatives, the first of which is $\dot{\epsilon}\lambda\pi\dot{\iota}\sigma\alpha\tau\epsilon$, "take on an attitude of

---

[1] Note the special anthropology of the writer, so unlike that of Paul. There is, of course, no reference to the Greek soul/body distinction.

[2] Selwyn (*op. cit.*, p. 134) includes the prophets of the Christian community.

[3] See Selwyn, *op. cit.*, pp. 138–39; Spicq, *op. cit.*, pp. 57–58. A more common interpretation of modern commentators sees in this text the failure of the angels to have a glimpse of the realities of Christian faith.

hope" (1:13).[1] What they have to hope for is the grace "that is coming to you in the revelation of Jesus Christ". Here χάρις, normally used of present Christian life,[2] describes the final fulfilment. The attitude of hope requires that they be sober (νήφοντες). This injunction is part of regular New Testament eschatological exhortation.[3]

The next development centres around the following imperative, καὶ αὐτοὶ ἅγιοι . . . γενήθητε (1:15), but this holiness is not presented statically: it is a movement from the passions of their past ignorance in response to the call of a holy God (1:14–15).

In the next small section (1:17–21), the key word is the imperative ἀναστράφητε (1:17). Here we see that this holiness belongs to a people who are, at the moment, passing through the time of their "temporary stay", an expression which recalls the opening description of the letter's readers and anticipates the emphatic beginning of the next major section: "Beloved, I exhort you as pilgrims and immigrants to abstain from the fleshly lusts that war against the soul" (2:11). Thus, while God's holiness is eternal, the holiness to which he calls his people must be worked out in the struggle of a pilgrim existence.

The God whom they call "Father" is a God who judges according to each man's works (1:17). While the participle κρίνων is present, here it is used as an attribute of God. The reference is not to God's judgements in this earthly life, but, as is usual in the New Testament, to his final judgement. So the Christian, in his life of obedience and holiness looks forward with filial fear to the end.

The participle εἰδότες (1:18) gives further ground for obedience to this exhortation by recalling traditional catechetical teaching. The thought goes back to the liberation wrought through the blood of Christ, who in God's eternal plan was made manifest at the crucial stage in human history, ἐπ᾽ ἐσχάτου τῶν χρόνων. This important phrase recalls the καιρῷ ἐσχάτῳ of 1:5 and with other expressions of time in 1:11 and 1:17 helps to structure the whole text of 1:3–25. It covers in its meaning the whole span, a short one in the thought of 1 Peter, between the earthly life of Jesus and his last coming, and so the mind of the reader is once more turned to the final end.

With the δι᾽ ὑμᾶς at the end of 1:20, the writer moves from the ready-made catechetical section introduced by εἰδότες (1:18) to a more personal note. All that God has done in Christ is for them, the readers, who are faithful[4] to the God who raised Jesus from the dead and gave him glory. The term δόξα is a favourite one of 1 Peter, occurring altogether ten times.

---

[1] The sharpness of these imperatives is lost in most English translations, which, naturally enough, translate the accompanying participles also as imperatives.

[2] E.g., 1 Pet. 1:2, 10; 2:19; 3:7; 4:10; 5:10, 12.

[3] 1 Pet. 4:7; 5:8; 1 Thess. 5:6, 8; 2 Tim. 4:5.

[4] The reading πιστούς is to be preferred to πιστεύοντας both as *lectio difficilior* and as better attested.

While it often refers to the resurrection of Christ (1:11, 21; 4:13; 5:1), it refers also to the final glory of the Christian (1:7; 5:4); and, in fact, the two are expressly linked in 5:1, where the writer speaks of himself as "a partaker in the glory which is going to be revealed". Thus the reference to "glory" in 1:21 prepares the reader for the final stage of this section, which sums up all that has gone before: "so that your faith may also be your hope in God".

It is difficult to know whether the ὥστε of this clause expresses a consequence or an intention.[1] Much depends on the importance given to the phrase. If it is regarded as an emphatic summing up of the whole earlier section, then it should be seen to share the exhortative nature of the passage and so express an intention. If, on the contrary, it is closely united to and limited by the immediate context, merely a development of the preceding πιστούς, then one would more naturally understand it as a consequence.

Structurally, the phrase comes at the end of a development. The next section, 1:22–25, is governed by the imperative ἀγαπήσατε and, in any case, is marked off from the preceding section by the absence of any connecting particle. As we have seen, the whole of the passage we are considering (1:3–25) is divided into two larger sections (1:3–12 and 1:13–25). We have already indicated how the text, so far, is dominated by hope and eschatological expectation. But, apart from this, we have the express mention of hope at key points: at the beginning of the whole passage, εἰς ἐλπίδα ζῶσαν (1:3) and at the beginning of the second section, τελείως ἐλπίσατε (1:13). We are thus invited to see in the ἐλπίδα of 1:21 a recall and a summing up of all that has gone before. In this way, the ὥστε can best be understood as introducing an intention: "so that your faith may also be your hope in God".

It must be admitted that there is some tension in the structure. This, to my mind, really presents no difficulty, but provides rather a warning against an understanding of structure which is too mechanical. It is true, as we have seen earlier, that there is good reason for considering 1:13–25 as a unit in the greater whole of 1:3–25. This, however, does not mean that the four small sections which make up 1:3–25 are bound to one another with equal closeness. We have already noted the absence of any connecting particle at the beginning of 1:22. This, of itself, indicates a break in thought. But, in addition, in the small section 1:22–25, the writer is consciously or unconsciously influenced by the already traditional triad of faith, hope and love. He has already shown this at the beginning of the letter, where he has introduced them in the order of hope (1:3), faith (1:5) and love (1:8). Thus, although the thought of hope rather than that of love dominates all that precedes, it is natural that the passage should

---

[1] For a full treatment, see Selwyn, op. cit., pp. 147–48.

respect the traditional order and end with love. Hence the dominant imperative ἀγαπήσατε in the final sub-section, 1:22-25.[1]

It seems reasonable, then, to see in the ὥστε clause at the end of 1:21 a sort of climax to the whole passage. We start with a strong reference to hope in 1:3. The section, 1:3-12, develops along eschatological lines, but with references to faith in 1:5, 7, 8, 9. Another strong reference to hope in 1:13 sets the tone for the section, 1:13-21 (with 1:22-25 as a more loosely connected development). Again there is reference to faith, in 1:21. One is justified, then, in attaching great importance to the bringing together of faith and hope at this precise point in the text.

But now the question must be asked *how* we are to bring them together. The translation proposed in the title of this article takes ἐλπίδα as a predicate after the infinitive. This is against the more common view of translators and commentators, but is supported, among others, by R. Bultmann,[2] J. Moffatt,[3] R. Leconte.[4] Beare tends to favour it.[5]

There is no doubt that the sentence itself is grammatically open to both meanings: "so that your faith and your hope may be directed to God" or "so that your faith may also be your hope in God". The absence of the article before ἐλπίδα, together with the insertion of ὑμῶν after πίστιν would seem to favour slightly the second meaning, but certainly cannot be said to decide the issue. Again, in the third century Bodmer Papyrus VIII (P72), the article is repeated before ἐλπίδα, thus indicating that at this early date the former of the two meanings above was followed. But this papyrus shows an inclination to avoid the *lectio difficilior*. In the very same verse it reads πιστεύοντας which can best be understood as a faulty reading for the more difficult πιστούς. Similarly, the addition of the article before ἐλπίδα may well show that the scribe was unhappy with the unusual meaning (the second indicated above) which flowed from the original text and so adapted it to produce an acceptable, if pedestrian, result.

A number of commentators see some sort of climax in 1:21 and put the stress on εἰς θεόν. Yet this would be an extremely lame climax, since we find the phrase πιστοὺς εἰς θεόν a few words before. As we have seen, in the greater context of 1:13-21, the emphasis falls strongly on ἐλπίδα. And even in the more immediate context of 1:21, the thought moves from the faith of the readers to the resurrection and glorification of Jesus, which is associated, as we have seen, with the Christian's own hope of glory. Thus the thought of the writer could be expressed: "Yes, you are faithful to God, but, in the light of all that I have said from the beginning of this letter, in the light of the glory of Jesus which you are to share, this faith

[1] This break in the text is felt by a number of translators, who start a new paragraph at 1:22, e.g., NEB, JerB, Beare, *op. cit.*
[2] *TWNT*, VI, pp. 208-11.
[3] *The General Epistles* (London, 1928).
[4] *Les Épîtres catholiques* (Paris, 1953).
[5] *Op. cit.*, p. 104.

of yours must pass over into hope." Thus faith in God, implied in πιστοὺς εἰς θεόν, is taken up again in τὴν πίστιν ὑμῶν, not in a lame repetition but in a new development which worthily sums up the whole passage. Thus the text can grammatically bear this meaning; the context indicates it. Is it too strange to be adopted? It is true that faith and hope overlap in the thought of 1 Peter and, for that matter, in the New Testament generally; but they are not synonyms. In fact, the thought of our text is not so different from that of Rom. 15:13: "May the God of hope fill you in your believing with all joy and peace, so that, by the power of the Holy Spirit, you may overflow with hope."

I suggest that the author of 1 Peter be credited with a piece of effective writing, which reaches a fine climax in the composition of 1:21. Let us grant him a turn of phrase which is mildly original.[1]

We have still to deal with the last small section (1:22–25) of our text. At first sight, it seems to contribute little to its general eschatological theme. After the climax of 1:21, it fills in the traditional picture of Christian life by exhorting the readers to love. The earlier themes of holiness, obedience (1:22) and re-birth (1:23) are recalled, while the "corruptible seed" of 1:23 re-echoes the "corruptible things" of 1:18. The last phrase, τὸ ῥῆμα τὸ εὐαγγελισθὲν εἰς ὑμᾶς, recalls the εὐαγγελισαμένων of 1:12. This concentration of themes previously mentioned, together with the massive scriptural citation, suitably finishes the whole section, 1:3–25.

Yet, if this whole passage is read sensitively, some correspondence will be seen between the re-birth "to a living hope . . . to an inheritance which is incorruptible" (1:3–4) and the re-birth "not from corruptible seed but from incorruptible, through the living and abiding word of God" (1:23). In the first case, the inheritance in heaven is incorruptible; in the second case the seed is incorruptible, but the very terms, "re-born" and "seed", imply growth and development. The incorruptible seed, received through the proclamation of the gospel, is a beginning which leads to a full sharing of God's life, which, like his word, is abiding. This idea is expressly formulated at the beginning of the section, 2:1–10, which, as we have seen, is structurally linked with 1:3–25: "As new-born babes, crave the undeceitful milk of the word, so that by it you may grow up to salvation" (2:2). Thus the love which is commended in 1:22–25 shows itself in a new life which grows from birth towards God. Set in this passing world, which withers away like grass, it is the life of Christian hope.

---

[1] He can be original; 3:19–21 is certainly a very original text.

CHAPTER XVIII

HOW CHRISTIAN IS THE BOOK OF REVELATION?

G. R. Beasley-Murray

Marcion's answer to the question would have been plain, even if we had not possessed Tertullian's record of his rejection of the book: "Not Christian at all, far too Jewish!" That answer has been echoed down the centuries by many who would have no desire to be linked with Marcion in any way. Apart from the effect of Dionysius' rejection of the apostolic authorship of the Revelation, its uncertain place in the canon of the New Testament and the ambivalent attitude of many Christians to it have in no small measure been due to the sheer obscurity of the book and the difficulty of discovering its specifically Christian message. It is well known that Luther found the Revelation offensive; he judged it as neither apostolic nor prophetic, for he could not find "Christ" in it – i.e. Christ in the Gospel. Calvin was also dubious as to its worth, and passed over it in eloquent silence in his exposition of the New Testament.

Modern writers frequently experience the same difficulty as Luther, and the charge of the Jewish character of its outlook is often made. This may be illustrated in C. H. Dodd's comments on the book in his early work *The Apostolic Preaching and its Developments*. Dodd regarded the book as manifesting a revived Jewish eschatology; in his view its excessive emphasis on the future has the effect of relegating to a secondary place the distinctive elements of the Gospel, namely the finished work of Christ and the sense of living in the divine presence here and now. He further asserted that its conception of the character of God and of Christ falls below the level not only of the teaching of Jesus but of much of the Old Testament. "The God of the Apocalypse can hardly be recognized as the Father of our Lord Jesus Christ, nor has the fierce Messiah, whose warriors ride in blood up to their horses' bridles, many traits that would recall him of whom the primitive kerygma proclaimed that he went about doing good and healing all who were oppressed by the devil".[1]

Rudolf Bultmann maintains a similar viewpoint. He describes the Christianity of Revelation as a "weakly Christianized Judaism", wherein the significance of Christ is practically limited to his giving assurance to the eschatological hope. He writes:

[1] *Op. cit.*, pp. 40 f.

The peculiar "between-ness" of Christian existence has not been grasped. In fact, not even in the chronological sense does the present possess the character of an interval, because the author does not reflect about the past which in Christ has been brought to its end and out of which believers have been transplanted into a new beginning. Hence the present is understood in a way not basically different from the understanding of it in the Jewish apocalypses: namely as a time of temporariness, of waiting. The clear symptom of this understanding is the fact that *pistis* is essentially conceived as "endurance," as in Judiasm.[1]

The chief objections to the book therefore relate to the allegedly sub-Christian nature of its Christology, its eschatology and its doctrine of God, and the combination of all three is believed to result in an obscuring of the apostolic gospel which lies at the heart of the New Testament. These are serious charges to make. If they are true we ought presumably to imitate Luther's courage, and insist that the book be placed in a kind of New Testament apocrypha, and warn Christian people of its lack of Gospel truth. The issue is sufficiently important to warrant an examination of such elements of the text as can shed light on it. In this article we can do no more than give pointers to the direction which the exegete must take.

Before we start, however, it may be worth recalling the pilgrimage of R. H. Charles in this field. His Jowett lectures on eschatology were based on a first-hand investigation of the eschatological teaching contained in the Biblical, apocryphal and pseudepigraphical writings of the Jews. In the first edition of the lectures, published in 1899, he anticipated Dodd and Bultmann by characterizing the thought of the Revelation as "unadulterated Judaism" (p. 347). In the second edition of the lectures, 1913, that remark was expurgated, although Charles still considered that the author's attitude to the world reflects the temper of Judaism rather than of Christianity (p. 403). In 1920 he brought twenty five years of study of the Revelation to a conclusion in the issue of his great commentary on the Book of Revelation; in the introduction he resists the view of scholars who affirm the Jewish character of John's doctrine of God, and affirms, "To draw such a conclusion betrays a total misapprehension of the question at issue" (vol. 1. p. cix), and time and again he extols the virtues of the book which he has now come to regard as in some respects the greatest in the New Testament. Charles's experience suggests that first impressions as to the teaching of the Revelation may require revision on patient investigation into the book itself.

One observation, however trite it may appear to the scholar, should be made at the outset, namely the necessity to distinguish between the form and content of a work like the Book of Revelation. In form, as all know, the Revelation is one with the Jewish apocalypses which proliferated in the

---

[1] *Theology of the New Testament*, vol. II, London 1955, p. 175.

last two centuries B.C. and the first century A.D. These works were rooted in the thought of the Old Testament prophets, and followed in the wake of their great exemplar, the Book of Daniel. Their authors took over the poetic and symbolic language of the prophets, and developed to a degree unknown before the cartoon method of presenting religious ideas. This is particularly well seen in the seventh chapter of Daniel, but perhaps no author presented his teaching with such luxuriant imagery and with such a profusion of symbolism as the prophet who wrote the Revelation. So far as form is concerned, John is the apocalyptist par excellence. The point at issue however is not John's expertise in the employment of religious cartoons, but what he teaches through them.

This may be illustrated by comparing two characteristic apocalyptic passages, wherein the deliverance of the Messiah is portrayed under the unusual image of the intervention of the Lamb; the one comes from the Testaments of the Twelve Patriarchs and the other from the Revelation. The Testament of Joseph ch. 19 presents the highly original doctrine of the Testaments concerning the Messiahs, the one from Aaron and the other from Judah, in the following passage:

"Hear ye the vision which I saw. I saw twelve harts feeding. And nine of them were dispersed. Now the three were preserved, but on the following day they also were dispersed. And I saw that the three harts became three lambs, and they cried to the Lord, and he brought them forth into a flourishing and well-watered place, yea he brought them out of darkness into light. And there they cried unto the Lord until they gathered unto them the nine harts, and they became as twelve sheep, and after a little time they increased and became many flocks.

And after these things I saw, and behold twelve bulls were suckling one cow, which produced a sea of milk, and there drank thereof twelve flocks and innumerable herds . . .

And I saw in the midst of the horns . . . a lamb, and on his right was as it were a lion; and all the beasts and all the reptiles rushed against him, and the lamb overcame them and destroyed them.

And the bulls rejoiced because of him, and the cow and the harts exulted together with them.

And these things must come to pass in their season. And do ye, my children, honour Levi and Judah, for from them shall arise the salvation of Israel."

Once it is recognized that the harts are changed into lambs, and the lambs into bulls, and that all of them represent the people of God, the meaning of the passage becomes tolerably clear: Israel is surrounded and attacked by the nations, but a Lamb will arise from the flock of God and will overcome and destroy the mighty nations; so the salvation of Israel will come, and God's people will rejoice in the peace of his kingdom. It is notable that this deliverance, featuring the exercise of messianic power over the enemies of God's people, is wrought by the Lamb and not by the Lion. Self-evidently the deliverance lies in the future.

In Revelation ch. 5 we are presented with another apocalyptic picture of the deliverance of the Messiah, portrayed as the Lamb. God on his throne holds in his hand a scroll written within and without and sealed with seven seals; the scroll represents either the common doubly-inscribed contract, here signifying God's covenant promise of the kingdom, or a testament declaring his will to bestow the kingdom to mankind (the ultimate meaning is virtually the same). No one in the universe, however, can bear to look upon the scroll, or take it and open it. But an elder says, "Weep not; lo, the lion of the tribe of Judah, the Root of David, has conquered, so that he can open the scroll and its seven seals".

> "And between the throne and the four living creatures and among the elders, I saw a Lamb standing, as though it had been slain, with seven horns and with seven eyes, which are the seven spirits of God sent out into all the earth; and he went and took the scroll from the right hand of him who was seated on the throne . . .
>
> And they sang a new song, saying,
> Worthy art thou to take the scroll and to open its seals,
> for thou wast slain and by thy blood didst ransom men to God
> from every tribe and tongue and people and nation,
> and hast made them a kingdom and priests to our God,
> and they shall reign on earth . . .".

The innumerable angels in heaven join in offering worship to the Lamb who was slain, and finally every creature in the universe ascribes glory and honour and power to God and the Lamb.

We will ignore the comparative banality of the employment of the imagery in the Testament of Joseph, as against the majesty of the picture in Revelation 5, and concentrate on the meaning of the two passages. The Jewish document reproduces the traditional expectation of Israel's deliverance from its enemies and its felicity in the kingdom of God. The unusual element in it is the idea that God will send two Messiahs for this purpose, the kingly Messiah from Judah, fittingly represented by the Lion, and the priestly Messiah from Aaron, depicted as the Lamb. But the deliverance comes in the orthodox way, i.e. by conquest in battle, for the Messiah Lamb is a mighty warrior. His representation as a Lamb has nothing to do with sacrifice, but with his origin as the young champion of the flock of God. He will be thought of as a strong, horned ram.

In the Revelation the figures of Lion and Lamb are fused together; the Christ is the Lion of Judah, the Root of David and the Lamb of God. The Jewish background is assumed, so there is no intention of conveying a paradox in the picture. This is emphasised in the statement that the Lamb has "seven horns and seven eyes". In the Old Testament horns represent strength (Deut. 33:17) and royalty (Dan. 7:7). Seven horns will signify immense strength, the fulness of might. As in the Testaments, the Lamb is a horned ram, and so a powerful fighter. Similarly seven eyes would originally have represented fulness of knowledge, or omniscience, as in Zech. 4:10; John however identifies them with the seven spirits of God sent out into all the earth; i.e. they represent for him the energies of the sevenfold Spirit loosed into the world. This reinterpretation has been made possible because an event unprecedented and unprovided for in Jewish apocalyptic has taken place: the Lamb stands "as though it had been slain", i.e. it has been slaughtered, but lives again. In view of the constant appearance of the exodus typology in the Book of Revelation it is almost certain that John wants his readers to recognize in the Messiah-Lamb God's passover Lamb (in 5:9 the Lamb has "ransomed" men to God, i.e. freed them for life in the fellowship and service of God, as in the doxology of 1:5). The warrior Lamb thus has "conquered" through his accepting the role of the sacrificed passover Lamb, and so made possible a second exodus. It is in consequence of his death and resurrection that he has sent into the world the seven Spirits of God. Here we have passed over from the traditional Messiah of prophetic and apocalyptic hope to the crucified and risen Redeemer of the new covenant.

The significance of this transformation cannot be exaggerated. It is more than the change of an apocalyptic figure into a Christian symbol for the Saviour. The very nature of salvation and of eschatology has been transformed in this change of concept of the Messiah. We are told that by his death and resurrection the Lamb has "conquered", and that through his sacrifice he has "ransomed men for God and . . . made them a kingdom and priests to God". The long awaited deliverance that initiates the new age has then been achieved. The new exodus has come to pass. And the Christ Redeemer, unlike Moses, whom the Jews viewed as the first Redeemer, is not merely on the march to the promised land; he has entered upon the inheritance and ascended the throne prepared for him by God. Accordingly in Rev. 5:12 all heaven ascribes to the Lamb the honours due to the divine King (the worship given to the Lamb in 5:12 is given in terms almost identical to that given to God in 7:12). The "worth" ascribed to the Lamb in 5:12 does not relate to a future gift of sovereignty, but to that which he has already "received". We must take it therefore that the handing to the Lamb of the scroll of the kingdom in v. 7 is in virtue of the victory which he has won in his death and resurrection, and that it marks his assumption of authority. Only so can we comprehend the adoration which is rendered to him in the subsequent hymns. The purport of the vision of the Lamb in Revelation 5 therefore is to declare that *in the redemptive acts of the Lamb of God the turn of the ages has taken place*. The Christ has commenced his rule, and he incorporates his people into his royal priesthood. Heaven has acclaimed his sovereignty already, but the rest of creation has yet to render the acknowledgement due to the Lamb, much as in the early Christian hymn cited in Phil. 2:6 ff. The later visions of the Revelation make it evident that a special exercise of the sovereignty of the Lamb must take place before all rebellion is ended and the universe owns its Lord; but this does not represent a further elevation of the Lamb to a position of exaltation not yet accorded to him, it is the consequence of the central action described in the vision.

The same understanding of the significance of Christ's redemptive action lies at the heart of John's version of the Redeemer myth in ch. 12. Whereas the story taken over by John depicts the overthrow of the Devil as due to his ejection from heaven by Michael and his angels, John's addition in v. 11 shows that the conquest is in reality due to the sacrifice of Christ. The event is celebrated in the song of v. 10: "Now the salvation and the power and the kingdom of our God and the authority of his Christ have come, for the accuser of our brethren has been thrown down . . .". The nature of John's sources however does not allow him to present the fulness of meaning entailed in this song as he has done in ch. 5. He develops the story of the Dragon's persecution of the messianic community, and the Church's sufferings under the Antichrist, culminating in an account of the messianic judgements and the parousia of the Son of Man (chs. 13–14). The picture in ch. 5 is more self-contained. It ignores the processes which have to be worked out in history, and so the passage of time between the resurrection and the parousia, and concentrates all attention on the Lamb. The result of this is to present the action of Christ in redemption and establishing the kingdom as an indivisible event. Since the song of vv. 9 f. has in view the death and resurrection of Christ, and the adoration of creation in v. 13 the outcome of history in the rule and glory of God and the Lamb (21:22 ff., 22:1 ff.), we must take it that the vision of ch. 5 takes into a single sweep the whole action of God in Christ from the incarnation to the end of the parousia in the new creation. This is a different way of representing the "now" and the "not yet" of the kingdom of God, such as we find in Paul and even in Jesus, but it embraces the great moments of God's saving sovereignty in a unity, such as perhaps is natural when one enters heaven's door (4:1) and views history *sub specie aeternitatis*. The idea therefore that the prophet John has no understanding of the significance of the present, or of the Gospel facts of Christ's death and resurrection, is irreconcilable with the meaning of his central vision in ch. 5. To my knowledge there is no analogy in all Jewish apocalyptic literature to the eschatological teaching of Revelation 5, and for that there is a simple reason: the vision is an exposition of the Gospel of the crucified and risen Christ such as only a Christian prophet can give.

Strange as it may seem, it is in this context that John's millennial teaching falls to be considered. That it has parallels in contemporary Judaism is well known, though the complexity and variety of that teaching is seldom appreciated. The thousand years duration of the kingdom of Christ is probably rooted in Jewish speculation, but it is equally likely that for John the significance of the thousand years lies not in its measurement of time, but in its characterizing the kingdom of Christ as the sabbath of the week of history, so fulfilling the type of the kingdom in the sabbath of creation.[1] The Biblical origin of the concept will have been seen by John in the prophecies of Ezekiel 36–39, for the pattern of these prophecies seems to have determined the presentation of his visions of the kingdom in chs. 20–22. To what extent his thought may have been determined by traditions of the teaching of Jesus we cannot possibly know, but John can hardly have been ignorant of the Lord's Prayer, with its burden that the kingdom of God should come "on earth as it is in heaven", and the beatitudes, wherein blessing is pronounced on the meek, who will inherit the earth, and on those who hunger and thirst to see right prevail, whose desire will be satisfied. Above all however there lies at the heart of John's doctrine of redemption the conviction that in the life, death and resurrection of Christ the turn of the ages took place, so that in and through the work of Jesus as the Christ the kingdom promised through the prophets came among men. John was led to believe, through the Scriptures and the prophetic understanding of the word and work of Christ, that the kingdom which came in grace and power among men through Jesus Christ, thereby determining the course of history and of the universe itself, shall have a glorious revelation *in history* by the intervention of Christ at his parousia. That same kingdom of grace and glory will reach its consummation in the transcendent order of the new creation. Through all times it is the one sovereign act of God in Christ which manifests itself among men. Whatever debt this eschatology owes to Jewish apocalyptic, it can hardly be denied that it is fundamentally a christologically determined eschatology.

The like is true of John's view of the City of God. There are various hints in Revelation 20–22, above all in 20:9, that the City which descends from heaven to earth is manifest in the kingdom of Christ and continues into the new creation. Was John familiar with the idea, prominent in Hebrews (12:22 ff.) and known to Paul (Gal. 4:26), that the Jerusalem which is above is our City even now, and that it vitally affects the life and worship of the Church of Christ in this time? We cannot tell, but it should not appear alien to us to contemplate that that same City should become the determinative factor in the story of man, as represented in the highly pictorial fashion of Revelation 21–22. There is not a line of John's description of the City of God which is not capable of realization in

[1] For the idea of the world week, and the relation of the kingdom of God thereto, see Enoch 32–33 and the Epistle of Barnabas ch. 15. On the various uses made of this idea in Rabbinical literature, and other speculations regarding the length of the messianic kingdom, see Strack-Billerbeck's *Kommentar zum Neuen Testament aus Talmud und Midrasch*, München 922, vol. III, pp. 824 ff.

measure within history, although its perfect expression requires the transcendent order, as John makes plain. Whether in this or any other order, it is Christ alone who brings the City of God to man, for the City is the context of man's existence under the divine sovereignty. To characterize such teaching as "Jewish", in a pejorative sense, is difficult to comprehend; undoubtedly it is rooted in the teaching of the Old Testament prophets, but it embraces also the hopes of mankind as known in John's day and voiced in ours, and it partakes of that kind of fulfilment in Christ which is the hall mark of New Testament Christianity.

Our main concern thus far has been the eschatology of Revelation. But the brief consideration we gave to the vision of Revelation 5 shows how closely interrelated are the three areas of eschatology, christology and the doctrine of God in the Revelation. The doctrine of Christ assumed in ch. 5 is clearly very lofty. Worship is offered to the Lamb such as belongs alone to God. And this is characteristic of the whole book. The risen Lord is described in the opening vision in terms reminiscent of the Ancient of Days and of his angel in the Book of Daniel (chs. 7 and 10). Christ is confessed as Alpha and Omega (22:13), as is God also (1:8). The implications of this claim are seen in the presentation of Christ as mediator of creation (3:14), as he is of redemption (ch. 5) and of the final kingdom (19:11 ff.). The kingdom which is to come is "the kingdom of our Lord and of his Christ" (11:15); in the closing vision of the heavenly City God and the Lamb are united as the Lord of the kingdom and the source of its blessedness (see especially 22:1 ff.). The unity of God and his Christ is thus consistently assured.

It is similarly evident that the doctrine of God in the Revelation cannot rightly be taken by itself, but should be viewed in the light of the Christology, soteriology and eschatology presented in the book. This has long been recognized, and it is seen with all clarity in the two-fold vision of chs. 4-5, for ch. 5 is not an independent vision. The two chapters together show us the God of creation as the God of redemption, accomplishing his sovereign and gracious will through the crucified and risen Christ. And the same holds good of the whole work. It is God in Christ who delivers mankind, and it is God in Christ who judges mankind. In the Revelation the concept of God as Father is exclusively reserved to express his relation to Christ. We are therefore inevitably led to perceive that God is revealed in the acts of Christ, and that Christ is the revelation of the Father. As is the Christ, so is the Father, as the Father so the Christ.

In Dodd's view, however, the God and the Christ of Revelation bear little resemblance to the God and Christ of the rest of the New Testament. Is that so? We have already seen how little appreciated is John's presentation of soteriology and eschatology in ch. 5. We are prepared to find that the same may apply elsewhere. Some years ago I received dental treatment at the hands of a dentist who was a mild and kindly Seventh

Day Adventist. While plying me with the tools of his trade he regaled me with some thoughts on the Book of Revelation, hardly characteristic of his denomination. "Of course, we know", he said, "that all that blood and thunder and lightning in the Book of Revelation was written to scare the wits out of sinners, but I don't agree with that sort of approach to people nowadays". Reclining in his chair and suitably gagged while under attack from the dentist, I was scarcely in a position to comment on his views. Is it not clear, however, that the Revelation was written not to terrify sinners, but to encourage Christians to persist in faith and win their inheritance? Inasmuch as the book obliges Christians to confess their faith, as well as hold on to it, it has in view the hope that men of all kinds should enter the City of God and not suffer the fate of the City of Antichrist.

In relation to John's presentation of the judgements of God, I have long been convinced that his method of composition has led many of his readers to misunderstand his visions. The three series of messianic judgements, depicted under the imagery of the seals, trumpets and bowls, are intended to portray from three different aspects a single, short period of judgement in history. Many readers, failing to recognize the parallelism, have received the impression that John views the course of history as an apparently endless succession of meaningless and cruel judgements. They have similarly failed to perceive that this brief, but fearful period of history is viewed as a repetition of Israel's experience in Egypt: the Antichrist is another Pharaoh who resists God and oppresses his people, hence he calls down on himself and on those aligned with him judgements like the plagues of Egypt. As in the Book of Exodus, so in the Revelation: the crucial event is not the plagues, but the redemption which opens up the way to the new world.

If the question be asked whether a book can be Christian in which the judgement of God prominently features, comparison must be made with the rest of the writings of the New Testament. It is easy, and tempting, to view the synoptic gospels in a generalised way and assume that Jesus spoke words of love alone and not of judgement; but that is to ignore so much of what Jesus said as to distort what remains.[1] The Sermon on the Mount begins with beatitudes of the kingdom and concludes with a parable of judgement. That balance of grace and judgement in the proclamation of the kingdom is characteristic of the teaching of Jesus.[2] It is equally observable in the Fourth Gospel, wherein the cross is viewed in

---

[1] For an example of what happens when the attempt is made to eliminate from the teaching of Jesus all reference to judgement see the book, *The Lord of Thought*, by Lily Dougall, and C. W. Emmet, London 1922. The procedures involved are, in my judgement, unscientific, and the end result remote from the reality which is interpreted.

[2] See e.g. Mt.8:11 f.; 11:5–24; 12:28–32, 38–42; 13:10–17, 24–30, 47 ff; 18:1–9; 25:1–13, 14–30, 31–46.

terms of judgement, as truly as in the Revelation.[1] The representations of judgement in the Epistles of the New Testament are too numerous to warrant mention. What of the Revelation? It should be admitted at once that its emphasis on judgement is more intense and prolonged than in any other work in the New Testament. That may have been due less to a divergence between John's theology and that of other New Testament writers than to his situation and the prospect which he believed the Church of his time faced. John contemplated a world giving its allegiance to the Antichrist and declaring war to the death on the Church. This he interpreted as the work of evil powers in an endeavour to make wickedness triumph in the world and so frustrate God's good purpose for it. For the "destroyers of the earth" (11:18), who debased themselves to the likeness of the devil whom they served (22:15), John foresaw annihilating judgement, unless they repented and listened to the eternal gospel (14:6 f.). Accordingly be applied the teaching of the Church's prophetic tradition to the situation as he saw it unfolding. It is significant that where Paul deals with the subject of apostasy under the Antichrist he too adduces elements of the prophetic tradition and speaks of judgement from heaven in unusually severe terms (2 Thess. 2:1-17).

It was the conviction of H. B. Swete that John's work is a revelation of the "severity of God" rendered necessary by the nature of the times, and that it forms a needful complement to the revelation of God in the Gospel and the Epistles.[2] The corollary of that is the desirability of reading the Revelation in conjunction with the rest of the New Testament, and the remainder of the New Testament along with Revelation, in order to secure a balanced view of the Christian faith. This, of course, is not unusual. The Synoptic Gospels without the Fourth Gospel would be wanting, and the Fourth Gospel without the Synoptics would be misleading. The Epistles require supplementing by the Gospels, and the Gospels by the Epistles if we are to gain a broad understanding of the New Testament revelation. So with regard to the last book of the Bible: if it may be viewed as the crown of Biblical eschatology, it requires to be read in conjunction with the books which preceded it. And they are incomplete without it.

[1] Cf. Jn. 12:31 f. with Rev. 12:10, and Jn. 3:16-21.
[2] *The Apocalypse of St. John*, London 3rd ed. 1909, p.clx.

CHAPTER XIX

APOCALYPTIC AND NEW TESTAMENT THEOLOGY

GEORGE ELDON LADD

W E ARE WITNESSING A RENAISSANCE OF INTEREST IN APOCALYPTIC literature and its theology. A little over a decade ago, one of Germany's most influential New Testament scholars, Ernst Käsemann, published an essay entitled "The Beginnings of Christian Theology".[1] Käsemann bases his argument on a form-critical analysis of the Gospel of Matthew and posits a theological movement after Easter in which the primitive Jewish Christians interpreted the meaning of Jesus' resurrection in terms of Jewish apocalyptic. Jesus was not an apocalyptist; he preached the "immediate nearness of God". Furthermore, the preaching of Jesus cannot really be described as theology. Primitive Jewish-Christian apocalyptic thus became "the mother of all Christian theology".[2] "The heart of primitive Christian apocalyptic ... is the enthronement of God and of his Christ as the eschatological Son of Man".[3] "Its central motif was the hope of the epiphany of the Son of Man coming to his enthronement; and it is a question whether Christian theology can ever make do, or be legitimate, without this motif which arose from the experience of Easter and determined the Easter faith".[4]

Käsemann's essay at once provoked a vigorous reaction from his German colleagues, particularly Ebeling and Fuchs. These essays, together with contributions by H. D. Betz, Frank M. Cross, David Freedman, and Robert W. Funk, were published together as volume 6 of the *Journal for Theology and Church* under the title "Apocalypticism".[5] In his essay, Freedman goes so far as to say, "The discovery and subsequent demonstration that the controlling factor in the literature of the New Testament is apocalyptic" is one of the developments of modern scholarship.[6] Käsemann's essay provoked a searching reaction from Wayne G. Rollins[7] who argues that the origins of Christian theology are much more complex than Käsemann suggests, and that apocalyptic was only one of several

---

[1] "Die Anfänge christlicher Theologie," *ZThK* 57 (1960), pp. 162–85. Published in English in *Journal for Theology and Church* 6, Robert W. Funk, ed. (New York, 1969), pp. 17–46. References are to the English Translation.
[2] *Ibid.*, p. 40.   [3] *Ibid.*, p. 43.   [4] *Ibid.*, p. 46.   [5] See n. 1.   [6] *Ibid.*, p. 167.
[7] "The New Testament and Apocalyptic," *NTS* 17 (1971), pp. 454–76.

influences forming early theology. Rollins also lists a number of important contrasts between early Christian theology and Jewish apocalypticism which set the former apart.

Renewed interest in apocalyptic has been expressed not only by New Testament scholars but also by the systematic theologian, Wolfhart Pannenberg. In obvious reaction to the prevailing existentialist theology, Pannenberg has argued that revelation occurs in history. It takes place indirectly and partially in the events of history, and fully in the whole of history as that whole is embodied in the end of history. Pannenberg discovers the full revelation in the eschatological event of the resurrection of the dead which can be understood only in the context of Jewish apocalyptic. The event of the resurrection has already occurred proleptically in the resurrection of Jesus.[1] Thus apocalyptic is made the vehicle for the understanding of revelation.

Pannenberg's thesis has been severely criticized by William R. Murdock who points out that Jewish apocalyptic sees no revelation in history. Essential to apocalyptic is the doctrine of the two aeons or ages. The future age is not the fulfilment of history but the end of history. For this reason, Murdock feels that Pannenberg has not caught the genius of apocalyptic.[2]

The growing interest in apocalyptic in America is illustrated by the fact that an entire issue of *Interpretation* was devoted to four essays on this subject.[3] William A. Beardslee first surveys the main characteristics of apocalyptic and then discusses the role apocalyptic thinking plays in the thought of Schweitzer, Buri, Käsemann, Pannenberg, and Altizer. Beardslee points out that while a renewed historical study of apocalyptic is now getting under way, there remain many unsolved problems.

Amos N. Wilder discusses the "Rhetoric of Ancient and Modern Apocalyptic". Paul D. Hanson writes on "Old Testament Apocalyptic Re-examined", in which he argues that Jewish apocalyptic has its roots in Old Testament prophecy.[4]

The issue concludes with a statement by a systematic theologian, Carl E. Braaten, "The Significance of Apocalypticism for Systematic Theology". He insists that "there is no unapocalyptic Jesus",[5] and argues that we must "cheerfully . . . acknowledge the apocalypticism of Jesus and . . . make it

[1] The work of Pannenberg and his co-labourers was published under the title *Offenbarung als Geschichte* (Göttingen, 1961), and translated as *Revelation as History* (London, 1968).

[2] See "History and Revelation in Jewish Apocalyptic," *Interp* 21 (1967), pp. 167–87. Murdock arbitrarily distinguishes between the eschaton and the age to come, the eschaton being the goal of history while the age to come lies beyond the end of history.

[3] See *Interp* 25 (1971), 419–99.

[4] This position is also held in essays by Cross and Freedman while Murdock holds that apocalyptic dualism and eschatology "together . . . formed the core of Zoroastrianism, and they were taken up together by apocalypticism under Iranian influence." (*Interp* 21 (1967), p. 174).

[5] *Interp* 25 (1971), p. 480.

the point of departure for systematic theology today".[1] Braaten sees the fundamental element in apocalyptic to be its doctrine of the two ages, and he insists that a Christian interpretation of history is impossible without the dualistic element in apocalyptic, namely, the dialectical differentiation of all reality into this present evil age and the new world of promise to come. Here are embodied the principles of negation and transcendence: negation of the structures of this present evil age by the transcendent power of the age to come. Braaten has now brilliantly worked out this thesis in his book, *Christ and Counter-Christ*.[2]

The revival of interest in apocalyptic in Germany is accentuated by the recent book by Klaus Koch, *Ratlos vor der Apokalyptik*, translated into English with the title *The Rediscovery of Apocalyptic*.[3] Koch surveys the situation in England as well as in Germany and bemoans the numerous efforts to "save Jesus from apocalyptic". He goes on to show that the problem of apocalyptic is the problem of Jesus. Koch insists that apocalyptic is one of the main links that joins together the two Testaments, and that Jesus must be understood against the background of apocalyptic.

Finally, the renewed interest in apocalyptic is reflected in the most recent publication of the one whom we honor in these essays: *Apocalyptic*.[4] This little book contains an analysis of the various characteristics of apocalyptic, both literary and theological, and concludes with a discussion of apocalyptic and the New Testament, particularly Mark 13 and the Revelation. Morris agrees that apocalyptic contributed something to Christianity, but he thinks that it is going too far to say that apocalyptic was the parent of the Christian faith.

> The Christian movement has its affinities with the apocalyptic movement. The language of the apocalyptists has influenced that of the Christians. The characteristic expressions of the Gospels often seem to receive more emphasis in apocalyptic than they do, for example, in the Old Testament.[5]

Morris insists that Jesus himself was not an apocalyptist,[6] and he emphasizes the fact that the characteristic literary form of Christianity was the gospel and not the apocalypse.[7]

In his discussion of dualism, Professor Morris seems to admit a larger debt to apocalyptic than his conclusion would allow. He first sketches the apocalyptic doctrine of the two ages – this age and the age to come. The present age is under the control of demonic spirits; it is full of evil and hopeless. All hope is posited in the age to come which will be the age of eternal life and immortality. Although Morris does not stress the point, this age will be brought to its end and the new age inaugurated by a

---

[1] *Ibid.*, p. 482.   [2] Philadelphia, 1972.
[3] *Studies in Biblical Theology*, Second Series, 22 (London, 1972).
[4] Grand Rapids, 1972.
[5] Leon Morris, *Apocalyptic*, p. 73.
[6] *Ibid.*, p. 86.   [7] *Ibid.*, p. 83.

cosmic act of God, sometimes in the person of a heavenly Messiah who comes to raise the dead and judge the wicked. In evaluation of this eschatological dualism, Morris comments, "To this day we are indebted to the apocalyptists for making this point so firmly that it has become an integral part of subsequent religion".[1]

This is a judgement with which I heartily agree, and in this essay I wish to exploit it and to expound its relevance for New Testament theology. If I seem to differ with Professor Morris, the difference is in emphasis, not in substance.

We must first note the important role eschatological dualism plays in apocalyptic thought. The fully developed idiom does not appear in Jewish literature until the last years of the first century A.D. "The Most High has made not one age but two" (IV Ez. 7:50). "The Day of Judgement shall be the end of this age and the beginning of the eternal age that is to come" (IV Ez. 7:113). "This age the Most High has made for many, but the age to come for few" (IV Ez. 8:1).[2] However, the terminology is implicit in Enoch: "The age shall be consummated" (En. 16:1); "this world of unrighteousness" (En. 48:7); "he proclaims unto thee peace in the name of the world to come" (En. 71:15). As Ringgren says, "Der Gedanke ist in den ältesten Apokalypsen nicht ausdrücklich formuliert, aber die Vorstellung steht deutlich im Hintergrund".[3]

The idea, which precedes the formulation of the idiom, is (to the present author) clearly rooted in the Old Testament prophetic hope.[4] The prophets continually look for a new redeemed order, which will be established by divine intervention, not by forces arising from within history. The Day of the Lord was conceived "as the time of the divine inbreaking into history in spectacular fashion. While God was believed to be always active on the plane of history, using nations and men to fulfil his ends, the Day of the Lord was thought of as a day of more direct and clearly manifest action". The prophetic predictions "were of a future not causally linked with the present".[5] The degree of continuity and discontinuity between the two orders is differently expressed by different prophets; but Isaiah expresses the hope of a new order in terms of new heavens and a new earth (Isa. 65:17; 66:22).

"This eschatological dualism is the essential characteristic of Apocalyptic

---

[1] *Ibid.*, p. 49. He quotes with approval the words of R. Meyer in *TDNT* VI, p. 827, "The idea of two world epochs ... was designed to outlast apocalyptic and become an enduring principle of faith."

[2] See also 2 Bar. 14:13; 15:7; Pirke Aboth 4:1, 21, 22; 6:4, 7. Volz cites a possible reference to Hillel (ca. 30 B.C.), but this is not certain. See P. Volz, *Die Eschatologie der jüdischen Gemeinde* (Tübingen, 1934), p. 65. For the whole subject, see Wm. Bousset, *Die Religion des Judentums im späthellenistischen Zeitalter* (Tübingen, 1926), pp. 243–49.

[3] H. Ringgren, "Apokalyptik," *RGG*³I, col. 465.

[4] This point is argued in detail in the author's volume, *The Presence of the Future* (Grand Rapids, 1973), chap. 2. See also S. Mowinckel, *He That Cometh* (Oxford, 1956), p. 265.

[5] H. H. Rowley, *The Growth of the Old Testament* (London, 1950), p. 179.

so far as its contents are concerned".[1] Ringgren devotes a third of his article on "Jüdische Apokalyptik" in the last edition of Die Religion in Geschichte und Gegenwart to a discussion of this dualism as the most essential feature of apocalyptic.[2] Von Rad says, "The characteristic of apocalyptic theology is its eschatological dualism, the clear-cut differentiation of two aeons, the present one and the one to come".[3]

The debt of the New Testament to Jewish apocalyptic has been expounded most vividly by Oscar Cullmann in his book Christ and Time.[4] Cullmann proves that the New Testament Gospel has as its background the Jewish concept which conceives of redemption taking place on a linear time line which divides time into the two ages: the present age and the coming age. For Judaism, the mid-point in the time line is the transition point from the present age to the future. Cullmann argues that the difference between Christianity and Judaism is that Christianity sees the mid-point no longer at the end of this age but in the historical mission of Jesus.

It is difficult to see how anyone can successfully challenge this position. The two-age terminology appears in every stratum of the Gospel tradition except Q.[5] The most important of these sayings, from a critical point of view, is that of Mark 10:30. When the young man asked Jesus how he might inherit eternal life (Mk. 10:17), he had no thought of life as a present possession in the Johannine sense. He was concerned about his future destiny, the life of the age to come. Probably he had in mind the words in Daniel when "many of those who sleep in the dust of the earth shall awake, some to everlasting life, and some to shame and everlasting contempt" (Dan. 12:2). In the subsequent discussion with his disciples, Jesus equated eternal life with the Kingdom of God (Mk. 10:23–25), and also with the age to come. In this age, his disciples will enjoy certain rewards in return for the sacrifice they are called upon to make, but they are also to expect persecutions (Mk. 10:30). The supreme gift, eternal life, belongs to the age to come. So far as this saying is concerned, apart from the age to come God's people will not experience eternal life.

The same eschatological dualism is reflected in a saying in the Fourth Gospel: "He who loves his life loses it, and he who hates his life in this world will keep it for eternal life" (Jn. 12:25). This is a saying which has parallels in the Synoptics.[6] Dodd has pointed out that "the Fourth Evangelist alone has given it a form which obviously alludes to the Jewish antithesis of the two ages: he who hates his soul ba'olam ha-zeh

[1] P. Vielhauer, "Apocalyptic," New Testament Apocrypha, Wm. Schneemelcher, ed., (Philadelphia, 1964), II. p. 589.
[2] H. Ringgren, op. cit., cols. 464–66.
[3] G. von Rad, Old Testament Theology (New York, 1965), I, pp. 301 f.
[4] Philadelphia, 1950. Rev. ed., 1964.
[5] Mark (Mk. 4:19; 10:30); M (Matt. 13:39–40; 28:20); L (Luke 16:8); Matt. 24:3; 12:32 and Luke 20:34–35.
[6] Mk. 8:35; Mt. 10:39, 16:25; Lk. 9:24, 17:33.

will keep it *la'olam ha-ba'* and consequently will possess *ḥayye ha'olam ha-ba'*.[1] Indeed, the very idea of ζωὴ αἰώνιος is eschatological.[2] It is the life of the age to come.

This eschatological dualism is also patent in Paul. Christ has been exalted far above every name that is named, "not only is this age but also in that which is to come" (Eph. 1:21). This present age is evil (Gal. 1:4). Satan has been allowed in the providence of God to exercise such power that he can be called the "god of this age" (2 Cor. 4:4). Because this age is evil, Christians are not to be conformed to its norms and patterns (Rom. 12:2). It was the rulers of this age who brought about the death of Jesus (I Cor. 2:8).[3]

Even in the book of Hebrews, which many critics interpret against a background of philonic, i.e., Greek, dualism, the eschatological perspective remains. "For it was not to angels that God subjected the world to come (τὴν οἰκουμένην τὴν μέλλουσαν), of which we are speaking" (Heb. 2:5). This is clearly an eschatological expression which is synonymous with *ha'olam ha-ba'*.[4]

Cullmann's thesis seems unassailable. The basic structure of New Testament theology is the same as that of Jewish apocalyptic.

At this point, a difficult question must be raised, if it cannot be finally answered. Did Jesus and the early Christians borrow the two-age scheme from Judaism? We have seen that the fully developed terminology of the two ages appears in Jewish literature first in IV Ezra. The witnesses for this terminology from the rabbinic writings before 70 A.D. are very infrequent and uncertain.[5] However, Sasse believes that "The NT borrowed the doctrine of the two aeons from Jewish apocalyptic".[6] So far as our literature is concerned, the Pauline letters are the earliest documents to use the idiom of the two ages; but if our Gospels correctly report Jesus' words, Jesus himself is the first one according to our texts to have used the idiom.

Many scholars believe that the Gospels do not correctly record the words of Jesus and that he could not have used the two-age terminology. While it is clear that several uses of the phrase are secondary, there is no convincing reason to conclude that the terminology does not in fact go

---

[1] C. H. Dodd, *The Interpretation of the Fourth Gospel* (Cambridge, 1953), p. 146.

[2] See H. Sasse, *TDNT* I, p. 209.

[3] It would take us far afield to discuss the critical problem of whether "the rulers of this age" are political rulers or spiritual powers. For a further discussion of Pauline dualism, see G. E. Ladd in *EQ* 30 (1958), pp. 75–84.

[4] See G. W. Buchanan, *To the Hebrews* (New York, 1972), p. 26. For the eschatological perspective of Hebrews, which many scholars have denied, see Wm. Robinson, *The Eschatology of the Epistle to the Hebrews* (Birmingham, 1950; a much-neglected little work), and C. K. Barrett, "The Eschatology of the Epistle to the Hebrews," in *The Background of the New Testament and its Eschatology*, ed. by W. D. Davies and D. Daube (Cambridge, 1956), pp. 363–93.

[5] H. Sasse in *TDNT* I, p. 206.

[6] *Loc. cit.*

back to Jesus. G. Dalman says, "It is clear that the ideas, 'this age', 'the future age', *if Jesus used them at all*, were not of importance in His vocabulary . . . The idea of the 'sovereignty of God' filled the place of that of 'the future age'."[1] This is a surprising statement in view of the fact that he had already said, "the true affinity of the idea of the sovereignty of God, as taught by Jesus, is to be found, not so much in the Jewish conception of *malkuth shamayim* as in the idea of the 'future age', or that of the 'life of the future age'."[2] However, if the *idea* of the two ages is found in Jesus' teachings, we should admit the probability of the terminology unless strong reasons prevent it. In the words of T. W. Manson, who was not inclined to "play up" eschatological concepts, "Parousia and Judgement mark the division between the present age and the age to come. They usher in what is described as 'the Kingdom of God' or as 'life'. These two terms appear to be used interchangeably".[3]

We must recognize the possibility that this terminology existed in Judaism and that both Jesus and Paul brought it into the Christian tradition. However, for this there is no final proof. It is more likely, in view of the appearance of the terminology in our sources, that it came into the Christian tradition through Jesus' teaching, and Paul uses the same terminology, which was also emerging simultaneously in Jewish idiom. Geerhardus Vos was convinced that

> there is no escape from the conclusion that a piece of Jewish theology has been here by Revelation incorporated into the Apostle's teaching. Paul had none less than Jesus Himself as a predecessor in this. The main structure of the Jewish Apocalyptic is embodied in our Lord's teaching as well as in Paul's.[4]

If Christianity took over the eschatological dualism of Jewish apocalyptic, it did so with a difference – a difference so striking and significant that it is easy to contrast the Gospel with apocalyptic, as Morris does.[5]

The fact is, if our thesis is correct that the doctrine of the two ages is a natural development of the Old Testament prophetic hope,[6] that this doctrine as it emerged in Jewish apocalyptic lost one of the most important features of prophetic theology: the truth that the God who is to act finally at the end of the age is also the God who acts in history and who reveals himself in historical events. The prophets believed that God had revealed himself in delivering his people from slavery in Egypt, in preserving his people from their enemies, and even in judgement in the captivity. The same God who had acted in history would intervene at the

---

[1] *The Words of Jesus* (Edinburgh, 1909), p. 148. See also the long note in W. G. Kümmel, *Promise and Fulfilment* (Naperville, Ill., 1957), p. 49.

[2] G. Dalman, *op. cit.*, p. 135.

[3] T. W. Manson, *The Teaching of Jesus* (Cambridge, 1935), p. 276.

[4] Geerhardus Vos, *The Pauline Eschatology* (Grand Rapids, 1952), p. 28. However, see p. 288, n. 4.

[5] *Apocalyptic*, p. 86.

[6] See p. 288, n. 4.

end of history to manifest his glory by bringing his redeemed people into the new order of the Kingdom of God.[1]

The apocalyptists lost the reality of God's acting in present history. Indeed, the evil plight of God's people in history was precisely their problem. In Maccabean times, the Jews rallied to the law, and many suffered martyrdom rather than violate the law. Yet God did not deliver them. Israel's historical experiences led them to the conclusion that history was irremediably evil. No hope for deliverance could be expected in history; all hope was focused on the eschatological event when God would rise up to judge the wicked and bring his people into the blessed age to come. Thus the apocalyptists reflect pessimism about this age. The blessings of the Kingdom cannot be experienced in the present, for this age is abandoned to evil and suffering.

This pessimism with regard to history is vividly reflected in the Dream Visions in Enoch. God has personally guided the experiences of Israel throughout its history until the Babylonian captivity. Then God withdrew his personal leadership, forsook the temple, and surrendered his people to wild beasts to be torn and devoured. God "remained unmoved, though He saw it, and rejoiced that they were devoured and swallowed and robbed, and left them to be devoured in the hand of all the beasts" (En. 89:58). Then God turned the fortunes of the nation over to seventy shepherds, instructing them as to the number of Jews who might be slain. However, the shepherds were self-willed and faithless, ignoring the divine directive and permitting fearful evils to befall God's people. When reports of the evil conduct of the shepherds were brought to God, he laid them aside and remained unmoved and aloof (89:71, 75). A record was made of the angels' faithlessness that they might be punished on the day of judgement when Israel would be delivered. Between the years 586–165 B.C., God was conceived to be inactive in the fortunes of Israel. God's people found themselves at the mercy of faithless angels. No deliverance could be expected before the messianic era.[2]

The apocalyptic rejection of history was the subject of a paper read at the hundredth meeting of the Society of Biblical Literature in America by Stanley B. Frost. He argues that far from having a philosophy of history, apocalyptic did not take history seriously, and did not view history as the medium of revelation. Salvation is to be sought not in this world but in a transcendent order. He points out that this fact has not been widely recognized.[3]

It is precisely at this point that the apocalyptic thought of the New Testament most notably differs from Jewish apocalyptic. In fact, the

[1] The term "Kingdom of God" is not used in the prophets, but the idea is constantly recurrent.
[2] For further illustrations see G. E. Ladd, *The Presence of the Future*, chap. 3.
[3] Stanley B. Frost, "Apocalyptic and History," in *The Bible in Modern Scholarship*, ed. J. P. Hyatt (Nashville, 1965), pp. 98–113.

difference is so great that many scholars would not call the basic structure of New Testament thought apocalyptic. It was this primary difference that led the present writer some years ago to suggest that we ought to distinguish between prophetic-apocalyptic and non-prophetic apocalyptic.[1] Non-prophetic apocalyptic has completely lost the sense of God's acts in history. It is completely pessimistic about history; history is surrendered to the powers of evil. Prophetic apocalyptic builds its world view on the apocalyptic doctrine of the two ages, but it retains the consciousness of God's acts in history. This is what led Cullmann to say that the main difference between Judaism and Christianity is that the latter places a new centre in the time line without surrendering the eschatological dualism.[2]

Long before Cullmann wrote his influential *Christ and Time*, Geerhardus Vos had expressed the same idea in what seems to the present writer to be an even more effective way. Instead of a straight line with two climactic points[3] – the incarnation and the parousia – Vos suggested the following diagram.[4]

The world to come,
realized in principle

	[in heaven]		
Resurrection of Christ		Parousia	Future age and world fully realized in solid existence
	[on earth]		

This age or world

This diagram is intended to suggest that all of the redemptive blessings already enjoyed in Christ are, to use Vos's words, "semi-eschatological" realities. *This is to the present writer the unifying centre of New Testament theology.*[5] The Kingdom of God, which is the central theme of Jesus' preaching, belongs essentially to the age to come. God's rule will never be fully realized in this age. The Gospels, like Jewish apocalyptic, recognize the role of evil spirits in this age. Satan and his angels must be destroyed (Matt. 25:41) before God's Kingdom is consummated. However, this does not mean, as in Jewish apocalyptic, that God has abandoned his world and

[1] G. E. Ladd, "Why Not Prophetic Apocalyptic?" *JBL* 76 (1957), pp. 192–200.
[2] See p. 289, n. 4.
[3] It can be argued that Christ did not in fact put a new *center* in the time line, for what he will do at his Parousia is as essential to the full realization of salvation as the incarnation, cross, and resurrection.
[4] G. Vos, *The Pauline Eschatology*, p. 38.
[5] See G. E. Ladd, "Eschatology and the Unity of New Testament Theology," *ExpT* 68 (1956–1957), pp. 268–73.

human history. In fact, *history has become the scene of the conflict between the Kingdom of God and the powers of evil.* "But if it is by the Spirit of God that I cast out demons, then the kingdom of God has come upon you" (Matt. 12:28). The Kingdom of God belongs to the age to come, but in the person and mission of Jesus, that Kingdom has invaded history to bring to men living in the old age the blessings of the age to come.

Eternal life also belongs to the age to come.[1] In the Synoptic Gospels, eternal life is always an eschatological blessing. But in the Fourth Gospel, Jesus has brought this eternal life to men while they still live in dying mortal bodies. "He who believes in the Son has eternal life" (Jn. 3:36). There is a distinct analogy between the concept of the Kingdom of God in the Synoptics and eternal life in John. Both belong to the age to come and are eschatological; in fact, eternal life is in reality the life of the future age. But by virtue of Jesus' mission, both the Kingdom of God and eternal life have become objects of present experience.[2]

The same historicising of eschatology is found in Paul's teaching about the resurrection, justification, and the Spirit. Paul makes it clear that the resurrection of Jesus was an eschatological event. His resurrection is the first fruits of the eschatological resurrection (I Cor. 15:23). First fruits is more than promise or hope; it is actual realization. The resurrection of Christ was an event in history, but it was not an "historical" event in the sense that it could be explained by antecedent historical events. It was an eschatological event. In the resurrection of Jesus, a piece of eschatology was split off from the end of the world and planted in the midst of history.

The same is true of justification. Justification is essentially the sentence of righteousness by the divine Judge in the eschatological day of judgement. This is what Paul expected when he was a Jew.[3] But now because of the cross, God has already pronounced the verdict of acquittal – and that not on the basis of good works but of faith in Jesus because of what he has done in history.

The gift of the Spirit is also an eschatological gift. The promise in Joel 2:28–29 of the outpouring of the Spirit was an event that belonged to the day of the Lord. Ezekiel (36:26–28) also predicted the gift of the Spirit but again it is in an eschatological setting. On the day of Pentecost, Peter proclaimed that the eschatological promise of the Spirit had been fulfilled – in history. And Paul's calls the gift of the Spirit both first fruits (ἀπαρχή Rom. 8:23) and a down-payment (ἀρραβών, 2 Cor. 1:22; 5:5; Eph. 1:14) of the eschatological fullness.

It is because these eschatological blessings have come to men in history that Paul says that Christ gave himself for our sins to deliver us from this present evil age (Gal. 1:4), and that we are no longer to be conformed to

---

[1] See p. 290, n. 2.
[2] Leon Morris, *Commentary on the Gospel of John* (Grand Rapids, 1971), p. 214.
[3] See F. F. Bruce, *The Epistle of Paul to the Romans* (London, 1963), p. 102.

the pattern of this age but to be transformed by a new inner dynamic (Rom. 12:2). Although Paul does not say so, this new dynamic can be nothing less than the powers of the age to come (Heb. 6:5) which have come to men while they are still living in the old age.

This fact has led many scholars to the conclusion that in fact the turn of the ages has occurred. "Mit Jesu Person und Wirken als Gottessohn und Messias ist die zukünftige Welt, das ewige Leben mit seinen göttlichen Kräften, Gegenwart geworden, der zukünftige Äon reicht mit ihm in diesen Äon hinein".[1]

> In its view of the two aeons, the NT is in essential agreement with first century apocalyptic. The framework of eschatological notions is broken only by the fact that the *αἰὼν μέλλων is no longer merely in the future*. Believers are already redeemed from this present evil *αἰών* (Gal. 1:14) and have tasted the powers of the future *αἰών* (Heb. 6:5) . . . *The new aeon has already begun, though as yet concealed from the eyes of men*.[2]

Michaelis strenuously objects to this notion that the turn of the ages has already occurred.

> "Ein 'zukünftiger Äon' sollte, wenn er Gegenwart geworden wäre, eben nicht mehr zukünftiger heissen, bzw, wenn er nach wie vor 'zukünftiger Äon' genannt wird, sollte er nicht als gegenwärtig vorgestellt sein. Von einer Gegenwart des zukünftiger Äons zu reden stellt einen Widerspruch in sich dar."[3]

This is certainly utterly logical. However, God transcends both time and history, and if not the new age itself, then at least the "powers of the age to come" have reached back into the old age. Vos's diagram certainly illustrates the situation in New Testament theology. Believers are living to all intents and purposes in two ages at the same time. We still sin, we are still weak, and frail, we still die; but we are nevertheless living by the power of a new life which is nothing less than the life of the age to come. The blessings of the new age do not constitute a worldly phenomenon. They are visible only to the eye of faith. They are now realized only in the spiritual realm.[4] In the age to come, the entire man – body as well as spirit – and creation as well (Rom. 8:21) will enjoy the blessings of God's salvation.

In any case, we have tried to show that the New Testament owes its basic structure to Jewish apocalyptic, which was in turn derived from the Old Testament. Apart from the inauguration of the age to come, God's

[1] Josef Schmid, *Das Evangelium nach Markus* (Regensburg, 5 1963) p. 37.
[2] H. Sasse, *TDNT* I, p. 207. [Italics mine].
[3] Wm. Michaelis, "Reich Gottes und Äonenwende" in *Neutestamentliche Aufsätze* (J. Schmid Festschrift; ed. by J. Blinzler, *et al.*, 1963), p. 162.
[4] Charismatics who believe that miracles and healings are normative for the entire church age will dispute this statement.

work of salvation remains ever incomplete. Because we have already experienced the powers of the age to come, it remains more than a hope; it is a certainty based both on the teaching of Scripture and on Christian experience.

INDEXES

INDEX OF MAIN SUBJECTS TREATED

INDEX OF MODERN AUTHORS

INDEX OF REFERENCES TO HOLY SCRIPTURE AND TO OTHER ANCIENT WRITINGS

C.   THE NEW TESTAMENT

F. OTHER ANCIENT AUTHORS AND WRITINGS